LAST SEEN ALIVE

The Search for Missing POWs
from the Korean War

LAST SEEN ALIVE

The Search for Missing POWs from the Korean War

LAURENCE JOLIDON

INK -SLINGER PRESS

AUSTIN, TEXAS · WASHINGTON, D.C.

It is the policy of Ink-Slinger Press, recognizing the importance of preserving both the world's writing and the world's natural assets, to publish on acid-free paper.

Cover photograph: Unidentified POW, Korea; courtesy U.S. Department of Defense

Cover Design: Richard Curtis

Library of Congress Cataloguing-in-Publication Data

Jolidon, Laurence
Last Seen Alive—The Search for Missing POWs from
  the Korean War
 —1st ed.

 p. cm.
 Includes index.
 ISBN 0-9646982-0-X
1. Prisoners of war. 2. Korean War—History. 1. Title

               95-077958

ISBN 0-9646982-0-X

Dedication

This book is dedicated to the memory of my father,
Laurence Jolidon, and to my mother,
Mary Imogene Cotter Williamson Jolidon.
In appreciation of the lessons they taught —
to respect others, to seek the truth
and to persevere.

If I should die in a foreign land,
Honey, honey,
If I should die in a foreign land,
Babe, babe,
If I should die in a foreign land
Bury me in the finest sand,
Honey oh ba-by mine...

—Marching cadence rhyme,
U.S. military, Anon.

Contents

Preface

THE BOOK IN YOUR HAND contains only part of a story that may never be known in its entirety, because the truth can be suppressed and the passage of time can erode even the most concrete facts.

Like all wars, the conflict that exploded on the Korean peninsula in 1950 left unimaginable cruelty, death, destruction and grief in its wake. But the Korean War also left an especially persistent legacy—of loss, of division of families, of parents and survivors. Koreans, Americans, other Asians and westerners from more than a dozen countries drawn into the war were left with no opportunity to place a seal on their grief or imagine the final fate of a loved one.

In telling about the continuing, incomplete efforts to unlock one of the Korean War's long-suppressed secrets—POWs never accounted for— this book risks creating doubts where no doubt existed, and of raising hopes where no hopes are warranted. But it does so in an attempt to shed light and replace myths with information.

And while the information includes reports of acts for which government officials, military commanders and some individuals ought to be held accountable, acts that without question deserve to be condemned, it is not my intention to blame or condemn entire countries.

Nor is my purpose to urge retribution. The best use of the truth about the events dealt with here is to light the dark pathways of the past, so that we can better see the future.

What you will find within these pages is clear, ample and unambiguous proof of the complicity of the former Soviet Union, People's Republic of China and North Korea in the disappearance and probable death of at least dozens, perhaps hundreds, of American soldiers, sailors, Marines and aviators. They are men who fought and were captured in Korea or Manchuria between June 1950 and July 1953, or were downed in the Far East while flying Cold War reconnaissance missions in the 1950s and 1960s.

As prisoners of war in military custody, under international conventions, not to mention by common decency, they should have been returned unharmed and without delay to their country and families, like the thousands who were repatriated by both sides under the terms of the 1953 Korean War armistice. Of course governments have their reasons, and their policies and excuses. What cannot be excused is further silence, further refusal to face the truth.

Where they or their remains are today is the most pressing, but also the most difficult question. The trail is cold, very cold, and for every person brave enough to disclose the ugly secrets of the past, and confront the consequences, a dozen shirk from the truth and maintain a discreet silence.

The attention of the public and the media is often focused on MIAs from the Vietnam War, while those missing from Korea seldom appear on the agenda. Today's students refer to the Vietnam War as "ancient history." That puts the Korean War in the category of pre-history.

But it is very much a part of the lives of hundreds of thousands of men and women, the survivors of the 2.2 million men and women who saw duty in the Korean War theater and their families and friends who waited in anguish for their return. For them and for the rest of us as well, this story is as current as today's newscasts and headlines.

The U.S. government is currently in negotiations with the Democratic People's Republic of Korea in an attempt to slow—it is too late to stop it—the Pyongyang government's program to develop nuclear weapons. While the danger of a nuclear conflict obviously is paramount, it would seem an opportune time to raise the issue of American servicemen still unaccounted for from the Korean War, and put North Korea on notice that we have not forgotten this long-unresolved topic. But the U.S. government chooses to ignore or blunt this opportunity.

The case of China is another disappointment. While much is frequently made of China's human rights violations when the debate over MFN rights is joined in Washington, China is never reminded that it should own up to its responsibility for helping answer MIA questions about Korea—the only full-scale war in which American and Chinese troops engaged in direct combat against each other.

As for the former Soviet Union, the political collapse of the old Communist power structure several years ago at last created an opportunity to explore what had been forbidden for decades—reports that American POWs were shipped to the USSR from the Korean War. A brief window of opportunity created by the slippage of massive political plates may be closing, but at least on the surface there is progress.

The Russian and U.S. governments over the past few years have supported a joint commission assigned to track down reports of American prisoners held in the former Soviet Union. It is an expensive and wide-ranging effort, requiring great skill, patience and persistence.

Good people have rendered honorable service to the missing through the joint commission. It is left to the reader to judge whether others have done as much.

Malcolm Toon, former U.S. ambassador to Moscow and other American members of the commission often praise Gen. Dimitri Volkogonov and the other Russian members for their cooperation. But the commission's own working papers and minutes make it clear that Russian cooperation is usually grudging, that the Russians distrust the United States' motives, that the United States' program is plagued with turnover and bureaucratic in-fighting that only disrupts or undermines the real goals, that both sides are restricted by an underlying political agenda, that Soviet veterans remain fearful even today when they speak out honestly about their activities in Korea, and that Russian pledges to turn over all relevant material are often mere words.

But despite efforts to conceal, misrepresent and even alter the history of Soviet involvement in Korea, enough records have come to light to form a body of credible evidence pointing to Soviet misdeeds. This book cites many documents that have survived and which help pinpoint the location of dozens of American POWs when they were last seen alive, before an opaque curtain of repression, apathy and prolonged secrecy obliterated most visible traces.

The fact that many were reported alive in Communist custody— some both prior to and after the 1953 armistice—places the burden of accountability on their captors, and their captors' successors. The passage of time—the first battles of the Korean War were waged 45 years ago this summer—may shift the path by which the complete story of their captivity may emerge, but does not relieve anyone with access to the truth, or knowledge of their fate, of the responsibility to state it, indeed to demand it be made public.

On occasion since the joint commission on American MIAs in the former Soviet Union was formed in 1992, there have been strong signals that the Russian government would like to wrap up the investigation and close down the commission.

Sadly, the U.S. government has been derelict in honoring its own overdue pledges to lift the seal of secrecy from much of the official, but long suppressed, history of the Korean War as seen from our side.

In light of even the faltering and modest disclosures made by

Russia's post-Communist government, the refusal to fully open 40-year-old military and diplomatic archives in the United States leaves the unfortunate impression that America, not the former Soviet Union, is the country that fears the truth, the party with something to hide.

The intent of this book—in keeping with the hopes of many families still waiting for information about their loved ones still lost in the bloody mist of the Korean War and its aftermath—is to help build interest to ensure that the work continues.

The path cleared so far should not be lost. The responsibility of Chinese and Soviet Russian officials in the case of American POWs from the Korean War is clear from an accumulation of documentary evidence.

There is no disputing the overriding fact—confirmed by U.S. and Soviet records and the testimony of American and Soviet veterans—that American prisoners were singled out for special questioning and indoctrination by Soviet officials.

Much of the Chinese-run POW system extended into Manchuria, north of the Yalu River, and the Russians' clandestine handling of American prisoners took place behind the guise of official neutrality by the Soviets. Only the Communist Chinese and North Koreans were the declared enemies of the United Nations in Korea, and officially only they had control over, and contact with, United Nations prisoners. The truth, as was suspected then, and is known now, was not that simple.

When the difficult negotiations were complete, and thousands of American POW/MIAs were not among those repatriated, it was clear that the worst fears already expressed by U.S. officials—that the Communists would hold back United Nations prisoners—had come true.

But the missing POWs didn't simply vanish into thin air after answering, or refusing to answer, their interrogators' questions. Indeed, reports of American POWs from Korea being shipped out of the war zone in trains, and held in work camps and hospitals throughout Manchuria and the farflung Soviet Gulag, surfaced during the 1950s and into the 1960s from many quarters, including U.S. and foreign intelligence reports and debriefings of former Gulag inmates who survived to bring out word of the secret transfers.

Some may weigh the evidence of POW transfers to the USSR and find it compelling, but incomplete. No American unaccounted for from the Korean War or after a Cold War shootdown, after all, has ever emerged from the former Soviet Union, Manchuria or North Korea.

It is necessary to remember that as recently as ten years ago, the former Soviet Union was one of the most closed and repressive countries on earth, and that one of the few countries whose repression and isolation exceeded it was North Korea, where no American—and few foreigners—have visited unescorted since the war.

Given the failure over months of rancorous talks to persuade the North Koreans and Chinese to allow international inspection of the rear areas where POWs were held and buried, the only way the United States could have determined how many and which POW/MIAs—of any nationality—had died, been put to death or held back alive would have been to renew military action on a massive scale not only in North Korea but in Manchuria and Siberia, win control over the places intelligence reports said prisoners were being held, and put the matter—along with thousands of new casualties—to rest.

The reason for the lack of living proof of Korean War POW/MIAs transferred to the former Soviet Union may be as convoluted as the theory that every single report since the start of the Cold War of Americans in the Gulag, scattered the breadth of Eurasia, was baseless. This theory holds that—as undoubtedly happened in some cases—wily inmates of varied nationalities claimed to be Americans when they were not, to win release.

Or, the reason may be as simple as the old saying that dead men tell no tales. The confirmed atrocities of the Korean War give particular weight to that reasoning.

Given the political conditions in the Soviet Union at the time, it is reasonable to speculate that American POWs shipped to Manchuria or Soviet territory were executed, or held until they died in labor camps or psychiatric hospitals. If so, then a plan to find their remains and honor their service is in order. The supposed location of graves of some American POWs who were Gulag casualties constitutes part of the record that has come to light since the Korean War.

Nor is it difficult to imagine that some American POWs who weren't among the repatriates at Freedom Village in 1953 were unannounced defectors who chose to remain behind quietly as sympathetic new citizens of Communism.

After all, the Americans taken prisoner in the Korean War did include more than 20 publicly known "turncoats," graduates of the Communists' infamous "brainwashing" program. These 21 U.S. Army enlisted men and a British commando outspokenly declined a chance to come home—although eventually the attraction of Communism faded and all but one of them returned to the West. Perhaps the attraction faded even later—too late—for some others.

As for whether the acts that Chinese and Soviet officials are now known to have committed during the Korean War with regard to POWs constitute crimes or merely guilty knowledge of crimes is for others better schooled in the law of conflicts and international relations to decide.

Many would say that a war fierce enough to leave almost as many U.S. dead—54,000—in three years as the Vietnam War did in a decade, that took the lives of millions of Koreans and Chinese, left an estimated 40,000 South Korean MIAs and also produced some of the most gruesome atrocities of modern times, including outright executions by forces on both sides, had already exacted more than its share of human loss.

Much of the material that comprises this book lay in the closed archives of the United States or the former Soviet Union until recently. Some was unearthed by public-financed researchers, working with the authority of their governments to interview witnesses, follow leads and declassify documents that had been kept from pubic view since the 1950s. Some facts were unearthed by the author and other journalists and private researchers supported by private funds and working with the assistance of the Freedom of Information Act. The rest comes from interviews done by the author in this country and the former Soviet Union with veterans of the conflict, their fellow POWs and surviving relatives.

Ambassador Toon and a small staff of military and civilian analysts and researchers are still searching for a more complete history of Soviet involvement with American POWs, although the most promising effort—produced in the joint commission's first year by a special group of analysts known as Task Force Russia—was basically disowned by the U.S. Defense Department bureaucrats who still control the POW/MIA issue inside government.

The information turned over so far represents at least some improvement over the uninformative declarations of the Defense Department at war's end, the official so-called "findings of death," based on nothing more than an absence of facts.

The U.S.-Russian Joint commission in May 1995 summed up its findings in an interim report covering the work completed since it was formed in early 1992.

The general conclusion, which includes a qualification that students of diplomatic language must admire, re-states that the commission is satisfied that "no American citizens, either military or civilian, are being held against their will on the territory of Russia today."

This characterization was first used after an initial flurry of reports of Americans still behind bars in what is left of Stalin's Gulag. Boris Yeltsin raised the issue with little warning soon after he took over the presidency by conceding that Americans had been imprisoned in the Gulag, saying that some might still be alive, and promising to find out what had happened to them.

Some of those reports have been investigated and the commission's report cited "a number of positive results." But the American members of the commission have worked under rules requiring them to run down most leads in tandem and to interview Russian witnesses with Russian commission staffers present.

The phrase "against their will" is an obvious concession to the Russian line that any Americans who came onto Soviet territory prior to Perestroika and the collapse of the Soviet empire were defectors, not MIAs.

In the case of POW/MIAs from World War II, when thousands of U.S. prisoners were liberated from Nazi-POW camps by the Soviet Red Army, the commission has determined that while some suspicious cases remain, reports of mass detentions of American GIs who were marched east rather than west after Germany's surrender were unfounded. The commissioners consider the World War II period its least controversial, and approaching a closed case.

As for the Vietnam War and Cold War shootdown cases, the commission's interim report concludes there is "no credible evidence" that American POWs were detained in the former Soviet Union. POW/MIA activists who specialize in the Vietnam era disagree vehemently.

They cite evidence collected for and testimony presented to a U.S. Senate Select Committee on POW/MIAs in 1992 about "Moscow-bound" American POWs from Southeast Asia. Volkogonov and his Russian staff have fenced off a position that concedes the presence of a handful of American "defectors" from Vietnam passing through the Soviet Union briefly on a propaganda tour, but no seized POWs.

The problem of Korean War POW/MIAs sighted in Manchuria and the former Soviet Union is far different—nearly 8,200 U.S. servicemen remain unaccounted for from the fighting in Korea, four times the number from Vietnam. And the type and amount of evidence makes it more troubling for the Russians and Chinese.

There is too much evidence pertaining to the transfer of Korean War POWs to Manchuria and the Soviet Union to ignore. Ambassador Toon himself has called it "compelling." And the Russians would have defied common sense had they not been intensely interested in all they could learn first-hand about U.S. fighting strength, equipment and morale from Americans captured in Korea.

After all, the Americans had burst onto the Russians' Far Eastern doorstep, sending ships, air squadrons and whole divisions of troops to a country that bordered the Soviet empire and shared an even longer border with Manchuria, where the Russians were still installed as a powerful landlord and defender after driving out the Japanese.

In August 1993, the U.S. side of the commission compiled a report entitled "The Transfer of U.S. Korean War POWs to the Soviet Union." The report cited written and oral evidence that was characterized as "a consistent and mutually reinforcing description" of the transfer process.

Since then, not fewer but more records and witnesses have surfaced to buttress that report's findings. But when pressed to characterize the report, U.S. officials speaking for the commission have gone to great lengths to diminish and qualify their own findings, apparently to soften the impact on Russia's nascent non-communist government.

And some Russian witnesses have been coerced into revising or disavowing their initial testimony under pressure from Russian officials.

Nonetheless, at the signing of the May 1995 interim report, Toon pointedly repeated his belief that while the case of the "Korean transfers" to Siberia is not airtight, it is firm. He said he shares "a strong suspicion" that "a number of American POWs wound up in Soviet hands." He has been even more straightforward in interviews where Gen. Volkogonov was not seated inches away.

Since the first groups of western and South Korean prisoners were marched north behind the lines of the Soviet-led invasion by North Korean troops, the grounds for that suspicion have been carefully hidden by the North Koreans and a succession of Soviet and Chinese regimes, all ready to swear that no U.S. prisoners were transferred to the USSR.

Now the shape of that lie is coming into view, and the suspicions have become facts demanding an explanation.

Some who read this account may think of it as a detective story, with a great many clues provided and some withheld. But they should remember it is a true detective story; the author claims no fictional license and has created no quotes or conversations from the context of an event.

The crimes are documented; many of the culprits have fled, or perished along with many of the victims. The chase continues.

Much of it is history, dealing extensively with events that occurred more than 40 years ago, when the world was a very different place. The reasons people acted the way they did and governments chose the policies they did were often different than they would be today. Each person, government and society is rooted in the atmosphere and tenor of the times.

But it also deals with the search for truth in the present, of what people and governments now are doing and saying about the past—to reveal it, suppress it or cloak it in lies.

In that sense what follows is both history and current events, like journalism between book covers. To help understand what kind of world we live in, we owe it to ourselves to reconstruct the truth, or as much of it as survives, especially about events as basic and significant as war and prisoners of war. To do otherwise is to dishonor the successes we achieved through the sacrifice of thousands, and the penalties we paid then. By doing that we forsake solemn pledges we made then, and render meaningless similar promises we make in the future.

The decisions behind the story of the POW/MIAs recounted in this book began with the sending of an international military force, under the United Nations flag and led by the United States, to the Korean peninsula in the summer of 1950 to help the South Korean government repel an invasion by the Soviet-trained military of North Korea. One promise inherent in that decision was that the United States would seek a full accounting for every American sent in harm's way on that mission.

That promise was not kept because America's leaders, intent on containing the Korean War within the boundaries of the peninsula, knew it would necessitate or provoke a wider war, perhaps a nuclear war. The U.S. military and civilian representatives who attempted while the fighting continued to learn the whereabouts of missing American servicemen—and nationals of other countries allied under the UN banner—worked diligently and honorably.

In addition to the limited war doctrine, the U.S. and the rest of the free world adopted new attitudes and aims regarding POWs during the Korean War. The policy that no Korean or Chinese who wanted to remain on democracy's soil and under UN protection should be forced to return to ideological slavery set a new, moral standard.

Some then and now believe that those Americans, South Koreans and allies from a dozen other nations taken prisoner in the war to defend democracy in Korea paid a terrible price for the decision to adopt a policy of no-forced-repatriation.

But forced repatriation of reluctant POWs would not have guaranteed that fair play and humane treatment would suddenly appear in the Communist prison-camp glossary.

The Communists would no doubt have employed their tactics of using POWs as propaganda tools regardless of the course of negotiations over prisoners. In fact, propaganda was inseparable from the negotiations.

In the end, some who went into battle on democracy's side survived the war but were kept from seeing freedom's light again. No compromises at the bargaining table or change of UN policy would have prevented that.

American governments since the 1950s have not devoted enough attention and resources to forcing our adversaries in that war to come clean. A day should not pass when North Korea, China and the Russian inheritors of Soviet power are not asked to account, by name, for the missing.

As some like U.S. Sen. Robert Smith of New Hampshire and the dedicated family members who comprise a devoted battalion of activists argue, it is time to give the question of MIAs from the Korean War and the Cold War a higher priority. In doing so, we should always remember that those who kept American prisoners from coming home bear the heaviest guilt for their absence and for their families' pain and grief.

But we are not blameless if we forget them. Our duty is to seek answers, demand explanations and discover the entire truth, no matter how long it is held hostage.

—**Laurence Jolidon**
Washington, D.C.
June 1995

Acknowledgments

I would like to first thank all of those men and women, veterans of the Korean War and their survivors, who agreed to share with me their experiences, their pain, and their thoughts and memories of the war and of the prisoners who are still missing.

I have walked a vigil with them, but I have not had to bear the grief or uncertainty they do. They have my admiration and appreciation. My fondest hope is that something I've written brings the resolution of their cases a moment closer.

I am grateful for the unquenchable support of my sisters Mimi and Marilyn and the rest of my small but loyal family, and the friends who have listened to my ideas, encouraged and helped me.

This project could not have seen completion, either, without the assistance and support of Dolores Alfond and the other founders and members of the National Alliance of Families. Their faith in what is right has never faltered, nor should it.

My thanks also to the many people associated with the Defense Department's POW/MIA effort, Task Force Russia and the U.S.-Russia Joint Commission for their assistance. Institutionally, I would also like to say how much I appreciate the courteous and professional staff at the Library of Congress and National Archives, the two places I know as intimately as the creases on my researcher's card.

For assistance in Russia and the former Soviet Union, my appreciation goes to Marina Kholina Labonville and Dimitri Mishlevchenko.

Chapter One

Caught in the Net

"I don't think that our forces should be mixed up in that. The Russians would love to see that situation come about and they would sit back there and laugh their heads off if we got our forces engaged with any Koreans at all…If it is a question of Russian forces, that is an entirely different matter."

—Former U.S. ambassador to Moscow George Kennan, testifying before the House Committee on Foreign Affairs, June, 1949.

"It's true that the presence of the 64th Corps was a secret. It did not appear in the Soviet press…But it was not possible to hide three divisions, a regiment, 500-600 flights per day plus a lot of planes shot down. You couldn't hide this in Korea."

—Viktor A. Bushuyev, deputy chief of intelligence for the 64th Fighter Aviation Corps, the major Soviet military unit involved in combat against the United Nations in Korea.

In the spring and early summer of 1950, the Soviet Union's embassy in Pyongyang, North Korea, swarmed with activity, like a submarine's conning tower just before it submerges to slip beneath the enemy.

Even the embassy's lowest clerks could sense that major events were in the works. There were so many meetings, so much paperwork, correspondence and message traffic. A buildup was on, and the supply lines into North Korea from China and the Soviet Union were choked with new Soviet T-24 tanks, airplanes, crates of ammunition and supplies freighted in by rail and sea from factories and steel and fabric plants that hadn't been this busy in years.

The Yellow Sea south of Port Arthur, all the way to Shanghai and back, was a floating warehouse of Soviet war materiel. And everything that arrived on the peninsula had to be unloaded, tested, and either hidden away or distributed to the military units that had trained for this day. The forces that would lead the attack were moving into position, surrounding their emplacements with camouflage, and key personnel were being shifted into place.

In late May, Lt. Gen. Kuzma Derevyenko, chief Soviet representative on the allied council for Japan and head of the large Soviet mission in Tokyo, made his move.

With his wife and luggage in tow, he set sail aboard Soviet trawler No. 284 along with 45 other Soviet nationals. He had given only one day's notice to the council's headquarters. U.S. intelligence believed the sudden, massive turnover of personnel was intended to keep the Soviets from being entangled in an imminent crackdown on Japan's aggressive Communist Party. But no one seemed to know for sure. One of the officers who worked for Derevyenko even suggested that he was being recalled to Moscow because he'd gotten too chummy with Gen. Douglas MacArthur.[1]

As would soon be evident, there were other, unseen motives. Derevyenko left a deputy in place, but his replacement, Maj. Gen. A.P. Kislenko, wouldn't arrive until August. That would mean the allied peace council (like the USSR's seat in another high-level public forum—the United Nations' security council) would be left without a permanent Soviet delegate just when the Far East was about to erupt in flames. If there were a design that might have been apparent to anyone connecting the dots of these diplomatic signals, it was masked by the all-too-common reports that trouble was brewing on the Korean peninsula.

Reports of imminent war on the Korean peninsula were as constant as the tide at Inchon.

Derevyenko had been in the Far East only since 1945. He'd gotten acquainted with MacArthur, the U.S. pro-consul in Japan, when he was designated by Stalin to sign the Japanese surrender aboard the USS Missouri for the Soviet Union. Derevyenko's theater of operations during World War II had been Europe, the cradle of the Soviet Union's most bitter defeats and most glorious victories. So it had been a great and unexpected honor to be selected to represent the Soviet Union in the official declaration of victory over the Japanese.

The duty in Tokyo—where the American influence gave postwar life a certain western looseness, and official matters often involved some new intrigue one moment and a flower-accepting social ceremony the next— could be diverting. But with the other parties to the allied council continually bringing up the unpleasant issue of Japanese prisoners of war, the tens of thousands of defeated troops who were still, years later, incarcerated in Siberian labor and indocrination camps, the atmosphere had grown tense and argumentative.

Trying to breathe life into the Marxist-Leninist cause under the direct gaze of such a powerful figure as MacArthur had not been easy, nor particularly successful. But Derevyenko's departure didn't signal a defeat.

While the Tokyo and Hong Kong press reported that Derevyenko was returning to Moscow via Vladivostok, he was actually headed for a new assignment in the region. He would be assuming high-level advisory duties related to a military surprise that was about to unfold.

Once the trawler reached the open sea, it made for a pre-arranged rendezvous with a Soviet submarine, which took Derevyenko to a port in French Indochina. From there, he traveled north to Peking, where he met with the political and military leaders of China's new communist government.

His message was that everything was in place for the dramatic move on the Korean peninsula. After repeated appeals from the young, energetic leader of North Korea, Kim Il-Sung, Stalin had given his approval for a lightning strike to liberate the southern half of the country.

The Soviet leader had opposed Kim's plans earlier, saying the time was not right and that the North Koreans should be prepared only to counter-attack when the expected invasion from the south by Syngman Rhee's forces materialized. But with Mao Tse-Tung's victory in China, the North Koreans had continued to press for the chance to consolidate their authority over the entire territory they believed was theirs legitimately.[2]

Stalin and Mao were prepared to assist, but the basic assumption of the entire enterprise was that the North Koreans could claim victory before the world noticed, or could act.

The United States had left Rhee to his own fate.

All U.S. military forces with the exception of a few advisors had been withdrawn from the south the year previous. In January, President Truman and his secretary of state, Dean Acheson, had as much as said they were not prepared to come to South Korea's defense. And Derevyenko and Stalin's other advisors in the Far East had all assured him that North Korea's new Soviet-supplied and Soviet-trained military was up to the task of wresting complete control away from the south in 90 days or less. Stalin was only interested if the war was going to be a short one.

Once Korea was under the Communist tent, Mao's plans to take Formosa so that he could truly be the great leader of all of China, could be resumed. After that would come the difficult but tireless work of wresting Japan out of the grip of the West. That project would require a united front all across the Asian perimeter. A unified Korea was a linchpin to that strategy.

Now the time was at hand to let history bring another storm out of Asia, and help Kim Il-Sung forge his little country's future.

After bringing the Chinese up to date on plans for the rapid summer "liberation" of South Korea, Derevyenko moved on to his next assignment, which would take the 46-year-old general behind the scenes of a covert war aimed at changing the future face of Asia for good.

Since the fall of 1948, when the majority of the Red Army's occupation troops had been withdrawn from North Korea, the Soviet Union had worked to create a home-grown force to replace it. In December 1948, Gen. Terentii F. Shtykov, a young (43), ambitious Communist Party committeeman whom Stalin had tapped as the first Soviet ambassador to Pyongyang, arrived with three dozen generals, colonels and lieutenant colonels whose mission, according to one of them was "to form and train a new North Korean army in not more than 18 months."[3]

Thousands of North Korean volunteers who had fought alongside Mao's soldiers, led by a fiery young stalwart named Kim Il-Sung, who had impressed his mentors in Moscow and at the military academy in Khabarovsk with his shrewdness and charisma, had returned from China and been melded into the national force. Soviet-Koreans from the ethnic Korean communities in Siberia and elsewhere in the USSR were carefully selected and groomed to take over important party, labor and production jobs.

Many in this new cadre spoke better Russian than Korean, but it was their ideology that mattered, not their facility with the native tongue.

To arm this growing force of eager nationalists, the Soviets had turned up the quotas at the tank assembly lines in Chelyabinsk and Novosibirsk and summoned thousands of Soviet military advisers to the training fields and tank ranges of Manchuria and North Korea.

The plans for the summer 1950 invasion of South Korea had been in the works for months. Earlier in the year, the Russians had moved eight brigades from Khabarovsk into central Manchuria, establishing a temporary military headquarters at Tsitsihar.[4] The advance elements moved farther south, to Mukden, just a few hours north of the border with North Korea.

About 150 new T-34 Soviet tanks were brought in from the USSR, along with 30 Russian armored officers to train the North Koreans in tank warfare.

The Chinese were somewhat leery of the help the Soviets were extending them as the newest member of the international Communist movement. They knew the Russian hug could quickly become an uncomfortable vise. After the Japanese surrender, the Soviets had looted Manchuria of much of its manufacturing and business base. Stalin had agreed the province should belong to China, but the Russian presence there was still a kind of de facto occupation.

The North Koreans, on the other hand, were so grateful for the assistance they had received from Moscow since the rout of the Japanese colonialists that they had virtually deeded much of an entire province along the Yalu River in northwestern Korea to the Russians.

The Russians had renamed North Pyongyan "Chagang," and were running it as a classic special preserve, where they had extraordinary rights and privileges.[5]

The Russians were confident they had brought the North Koreans to the brink of military success. Stalin had no intention of committing Russian troops to the fight in Korea, but he had promised the Chinese and North Koreans that the advisors would remain at the highest levels of the military for support and guidance, and should the plan for a lighting-fast victory over the south by September require it, he was prepared to throw the overwhelming weight of Soviet sea and air power behind the effort.[6]

While planning for the invasion took priority, the other programs the Russians were operating on the Far East perimeter of the huge Soviet empire continued as well.

One of the most sensitive involved air-drops of North Korean agents into South Korea, carried out by a counter-intelligence group designated as "M" unit. Well aware that the U.S.-backed government of South Korean president Syngman Rhee was engaged in its own covert operations, and that hundreds of "guerrilla fighters" on both sides had been captured and summarily executed in recent years, all of the Soviet advisers were careful to guard against exposure or sabotage by enemy agents.

But given their unique mission, "M" Unit's commanders, Cols. Kubrak, Bovkun and Patin, Lt. Col. Sukharev and Sr. Lt. Valeyev, ordered their men to be especially security-conscious because saboteurs could be anywhere. In Sukharev's words, "the infiltrated enemy in Korea is carefully disguised, and it is therefore the duty of the advisors always to be on the alert, especially in the units where we constantly work with complicated mechanical equipment which is serviced by people who were formerly employed by the Japanese."[7]

The Russians had also helped the North Koreans organize their own training school for guerillas. One of Kim Il-Sung's assurances to Moscow was that the hundreds of secret agents he had sent south in the first half of 1950 would raise revolutionary consciousness below the 38th parallel to a fever pitch. Kim Il-Sung and his troops wouldn't be invaders, but welcomed as brothers.[8]

A principal target of the agitators and guerrillas sent south from Pyongyang was the U.S. military infrastructure the Rhee government depended on for its defense.

The effort to obtain military intelligence in South Korea had been made slightly more difficult by the arrest in August 1949 of Nikolai Kreosev, the lone caretaker of the Soviet consulate in Seoul. The South Koreans had charged him with stealing information about their military and passing it to Gen. Derevyanko's office in Tokyo as well as to the Soviet embassy in Pyongyang.

But in fact, the Soviet consulate in Seoul had lost much of its utility in 1947, when Rhee's secret police broke up a well-organized spying ring that relied on Soviet officials for financing and cover. The main Soviet ring-leader of that operation had been Anatoli Shabshin, then the Russian vice-consul in Seoul, who seemed to like nothing better than a good running spat with the U.S. occupation commander, Gen. John R. Hodge.[9]

With his hard-line, distrustful attitude toward the Koreans, Hodge made a perfect foil for Shabshin's jibes at the allied powers' "trusteeship" for the south, which thanks to frequent roundups and executions of communist guerrillas and sympathizers even many non-communists saw as little better than the hated Japanese occupation it had replaced.

Some of the Communists' covert operations had an almost comic-opera air. In August of 1949, North Korean infiltrators made off with a cabin cruiser owned by Brig. Gen. William L. Roberts, commander of the U.S. military advisory detachment.[10]

As the invasion date approached, covert operations increased.

On June 1, a 30-man party of North Korean guerrillas pulled away from the coastline and headed south, to an island just off Inchon, the main port for Seoul. They infiltrated the capital area and made contact with sympathetic agents in the south, cultivated over the five years since Korea had been freed from Japanese occupation. Their signal to recognize each other was a white bandage, worn on the right hand.

Once the invasion was launched, the guerrillas were to stay in the vanguard of the advancing North Korean forces, clearing bridges, staking out railway stations and otherwise paving the way for the main force. The guerrillas' Moscow-trained leader, Lt. Han, told his men the invasion was scheduled to begin in a few weeks, and it would be the "first step toward the liberation of Asia."

Han predicted the operation would be over in two months, even if the U.S. forces stationed in Japan came to the aid of the South Koreans. If they didn't, "it would take our forces only ten days to overrun South Korea," he told his men.[11]

Simultaneously, to mask their role in the preparation for the invasion, a number of the Soviet military advisers were ordered to withdraw. But they retreated only as far as the margins of the action, to longtime bases just beyond North Korea's frontiers—on the USSR-Korea border southwest of Vladivostok, to the Soviet-run naval facility at Port Arthur, or to newly-enlarged bases just across the Yalu River in Antung, Mukden and Tsitsihar. The Soviet embassy in Pyongyang retained its full complement of diplomats, technicians, security and propaganda experts and military and political advisors. Some, like Vladimir Grigoryevich Tolstikov, came under the cover of reporters for Pravda, the Moscow newspaper. Pyongyang was seen as a good post for ambitous young Soviets, Tolstikov said. Both he and his wife drew assignments there. And Mrs. Tolstikov didn't let a little thing like a war get in the way of starting a family. She and Vladimir had three children during the Korean War—all conceived in North Korea, but delivered in Moscow.

To those on frontline duty in Pyongyang, however, it was also clear that Mao's successful takeover of the vast Chinese land mass, with its millions of people, would bring major and significant changes to the Far East.

China's new Communist regime was rapidly and urgently pressing to regain control over Port Arthur and the other cities in Manchuria that the Red Army had taken back from the Japanese. An area the Soviets had run as a virtual Russian concession or fiefdom since 1945 was filling up with Mao's new ideologically loyal legions.

With its warm-weather ports and proximity to Japan, Korea had been important to the leaders in Moscow since before the Bolsheviks began calling the shots. The Russian czar Nicholas II had tried to extend his power along a number of salients in the Far East, including to Korea, which naturally enough the Japanese and Chinese saw as their natural habitat.

After years of feinting and negotiating, Russia spurned a Japanese offer to take only Manchuria and leave Korea, where both countries had encouraged large settlements, to Japan. The Russo-Japanese war (1905) that resulted was a disaster for the Russians' dreams of a Korean colony. The loss of Korea was followed by an even costlier loss of most of Manchuria, including Port Arthur and the serviceable railroad lines across Manchuria that knitted several ports with the Russian outpost of Vladivostok.

Considering this history, Stalin's 1945 re-capture of the old Russian frontier areas south of the Amur River, all the way to the dusty streets of Kaesong, was a sweet and long-awaited payback to Japan for the indignities and territorial losses of 1905.

From that perspective, it seemed quite natural for the Russians to be striding like re-born cossacks through Pyongyang and Wonsan in 1950. The Soviets were accustomed to moving around Korea's northern half openly, unworried that someone might interpret their presence as covert, illicit, or in any way inappropriate. After all, the Kremlin recognized Kim

Il-Sung's government—in fact had virtually created it. Moscow's diplomats, military leaders, political operatives, journalists, ballet instructors, propaganda workers and intelligence agents were just as welcome north of the 38th parallel as Washington's were south of it.

Perhaps that helps explain why once the war broke out, and the zone of North Korea's authority stretched very quickly to the far southern limits of the small peninsula, it seemed as though Soviets were popping up everywhere.

By late 1952, there were so many Russians and Soviet-manned and -operated installations in North Korea that the Pentagon's psychological warfare specialists considered dropping leaflets written in Russian, "to appeal directly to Soviet personnel."

U.S. policy was to downplay the presence of the Soviet military in the war, always carefully describing them as "advisors" or "technicians." But besides the aviation fighter and training squadrons and anti-aircraft batteries—some of which were deployed southward to the front lines of battle—all kinds of Soviet military units were engaged in the struggle. Victor Ilyinsky, a Soviet soldier who defected to West Germany soon after the war, said he was attached to a signal corps unit in North Korea from 1951 until the armistice was signed in July 1953.[12]

Since the Soviet Union's role in the war was quasi-covert from the beginning, no indisputable figures exist for the total number of troops deployed there. But the presence of an aviation corps with its pilots, maintenance and fueling crews, radar sites, numerous artillery brigades, border guards and military intelligence personnel argue for a figure not less than 20,000—and perhaps much higher.

There had certainly been a strong Soviet presence behind the rousing anti-American propaganda drive, aimed at ridding the Korean peninsula of United States "imperialism." The full-throated cry against Uncle Sam's heavy-handed rule continued unabated as war preparations in the north proceeded.

In Washington, D.C., late in the evening of Sunday, June 25, an official from the U.S. embassy in Seoul, Arthur M. Schechter, 42, landed aboard a Northwest Airlines flight carrying an embassy pouch stuffed full of Russian-language material.[13]

The pouch was from John Muccio, U.S. ambassador to Seoul, and contained handbills, brochures, radio transcripts and documentary films to be shared with influential members of Congress as evidence of the Soviet-financed "culture and propaganda" campaign the North Koreans were carrying out in conjunction with acts of sabotage, subversion and arson to ruin American prestige in the region and destabilize the South Korean government.

Complaining of having to listen while Radio Pyongyang "for 13 hours daily spews insult after insult" against Americans, Muccio wanted Congress to know just what the barricades of freedom looked and sounded like from his post halfway around the world.

But by the time Embassy Pouch 696 reached Foggy Bottom, so had other, more ominous messages. Only hours earlier, the Soviet-trained and supplied army of North Korea had mounted a full-scale invasion across the 38th parallel. Anti-American and anti-South Korean propaganda had escalated to all-out war.

The Soviets were betting on a quick, knockout blow. Derevyenko and Shtykov's chief political adviser, Shabshin, had reassured the ambassador and party leaders in Moscow that the United States would not intervene militarily to save the South Korean regime. Hadn't MacArthur basically ignored the situation in Korea, relegating it to secondary importance while giving top priority to helping Japan rise from the war's atomic ashes?

An incident over the Baltic Sea in April in which Soviet fighters shot down a Navy Privateer with a crew of 10 had also provided support for the belief that the American were not up for a fight. The shootdown had raised only a small ripple of official protest.

And in South Korea itself, it was well known that American military planners were nearly as worried that Rhee's militant speeches and constant demands for more weapons would draw them into a military adventure as they were about the threat from the north. Concerned that the South Korean president might use U.S. weapons to mount his own invasion northward, U.S. authorities had deprived Rhee's troops of all but "defensive" weapons stocks.

Shabshin, the top Communist Party representative in Pyongyang and a top advisor to Gen. Shtykov, had logged a lot of experience with the Americans in Korea since the Soviets had won the race to the ancient kingdom to accept the surrender of the Japanese warlords. But he, Derevyenko and the others who wagered the United States wouldn't try to block the north's bold bid to carry out its Marxist destiny were about to be proven wrong.

The first days of the North Korean invasion went as predicted. The repeated warnings of an invasion had lulled the enemy into dropping its guard. But a few weeks later, with President Truman asking for international help to repel Kim Il-Sung's forces, it was clear that Shabshin and Shtykov had guessed wrong.

Shabshin had left Pyongyang for Berlin the day after the invasion, suddenly worried that the situation was explosive, given President Truman's instant, angry reaction. It was already clear to him that the Chinese troops massed in reserve in Manchuria would be needed, even though Mao was not at all eager to get involved.

Mao had believed the Soviets when they said entry into the UN was a sure thing, probably by that fall. Now those prospects were beginning to dissolve.

For Gen. Shtykov, who was obligated to make periodic reports on the war to the Communist Party's Central Committee in Moscow, it was time for a full-blown reassessment. He summoned his top military and political aides to the embassy on July 6 for a complete appraisal.

As some 50 officials made their way to the meeting, not everyone had these geopolitical concerns uppermost in their mind. Ivan Gribanov, who supervised the garage at the mission, could be forgiven a few minutes' worry about his main personal concern: whether the 200 rubles he was wiring home each month was enough to take care of his mother, who lived many time zones away, all the way across Russia, in the Novgorod region between Moscow and Leningrad.[14]

Sergei Kim, a short, round-faced, Russian-speaking Korean who was the official interpreter for ambassador Shtykov, wore his usual serious look. He knew his linguistic skills would be in great demand. But as one of the Soviet-Koreans specifically recruited to bring about a transformation of his ancestors' birthplace, he felt chosen for a great honor.

As they gathered for the important appraisal session, the ambassador and his guests needed to remain alert, keeping a watchful eye on the sky. American planes had begun flying daily bombing raids from Fifth Air Force bases in Japan, destroying much of North Korea's tiny air force on the ground. And fighter-bombers launched from U.S. and British aircraft carriers off Korea's eastern coast were hitting airfields near Pyongyang, as well as convoys of North Korean troops.

The sleek, fast aircraft the Americans were able to bring into the battle were proving devastating for North Korea's tiny air force. With barely 120 planes, about 40 competent pilots, and crude communications gear, the North Koreans were no match for the Americans in the air.

Even worse, the U.S. bombing and strafing runs were taking out entire groups of airplanes at once, while they were parked at unprotected airfields, wrapped in red and green blankets that served more to point them out than to camouflage them. Ammunition and fuel storage areas were similarly vulnerable. The 15 Soviet advisers attached to the aviation section had their work cut out for them.[15]

Eventually, the bombing of Pyongyang and other cities in North Korea would reach even more intense, saturation levels. North Korean officials and their advisers from the Soviet Union, Poland, Czechoslovakia, East Germany and other Communist bloc countries would have to abandon much of the flattened capital and operate out of a few major buildings with below-ground rooms and spend days moving in and out of the caves that honeycombed the area, dug into hillsides by the resourceful North Koreans.[16]

But in early July, 1950, Pyongyang was still safe enough for a large gathering of Russian and North Korean VIPS. And the ambassador and his North Korean colleagues had reason to be extremely pleased with the latest news from the front.

Seoul had been seized with virtually no resistance. A number of Soviet advisers had accompanied their North Korean units into the city and reported that parades, political rallies and some expected scavenging were underway. Before fleeing, the U.S. military advisors had tried to organize the South Korean troops into hasty defensive positions to slow the North Koreans' advance, but the North Koreans' superiority was unstoppable. The first American combat troops had just arrived from Japan, but appeared to be making little headway against the tide of the attacking forces.

In a way, Shtykov and his aides may have mused, what the western powers were claiming was a new example of "Communist aggression" was no more than a long-delayed resumption of "August Storm," the Red Army's smashing drive through Japanese-occupied Manchuria and Korea in the late summer of 1945.

In that lopsided victory, only days after the first atomic bombs were used on Japanese cities, Soviet troops had rounded up whole divisions of Japanese troops while racing to stake out as much of the peninsula as they could lay claim to before the Americans arrived. But the Americans had flown into Seoul just as the war ended, and the Kremlin had to be satisfied with the Far East clauses of the agreement reached at Yalta.

In the confusion and chaos of the war's end, the allies had agreed to divide the country at the 38th parallel. Now that arbitrary line of separation could be forgotten.

Neither the Soviet-backed government in the north nor the U.S.-supported government in the south had much liked the arrangement, anyway. Each side had basically chosen and nurtured its proxy for a struggle to determine whether the Communists or the democrats in the west would control the whole peninsula. It was no surprise that, over the years following the Japanese surrender, the 38th parallel had become as tense and contested as the lines dividing the big powers in Vienna and Berlin.

Now, with a force of more than 135,000 North Korean troops led by Soviet-supplied tanks slashing rapidly toward a convincing victory, the stunned South Koreans, assisted by only a handful of U.S. military advisers and a single battalion of U.S. Army ground troops just arrived from Japan, were falling back in bloody confusion. In their haste to flee Seoul, the South Koreans had dynamited the main highway bridge over the Han River well before North Korean forces arrived, killing hundreds who were trying to cross and stranding thousands north of the river.

On June 30th, Brig. Gen. John H. Church, head of a survey team MacArthur had sent from Tokyo to assess the situation, reported that the lightly armed South Korean troops "will not stay any length of time under artillery fire—they are almost as frightened of it as of tanks."

In their futile attempts to block the North Korean advance at several junctures, South Korean army commanders were forced to order retreat after retreat. Many vehicles and heavy weapons like howitzers, mortars and anti-tank guns the U.S. had supplied for South Korea's defense were simply abandoned. Within days, so many positions were overrun, and units scattered, field officers were able to muster fewer than half of Rhee's 98,000-man army.

Two of the Soviet mission's highest-ranking members—Grigori I. Tunkin, the Soviet foreign ministry's eminent Far East expert who had been a key member of the failed U.S.-USSR Joint Commission on Korea, and Col. Alexandr M. Ignatyev, a principal figure in the creation of a Communist-directed civil administration above the 38th Parallel—were not able to attend Shtykov's meeting. Perhaps they had already been recalled to Moscow, to explain to Stalin how they intendedto deal with this unexpected war with the Americans.

But the gathering did draw some of the principal figures who had worked since 1945 to consolidate a Communist beachhead in the Far East and others who had been even more directly involved in the launching of Kim Il-Sung's surprise attack.[17]

They included Aleksei Sokolov, a future ambassador already embarked on a notable diplomatic career; Maj. Gen. Nikolai G. Lebedev, executive officer of Soviet occupation forces in North Korea; Gen. Alexei Antonov, deputy chief of staff of the Soviet Army; Col. Sevastyan Polyashenko, acting chief of the Soviet mission in Occupied Japan; Mikhail M. Belov, also from the Tokyo mission; N.I. Timofeyev, from the Soviet embassy in Peking; and Col. Bodyagin, head of the KGB's regional office and internal security adviser to the North Koreans.

While the officials meeting at the Soviet embassy assessed the situation, the first western prisoners of the Soviet-trained and -supported forces of North Korea were nearby.

Under constant guard in the barbed wire-enclosed headquarters of the Internal Security (secret police) in Pyongyang that day were several dozen foreigners—diplomats, missionaries, journalists, technicians, doctors, advisors, merchants and ex-military personnel who had been caught in the net the North Koreans had drawn so quickly around Seoul, Kaesong, Taejon and the smaller communities that lay between them on the North Koreans' invasion route.

Men and women of various ages, callings, backgrounds and nationalities—including at least 13 Americans—some of those captured had been prisoners of the Japanese in World War II. One was a Jewish physician from Vienna who had survived the Nazi prison camp at Buchenwald. Some of the French priests were among the frailest, born in the 1870s but, according to their younger fellow prisoners, uncomplaining.[18]

Captured in the first days of fighting, they had spent the Fourth of July in a truck being transported to the North Korean capital from Kaesong, Seoul, and other cities where roundups of foreigners and Koreans suspected of pro-Rhee sympathies were an hourly occurrence.

To be sure, these 60 or so foreigners represented only a fraction of the total number of prisoners in the hands of the invaders. Except for the network of North Korean agents working undercover, virtually the entire population of South Korea had been surprised by the attack, and tens of thousands were too slow or too trusting to elude the invaders as the North Koreans easily occupied Seoul on the fourth day of the war.

Everett Drumwright, vice consul at the U.S. embassy, confided later that when he first heard of the North Korean attack, "I dismissed it as just another rumor."[19]

The hundreds of Korean prisoners included several dozen members of the recently elected South Korean assembly (none of whom was ever repatriated). Lulled into staying too long by reassuring government radio broadcasts that misled them into thinking the invasion was being repulsed, they had missed the last train carrying government officials out of the capital.

After the war, South Korean officials trying to measure the human cost of the war compiled a list of 86,000 intellectuals alone—novelists, surgeons, professors and administrators—who remained missing.

Even partial figures for the first fall of Seoul on June 28 (the city would change hands three more times between September 1950 and March 1951), pieced together in the fall of 1950 by South Korean and American officials, estimated nearly 1,000 residents killed, more than 2,400 taken prisoner and another 1,200 missing.

Besides the U.S embassy staff, Catholic and Protestant missionaries and Red Cross personnel, the American community in Seoul included a CIA station of several hundred agents and workers, a regional office of the Economic Cooperation Administration (forerunner to the Agency for International Development), hundreds of technicians working under contracts supervised by the ECA, about 50 U.S. military advisers and their dependents, and a handful of businessmen and journalists.

An embassy list of U.S. civilians living in South Korea, including dependents of U.S. military advisers, compiled just days before the war broke out contained 1,560 names. Most of the 1,230 in Seoul, including U.S. ambassador Muccio, evacuated the capital by plane and ship on June 26 and 27.

One boat rigged to accommodate only a dozen passengers left Inchon with 690 American dependents on board, jammed into every crevice and pressed so tightly together they could barely move. But all arrived safely in Tokyo, and relieved U.S. officials congratulated themselves on escaping the Communist onslaught.[20]

Their relief was short-lived. U.S. and South Korean military losses were high, and by July 8, newspapers in Communist-controlled Seoul were reporting that 501 U.S. troops were being held prisoner in the city's West Gate prison.

The new Communist occupiers allowed many Seoul residents to go on with their lives, as long as they were willing to participate in daily demonstrations on behalf of Kim Il-Sung.

But the hunt for spies, saboteurs and informants went on. Officials in charge of sorting out thousands of prisoners isolated anyone whose background included links to the U.S., or to Rhee's U.S.-supported government. Prisoners who had traveled beyond the borders of Korea, or worked for foreign powers, were highly suspect.

One such case was Kim Kon Hu. A 47-year-old mining engineer fluent in several languages, Kim told his captors he had studied at a college in the U.S. from age 19 to 26, then worked in both the Soviet Union and China. In 1946, he was employed as an interpreter at the U.S.-USSR Joint Commission in Seoul, and from 1946 to 1948 he had worked as an advisor to the U.S. military.[21]

After moving into the management of the South Korean tungsten industry, Kim returned to the U.S. to study mineral experimentation. Since January of 1950, he had been technical chief of South Korea's Tungsten Mining Co.

When Seoul was back in the hands of the United Nations command in the fall of 1950, U.S. intelligence units recovered Kim Kon Hu's interrogation sheet. A notation in pencil read "transferred to Home Ministry," an indication that higher-level interrogation was in order.

But the prize catches of the invasion were the first group of western civilian POWs, who were quickly hustled to secret police headquarters in Pyongyang.

Besides more than a dozen Americans, the contingent rounded up in Seoul and Kaesong in June and July 1950 included the top British and French diplomats in Korea, Capt. Vyvian Holt and Georges Perruche, and their chief aides, Bishop Patrick Byrne of Washington, D.C., the papal representative in Korea, the British head of the Salvation Army in Seoul,

Herbert Arthur Lord, a Swiss hotel manager and a few shadowy figures whose identity was not clear even to their fellow prisoners.

Quickly separated from the other captives, the foreigners were treated harshly, but not brutally. Their worst experiences came after some weeks in and near Pyongyang, when they were marched north with the first groups of U.S. military prisoners, along a rugged route that after ten days was littered with the corpses of stragglers who were executed where they fainted, or grew too weak to stand, or defied their guards' warning not to try to assist any who fell behind.

But Korean nationals caught in the same net appeared to fare even worse, from the conditions the western civilians witnessed in the first phase of imprisonment at a Pyongyang schoolhouse. The screams, pounding, and repeated gunshots coming from nearby rooms were unmistakable evidence of a steady stream of executions in the secret police compound.

The foreigners were taken one by one away from the group for questioning by teams of interrogators about their politics, their reasons for being in Korea, and their ties to the U.S. and South Korean governments and military.

Like the other Americans, Rev. Larry Zellers, a Methodist missionary from Texas who had been living in Kaesong, just two miles south of the north-south dividing line, was accused of working with U.S. counter-intelligence. His fellow POWs were worried that his predicament was more serious than theirs, however, because their captors knew—presumably from a North Korean intelligence file on him, since he hadn't disclosed it—that Zellers' military experience in World War II included flying in airplanes and using field communications gear.

When other POWs were returned to their cells, they often warned Zellers that the interrogators had asked them many questions about him, and about the apparent contradiction between his military expertise and his statement that his only job in Kaesong had been teaching English to school children.

As the interrogations continued, Zellers' captors began stating matter-of-factly that they had proof he had been passing intelligence to officials in Seoul, and that he would be executed as a spy. "You know it is a very bad thing for a soldier to be captured when not in uniform," one of Zellers' interrogators told him. "Things are very bad for you."[22]

This intense questioning of foreign prisoners at the Pyongyang jail went on non-stop for several days. The interrogators treated Zellers and the others as though they truly suspected that somewhere among the motley collection of elderly priests, missionary teachers, limping nuns and traders, middle-aged technical advisers and diplomatic dependents there might very well be a valuable captive or two, someone with close and perhaps highly classified ties to the U.S. occupation forces, someone who actually possessed a valuable military secret or two.

Zellers and the other missionaries, diplomats and journalists who were taken initially to Pyongyang say the questioning there was done by North Koreans, and the first Russians they encountered did not appear until the winter of 1950-51.

But they knew the Russians weren't far away. Some of their fellow prisoners were being taken away for interrogation by Soviet officials.

The day after Shtykov's meeting at the Soviet mission, the American bombing did increase markedly, making life there so hazardous that much of Pyongyang was temporarily evacuated. The foreign prisoners were placed in an open truck and moved to a schoolhouse several miles outside the city.

There Zellers and the other Americans in his group found there were even more foreigners who had been caught in the invasion net, including more diplomatic employes of different nationalities and several whole families, about 20 stateless people—often known as "White Russians" because of the long history of Russian settlement in the Far East under the czars.

Their family names—Vorosoff, Daylaisha, Kilin, Kuchikoff, Salahutdin—marked them as products of the polyglot migrations that brought people to the Korean peninsula from various nations and many cultures. The White Russian families had been living quietly and peacefully in Seoul, thankful that the U.S. military and the civilian assistance programs were injecting a boost of economic life into the war-battered land.

But with no official papers, having passed on the recent offers by the USSR throughout China and the Far East to claim their "rightful" status by signing papers granting them Soviet citizenship, they were "stateless persons," fair game for the prison camps.

They were some of the first to be captured, and their future would remain undecided long after the armistice and repatriation that ended the imprisonment of the western visitors to Korea.

Among these several groups of civilians captured by the North Korean troops and taken to Pyongyang within days of the invasion were two people—a man and a woman—whose paths took a course different from the rest. Their fellow prisoners knew them as Helena Orchestraia and Andre Merzlitsky.

Helena had worked with Maisara Vorosoff, a native of Hailar, Manchuria, one of the White Russian prisoners, as a clerk at the U.S. civilian commissary. When the North Korean tanks rolled into Seoul, Maisara recalled, she and Helena took refuge first in a downtown hotel, then moved to a compound at the French legation, where a number of foreigners had congregated.

They knew the French consul, Perruche, and hoped that a western diplomatic compound would offer immunity, some protection from the suspicious bands of North Koreans going neighborhood to neighborhood, house to house, store to store, looking for subversives.

But the North Koreans, recognizing none of the niceties of international protocol, took the French consul and everyone in the compound prisoner. Within days, Helena and Maisara—both then in their 20s—were put among the stateless families, then as the days wore on, merged with the larger group of non-Korean POWs being held at the schoolhouse outside Pyongyang.

It was here, said Maisara, that she, Helena and others were questioned by Soviet military officials. She and Helena drew their curiosity, Maisara believes, because they both worked at several agencies and commissaries frequented by or operated mainly for the use of the U.S. community in Seoul. The interrogators were looking for any link to the Americans.

Helena told the Soviet questioners that she was of Polish extraction and that her father was in the diplomatic service. But then, said Maisara, Helena "started changing her name" under questioning and the men interrogating them—two Russians dressed in military uniforms and a third in civilian clothes—"got suspicious."

A few days later, said Maisara, "they took her away and I never saw her again." When she asked the officers about Helena, "they said they'd sent her to Harbin, where she had a brother."

Then there was the man, Andre, who only spent a few days with the group of western civilian prisoners. He also had ties to the U.S. community in Seoul. But exactly what those ties were, even his fellow prisoners weren't certain.

Maria Kilin, who was 26 when the North Korean soldiers and security police came to her father's small retail store in Seoul and marched her whole family off to prison, said she knew Andre "very well. He lived in our house for awhile."

A large, physically imposing man in his 40s or 50s, Andre had told Maria and other acquaintances in Seoul that he had come to South Korea at the close of World War II after serving with the U.S. military. He never talked much about the war, or what his duties had been, said Kilin, but when the U.S. forces withdrew from South Korea in the summer of 1949, leaving only a few military advisors, he stayed on, working as an engineer and diver on an American-operated barge at Inchon, the seaport just west of Seoul.

Philip Deane, a British war correspondent for the London Observer who was among the civilian prisoners in this group, described Andre as "a White Russian diver who had worked for ECA," the U.S. foreign assistance agency.[23]

"He was tall and very strong," Kilin recalled. "I remember when my daughter Olga drew a picture of him, she put a big belly on him."

As for his nationality, no one knew for certain. "Andre said he was from Australia," said Kilin. But Maisara, who also became acquainted with Andre through others in the Seoul's non-Korean, Russian-speaking community, said he was actually a native of Manchuria, but had lived in Australia either during or after World War II.

Sagid Salahutdin, who was a teenager in a family of Turkish descent living in Seoul when he and all of his relatives were taken prisoner a few weeks after the invasion, also knew Andre as a frequent customer at his family's store. Because he could speak both English and Russian, had a job with good connections to the U.S. community and yet blended easily into the diverse culture of Seoul, Sagid suspected that Andre was working in some capacity for the U.S. military, probably in intelligence. He fit the profile, said Salahutdin, for someone the Americans or British would enlist to keep them informed of what was happening within the Russian-speaking community.

Andre drove around town in U.S. Army jeep, reason enough for his eventual Communist captors to question him closely, several acquaintances agreed. But Kilin thought of the jeep as a means of escape, not the cause of being arrested.

"If he had only come to get me," she said wistfully, "we could have gotten away, to Pusan, in his jeep."

But like Salahutdin, Kilin, Maisara and their entire families, Andre was caught in the net, too.

Zellers and other repatriated POWs who encountered him in the first days of their captivity remember him as a gentle giant around the police compound, assisting another POW, Walter Eltringham, a mining engineer from Pennsylvania beaten so severely that he later died from his injuries.

By the time she and her family reached the transit prison in Pyongyang, said Kilin, Andre had been singled out and taken away. She and the other prisoners were told only that the Soviets wanted him—as they had wanted Helena Orchestraia—for "questioning." He was "removed by the authorities," wrote Deane, "and was never seen again."[24]

On July 30, a few weeks after the last groups of prisoners had been rounded up in Seoul, Gen. Shtykov gave a dinner at the Soviet embassy in Pyongyang, to toast the war.

The U.S. and nearly 20 other countries were gearing up to send a sizable military force to the region, with the mission of halting and reversing the gains the North Koreans had made. With their many bombers and squadrons of modern fighters, the U.S. Air Force had complete air superiority over the battle zone. But the prospects for Kim Il-Sung's forces were still favorable.

North Korean troops were driving relentlessly southward. If they could shove the South Koreans into the sea within the next few weeks, the UN effort would be too late.

From August through the following January, the war took several sharp turns. First, North Korea's gamble failed, and the United Nations forces clung to a tiny foothold on the southeastern tip of the peninsula, the "Pusan perimeter." Then MacArthur's big gamble—an amphibious landing at Inchon, behind the North Koreans' main force—succeeded.

U.S. troops encircled the invaders and hammered them to the brink of defeat.

But MacArthur's units had no sooner occupied Pyongyang—with U.S. and South Korean units bivouacked on the Manchurian border and the USS Missouri shelling the city of Chongjin, only about 60 miles south of Vladivostok, until it erupted in flames—than the pendulum swung again.

The new Communist Chinese government of Mao Tse-tung sent in 39 divisions of "volunteers" and the Soviet Union dispatched an entire corps to the theater composed of anti-aircraft batteries and squadrons of new MIG fighter planes to push the United Nations forces away from their frontiers.

Mao's and Stalin's responses had been foreseen by George Kennan, a former U.S. envoy to Moscow, in an August, 1950, memo to Secretary of State Dean Acheson:

"The Soviet leaders must be seriously worried over the proximity of the Korean fighting to their own borders and over the direct damage which can conceivably be done to their military interests by any extension of the area of hostilities….When we begin to have military successes, that will be the time to watch out. Anything may then happen—entry of Soviet forces, entry of Chinese Communist forces, new strike for UN settlement, or all three together."

The Soviet Union tried to keep its forces from public view in Korea. There were incidents in which the underlying grid of Russian aid and combat involvement showed itself—the shooting down of Soviet pilots and crews, the capture of eight Russian "civilians"—who were more than likely Soviet advisors fleeing in civilian garb—when UN forces retook Seoul in the fall of 1950.

And then there were the interrogators, the Russian officers—men and women, sometimes in Soviet uniforms, sometimes in Chinese military dress, sometimes in civilian clothes—who invariably appeared when an American found himself a POW—in Pyongyang and many other places throughout North Korea, Manchuria, and even mainland China.

The North Korean capital was reduced to rubble before the war was over. Yet Gen. Shtykov and his successor, V. N. Razuvayev, who replaced him in August 1951, kept a Soviet embassy functioning throughout the war as both a diplomatic and military headquarters.

And the Pyongyang area near the Yellow Sea coast remained a transit site for thousands of American and other allied POWs. The foreign civilian POWs—including the seven Americans who survived—passed through Pyongyang to change trains for Moscow when they were released in April 1953. After the armistice, many military POWs spent their last night in captivity there before being trucked to the exchange point at Panmunjom.

But the fate of Andre, the Jeep-driving, Russian-and-English-speaking engineer last seen alive two weeks after the war began, would remain a mystery for more than 40 years.

Not until 1994 would a retired Soviet military officer—who was convinced he had encountered a fellow Ukrainian in a little piece of hell called Korea—find the courage and the opportunity to tell his story.

And that story would unlock a still greater mystery.

Chapter Two

Trains to Manchouli

"A plan has been formed by use of clandestine systems to obtain recovery of one or more such persons to establish the case beyond doubt before the world that such persons are being held."

—1954 Department of Army memo reporting on
efforts to account for American POWs in the Korean War
who were not repatriated and were believed
still held by Communist forces.

"Transportation by rail has greatly improved in China and N. Korea. Emergency repairs, working efficiency and traction have increased, and are being carried out with amazing speed despite continued destruction by the U.N. Forces."

—September 1951 U.S. Air Force intelligence report on
rail conditions in China during the Korean War.

When the Communist ruling class in the Soviet Union finally began to collapse and scatter in the early 1990s, the door looked ajar to an enormous thieves' den.

Russia, Ukraine, the Baltics and a score of previously repressed republics from the Polish border to the Mongolian frontier, gripped for most of a century in an economically stunted but manifestly dangerous empire of collectivism, were suddenly ripe for giving up a long list of well-kept, perhaps unspeakable, secrets from Stalin's time to the day before yesterday.

As Mikhail Gorbachev was replaced by Boris Yeltsin, the hero of the Moscow barricades, a shudder of hope rippled through a small community of Americans.

They were very interested in what could be in the KGB's musty files, but their interest was far more personal than professional or academic. They would let others hunt down the thick dossiers on Lee Harvey Oswald, or identify the full-time Communists the Soviets had kept on the payroll in the west, from Berlin to London to New York. They weren't concerned with which western scientists or secretaries might have shared secrets or cocktails with Stalin's nuclear physicists.

Their minds and emotions were fixed on the unknown fate of thousands of American POWs from the Korean War, Indochina and the numerous Cold War shootdowns during the 1950s and 1960s that had left the pilots and crews of several dozen long-range reconnaissance missions on the ground in Soviet territory, either dead and unrecovered, or alive and in peril.

They were people like Rita Van Wees, the aging but indominatable mother of Army Pfc. Ronald "Dutch" Van Wees, missing in action in Korea since Nov. 30, 1952. Seeing the old guard in Moscow finally giving way, she was moved to write yet another of her polite but stern letters to President Bill Clinton, the current occupant of the White House:

"Sir, as you go on your trip to Russia, when you look at your beautiful family, saying good-bye think of us as we have also beautiful loved ones so unbearably missed.

"These wonderful men should be first before any trade agreements and (be) allowed to either come home or be in touch with those that can never find peace again."[1]

The long, agonizing search for answers by Rita Van Wees and the other Korean War POW/MIA families and survivors for whom she is a kind of beacon and role model is rooted in the history of the Cold War and the standoff between two powerful superpowers that began moments after the joyous victories of World War II in Europe and Asia.

As the standoff became a land war, although a "limited" one, fought through proxies on the Korean peninsula—a war that Stalin had launched, or at the very least sanctioned and encouraged—reports soon surfaced that American prisoners were being transferred by the hundreds into Manchuria and from there to Siberia.

It took only a glance at a map to see that Siberia was a place that could hide whole divisions of prisoners; and only a cursory study of history to know that it had served that purpose in the past. And while the Truman and Eisenhower administrations in Washington chose to play down the Soviet role in the Korean War, there were sufficient allegations made about

Soviet involvement to leave the American public no doubt about the Kremlin's stake in it.

The fighting was still underway when an article appeared in a national magazine that took the hints, suspicions and fears about the Soviets' role and stake in Korea, as expressed by an assortment of columnists, commentators and editorialists, to their logical conclusion. Here, finally, was a story that seemed to explain the growing mystery over disappearing prisoners in Korea.

The account in Esquire, by Zygmunt Nagorski Jr., was entitled "Unreported GIs in Siberia," and rested on the word of an anonymous "informant, a short husky little man" the author said he had met in Berlin the previous year, and who had proven his reliability by filing dispatches to Nagorski's news agency on political developments behind the Iron Curtain that had proven to be correct.[2]

Nagorski's informant said the Communists had shipped both South Korean and American prisoners north from the battle area and, through a sophisticated selection process, were parceling them out to various prisons, interrogation rooms and labor camps spread across the Siberian wastes for use as slave labor and instruments of propaganda.

While most South Korean POWs were sent to Yakutsk, a remote and largely isolated city in the very heart of Siberia on the Lena River, the American prisoners were first sent to camps on the Chinese side of the Yalu River, in southern Manchuria, for screening, to determine their usefulness and politics. After being separated into groups slated for further punishment, interrogation or indoctrination, the Americans were "turned over to the Russians," Nagorski wrote, and "marked dead on POW lists."

That was certainly a phrase that struck home with the families of thousands of American GIs whose names had appeared on the lists the Communists were passing to UN negotiators of POWs they said had died in their prison camps.

The prisoners, according to Nagorski's informant, were then transported to Posyet, a Soviet port and naval station just inside the USSR where the Soviet and North Korean boundaries meet, and from there in a series of journeys to Khabarovsk, Komsomolsk and Chita, cities on the southern rim of Siberia that historically served as hubs for the intake and management of large groups of foreign and domestic prisoners.

The "coordinating center" for the process, and for many prisoners the final stop, Nagorski wrote, was the city of Molotov (now Perm), an industrial city that also housed a large secret police headquarters and prison.

The object, in Nagorski's account of his source's findings, was to hone the original groups of POWs down to the few willing to become agents or propagandists for the Soviet Union. Only a few ever reached the end of the indoctrination line, he wrote, because "the overwhelming majority of the transferred prisoners" refused to be used for propaganda work.

The operative tool in the process, he wrote, was an emotion: fear. "The men are transported by rail in trains heavily guarded by MVD men accompanied by dogs. At the transit camps there are more interrogations, and then selected POWs are sent to Chita, located east of Lake Baikal and near the Chinese frontier. The town, one of the largest on the Trans-Siberian Railroad, has an impressive MVD prison.

"Here the Communists start talking force. The prisoners know that their fate is entirely in the hands of the Soviet police; they are told that the North Koreans have declared them dead." The prisoners who chose to cooperate would then be rewarded with a transfer to a "rest camp," while those who continued to resist would be sent to "one of the stricter camps."

Those granted a pass to the rest camp at Shivanda, near Chita, Nagorski's informant said, received "good food, clean accommodations and general conditions far above anything known by the average Russian." The others found themselves "used as forced labor" in any of dozens of "disciplinary" prisons in the Komi-Permsk National District such as Kudymkar, Chermoz and Gubakha.

The special and isolated camps for American POWs were under dual supervision, Nagorski claimed, with political control in the hands of a special Communist Party delegate named "Comrade Edovin," while military control was exercised by a man named "Kalypin."

After reading about "GIs in Siberia," families that had been told no more than that a son, or husband, or brother was "missing in action" or a prisoner of war in Korea could only wonder if he was among those unfortunate souls already or soon to be packed into train cars for shipment to Manchuria, Molotov, Khabarovsk, Chita and—if he survived that long—points beyond.

What the families didn't know—couldn't know because it was classified intelligence information—was that when Nagorski's article was published the Central Intelligence Agency was already in possession of this same information about American POWs shipped to Siberia from Korea. And the agency's information so closely tracked the data found in Nagorski's article—down to the names of the political officers in charge of the camps for Americans—that it was unquestionably written from the same notes and sources.[3]

Dated July 15, 1952, nine months prior to the Esquire story, the report said that by December 1950, "it was known that transit camps for prisoners of war captured by the Communists in Korea had been established in Komsomolsk on the river Amur, Magadan...in the Sea of Okhotsk, Chita and Irkutsk. Through these transit camps are passing not only Korean POWs but also American POWs."

South Korean POWs were transported in ships that contained 1,000 or more prisoners each and landed at a number of ports along the Siberian coast, the report said. From there, the prisoners were put to work building roads, electricity plants and airfields, although under conditions that caused "high mortality." The camps for POWs in the Yakutsk region, the report stated, were near coal mines and dams and also were operated "under primitive conditions" that caused high rates of sickness and death.

Information on the "non-Asiatic," or American, prisoners, the intelligence report stated, "was received on 30 April 1952 from Gubakha railway in the Komi-Permsk National District in northwestern Siberia.

"According to this information, about 300 POWs were transported by rail from Chita to Molotov in February 1952. The prisoners were clothed in Soviet-style cotton padded tunics with no distinctive marks. They were first transported from the railway station to the MVD prison and then sent by rail, in a train consisting of 9 wagons, to Molotov on or about 5 April 1952. The train was heavily guarded by a railway guard of the MVD."

Previous shipments of American POWs from Chita to Molotov had occurred in August and November 1951, the report said: "The total number of POWs transported in this direction amounted to about 6,000 at the end of 1951. Their fate is not known."

Shipments passed through Khabarovsk, to Chita and Molotov "roughly every fortnight," the report said, "in small groups of up to 50 persons." "It is most probable that POWs are undergoing some sort of investigation and selection process while in the MVD prisons in Chita. Some of them are retained in prisons in Chita for a long time, while others are sent directly by rail to Molotov and other industrial regions in the Ural Mountains."

The CIA's informant was able to provide such detail as could only be known by someone who was close enough to this POW-transfer process to not only see, but hear, what was going on.

The report asserted that "several railway transports of American and European (probably British) POWs were seen passing at intervals of 10 to 20 days...clad in cotton padded, grey tunics...civilian caps...no military insignia. They spoke among themselves in English, and they knew no other language except a few words in Russian.

"During the journey they remained locked in heavily guarded wagons and were not allowed to leave them. They received their meals from MVD (Soviet security agency that was precursor to the KGB) guards. Each wagon had small windows at two levels. Each window was barred and covered by opaque glass."

Then the report spelled out specifics dealing with the American prisoners, relating that "a certain number of American POW officers, among whom was a group referred to as the 'American General Staff,' were kept at that time in the Command of the Military District of Molotov. Some of the POWs were accommodated in the building of the MVD in Molotov, having been subjected most probably to interrogations. They had been completely isolated from the outside world."

Then came the specifics of how the POWs were actually used by their Russian interrogators, and bosses. The report was drawn in convincing detail:

"In the town of Gubakha and in the industrial regions of Kudymkar and Chermoz there were three isolated camps and one interrogation prison for American POWs from Korea...Prisoners kept in the three labor camps were employed on the construction of a new railway line. In one of these camps, called GAYSK, about 200 Americans were kept. They were employed in workshops assembling rails and doing various technical jobs. These camps were completely isolated from any civilian camps located in the neighborhood. Political control was carried out by the local Party organization, headed by (fnu) (ed: first name unknown) Edovin, a delegate from the Obkom of the Komi-Permsk National District. All three camps were under the charge of (fnu) Kalypin, a Soviet officer of unknown rank who was sent from Molotov in February 1952."

In a scene that could have come straight out of a book about Communist "big brother" methods, the intelligence report said that in other camps near the Gubakha railway, "about 150 Americans were kept, probably soldiers and NCOs. An interesting thing was that from these camps one to three POWs were taken every few days by officers of the MVD for transportation to Gubakha or Molotov. They never returned to their camps, and their camps (sic) and their fate remained unknown. According to the supposition of persons acquainted with MVD methods these POWs had been observed in their camps by specially assigned agents of MVD, who knew the English language and thus were able to find out those who were very hostile to the Communist regime and ideology and those who could be considered sympathetic.

"Those belonging to the first group were most probably sent either to prison or to especially hard labor camps for extermination; the others were probably sent to special political courses in Molotov."

Asked about the similarities between his magazine article and the CIA report, Nagorski acknowledged having extensive contacts with the CIA during that period, and agreed the report and his story obviously share the same source. He surmised that a CIA employe might have used his story as the basis for the agency's classified report but failed to cite it explicitly to make it appear the employe had cultivated a very good source.

"He probably got a promotion out of it," said Nagorski.[4]

But that doesn't explain one fact: the CIA report was dated some months before the publication of the magazine article.

Regardless how it was being circulated, the story of American POWs being shipped into the Gulag was gaining some currency both in the public domain and in the intelligence community.

With such deadly prospects in store for any American captured by the Communists in Korea, it was no wonder that many citizens back home were suspicious of an idea that had gained considerable ground among U.S. policymakers since the war stalemated in the summer of 1951—so-called no-forced repatriation, to return only those Chinese and North Korean prisoners who wanted to go back.

The idea that the Communists would keep UN POWs in retaliation—claiming, of course, that all those who wished to return had been allowed to—was enough to flood the mail to Washington with letters and petitions, even though the majority of public opinion and newspaper editorials appeared to favor voluntary repatriation.

A State Department memo in December 1952, in the final months of President Truman's administration, reported: "Editorial opinion has been almost unanimously in favor of the UN position. However, there has been a constant under-current of privately circulated petitions demanding the return of our prisoners as a first concern. One such petition, started some months ago by the parents of a prisoner and with no known Communist inspiration, is believed to have gathered about 250,000 signatures. At present the department has received about 12,000 petitions or form messages calling for a cease-fire and a large proportion of them demanding the return of our prisoners."[5]

But what the State Department referred to as "the UN position" prevailed, and the die was cast. Now the POW/MIA families scanned the lines of every story from the negotiating and prisoner-exchange front to find proof of what they considered the war's biggest folly.

On July 27, 1953, a cease-fire went into effect, setting the stage for the mutual exchange of prisoners. On Sept. 6, 1953, the mutual repatriation was completed. Three days later, the UN Command demanded that the Communists account for 3,404 names (including 944 U.S.) that were not among the repatriates and not on their lists of those who died in enemy hands.

Two weeks later, the Communists replied that most of those the UN negotiators had asked about had never been captured. As for those who had been POWs but were now missing, they said most had in fact been repatriated (they gave a number, 580, but no names) and the rest were either dead, escaped, or had been "released at the front" during the fighting.

On Oct. 3, instead of further talk about the missing UN POWs, the Communists countered with a list of their own: 98,783 Chinese and North Korean troops they claimed must still be in UN hands. The hard-won agreement that had led to the release of thousands of POWs on both sides had reached the limits of its effectiveness. All that was left to decide was the fate of those prisoners on both sides who were having their options explained to them by a commission of "neutral nations."[6]

But the dividing line between the antagonists on the ground remained porous. On Nov. 23, three South Korean soldiers dashed across the demilitarized zone seeking refuge with the UN Command. Where had they been when the prisoner-exchange was underway? They said the Communists still held a great many POWs.

When the UN asked the Neutral Nations Commission to call a joint investigation of the soldiers' charge, it declined.

A few weeks later, on Dec. 14, two more South Korean soldiers made a delayed exit from north of the demilitarized zone. They confirmed what the earlier escapees had said about POWs secretly held back. By this time, the UN Command was having an internal debate about what to call these late-arriving POWs. Were they escaped prisoners? Defectors? Deserters? The term they used temporarily was defectors. But the important aspect of their defection—the stories they brought with them of POWs that had become hostages—remained beyond the power of the UN to investigate or resolve.

By early 1954, Washington's possible "courses of action" for giving "positive assurance to the American people that the U.S. government is seeking the release or a satisfactory accounting for missing Prisoners of War apparently still held in Communist custody" had been reduced to three, all summarized in a one-page memo to the Pentagon from the Department of the Army:

"a. Seek the release of personnel through the diplomatic efforts of the United Kingdom.

"b. In the United Nations General Assembly charge the Governments of Communist China and North Korea with a violation of the Armistice Agreement.

"c. Release to the press a joint State-Defense public announcement."[7]

Needless to say, these optional "courses of action" didn't begin to satisfy people with a special interest in the outcome—the families of thousands of servicemen who had not returned, but their government couldn't tell them what had happened to them.

In April 1954, a group of 72 women from 40 different states—including Rita Van Wees of the Bronx, N.Y.—gathered in front of the United Nations building in New York. On the lapels of their coats or sweaters they wore the name of their missing son, fiancee or husband and blue ribbons inscribed, "Mothers of Forgotten Men."

Other mothers and daughters had flown to Hong Kong, or Geneva, Switzerland, where the International Red Cross has its headquarters and where a UN conference was scheduled to convene to validate the agreements reached at Panmunjom. They were determined not to let the issue drop. They all wanted the question of POWs and MIAs placed on the agenda of the upcoming conference in Geneva on the aftermath of the Korean War. Their adviser and patron was Eugene Guild of Colorado, a retired Army captain who had returned the Navy Cross that was awarded posthumously to his Marine captain son to protest what he called President Truman's "appeasement" of the Communists in Korea.[7]

Rebuffed in their attempts to speak with Secretary General Dag Hammarskjold, who sent word he had no authority over member countries, the women attempted to speak with U.S. officials.

A few from the group met briefly with Henry Cabot Lodge, the U.S. ambassador to the UN, leaving the petitions they had gathered from speaking with veterans' groups and from letter-writing campaigns. These first voices and pleas from the families of MIAs were much milder than today's and more in keeping with the gentler form of public discourse in the 1950s.

Basically, their demands amounted to an appeal to the government for information about men who had been seen in prison camps, had been photographed on prisoner marches, had written letters from the prison camps, had even been listed as prisoners by the Communists, but were not among the repatriates or sets of remains sent back from Korea.

They moved on to Washington, where they hoped to present their plea to President Eisenhower, but were not granted a personal visit. They did participate in ceremonies at the Tomb of the Unknown Soldier in Arlington Cemetery, and Guild testified before the Senate Armed Services Committee, but their impact was limited to a few short stories and photos in the next day's papers.

"All we want to know," Peggy Doorley, of Uniontown, Pa., told a reporter in Washington, "is are they living or are they dead, and we want proof. We don't want to make any trouble. We have had sympathy, but we need more than that." But sympathy was all the government was prepared, or equipped, to offer by that time.

Doorley's fiancee, Air Force Lt. John R. Coulter, had been missing since Dec. 1, 1950.

His case remains one of 187 in which Air Force records indicate a high degree of probability that a pilot or crewman was captured by the enemy. Coulter was never listed as a POW. His B-26 was scouting for bombing targets in the vicinity of Seoul, which was then in Communist

hands, when he last had radio contact with base control. He disappeared
without a trace.

But the sympathy many felt for the families of the MIAs was
countered by the national obsession with Communism. The very fact that a
serviceman had been captured by the Communists seemed to place a taint
on his reputation. The fact that some POWs had become known collaborators
in the Communist camps in Korea left a brand on many who had resisted
bravely and fiercely.

In the very week the delegation of "Families of Forgotten Men" was
seeking attention for its cause, the U.S. Army court-martial of Cpl. Edward
S. Dickenson, one of the POWs charged with collaborating with his
communist captors, was underway in Washington.

Also working against the MIA families in their campaign were the
publicized results of studies by psychologists who had gauged the reactions
of American prisoners to life in the Korean camps. One such study found
that 70 per cent of American POWs "contributed wittingly or unwittingly
to Communist propaganda efforts."

The campaign by the POW/MIA families was attributed by the
chairman of the House Committee on Un-American Activities to a
Communist-inspired "fifth column" that had tried to use the plight of the
prisoners of war to pressure the U.S. government to "abandon the Korean
War."[8]

The notion was absurd. There is no doubt the governments of the
Communist bloc used the grief and frustration of POW/MIA families for
their own political ends. But in their writings and speeches, the families of
Korean War MIAs were among the most outspoken and resolute in their
opposition to communism. It was a sign of the politically malignant times
that charges of pro-communism could be uttered by a national politician to
smear families who firmly believed their own government wasn't being
tough enough in negotiating with the Communist Chinese and the Soviet
Union for the freedom of U.S. POWs.

Whether because of attacks from the right, confusion from the left,
or the apathy of the center, no media or public groundswell collected around
the families or their concerns. A federal court suit they filed was short-
lived. Charges that the U.S. government wasn't being tough enough in
bargaining with the Communists over missing POWs melded into the
cauldron of Cold War rhetoric over how to deal with the Communist
menace—the spies at the UN, turncoats in the POW camps and sympathizers
in the federal government.

Some in the military, however, decided their obligation to the missing
POWs in Korea was not over. The U.S. Air Force initiated a secret program,
"Project American," in which intelligence squadrons in Japan were ordered

to comb the wartime MIA files, re-interview repatriated POWs and interrogate the continuing flow of Japanese repatriates from the USSR for signs of the American POWs still unaccounted for from Korea.

While no live prisoners were rescued from postwar captivity, the 6004th Air Intelligence Service Squadron gathered enough testimony and data to compile a list of "USAF Personnel Possibly Alive in Communist Captivity" (August 1955). Supported in part by the word of two returned Air Force POWs, the report said at least 14 men had either been "in Kaesong awaiting repatriation" or last seen alive elsewhere in the Chinese-supervised POW camp system, but were never released. The aviators were:

Capt. Jack V. Allen, a World War II veteran from Lennox, S. D.; Capt. Harold Beardall, son of a former mayor of Orlando, Fla; 1st/Lt. Donald Bell, a former FBI clerk from Yuba City, Calif.; 2/Lt William J. Bell, a Naval Academy graduate from Washington, D.C.; A/3c John C. Brennan, a wing gunner from Boston, Mass.; S/Sgt. Joseph S. Dougherty, a radioman and World War II veteran from Zanesville, Ohio; T/Sgt. Robert F. Gross, a radio operator from Greensboro, Ala.; 1/Lt Edward S. Guthrie Jr., navigator, from Asheville, N.C.; T/Sgt. Robert W. Hamblin, a flight engineer from New York City; Capt. Luther R. Hawkins Jr., a pilot from Keysville, Va.; Maj. Kassel M. Keene, a bomber pilot from Georgia who had received the Soviet "Order of the Red Star" decoration for his cooperative missions in World War II; 2/Lt. Frederick R. Koontz, pilot, from Akron, Ohio; 1/Lt Waldemar W. Miller, of San Francisco; Capt. Fred B. Rountree, who attended West Point, from Egypt, Ga. All but Miller are also on the Air Force's long-standing list of 187 MIAs whose last known location or situation indicated survival and probable capture.

Air Force intelligence could collect all the data and sightings of American aviators last seen alive in the prison camps of North Korea and China. But Air Force intelligence couldn't bring them home.

A Department of the Army memo referred to "overt and covert (efforts) to locate, identify and recover" missing POWs, saying Army intelligence "is making an intensive effort through its information collection systems worldwide to obtain information on these people and has a plan for clandestine action to obtain the recovery of one or more to establish the case positively that prisoners are still being held by the Communists."[9]

But no military action, clandestine or otherwise, brought a live American POW back from the ranks of the missing.

From time to time, events that brought back memories of the "forgotten" war helped raise the MIA issue for the families. In 1955, China finally released more than a dozen airmen it had held as "war criminals" after they were shot down in—or taken into—Manchuria during the war, charging them with crimes against the Chinese people.

While the stories these repatriates from Chinese prisons told military and intelligence debriefers—of other, unacknowledged American POWs still in captivity—were not made public at the time, the fact that anyone who had been captured in the Korean War and imprisoned behind the Bamboo Curtain had re-appeared—alive and well—was enough to raise hopes.

Peking's freeing of a Canadian fighter pilot, Squadron Leader Andrew R. Mackenzie, on Dec. 4, 1954, and 15 American pilots and crewmen the next year prompted another wave of letters and telegrams to the United Nations, the Red Cross, the State Department, Pentagon, White House and members of Congress from families who still had no definitive answer to their questions. Some had heard their son's name broadcast over shortwave radio from Moscow or Peking. Some had received letters from prison camps signed by a husband or brother saying he wanted to come home, but was being treated okay. Some had seen a father's or a friend's face in a blurry photograph from one of the Communist prison camps or in a line of hollow-eyed POWs being marched through an unidentified town in North Korea or China.

But the account that—more than any other single report or piece of evidence—began to symbolize the awful predicament that any un-returned POW from Korea might have faced in the fearful imaginations of their loved ones dealt with men being placed in train cars and shipped north. Most of the POW/MIA families and those who had begun to read and follow the issue had heard the same story.

If they knew anything about Korean War MIAs, they had heard about the trains to Manchouli.

In March, 1954, Julian Harrington, the U.S. consul general in Hong Kong, pouched a secret dispatch to the State Department that read:[10]

"A recently arrived Greek refugee from Manchuria has reported seeing several hundred American prisoners of war being transferred from Chinese trains to Russian trains at Manchouli near the border of Manchuria and Siberia. The POWs were seen late in 1951 and in the spring of 1952 by the informant and a Russian friend of his. The informant was interrogated on two occasions by the assistant Air Liaison Officer and the Consulate General agrees with his evaluation of the information as probably true and the source as of unknown reliability."

The full report, from Air Force Col. O. Delk Simpson, said:

"This office has interviewed refugee source who states that he observed hundreds of prisoners of war in American uniforms being sent into Siberia in late 1951 and 1952. Observations were made at Manchouli ... on USSR-Manchurian border. Source observed POWs on railway station platform loading into trains for movement into Siberia. In railway restaurant source closely observed three POWs who were under guard and were conversing in English. POWs wore sleeve insignia which indicated POWs were Air Force noncommissioned officers. Source states that there were a great number of Negroes among POW shipments and also states that at no time later were any POWs observed returning from Siberia. Source does not wish to be identified for fear of reprisals against friends in Manchuria, however is willing to cooperate in answering further questions and will be available Hong Kong for questioning for the next four days."

When the Air Force received Simpson's report, they asked for more details about what the POWs looked like and what they had been wearing, who had been guarding them,and when these events took place. Simpson re-interviewed the "refugee source," and sent answers to the Air Force's seven questions:

(1) (Description of POWs' clothing?) "POWs wore OD (olive drab) outer clothing described as not heavy inasmuch as weather considered early spring. Source identified from pictures service jacket, field, M1943. No belongings except canteen. No ornaments observed."

(2) (POWs' physical condition?) "Condition appeared good, no wounded, all ambulatory."

(3) (Nationality of guards?) "Station divided into two sections with tracks on each side of loading platform. On Chinese side POWs accompanied by Chinese guards. POWs passed through gate bisecting platform to Russian train manned and operated by Russians. Russian trainmen wore dark blue or black tunic with silver-colored shoulder boards. Source says this regular train uniform but he knows the trainmen are military and wearing regular train uniforms."

(4) (Specific dates of observations?) "Interrogation with aid of more fluent interpreter reveals source first observed POWs in railroad station in spring 1951. Second observation was outside city of Manchouli about three months later with POW train headed towards station where he observed POW transfer. Source was impressed with second observation because of large number of Negroes among POWs. Source states that he was told by a very close Russian friend whose job was numbering railroad cars at Manchouli every time subsequent POW shipments passed through Manchouli. Source says these shipments were reported often and occurred when United Nations forces in Korea were on the offensive."

(5) (Destination in Siberia?) "Unknown."

(6) (Russians in uniform or civilian clothing?) "Only Russian accompanying POWs were those who manned train."

(7) (Complete description of three POWs mentioned?) "Three POWs observed in station restaurant appeared to be 30 to 35. Source identified Air Force non-commissioned officer sleeve insignia of Staff Sergeant rank,

stated that several inches above insignia there was a propeller but says that all three did not have propeller. Three POWs accompanied by Chinese guard. POWs appeared thin but in good health and spirits, were being given what source described as good food. POWs were talking in English but did not converse with guard. Further information as to number of POWs observed source states that first observation filled a seven-passenger-car train and second observation about the same. Source continues t emphasize the number of Negro troops, which evidently impressed him because he had seen so few Negroes before.

"Source further states that his Russian railroad worker friend was attempting to obtain a visa to Canada and that he could furnish more information, the railroad worker's name is Leon Strelnikov whose mother's sister lives in Canada and is applying for a visa for Strelnkov (phonetic). Comment reporting officer: Source is very careful not to exaggerate information and is positive of identification of American POWs. In view of information contained in Charity Interrogation Report No. 619, dated 5 February 1954, Reporting Officer gives above information rating of F-2.Source departing Hong Kong today by ship. Future address on file this office."

Charity Interrogation Report No. 619 had this to say:

"A reliable, friendly foreign intelligence service reports to the U.S. information they had received from a Turkish source traveling in Central Asia. The source, who had been interrogated in Turkey, states that while at Mukden, Manchuria, he 'saw several coaches full of Europeans who were also taken to the USSR. They were not Russians. Source passed the coaches several times and heard them talk in a language unknown to him.' Source states that one of the coaches was full of wounded caucasians who were not speaking at all."

The Hong Kong refugee's story, backed up by the "wounded caucasians" intelligence, was credible enough to persuade the State Department to broach the subject at the embassy level in Moscow. The U.S. ambassador informed the Soviet foreign ministry that Washington had reason to believe the Kremlin would know the whereabouts of some of the American POWs missing in Korea. The Soviets swatted away the notion with a curt denial.

Any suggestion that American POWs had been transferred to the territory of the USSR was a total fabrication, the Soviet Foreign Ministry insisted.

Official denials aside, however, the rational structure for belief in the so-called "Siberian transfer" of POWs was soundly based on experience, history and logic. Since the Wilson administration's brief and disastrous military expedition to Russia in 1918, which claimed American casualties while failing to stop the Bolsheviks from surging to the top of the social and political revolution that accompanied the fall of the czar, there had been military prisoners—some of them Americans—reported missing in Siberia.

Russian leaders going back many generations had used the forbidding terrain and climate of Siberia as a natural place of exile and prison. Foreign military personnel visited the approaches of Russian territory at great risk of being treated as badly as the average Russian thief or political dissident.

After World War II, the vast and largely isolated network of labor camps, mines and closed cities, industrial areas, laboratories and towns known as the Gulag was brimming with not only the variety of ethnic populations that Stalin had ordered moved off their ancestral lands within the Soviet empire, but with an array of captured military prisoners of many nationalities.

The result of the chaos of years of world war, these Italian, Spanish, French, German, Austrian, Chinese, Korean and Japanese troops were disarmed where they surrendered, then imprisoned and worked under inhuman conditions alongside millions of the Soviet republics' own citizens. Many of the latter were Red Army troops who virtually overnight went from being prisoners in Hitler's camps in Germany to prisoners—or corpses—in Stalin's camps in Russia.

Even a cursory reading of publicly-available information about the extensive use Stalin made of the Gulag as a repository for foreign and Russian military prisoners is enough to force the conclusion not whether the Soviets might have kept foreign prisoners after World War II, given the opportunity, but why the rest of the world didn't object more loudly and forcefully when these crimes became widely known.

For example, Spain's "Blue" Division of soldiers who fought alongside the Germans in World War II surrendered to the Soviets in 1945. Not until 1954 did they see home again. More than 4,000 officers and men spent the intervening nine years—which included the Korean War—in Gulag camps, as laborers and virtual slaves. Their return to Barcelona was chronicled in Life magazine.

That same year, as the U.S. was presenting the Soviets with evidence of the seizure of Korean War POWs, the UN was attempting to get Stalin to acknowledge his government was still holding hundreds of thousands of German and Japanese soldiers from World War II.

During the decades of official silence from the Soviet Union, there were numerous reports of live-sightings in the Gulag. More than a handful even mentioned that an American prisoner said he had been captured in the Korean War. But the accounts often mentioned only first names, or half-names, or non-names, some version of what might have once been an

American's name, but garbled by translation into one or several languages and back again.

Besides the problem that language posed, there was another reason for the vagueness and uncertainty of the reports. Some of the Americans who could be found in the Gulag were from families that had emigrated in the 1930s to the Soviet Union, when it was viewed by some as a great social experiment. Thus they might be listed in court and prison records as Soviet citizens, not foreigners. They had taken their chances with the Communist system, it could be said, and one of those chances had involved the risk of incarceration. Unfair, perhaps, but understandable.

But people sentenced to prison in a country they didn't willingly come to—there were special camps for such people. And the people in those camps, according to Russians with some experience in these matters, might lose their own names as one of the first orders of business.

They would receive a new name, or perhaps just a number. That way there is never a need to write down a name, or record the transfer or illness or death of something as anonymous as a number. And after serving a sentence, they might even be released—allowed to move into the remote town nearest the prison, but not farther, and forbidden from communicating with friends or family elsewhere.

These kinds of practices had become known long before the Gulag began to empty out, thanks to the smuggled writings of the once-imprisoned—dissidents, thinkers, actors, writers, and victims of religious persecution.

By the time their country had opened to the West, Russians found that the world had known a great deal about their Magadans and Vorkutas, their Tambovs and Lubyankas for many years. Many of them had known all along, of course—especially those whose relatives were among the millions arrested and sent to prison.

Official Kremlin denials aside, the story of trainloads of Americans shipped north out of Korea through Manchuria and Siberia left a trail of evidence that cried out for investigation. There is no evidence that the U.S. government did much to prove the case one way or the other.

The accounts and memos and names are firmly planted in the U.S. government's own files, however, and by themselves form a reasonable premise. And that is without the testimony of a former military officer and White House aide, Phillip Corso, who was present at the story's genesis, and has always known it was true.

Corso was in an excellent position to know the source of the Manchouli story and, not only that, to let people in a position of high authority know about it as well. He says he tried.

He was a lieutenant colonel working at MacArthur's headquarters in Tokyo during the Korean War as chief of special projects in the intelligence division. When he returned to the U.S. in 1953, Corso was assigned to the National Security Council at the White House, on the staff of President Eisenhower. He says he and others who worked on intelligence matters made sure the president was informed of the story.[11]

Among Corso's duties in Japan was the job of tracking "all prisoner of war camps, our prisoners, how they were being treated and where they were, and who was in charge and how they were being interrogated...."[13]

His sources for the status reports of American prisoners—sometimes 100 or more a day—included the UN's clandestine agents in North Korea and China, allied intelligence services, captured North Korean and Chinese troops and the UN's own liberated POWs.

When the Little Switch prisoner exchange occurred in April 1950, Corso recalled, he messaged Washington that he was certain—from the type and number of American POWs returned—that the Communists were intent on holding back some prisoners. Of the 149 Americans who were returned in that exchange, many were not seriously ill nor gravely wounded.

After meticulous study of his status reports on individual POWs, Corso compiled an intelligence finding estimating the Communists still held 500 sick and wounded American prisoners. "The condition of these POWs was such," he said, "that if they did not receive adequate treatment immediately, they would surely die."

He said his intelligence report was read into the record of armistice negotiations by the U.S. delegate to the Panmunjom talks, but the issue was never pursued. Hundreds more American POWs did in fact die in prison camps before the armistice was signed, he observed.

While on duty in the Far East, Corso said, his daily duties of tracking prisoners and reports of where they were held and how they were being treated and exploited by the Communists put enough information in his hands to convince him that American POWs were being shipped to China and the Soviet Union from Korea.

"I secured this information," he said, using the jargon of the military, "from, I'd say, hundreds of prisoner of war reports, from Chinese and North Koreans, who actually saw these prisoners being transported and talked to some of them. Also, we had guerrillas and agents in the area who saw these prisoners being transported...."

How many? "I had definite information of train loads, two certain, possibly three. Each train held 450 prisoners. These prisoners were taken from North Korea through Mukden, Manchuria, to Manchouli."[12]

Manchouli is the last Chinese stop on the railroad that extends into southern Siberia. There, the width of track, or gauge, used in China ended. The track through Siberia was a different, wider gauge, used throughout

Russia.

After the Communist victory in China in 1949, as the new government of Mao Tse-tung moved in to take over the railroads in Manchuria from the Soviets who had administered the province since ousting the Japanese in 1945, they found that the Russians had widened the tracks so that Soviet trains could enter and leave Manchuria from Siberia unimpeded. Soviet tracks were five feet apart, Chinese tracks four feet, eight-and-a-half inches.[13]

The Chinese, however, re-converted the tracks within Manchuria to the narrower gauge, and it remained that way through the Korean War. It was a small difference—only three-and-a-half inches—but crucial. It meant stopping the trains at Manchouli, coming and going.

"That meant that prisoners would be transferred from one train to the other," Corso said, "over a landing. And that was the point where most of the prisoners were seen and recognized as Americans...."

One of the reports of transfers that Corso gave a great deal of credence to came from a North Korean prisoner who, in the fall of 1950, was marched into a UN prison camp claiming to be a lowly private.

In fact, Corso said, "private" Pak San Yung was a lieutenant colonel and a member of the North Korean Communist Party's central committee. Corso said he learned that as he debriefed Pak for a week, during which time the North Korean officer told him that American POWs were shipped to the Soviet Union, after being rated and ranked according to their specialties and skills.

Besides reports from guerrillas and enemy POWs, Corso said, there were the "few high-level Soviet defectors" he spoke to "who confirmed it—that this transfer was going on, which was in violation of what rules the war was supposed to be fought under—if there were any rules."

His informants told him the American POWs were taken to the Soviet Union "for intelligence purposes. The operation, as far as we were concerned, was a GRU/NKVD operation (acronyms for the Soviet military intelligence and internal security police organizations) in those days. And it was mostly to elicit information from them, possibly take over their identities or use them as agents, or use those as nationals to assume their identity."

Not only were such operations "normal" for intelligence agencies at the time, Corso explained, "but Soviets had perfected the system, and it was very sophisticated in the way that they operated."

And "once the information was taken from them," he said, "and they were used, how the Soviets saw fit to use them, they were eliminated, and they would never come back.

"Which actually happened—they never came back. They were killed, which was Soviet policy also."

Corso said the information he obtained from Soviet defectors dealt with the operational aspects of the transfer policy, "not so much that prisoners were being taken to the Soviet Union, because we already knew that...We knew that some were being used for espionage and maybe some for sabotage and we wanted to know what we could find out."

Corso described his sources this way: "...hundreds of prisoner reports, North Korean and Chinese prisoners that we took, defectors and other intelligence that I can't describe for certain reasons. And, as I say, photographs, because we photographed camps, and so we saw movements, and people on the ground, civilians, also would come through.

"This was the intelligence process, put together very, very carefully, for a long period of time, matching all information and putting them together to show a pattern in the picture."[14]

One of the people who helped complete the picture for Corso was a Soviet defector named Yuri Alexandrovich Rastvorov.

Rastvorov became one of the United States' most prized Cold War trophies almost by chance. During the Korean War, he had served as an intelligence officer at the Soviet embassy in Tokyo. In January, 1954, he decided to defect to the West because, he said later, "I wanted to live like a decent human being."[15]

He had first sought help from British officials in Tokyo. But when a flight to London in the company of British embassy officials was thwarted by bad weather, he switched plans and made contact with U.S. authorities, who flew him out the next day. He was granted political asylum and over the next few years, before disappearing into obscurity in the U.S., delivered reams of Soviet secrets and intelligence operations into the lap of the U.S. government. He was featured in Senate hearings of the Internal Security subcommittee in 1956 that probed Soviet intelligence and spying activities in the U.S. and abroad.

But the portion of his past that related directly to the Korean War was his assignment for the Soviets before he was sent to Japan. As a young captain in the MVD (later renamed the KGB), he spent more than six months during 1948 in a program aimed at recruiting intelligence agents from among Japanese POWs held in Siberian prisons.[16]

He told American debriefers that his "special group of ten men was spread between Khabarovsk, Krasnoyarsk, Chita, Vladivostok and Barnoul"—all cities that were central hubs in the vast network of Siberian prisons housing hundreds of thousands of Japanese POWs captured in Korea and Manchuria at the close of World War II.

When he arrived at his post in Tokyo in July 1950, a few days after the war had begun, Rastvorov was intimately familiar with the techniques his government was using to capitalize on the large pool of manpower and potential agents being held behind barbed wire in the Soviet Far East.

By the time of Rastvorov's defection, Corso had been transferred to Washington to work on Eisenhower's National Security Council. He asked permission to speak to the defector. Corso said he was concerned that the Russians could be planning to use the identities of American POWs from Korea to build "legends"—or life histories—for Soviet agents who would later infiltrate the United States or its government facilities or private sectors abroad.

"Rastvorov revealed," Corso testified (to the Senate committee on POWs and MIAs), "he had been aware of U.S. POWs heading into Siberia after changing trains at the Manchuria-Russia border. Rastvorov told me he believed that selected U.S. soldiers—especially those with no roots nor family ties—were taken to Russia as part of a joint KGB-GRU operation to be debriefed on details of their backgrounds. Then, Russian nationalists would be able to assume the identities of these POWs and be 'played back' at appropriate times to carry out espionage activities in the U.S. and Canada."

Rastvorov's account of using American POWs' identities to create "legends" bore a striking resemblance to an earlier piece of intelligence that was produced during the war by CCRAK, the Army's reconnaissance operation in which U.S. intelligence units sent Korean agents behind enemy lines. The report originated with the Nationalist Chinese embassy in Seoul:

"According to reliable information, the Communist Chinese forces have transferred UN POWs to Russia in violation of the Geneva Conference. These POWs will be specifically trained at Moscow for espionage work. POWs transferred are grouped as follows: British 5, Americans 10, Canadians 3, and 50 more from various countries."

In addition, the CCRAK report said, Russia had established a "Higher Informant Training Team" in Siberia in October 1952, where 500 Japanese, Korean, Filipinos, Burmese and Americans were undergoing espionage training."

Corso said he wrote a one-page summary of his concerns based on his conversations with Rastvorov and sent it to the attention of President Eisenhower. "I recommended that the report not be made public," he testified, "because the POWs should be given up for dead since we knew the Soviets would never relinquish them. Out of concern for the POWs' families, the President agreed."[17]

Eisenhower agreed that a copy of his report on the Korean War transfers should be submitted to the Pentagon, Corso said. But nothing was to be said publicly about the report.

And Corso's reports weren't the sole source of Siberian-transfer intelligence. In January 1954, a report from the U.S. Army Intelligence and

Security Command, basing the information on debriefings of Japanese POWs just released from camps in Manchuria, said the Soviets were running a large interrogation center for U.S. POWs from Korea—mostly aviators— in the Chang-pai region on the upper Yalu River.

In 1952, the Japanese repatriates said, it was moved to Antu, north of the Tumen River in southeastern Manchuria. After being interrogated, the American aviators passed through Mutanchiang, Manchuria, a railhead even farther northeast, toward the Soviet border, and from there were "taken to the USSR."

Corso maintains that the holding back of American POWs and their transfer to China and the Soviet Union were common knowledge in the Eisenhower White House, and that some people working there—he calls them "heroes"—spoke up on the behalf of the POWs, who had become the targets of Communist exploitation and propaganda, yet couldn't win active or majority support at home.

The overriding fact that prevented the U.S. government from pressing for their release, he believes, was a fear of causing an all-out war with either the Soviet Union, China or both, had the United States pushed the issue beyond the negotiating table at Panmunjom.

As evidence of this mindset, Corso read from National Security Council papers containing statements such as "The United States should not refer to the USSR as an aggressor in Korea," "Agree to the term that Chinese communists in Korea were volunteers," and this: "Korea is an inconclusive operation, and continued maintenance of military operations would create the grave danger of general war."

Corso ended his 1992 testimony with sharp criticism for "ill-advised people in our State Department, the CIA and other government agencies who, for reasons known only to themselves, allowed their actions to be influenced by foreign ideology and slanted intelligence."

Tragically, he believes, the American POWs shipped to the Soviet Union—at least 900, he told the Senate hearings and Task Force Russia, and perhaps as many as 1,200—were the price of keeping the war in Korea from spreading farther.

After interviewing him, to check his documentation, the military analysts and researchers working on the Korean War POW/MIA issue sent a team to the Eisenhower Library in Abilene, Kan.

A report (from the task force in March 1993) said documents in the library "fully supported Lt. Col. Corso's statements as to what the U.S. government knew or had reason to believe about prisoner transfers during the Eisenhower administration."

Once inside Manchuria, headed northwest across the rugged Chinese terrain, two or three trainloads of American prisoners would have amounted to a tiny fraction of the rail cargo shipments that criss-crossed Manchuria for more than three years before and during the Korean War.

The Chinese and Russians poured weapons and supplies into North Korea aboard thousands of clacking railroad cars, transporting tanks, artillery, MIG jets, fuel, ammunition, supplies, medicine, troops from several Soviet republics, captured planes and equipment, high-level delegations from Pyongyang and Moscow and, when the fighting was nearly over, even gentle missionaries, bedraggled diplomats and a newly minted spy for Moscow, British vice counsel George Blake, all recently freed from lice-ridden prison camps.

Like the prisoners the refugee saw waiting at the Siberian border station, all rode the trains to Manchouli.

Chapter Three

On Stalin's Instructions

"Miss James...said we are still including his name in all of our representations to the Soviet Foreign Office but...pointed out that this puts the United States in the anomalous position of asking the Soviets for the release of an American citizen at the same time that we ask for a death certificate."

—State Dept. memo of Jan. 13, 1956,
regarding the case of Charles Clifford-Brown,
a U.S.-born engineer who claimed German citizenship
but was executed as an American spy.

"Paralysis of the heart owing to acute sclerosis of the coronary artery with associated angiospasms and papillary carcinoma of the urinary bladder."

—Cause of death listed on false death certificate dated Jan. 13, 1947,
for Isaac Oggins, an American executed in Norilsk, USSR,
sometime after mid 1947 while in prison for espionage.

If Joseph Stalin were still alive, it's safe to say it would be pointless to be asking for information about American prisoners of war in the Soviet Union.

And not just because Stalin was one of the most monstrous, bloody-minded tyrants of this century or any other, and a man who never did anyone or any country a favor—unless we agree that he did the world a favor by living no longer than he did.

It's because for Stalin, there never were—never could be—"prisoners of war" held in the Soviet Gulag, that vast, secretive system of dust-choked mines, forced-labor camps, disciplinary prisons and frozen, mostly unmarked graveyards stretching from the eastern plains and czarist tombs, through Central Asia and encompassing most of the forested and forbidding tundra, frozen lakes and stony, uninhabitable islands that needed no bars and a minimum of stakes and wire because they were located beyond time, and sometimes past the Arctic Circle.

The thousands of Polish officers slain in the Katyn Forest were prisoners of war of the Soviets, but not for long. No comfortable cell in Vorkuta for them.[1]

Now if it's American "war criminals," or spies, or people suffering from lingering illnesses that require the relief of fatal injections in lieu of permanent hospital care you're looking for, Stalin's thick-shouldered, brutality-dispensing experts in bad suits could probably oblige.

The Korean War was only a few weeks old—and Stalin in the final years of his long, murderous reign—when Jacob Malik, the deputy foreign minister of the USSR who was also its representative in the UN Security Council, issued a stern rejection to a demand from the United States and other nations for information about German POWs still in Russian hands.

The charges that hundreds of thousands of German troops—five years after World War II ended—were still in Russia, Malik said, "were absolutely ungrounded and do not correspond to reality." On the other hand, he admitted, there were some 9,717 prisoners who had been "convicted of grave war crimes," another 3,815 under investigation for similar offenses, and 14 others "detained as a consequence of illness."[2]

When the U.S.-Russian Joint Commission on American Prisoners in the Former Soviet Union in 1992 began peeling back the layers of deceit and suppression that had concealed the true fate of Americans under the Soviet dictatorship, from Malik's time on, some of the first secrets to emerge had to do with individuals the Stalinist bureaucracy had categorized as sick, criminal types or individuals with subversion and sabotage on their minds. Some were healthy when first arrested, but their health suffered a steep and mysterious decline soon after they were subjected to a routine mixture of ghoulish incarceration and hopelessness. The fact that they happened to be Americans meant the researchers going through the archives of the prisons and secret police agencies of the former Soviet Union in the 1990s encountered their cases in the course of the work for the joint commission aimed at resolving POW/MIA cases.

At first glance, the material seemed mostly arcane, the stuff of historical footnotes. There were the cases of the children of American citizens who had immigrated to the Soviet Union in the 1930s, when hundreds of well-meaning people of socialist bent decided that they could best apply their idealism to the problems of the world by joining the new, classless society that Stalin was advertising. They moved to the USSR and pitched in, manning assembly lines, working in the mills, becoming good Marxists, sending their children to schools decorated with statues of Lenin and stocked only with the books suitable for good little Reds.

Stalin's ideological guardians rewarded many of them by pointing out their ethnic origins to the secret police, who regarded with great suspicion anyone with the bad luck to have been born with East European, Ukrainian, Jewish or Slavic-sounding names. They often featured in the periodic roundups of suspected grafters, soldiers liberated from German POW camps, capitalists, bandits and slackers who corrupted the otherwise stellar work force making the revolution come true behind the Iron Curtain. In his first appearance in the U.S. as the Russian co-chairman of the joint commission, Volkogonov acknowledged this pattern in the Soviet records.[3]

In July, 1992, he released a list of 39 names of American citizens, all with Slavic, East European or Baltic family origins, he said had been falsely charged with espionage. And he asked for help in locating them, expressing optimism that some could still be alive. "Up to 30 percent of the inmates of the Stalinist camps survived and left the camps," he said. "That is why we have every reason to hope that we can find some of these people."[4]

Volkogonov—a scholar, an historian, a famous biographer of Stalin—was just feeling his way as an advance man with the humanitarian, POW/MIA-resolution portfolio for Yeltsin, who was just launching his westward-pointing presidency. Volkogonov, it was assumed, was speaking for the new Russian president when he offered some tidbits about American civilian prisoners in the Gulag, and saying he favored allowing "one, two, three American historians or specialists" to work with the joint commission in Moscow. And he also spelled out what the Russian leader hoped to receive in return: "We need not only help with bread and with money," he said. "The most important help we need is help in how we should build our market. We need technical help, we need intellectual and organizing help."[5]

While the delicate work of looking through the Soviet Union archives for material that could safely be released to the Americans took a quick detour down the path of Marxist sympathizers, it quickly returned to the trail of prisoners of war. The stories of the American civilians sentenced to the Gulag because Stalin didn't like their foreign-sounding names soon faded from the headlines, and the joint commission settled into its main task of debating the evidence that pointed toward the holding or transfer to Soviet territory of men in uniform—aviators, soldiers, reconnaissance pilots and crews.

But in the grand, evolving scheme of looking into the ugly Soviet closet, the Gulag documents dealing with American civilians, deserters, tourists, priests and fellow travelers that were churned up early in the archival search for the fate of missing military prisoners had the result of shedding light on the main issue, in this way:

If the American prisoners from World War II, Korea, Vietnam and the Cold War who were still missing—and were last seen alive in Soviet custody—had been transferred into the Gulag under Stalin and his immediate successors, what would they have encountered there? How would they have been treated? How long would they have survived? Would there be any trace of them after 30 or 40 years?

In learning the answers to these questions, the experiences of two men named Isaac Oggins and Charles Clifford-Brown provided American researchers with some fascinating, but not very hopeful, reading.[6]

* * *

To put it bluntly, by the time the U.S. government heard that Charles Arthur Clifford-Brown was in the Gulag, he was dead. Here's what the documents released from the former Soviet archives said about him:

He was born in Los Angeles, Calif., in 1918. His parents, Richard and Barbara, were also born in the United States. He had a high school education and had been residing until the mid-1940s in Hamburg, Germany, where he worked as a draftsman and engineer for the Blom-Vos firm. He was of medium height, lean, with a long neck, dark brown hair, blue eyes, an oval face, large nose, small mouth, thick lips, straight chin "with a transverse cleft" and "triangular" ears.[7]

That description of the man came from his Soviet jailers, who dutifully underlined the appropriate adjectives on the bureaucracy's long form for physical attributes, when he was arrested in Moscow on Aug. 30, 1951, by Junior Sgt. Mitrakov.

Charles Clifford-Brown's case wasn't long in adjudication. On Nov. 17 that same year, he was convicted and sentenced to 25 years in prison "for participation in preparing an aggressive war against the Soviet government." (In the aggressive war then taking place in Korea, November 1951 marked a crucial stage; pressured by the Truman White House and the Joint Chiefs of Staff, American negotiators for the UN Command agreed to a cease-fire line that gave the Communists control of Kaesong, an ancient Korean capital south of the 38th parallel.)

Charles Clifford-Brown's sentence was to be dated from Aug. 28, 1944, the time of his arrest by Soviet state security officials in Romania, presumably the place Charles Clifford-Brown was then carrying out his preparations for the "aggressive war" against the Kremlin.

It is not clear from the archival documents released by the Russians how long Charles Clifford-Brown had been in Romania, nor how long he remained in prison in Bucharest, only that he was re-arrested in Moscow in 1951, by MGB (KGB) Capt. I.S. Mamaev.

Whatever he had done in Moscow to draw attention to himself—beyond using identification papers that were evidently no different from the ones he carried into Romania during World War II—was not spelled out in the papers, either. But thanks to State Department correspondence from the 1950s, it is known that he spent some time in a Soviet prison camp in Alexandrovsk. An Italian citizen who was released in 1955 said he met Charles Clifford-Brown in that prison, and that Charles Clifford-Brown died there in about 1954.

The report found its way to U.S. consular authorities in Moscow, where they didn't know what to make of the Charles Clifford-Brown story. Since 1953, when Austrian POWs from World War II who had just been freed from prison in Siberia passed on his name among those of other Americans they had met there to U.S. officials, he had been on the U.S. government's classified lists of American citizens held in the Gulag. The constantly changing lists comprised not only the names of people someone, usually a wife, husband or other relative, had asked the U.S. government to find, but of names, or partial names, referred by released Gulag inmates. By the early 1950s, the list included dozens of names, or purported names, of American citizens believed to be "unjustly detained and unaccounted for" on Soviet territory.

No record existed of anyone asking the U.S. government to find Charles Clifford-Brown, although many such records remain uncollated and scattered throughout the volumes of diplomatic and consular records from State Department posts around the world. His name—sometimes with "Clifford" as his first name—had simply seeped out of Siberia along the Gulag grapevine. And its authenticity drew some suspicion at the U.S. embassy in Moscow, "from the way he changed his story from time to time it could very well be that he was a German with a knowledge of English trying to bluff the Russians into dealing with him as an American citizen."[8]

Whether Charles Clifford-Brown had actually "changed his story from time to time" or—which is more likely—several different versions or scraps of his story (and of his curiously kaleidoscopic name) had drifted out of the prison system on the fractured memories of several former Gulag inmates, the fact was that if the Soviets chose to regard Charles Clifford-Brown as a German citizen, there wasn't much the United States could do about it, except inform the Germans.

But the State Department could try. As a memo on the case stated, the U.S. "has never been able to identify Clifford Charles Brown, Charles Brown Clifford, etc.," but consular officials were "still including his name in all of our representations to the Soviet Foreign Office." Since it had also been reported he had died there, it was suggested they might also request a "Form 192," which was a consular report of the death of an American citizen.

This, one of the embassy memos pointed out, would put the U.S. "in the anomalous position of asking the Soviets for the release of an American citizen at the same time that we ask for a death certificate."

The Soviets prepared a death certificate for Charles Clifford-Brown. But it would not be seen by U.S. officials for nearly 40 years, when it passed to the American side of the joint commission on missing American prisoners as part of a small file on him. The death certificate shows that the series of memos on his case exchanged by U.S. consular officials in 1956 were beside the point. Even if the Soviets had granted the U.S. government's request to return him, it would have been in a casket. When those memos were written, the draftsman-engineer from Los Angeles was already dead, executed by the state.

The Soviet records show a more benign cause: severe health problems. The Charles Clifford-Brown papers include a letter dated Aug. 6, 1992, from the Russian internal affairs ministry saying "It has been established by a check done by the Main Information Center of the Russian MVD" that Charles Clifford-Brown was "serving his sentence in the Verkhne-Uralsk prison where he died on 17 May 53 from weakening of cardiovascular activity caused by active tuberculosis and hyperacidic gastritis."

Volkogonov apparently accepts the date of death, but says the cause of death "by disease" is obviously false. The general used the word "shot," but there is no indication in the archival documents of the instrument used, and it more than likely was by poisonous injection, a favorite method of the time.

Another document released by the Russian side of the commission adds a Gogol-like twist to his tragic story. It is entitled "Decision No. 3478/N" of the Military Board of the Supreme Court of the USSR, and is signed by three generals. It is a pardon, and it reads:

"We have reviewed the material on the early release of Brown-Clifford Charles, born in 1918, American, citizen of Germany, in court session on 25 May 1953. He was sentenced by a Special Session of the JGB of the USSR on 17 November 1951 under Art. 58-4 of the UK of the RSFSR to 25 years imprisonment. Taking into account that further confinement in prison of the convicted Brown-Clifford is not necessary—

IT IS DECIDED: Brown-Clifford Charles is released early from further serving his sentence."

The document is sealed and certified. It appears absolutely standard and authentic. But the date is jarring. Charles Arthur Clifford-Brown, pardoned on May 25, had been dead since May 17, according to the Russian internal affairs records. When the generals at Verkhne-Uralsk prison decided in their wisdom that "further confinement" was not necessary, they were absolutely correct.

Questions arise, as the mind reels. Is the parole document—like the death certificate—a fake, drafted to hide his death if that was deemed more in the state's interest? Faked death certificates were a specialty, after all, of the MVD. A faked parole document would be no more difficult to create. But why bother, if the parolee is already dead of "tuberculosis and hyperacidic gastritis."

Or did the bureaucracy grind too slowly in Clifford-Brown's case, putting him into a Gulag grave while, in another part of the prison, a camp clerk dulled by vodka dawdled over typing the document that could have spared his life? Was his salvation in the works when he was killed? Were the generals informed that their order for early release had been overtaken by events?

Perhaps if the authorities in charge of executions had known the "American, German citizen" Charles Clifford-Brown was to be paroled in a matter of days, they might have agreed to a delay. But then again, perhaps they did know, and proceeded anyway.

On July 24, 1992, just before Volkogonov handed over this particular file to the American side of the joint commission, he received a letter on the case from the Russian federation's attorney general, and included it in the documents turned over to the U.S. It is a "rehabilitation" letter, in accordance with the law passed in October 1991, when the Communist Party was being dismantled in Moscow, that orders the "rehabilitation of victims of political repression."

The letter states that Charles Clifford-Brown "was sentenced without grounds" in November 1951 when he received the 25-year jail term that ended less than two years later in execution. In other words, he hadn't really participated in "preparing an aggressive war against the Soviet Union." That was simply the charge used to arrest him and send him to prison.

He is buried, according to Volkogonov, "in the place where he was imprisoned."

For Charles Arthur Clifford-Brown, dead at age 35, parole came too late. Rehabilitation came even later. Justice came not at all.

* * *

When Volkogonov revealed in the late summer of 1992 that two Americans had perished while serving time in Soviet prison camps, he did so in careful stages.

In mid-August, an article in the Moscow newspaper Izvestia based on a statement signed by the general said "an American" had been sent to his death by Stalin. That was news enough for one day, apparently. The statement did not identify the victim by name, or say when he had been executed, only that he had been among several dozen Americans wrongfully jailed by the Soviet secret police during and after World War II. "They were accused of espionage and other crimes, threatened and intimidated, told their children would be taken from them, and so forth," Volkogonov's statement said.

Volkogonov did add that Stalin had approved a cover story alleging that the executed "spy" had died of a disease, not by liquidation. The execution and falsified documents were attributed to Viktor Abakumov, then Stalin's chief of foreign intelligence and creator of the wartime counterspy organization known as "Smersh."[9]

Five weeks later, Volkogonov gave a press conference in Moscow at which he spoke of two cases, but gave only the last names—Oggins and Clifford—, and said he didn't know their first names. His government was still looking for details, he told reporters. "I think in many cases there are simply no traces left." But he was merely parceling out the traces. The best details were in the documents Volkogonov was even then preparing to turn over to the Americans on the joint commission.

Only the next day did Volkogonov finally reveal the two men's full names, and it was in the midst of the delivery of a large notebook full of documents from the Soviet archives. Volkogonov emphasized that neither Oggins nor Clifford had been prisoners of war. Only a few months earlier, Yeltsin had made his startling pronouncement that the Soviets had held an undetermined number of American POWs in prison, including some from the Vietnam War, and that some might still be alive.[10] Volkogonov was still dealing with the fallout from that speech, which he often took great pains to say was not substantiated by anything yet located in the archives.

The only Americans taken to the USSR from Vietnam were six deserters, he has maintained. The six, who were known to the U.S. government, stayed only briefly before moving on to various propaganda stages in Europe. Sightings and reports of other, legitimate "Moscow-bound" prisoners transferred against their will from Vietnam prison camps—testified to by both American and Russian witnesses—are routinely dismissed by the Russian side of the joint commission.

In November 1992, while testifying before the Senate Select Committee on POWs and MIAs in Washington, Volkogonov again mentioned the Oggins and Clifford executions, saying more about them than he had previously. He called them tragedies "worthy of Shakespeare" and said that the two men were not spies at all. They were executed because they "knew too much" about the Gulag, and if released, would reveal its grisly secrets.

The documents that Volkogonov turned over on the Oggins case, however, presented a much more complex picture of the "spy" who "knew too much."[11]

Isaac S. Oggins was born in Massachusetts, in 1898. There was never any question of his citizenship. But the Soviet documents show he was arrested in Moscow on Feb. 20, 1939, tried, convicted of espionage and sentenced to eight years in prison. His term was to begin on the date of his arrest.

He apparently spent the war years in various Gulag prison camps, where he was sighted by Japanese POWs and other foreign inmates who were later freed. The next reference to him in the released Soviet documents is in a long memo dated May 21, 1947, from Abakumov, the foreign intelligence chief, to Stalin and V. M. Molotov, longtime member of the Politburo and one of Stalin's closest confidants.

The document released by Volkogonov is heavily censored in places. But enough information remains to make it clear that the U.S. Embassy had learned of Oggins' imprisonment and had asked Soviet authorities to release him to their custody. The Soviets convened two meetings—Dec. 8, 1942, and Jan. 9, 1943—at which Oggins, who was serving his time at a prison camp in Norilsk, was taken to Moscow where he was permitted to meet with U.S. officials. He told them he had been arrested as a Trotskyite, attempting to enter the Soviet Union on a false passport to contact underground, anti-Kremlin agents. The memo continues:

"In spite of such a declaration, the American Embassy in Moscow repeatedly raised the question before the MID (Ministry of Defense), USSR, on the review of the case and the early release of Oggins and forwarded Oggins' letters and telegrams to his wife, who lives in the USA. They also told the MID, USSR, that they recognize Oggins as an American citizen and are ready to repatriate him to his homeland."

On May 9, 1943, Abakumov wrote, the U.S. Embassy was informed that the Soviets did not "consider it necessary to review Oggins' case." In other words, he would remain in prison.

The memo then continues, with large portions omitted:

"On 20 February 1939, Oggins {CENSORED} was in reality arrested on the charges of espionage and treachery.

{CENSORED}

"While investigating these suspicions, we did not find corroboration and Oggins pleaded not guilty. However, a Special Session for the NKVD, USSR, sentenced Oggins to 8 years in the ITL, counting the term from 20 February 1939.

{CENSORED}

of Oggins in the USA might be used by persons hostile to the Soviet Union for active propaganda against the USSR."

Then comes the solution:

"Based on this, the MGB, USSR, considers it necessary to execute Oggins, and then to report to the Americans that after the meeting with Oggins and American Embassy representatives, in June 1943 he was returned to the place of confinement in Norilsk where he died in 1946 in a hospital as a result of aggravated tuberculosis of the spine.

"In the Norilsk camp archives we will reflect the course of Oggins' illness and medical and other aid rendered to him. Oggins' death will be recorded officially in his medical records along with an autopsy and burial certificates.

"Since Oggins' wife {CENSORED} is in New York, she has repeatedly asked our consulate for information about her husband, knowing that he was arrested, {CENSORED} we consider it useful{CENSORED} to summon her to the consulate and tell her of the death of her husband.

"I request your instructions."

The instructions from Stalin and Molotov were to proceed.

It is easy to visualize the diligent yet creative Abakumov (who had an appointment with the executioner coming up himself in a few years, but of course wasn't then aware of it) grabbing his black desk telephone with one hand to set Oggins's termination in motion, while with the other scribbling out a brief note, prescription-like, ordering a false certificate of death on medical grounds.

In the photographs taken of him in prison, Oggins appears to be an intelligent man, a man of ideas, certainly, but with rumpled hair and downcast gaze, a man preoccupied - as anyone serving a sentence in Norilsk prison for espionage had good reason to be - with his mortality.

The good doctor-forgers at the MGB dispensary came up with another fine, authentic-looking death certificate for Oggins, too, this one attributing death to "paralysis of the heart owing to acute sclerosis of the coronary artery with associated angiospasms and papillary carcinoma of the urinary bladder." That menu of medical symptoms should have won a Lenin's award of some kind for the author.

One final inconsistency is that, unless Oggins was already dead when Abakumov asked permission to have him executed (we begin to see how this game is played after awhile), the piece of paper attesting to his death simply jettisoned about four of his last miserable months of existence.

Abakumov asked Stalin in May 1947 if he should put Oggins away. The death certificate says he died in the village of Penza the previous Jan. 13.

Isaac S. Oggins, American Communist-secret agent, dead at 49. And buried in the Jewish cemetery of the village where he died - so the records say.

* * *

Volkogonov added another 1992 letter to the Oggins file, however, that was submitted to him by the Russian security ministry (KGB). "As a result of an investigation," it reports, "it was established that the U.S. citizen Oggins, who was groundlessly repressed, was buried in the Jewish cemetery in the city of Penza."

At the next meeting of the joint commission in August, 1992, Volkogonov remarked that the two executions showed that "The Soviet regime was capable of anything. Oggins was shot two weeks before his scheduled release by Stalin, and Abakumov gave the direct order, as we know, because Abakumov reported it to Stalin. It's clear."

Some of the blank spots in Oggins' life—if not in his KGB file— have been filled in by a key character in the secret history of the Soviet Union under Stalin, Pavel Sudoplatov. In an account of the Oggins execution in his book, "Special Tasks—The Memoirs of an Unwanted Witness—a Soviet Spymaster," Sudoplatov says Oggins was not an innocent American citizen wrongly accused, as Volkogonov alleged, but a full-fledged Communist spy who had somehow ended up on the liquidation list of his former superiors in the espionage trade.

Sudoplatov writes that he was "erroneously and unlawfully arrested...for anti-Soviet activities." Oggins, he asserts, reportedly had arrived in the Soviet Far East under false Czechoslovak papers. And there were other reasons for having him killed.

"The reality of his story is this: Oggins was a Communist sympathizer and a member of the American Communist party. He was also a veteran agent of the Comintern and NKVD (KGB) intelligence in China and the Far East. His wife, Nora, was a member of the NKVD intelligence network in charge of controlling safe apartments in France in the mid-1930s. Oggins was arrested in the Soviet Union in 1938 and began serving his term without attracting attention from the press. In 1939 Nora Oggins returned to the United States. I have every reason to believe that she began to cooperate with the FBI and other government agencies."

It was Nora Oggins, Sudoplatov writes, who was behind the U.S. Embassy's efforts to get her husband released. And Abakumov suggested Oggins be eliminated, he asserts, "because Molotov was concerned about the possibility of his being used as a witness against the American

Communist party by the House Un-American Activities Committee."[12]

Stalin's and Molotov's real fear, said Sudoplatov, was "that Nora would disrupt our agent network in America." It was then decided he should be killed, to silence him.

Sudoplatov wrote that the execution took place in 1947, but differs with Volkogonov on the method used in this case. It was done "in the course of a routine medical checkup in prison," he wrote, when he was given an injection of poison by Grigori M. Maironovsky, head of "toxicological research" for the secret police, a title that apparently encompassed live demonstrations of the toxic qualities of certain intravenous liquids. Maironovsky's research subjects, once dead, looked remarkably like people who had died of heart failure, Sudoplatov observed.

With mostly falsified records to go on, it's obviously not possible without more reliable evidence to say with any certainty Sudoplatov or Volkogonor is conect as to motive and method nor whether the executions were actually carried out on the date that the false certificates say death occurred by other means. It is curious, though, that Oggins, whose supposed date of death was 1947, was reported alive by a Japanese Gulag repatriate nine years later.[13]

The ghosts of spies must linger long in the Gulag.

Sudoplatov's account agrees that Oggins was given a funeral and buried in the Jewish cemetery in the city of Penza, 200 miles from Moscow. "I feel sorry for him," wrote Sudoplatov, "but in those Cold War years we did not concern ourselves with what methods were used to eliminate people who knew too much."

But if Sudoplatov is correct about Mrs. Oggins' contacts with the FBI and "other government agencies," the former Comintern agent's problem wasn't that he "knew too much"—anyone who had spent more than a week in the Gulag already "knew too much" about that unhappy place. Rather, Oggins' main problem seems to have been that he and his wife were apparently convinced that the mighty FBI and the U.S. embassy in Moscow could have some influence over Stalin, the KGB, the Gulag authorities, or all three.

When it got down to it, they also sadly underestimated the counterintelligence service's supply of doctored death certificates.

* * *

Reports of American POWs in the Gulag didn't originate in 1992, when Yeltsin made his speech saying that Russia's post-Communist reform government had begun looking into the Stalin era records for signs of

Americans grabbed up by the Soviets.

Beginning soon after the end of World War II, American embassies and consulates throughout Europe began hearing from refugees, former war prisoners from other countries and released inmates that they had met and talked to—in at least one case, taken photographs of—American POWs in the Gulag.

Following up on such reports was no easy matter, however. As one State Department official lamented in an office memo a few years after the war ended in Europe:

"We cannot make any representations to the Soviet authorities on behalf of prisoners of war. The Soviet Central Information Bureau is not permitted to furnish us with such information and the Foreign Office has never given us any information at all on non-American citizens—not only enemy POWs. The only channel open, therefore, is to attempt to contact the prisoner direct when his address is furnished by the inquirer."

Futile as this would seem, U.S. government offices did attempt to utilize this channel. To no one's surprise, it failed utterly. "...many of those people we consider to be American citizens are considered by the Russians to be Rumanians, or Hungarians, etc. and they are adamant in their refusals to give us the smallest drop of information.

"As for the letters we send direct—out of the hundreds we have sent not one has elicited a reply. A few days ago we got a whole batch of them back from the post office which had not even bothered to send them. They were taken back to the post office and the PO personnel said a big mistake had been made and they would forward the letters. The fact remains, however, there has never been a reply."

Until 1950, obviously, any American serviceman reported held in the Gulag would have been a POW from World War II. The imposing figure of 78,000 servicemen unaccounted for from that conflict left a great hole in the rolls of the returned, and after a few years, resignation had set in among those in Moscow whose job it was to continually appraise these reports. Take this May 4, 1948, reply by the Moscow embassy's military attache to communications from other embassies regarding a set of reports, including two (unnamed) U.S. Air Corps officers reportedly held in Odessa, and another reporting eight (unnamed) American military officers being held at a camp at Chelyabinsk, in Siberia:

"Several previous reports, without names, have been taken up with the Ministry of Foreign Affairs by the Embassy. In each case, their reply has been a categorical denial that there are any U.S. prisoners of war in the Soviet Union. Therefore, the Embassy feels that no useful purpose would be served in bringing this matter up again unless complete data is available on the individuals allegedly being held illegally by the Soviet authorities.

The Embassy feels that these "Americans" are probably English-speaking foreigners, dual nationals at best, who are attempting to pass as Americans in hope of release."

Much the same twin attitudes—adamant denials from the Soviets, cynicism from those in the U.S. government who faced frustratingly incomplete reports—prevailed into the mid-1950s, when identical reports began to come in mentioning American servicemen from the Korean War in the Gulag.

Even reports with sufficient information to base a search upon failed to light a fire under the desks of the embassy officials who logged in the accounts brought to the embassy grounds by well-meaning, often quite patriotic, foreign informants. A most complete report of a Korean War POW in a Soviet labor camp was presented in August 1956 at the U.S. embassy in Vienna by a repatriated Austrian prisoner, Adalbert Skala. He reported having met an American Army officer, "a lieutenant of armored troops," about 38 years old, in 1951 in a Soviet prison at Irkutsk. Skala said he and the American were cellmates both there and in Lubyanka Prison, in the heart of Moscow, where he last saw the man. Despite their many months together, Skala said he didn't know the man's first name, only the last, Racek.

But that would have been enough for at least a routine check back in Washington. For he said Racek had given him the name and address of his father, Thomas Racek, of 358 East 72nd Street, New York. (The corner residential building has long since been converted into a larger structure.) Skala described Racek as "not in particularly good condition, having a number of front teeth knocked out, having lost his hair, and generally having suffered the effects of mistreatment." He also said Racek had been receiving Red Cross packages through the Austrian Red Cross, and that he had received a card just that month (August 1956) from Racek, indicating he was still at the prison in Moscow.

Of course, if you worked at the U.S. Embassy in Moscow in 1956 you couldn't just stroll down to the Lubyanka prison, which was located in the basement of KGB headquarters, and ask to sign up for visitors' hours to see one Mr. Racek. Or could you?

Interviewed 35 years later (having done another, subsequent term in Soviet labor camps and then retired from the Gulag patrol for good), Skala confirmed virtually all the details contained in the embassy report of his visit, but said he could add nothing more. After telling the people at the American embassy in Vienna the New Yorker's home address, he'd never heard from Racek again.

* * *

The Gulag was not just a monument to inhumanity—it was an enterprise with an inexhaustible supply of slaves labor spread across an enormous land mass straddling the Eurasian subcontinent and from Mongolia to beyond the Arctic Circle. No wonder the Soviets weren't always sure who they had in there.

In February 1954, the head of the chief directorate of the MVD wrote to the Minister of Internal Affairs regarding six American citizens "arrested at various times on the territory of Germany and Austria" and "imprisoned in special camps and prisons" in the USSR.

The letter ends with an order to instruct the prison bureau "to identify all American citizens held in camps and prisons...since there have been situations when the presence of American citizens in camps became known only when the U.S. Embassy in Moscow posed questions about them" to the interior minister.[14] As in the vast majority of cases of missing Americans the U.S. government brought to the attention of the Soviet government until the post-Communist era, it wasn't very effective simply to pose questions to the Soviets about U.S. citizens reported locked away in the Gulag. But the reports kept arriving. And at the time of the Korean War, many of those reports came from repatriated Japanese prisoners of war, who knew exactly what it was like to be kept from returning home when the fighting was over.

The number of Japanese POWs the Soviets imprisoned in the Gulag after World War II is difficult to state with certainty. A report issued by MacArthur's headquarters in May, 1949, reported there were still more than 60,000 unrepatriated Japanese in Manchuria, about 85,000 on Soviet-held islands north of Japan, and about 325,000 in Siberia.[15]

The Russians had basically captured the entire Kwantung Army of Japan when they swept down out of the Soviet Union in the final weeks of the war in the Pacific and took the territories away from the Japanese in Manchuria and half of Korea. The Japanese troops they captured were utilized for labor in those places, as the Soviets took over the running of huge areas of formerly Japanese and Chinese territory, and many thousands were shipped into the Soviet Union itself, some to prisons and labor camps west of the Urals, even to Moscow and Ukraine.

The Soviets agreed to a staged repatriation of these POWs, in which a certain number would be sent home each month and each year. But the negotiations for this procedure were so protracted, and the conditions in which the Japanese prisoners worked and lived so harsh, that tens of thousands died before the Russians could deport them.

Freeing the Japanese POWs from their prisons in Siberia proved very difficult. Merely accounting for those who were missing there was next to impossible. In August 1950, even after a few years of periodic shipments of Japanese back to their home islands, the occupation government then running Japan was claiming that 370,000 POWs remained on Soviet territory. And the U.S. political adviser to Japan, William Sebald, reported that month that the Japanese were engaged in the monumental task of compiling a complete list of their missing soldiers.

"As of Aug. 20, 1950," Sebald wrote, "evidence had been received concerning presence or death in Soviet and Soviet-controlled territories of 210,803 named persons." It constituted a brave effort, Sebald wrote, but given the refusal of Soviet authorities "to supply any information concerning fate of Japanese in their hands, plus physical task of carding names, interviewing families and repatriates, eliminating duplicates, and classifying information...." All in all, Sebald concluded, "for obvious reasons will probably never be possible obtain names of all missing Japanese."

In one of his final acts of contrition for the sins of the Stalinist past, Mikhail Gorbachev, the last Communist president of the Soviet Union, hand-delivered to the Japanese foreign minister in April, 1991, a list of nearly 60,000 Japanese POWs who died while in Soviet captivity in Siberia. A senior researcher at the Academy of Science's Institute of Oriental Studies in Moscow, Aleksei Kirichenko, said he had found the names of 639,635 Japanese who had been imprisoned in Siberia. The more than 64,000 who had died, he said, were in more than 320 burial sites around the former USSR.[16]

However many there were, one Far East command floated a proposal in 1954 that never received much attention outside of Air Force circles: snatching them out with a massive airlift. The command suggested that, after using unspecified means to "intervene with the Russians, the Chinese or both to release the Japanese nationals being held," the U.S. announce "a proposal to have the United States Air Force fly to a mutually agreeable location, or locations, and airlift the liberated Japanese home."

The idea was presented in a message from the Far East Air Force commander to the Commander-in-Chief, Far East, in October 1954. The rationale behind the idea included the fact that, at that moment, Far East Air Force employed "some 45,000 Japanese nationals on whom it is, in great measure, operationally dependent." Busting tens of thousands of their fellow Japanese citizens out of the Gulag would undoubtedly, as the unsigned message suggested, "promote and maintain good relations" with the Japanese on the U.S. payroll.

The idea had great potential as a morale-booster. But its greatest value was seen in the fact that the Russians—who of course controlled Siberia and its air space—would almost certainly not permit it to happen.

"It would certainly interfere with USSR manipulation of the issue, and would put the U.S., in the event of a very likely refusal by the Communists, in a position to utilize Japanese pride and sense of honor to further alienate them from the Communist bloc."

And even if the Russians should surprise everyone by accepting the daring plan, and allow the U.S. to "intervene" and then carry out the airlift, it wouldn't be as expensive as it might appear, the Air Force command suggested. Even though the Japanese Welfare Ministry's figure of 71,165 unrepatriated Japanese "should be retained for its propaganda value, the actual number estimated to be alive by the Japanese is 46,314 of whom only 13,631 are in Soviet hands."[17]

Quite a number of the Japanese who were repatriated—a process that continued for many months after the war in Korea ended—mentioned seeing American POWs in their Gulag prisons, just as the European repatriates had following World War II. The U.S. military, at the urging of the Air Force, established two programs known as "Operation Wringer"— one for Europe and one for Japan—which carried out military debriefings of returning soldiers and civilians.

Many of the reports were concrete as to place, if not in terms of name, rank and serial number of the American POWs. A report in July 1956 of U.S. aviators from the crew of a B-29 shot down on June 13, 1952, said one or more U.S. servicemen believed to be from that crew were seen in October, 1953, in a Soviet hospital north of Magadan, "near the crossing of the Kolyma River between Elgen and Debin at a place called Narionburg." The prisoners were no longer prisoners of war, needless to say, but criminals convicted of violating Article 58 of the Soviet Penal Code, which outlawed subversion and espionage.

Another Japanese repatriate who had spent from 1950 to 1953— three years of Siberian imprisonment which also happened to coincide with the Korean War time span—in the massive Gulag prison hub at Khabarovsk told the Operation Wringer authorities that at POW Camp 21 there, he "heard from Soviet guards, prisoners and laborers that the crew of a military plane shot down by Soviets was in Khabarovsk prison."

The report said he believed there were "12 to 13 unnamed Americans" in the military crew. While there were no names to help trace the report, there were notable incidents involving the shootdown of U.S. military reconnaissance planes just off the Soviet coast during the war. (See Chapter 14, *Order of the Red Banner*.)

One of the most graphic reports of an American serviceman held after World War II in the Gulag involved a POW camp in Karaganda, which is yet another legendary outpost of the Gulag in the Central Asian republic of Kazakhstan (formerly the Kazakh Soviet Socialist Republic). The report, detailed in a letter that was circulated in the fall of 1950 to military and diplomatic posts throughut Asia and Europe, deals with conditions in the Gulag in the years prior to the outbreak of war in Korea:

"1. Interrogation of two Japanese repatriates from the USSR reveal the possibility that an American man was being held in Soviet forced labor camps as of 1948.

"2. One of the informants, who was repatriated 21 January 1950, reports having seen and talked with an American, name unknown, at the 99-13 PW camp in Karaganda between May and June 1948. The American was described as 25-26 years of age, 5'6" tall, weight 110 pounds, blond hair, blue eyes, lean face. The repatriate 'heard' that the American was an 'ex-GI' who was captured in Europe near a large river (possibly the Elbe) after being lost from his unit during the last war. He was reportedly tried at Moscow and Karaganda by a military court on charges of espionage and received a 15-yr sentence. According to the informant, the American spoke Russian fairly well and his German language ability was good.

"3. The second informant, repatriated 22 April 1950, reports that an American prisoner arrived at Karabas convict camp southwest of Karaganda about 22 August 1948. The American was quartered in the same room with the interrogee for three days. The informant states that the American was reportedly captured somewhere in Germany and sentenced to 25 years in prison on charges of espionage. He was described as 25 years of age, height 5' 7", weight 150 pounds, medium build, large mouth, long face, reddish-brown hair, blue eyes, fluent in German and Russian."

The informants seem to be describing the same man, but the letter cautioned "there is no corroborative information on hand at the present time" to back it up.

The letter also notes, however, that the second Japanese repatriate said the American was "ill-treated" by the other inmates, "who blamed the United States for their predicament," and that the American was transferred to "special quarters" at the same camp at Karaganda in late August 1948.

The Karaganda camp was a large facility, and located midpoint between Europe and Asia. At Karaganda, one might meet barrackmates not only from Japan but from Europe. One European POW gave this corroborating report, which deals with events at the Karaganda prison somewhat later, and was also cited in the letter that went to military commands around the world in the fall of 1950:

"Source states that he knows of one American who is interned in one of the camps in KARAGANDA (49 degrees 52 minutes N-73 degrees 10 minutes E), KAZAKH SSR. Source bases his statement on the following:

"One day in October 1949, after he had returned from work, one of his fellow PWs in the barracks told him of an incident he had witnessed that day. On his way to work with his group, he was passing the vicinity of the airstrip when he saw Soviet militia and MVD soldiers start beating a man who had been walking in the area.

"The man cried out that he was an American citizen. They then beat him and mistreated him all the more and called him a spy. A car of the MVD police arrived upon the scene, and the man was dragged into it and presumably taken to MVD headquarters. Source never saw the man again, nor did any of his comrades, but they heard that he had joined the other persons who were interned in the area."

But while the Japanese brought back some data about POWs, to the Air Force, the great value of the repatriated Japanese POWs was in their intelligence about potential bombing targets in the Soviet Union.

The Air Force was preparing—drawing contingency plans—for the next war, which everyone assumed would involve fighting the Soviets and would likely include atomic weapons. The Air Force wanted to know where to drop the atomic bombs where they could do the most damage to Russia's military-industrial complex and cause the maximum disruption of its war-making potential. A meeting of the Joint Atomic Energy Intelligence Committee in March 1950, a few months before the start of the Korean War, gives an idea of what was on the minds of the top intelligence people in the U.S. military and intelligence community:

More than 1-million Japanese POWs had returned from Siberia, an Air Force officer reported. "They have shown exceptional memory concerning the details of the places where they have been among which are all the industrial cities in the Urals and the cities in the Tashkent area. Excellent town maps have been made from these interrogations."

The Japanese POWs the Russians had stored in Siberia and were slowly allowing to leave were the mainstay of U.S. Air Force intelligence in the Far East in the years leading up to the Korean War.

An air-interrogation section under two Air Force officers and employing 20 civilian interrogators and five typists were thrown into this effort, which was coordinated with the CIA's station chiefs in the region. "The major portion of air intelligence produced by this command is from intelligence information collected through interrogation of Japanese repatriated from Soviet areas," according to a June 30, 1949 memo from the Far East Air Forces plans and policies officer.

The information, it cautioned, "necessarily is limited to that which can be seen or heard by a person in the status of a prisoner of war" and was usually from six months to one year old.

Despite these qualifications, the Japanese ex-inmates of the Gulag provided abundant data "on Soviet airfields, topography, urban areas, etc., and is excellent for the production of targets," the memo added.

One of the most useful pieces of intelligence discovered in the questioning of returned Japanese soldiers, however, was that the Russians had carried out an ambitious program to create a cadre of secret agents among the Japanese POWs. After sufficient indoctrination and training, these soldiers would be given assignments or coded methods of contacting subversive leaders back in Japan. The future agents were recruited out of the crowded POW camps and given an increasingly compromising course of instruction, culminating in their selection as secret agents.

It was this program that the KGB agent in Tokyo, Yuri Rastvorov, had participated in and explained in detail to U.S. intelligence after his defection in 1954. The future agents were weaned on spying assignments targeting their fellow POWs. "Such practices," said a Pentagon study of the Soviet training regime, "serve not only to train and test the person, but it also prepares the prisoner psychologically for his future intelligence mission. Becoming accustomed to secret agreements, secret contacts, and covert activities, the potential agent gradually learns to accept a double life as a matter of course."

North Korea sent thousands of South Korean POWs into Siberian exile during and after the war, according to Kan San Kho, a former deputy head of the North Korean internal security department. The Soviet Gulag also served as a convenient prison—with ready-made labor camps and no chance of parole—for North Koreans convicted of sabotaging the war effort, Kan said. He recalls at least two major cases of war profiteering by North Korean officials during the Korean War in which supplies furnished by the Soviet Union were used for private gain. At least a dozen North Korean officials found guilty in each case of running the criminal enterprises were sent north into the USSR, Kan said.[18]

Born in the Far East, near Vladivostok, Kan worked in North Korean propaganda and intelligence positions during the war. His appointment as deputy head of the North Korean security force—the equivalent of the Soviet KGB—came after the war. He also served as the chief North Korean representative at Panmunjom during 1957-58.

He was part of the group of military officers, Soviet citizens of Korean descent who, after helping drive the Japanese from the region at the end of World War II, were selected on Stalin's orders to form the nucleus of Kim Il-Sung's army and government. He returned to the Soviet Union in 1959, and lives today in Russia.

Americans on the joint commission visited the Russian Far East, where many thousands of the Japanese POWs had been held and died, in September 1992 to look into reports of Americans in the Gulag. The U.S. delegation headed for Khabarovsk, where the interior ministry's main prison camp administrative offices are located.

The Russian camp administrators they interviewed said they knew of no Americans who had been imprisoned or hospitalized in the Khabarovsk area, even after World War II when a number of U.S. plane crews crashed or made emergency landings on Soviet territory in the region.

Gannadiy Mikhailov Popov, who said that during the Korean War years he served as a political officer with the MVD, and afterward as director of camp administration in Khabarovsk, recalled no Americans in his camps, but said there were 123,000 Japanese POWs in the Russian Far East.

But the Task Force Russia office in Moscow and new U.S. embassies throughout the former Soviet Union continued to receive letters, calls and walk-ins with stories of Americans imprisoned in the Gulag from Korea.

• Bronius Skardzius wrote the U.S. embassy in Vilnius, Lithuania, that at a transit prison in Novosibirsk, about June 1952, two prisoners arrived who said they were American pilots who had been shot down over Korea. Part of a group of German prisoners, the Americans were dressed in khaki shirts and trousers. One, who was tall with a red beard, said he was a captain in the U.S. Air Force. Skardzius also passed on the names of two other ex-inmates who live in Vilnius who might have information.[19]

• Anton Keburis, also of Lithuania, said he met two captured American pilots from Korea in Moscow in July, 1952. He described them as "obviously cultured men in decent civilian suits," about 30 years old. Keburis said he spent four or five days with them, conversing in "school German," before he was sent to another prison in Chelyabinsk. He never saw them again.

• A former inmate of Soviet labor camp No. 307, in Yakutia, said he had met there two American POWs from Korea, an infantry lieutenant named Ted Watson and a sergeant Fred Rosbicki.

• Yuri Filippovich Yezerskiy, a retired MVD (KGB) general-lieutenant who served as a camp administrator in Vorkuta between 1954 and 1963, said there were four or five young American men in their mid-20s in the prison camp complex during that time. He didn't know if they were civilians or former prisoners of war, and could provide no names, but said he believes Americans would be extremely difficult to trace in the prison records with which he became familiar. (Yezerskiy speaks from close personal experience. His Jewish father, he said, spent 15 years in prison at Vorkuta and was released in 1953. A year later, Gen. Yezerskiy was given the assignment of supervising construction at the prison complex where his father had been incarcerated.)

"The prisons often kept what we called 'double accounts' of the people there," he said. "They would have their real names and also prison names." An American inmate's "prison" name, said Yezerskiy, might be a Russian-sounding name "or some common American name, like Smith or

Brown. He said prison regulations eased after Stalin's death, in 1953, and a number of foreigners at Vokuta began receiving packages of medicine and clothing and reading material via the International Red Cross. The chances of sending a letter or package directly to an inmate of any nationality were low, he said, although the Red Cross did have a system in which some prisoners had assigned numbers that would indicate a package was meant for them.

Yezerskiy told the American analysts for the joint commission that records of name changes might be on file still, but he wasn't certain.[20]

The reports came in letters from all across the vast expanse of the former Soviet Union. The analysts handling the chore of sifting and interpreting them for the American side of the joint commission evaluated each one for the information it contained and the source. Some of the sources were judged to be interested more in the attention that a Gulag-sighting report could generate than in passing along legitimate information. But none of the reports came closer to being exactly what the analysts of Task Force Russia were looking for than the testimony of a decorated Red Army veteran by the name of Nikolai Dimitriyevich Kazersky.[21]

Kazersky had spent four and a half years beginning in 1950 in a Siberian labor camp at Zimka, on the Veslyana River near the village of Knyazhogost. After a time, he said, the prison rumor mill had it that an American was among them, and in the fall of 1952, or the spring of 1953, he couldn't recall exactly, he had met this man.

He said the American told him he had been a pilot of an aircraft attacked over North Korea and forced to land in Soviet territory. All three men aboard had been taken prisoner, he told Kazersky, but by then had been sent to different prisons, although his "radioman" had spent some time at the Zimka camp as well. Kazersky said he and the American had difficulty conversing because the pilot had been in isolation for much of his sentence to that time, and each knew only a few words of the other's language. But he was able to describe "The American," as he was called at the camp, and his situation.

The pilot was about 30 years old, five-feet-seven, slender, with dark hair and a dark complexion, with a small, oval scar on one cheek. Kazersky thought he was of southern European origin. He lived in Barrack No. 6 (Kazersky drew a map of the prison for the analysts).

The analysts also showed Kazersky photographs of some of the Air Force MIAs from the Korean War, and combining his choice of photographs with the other information he had related, the analysts came up with a potential match: Capt. Ara Mooradian, of Fresno, Calif.

Mooradian was a bombardier on a B-29 that was disabled in a MIG attack as it was returning from a mission on Oct. 23, 1951. The plane was last seen in the air, on fire but under control. Two bodies from the plane were later recovered; six other crew members, including Mooradian, were listed as MIA.

Not everything fit exactly—Mooradian was taller than the height Kazersky gave; he was a bombardier, not the pilot; the B-29 had 13 crew members, not three.

When Task Force Russia investigators asked Kazersky a few months later to let them videotape his testimony a second time because the tape of his original interview was of poor quality, he refused. He said a friend of his had cautioned him about discussing Americans in the Gulag. But he'd already spoken out once. "The KGB is still active," Kazersky reminded the Americans. And that's enough reason to stop talking before its too late, he believes.

Kazersky remains certain he met an American POW from Korea in the Soviet prison camp. It might have been Capt. Ara Mooradian.

* * *

One of the most complete and persuasive stories involving an American POW in the Soviet gulag came from a person of unquestioned honesty and high reputation—Balys Gajauskas, a member of the new Lithuanian parliament.

Gajauskas told Task Force Russia that during the 1950s, when he was imprisoned in a Soviet mining camp in the Balkash area, he met two American inmates. One was named "Victor Shaeffer."

He said Shaeffer told him he was a Navy officer, born in Germany but a resident and citizen of the U.S., who worked for U.S. intelligence in the Far East during World War II. He said he was working behind Japanese lines when the Soviet Red Army invaded through Manchuria and northern Korea at the close of the war and arrested him. Before arriving in Balkash, he said he had been imprisoned initially in a "closed camp" somewhere in the Far East, and later in Karaganda.

Gajauskas remembered that, while Shaeffer had been born in Germany, he spoke German poorly, but was fluent in Korean and Japanese. He said that after Stalin's death in 1953, the American was moved once more, and he never saw him again.

The parliament member said he only saw, but never spoke to, the second American prisoner at his camp, but he understood him to be a U.S. Army officer who had been arrested by the Soviets in Berlin.

As a former inmate, Gajauskas was also able to describe—at least in the Lithuanian experience—how Gulag camps operated. He said so-called "closed" camps were those run solely by the KGB, but that even at "open" camps the security agencies would station personnel.

And rather than inmates being forced to change their names, he said it was more common for people in the general population to adopt a new name, fearing they could be on some list to be arrested under their real name.

But he said frequently Gulag inmates who managed to serve and survive long prison sentences were exiled to a remote village, not far from their prison, and ordered to remain in place and not communicate with relatives or old friends and tell them where they were, or risk being thrown back into prison.

Task Force Russia included Gajauskas's testimony as part of the evidence in its 1993 report and video on Korean War POW transfers to the former Soviet Union—based on an initial misunderstanding that the American intelligence officer had been a prisoner during the Korean War. When that point was cleared up, task force members apologized profusely to the Russians for having made an "honest" mistake.

But the underlying point was true, and sobering: Substantial evidence exists that the Russians took custody of an American military officer on the basis of his intelligence activity and shipped him off to Siberia.

But he only worked for the OSS, and not its successor, the CIA. And he wasn't a Korean War POW. During the Korean War, he was in the Gulag. Of course, if he hadn't been in prison, he might have volunteered.

* * *

Would Stalin's regime have returned the remains of 15 American servicemen who died on Soviet territory during World War II to the United States while—at the same time—his military and intelligence services were interrogating U.S. prisoners from the Korean War and shipping some of them to Siberia?

The answer might be yes, if both were carried out secretly. That would help explain an unpublicized event that took place in late December 1951 in Germany and the still-unfolding mystery of Soviet involvement with missing American POWs in Korea.

The old business on the agenda of the joint commission on POWs and MIAs is World War II. And that war was still very much in the minds of those who were running the U.S. government and military during the Korean War. (For that matter, much of the fighting in Korea was done by World War II veterans—Korean, Chinese, Russian and American—who brought a distinctly grizzled outlook to the battlefront.)

But the policy makers, and the general public, were not informed of what took place between the Soviet Union and the United States on Dec. 29, 1951, in the freight yard of the Warsaw rail station in the Soviet sector of East Berlin. Maj. George Gunderman of the 7887th Graves Registration Detachment out of Liege, Belgium, had been waiting in Berlin for more than a week, trying to contact the Soviet Liaison Office to set a date for the transfer of 15 American soldiers who died on Soviet territory during or just after World War II.

The Russians agreed to do it on Christmas Day, at 5 p.m. The Americans showed up, but the Russians inexplicably didn't, so more phone calls were made. Finally, a second appointment was scheduled for Dec. 29, and the remains were returned in caskets each bearing "a brass plate upon which was inscribed the name and service number in both Russian and English." Salutes and handshakes ended the ceremony.

Neither government issued a public statement about the transfer, and the records were classified.[24]

Chapter Four

Circling The Wagons

"I have ordered that all information relating to the U.S. citizens on USSR territory be carefully checked, and every possible measure will be taken so as to remove this problem between the Russian and American peoples."

—Russian president Boris Yeltsin,
in a letter presented June 12, 1992,
to the Senate Select Committee on POW/MIA Affairs.

"The fact is that in the last five years, our society opened up. If there had been an American, he would have had the chance to announce himself. Write a letter."

—Gen. Dmitri Volkogonov,
co-chairman of the U.S.-Russian Joint Commission on POWs and MIAs,
June 17, 1992.

On the icy cold morning of Feb. 10, 1993, in Moscow, Paul M. Cole, an analyst in the international policy department of the RAND Corp., and a Russian-speaking colleague paid a visit to the offices of a new foundation called the Reform Fund.

The head of the foundation was Vadim Bakatin, a former Soviet interior minister and ex-chairman of the KGB. He had been appointed to lead the legendary Soviet intelligence service by Mikhail Gorbachev, in the last stage of Gorbachev's rapid descent from world power and reknown as the last Communist head of state in Russia's history.

While the entire Soviet hierarchy rattled and shook from the massive political pressures unleashed during the turbulent last months of 1991, some creating and some working to derail a more open and democratic society and government, Bakatin had ridden the whirlwind.

But inevitably he also became a political casualty. He was dismissed in December 1991 by Gorbachev's successor, Boris Yeltsin.

An incoming president could be expected to want his own man in such a high-level post, but there was another reason many of the staunch, old-guard types at the Lubyanka headquarters of the KGB had lobbied Yeltsin to replace him.

As a gesture of goodwill, and an indication that matters had changed forever between the former Cold War enemies, Bakatin had turned over to U.S. ambassador Robert Strauss what he said were the blueprints for the bugs—eavesdropping devices—the KGB had planted in the new American embassy building that would allow Soviet agents to hear or record virtually every word and whisper voiced there.

Bakatin's act of openness was greeted by reformers as a hopeful sign. Yevgenia Albats, a Moscow reporter and author who covered the KGB for many years, called him "the only decent person ever to have headed that criminal organization."[1]

But the incident, among other signs that a real reformer was in charge of the KGB, caused Bakatin to be viewed by the KGB's traditionalists, who still wielded power in the hushed, secretive corridors of the agency, as a traitor, so eager to curry favor with the West that he would dismantle the old but serviceable practices of espionage and reveal the inner workings of the Soviet sanctum.

Bakatin was still managing to cling to his post at the head of the KGB when Cole had made his first call on him, in December 1991. The subject Cole wanted to talk to the KGB director about was missing American prisoners.

A Georgetown University and Johns Hopkins University graduate in diplomacy and international relations, and a veteran of Washington, D.C.'s think-tank culture, Cole had just been appointed director of a RAND project, financed through a Pentagon contract, to search the Soviet archives for clues to unaccounted-for American prisoners from World War II, Korea and the Cold War.

The traditional Pentagon perspective on POW/MIA affairs— bureaucrats, military officers and family members agree on this much— was that it was a tarbaby assignment, to be avoided at all costs for the sake of protecting a career. The only war that held any interest for the people in the Defense Intelligence Agency, which was supposed to be paying attention to the POW/MIA issue, was Vietnam.

And DIA's whole concern even in Southeast Asia was strictly intelligence, not resolution of MIA cases. Anything that might be of interest to survivors of MIA cases in Vietnam or any earlier conflict was first debunked, then filed away. The job of dealing with the emotional and fund-raising aspects of the POW/MIA issue was left to the League of Families, a private but government-endorsed association. The League's main concern was not resolution of cases, but recovery of remains—in Vietnam.

While POW/MIA affairs was anything but a high priority for the bureaucrats and paper turf-warriors in the Defense Department, the prospect of reviewing documents on Soviet secret assistance operations and Gulag inmates since 1945 was beginning to attract a lot of attention elsewhere in Washington and among POW/MIA activists not associated with the League.

A Senate Select Committee was preparing for hearings on the whole spectrum of POW/MIA affairs, and the idea for a U.S.-Russian Joint Commission on American POWs in the Former Soviet Union was taking root on Capitol Hill. As usual, virtually all of the committee's and the joint commission's attention was focused on the Vietnam era. Cole's RAND project was a bone thrown to the other wars and eras.

His team's research was to cover all the other wars in which there was reason to believe the Soviets knew what had happened to American POWs and MIAs: World War II, with 77,000 unaccounted for; Korea, with nearly 8,200; and the Cold War, in which dozens of pilots and air crewmen had gone missing while flying secret reconnaissance missions over and near Soviet territory.

The Korean War was chosen as RAND's first target. Given the USSR's covert role in that conflict, and the longstanding reports that American POWs from Korea had been spirited into Siberia during the war, it held great potential. Whether the Russians would come clean on Korea would be an excellent test of the larger issues: the extent to which the new Russian government was serious about ridding itself of the sins of Stalinism, and the depth and strength of the U.S.'s own resolve in facing what appeared on the surface to be a blatant case of POW abandonment in Korea.

As Cole and his colleagues Benjamin Lambeth and Sergei Zamascikov prepared a strategy for getting the most out of the former Soviet archives, they reminded each other that their time was limited.

Russia might appear to be opening up as never before. But no one knew how long the window of opportunity would remain open. It was important to gain access to the critical military and KGB archives before the window closed.

On their first trip to Moscow in December 1991, Cole and Zamascikov—who had defected from the Soviet Union in the 1970s and was sentenced to prison in absentia—set up an appointment with the then-head of the KGB, Vadim Bakatin.

If anyone could give them access to the documents they needed, it was this man. For as part of the mood of reform that was then sweeping the former Communist empire, the chairman of the KGB, the defense minister, the director of the Institute for Military History and the chiefs of various research institutions were authorized to conduct research into Soviet involvement with American POWs and MIAs. All decisions ultimately led back to Yeltsin, of course. The former Soviet Union had dissolved in form, but not entirely in substance.

Cole and Zamascikov were led into the dark-paneled corridors of KGB headquarters at Lubyanka in the heart of Moscow, only to find that Bakatin was tied up meeting with U.S. Secretary of State James Baker III and would be unable to keep their appointment. The KGB's deputy director, however, assured them that Bakatin was determined that the U.S., through Cole's research team, would be granted access to KGB files.

When he left Moscow, Cole reported the KGB's attitude to the Defense Department, saying that things looked very favorable for research in the critical area of POWs and MIAs: "There seemed to be a story to tell," he said, "and more importantly, the Russians were ready to tell it."

But Cole's optimism was premature. Bakatin was soon gone, ousted in the Yeltsin takeover. And in March 1992, another channel of research into the Soviet Union's past was officially created—the U.S.-Russian Joint Commission. Cole's intrepid foray into the lair of the secret-keepers was soon to be overtaken by events.

The commission came into being, those present at the creation say, out of the recognition that a number of entities within the U.S. government—Congress, President Bush's staff, State, Defense, the National Archives—had an interest in being aware of whatever records the Russians were willing to give up from their formerly secret files. There was also the usual competitive factor, which amounted to the Republican-controlled executive branch and the Democrat-run Congress wanting to know what the other knew, when they knew it.

The American side of the commission, headed by retired diplomat Malcolm Toon, a former U.S. ambassador to Moscow, made up of representatives from the House and Senate, the Pentagon, State Department and the National Archives.

To help interpret and analyze the material the commission was expecting to receive from the Russian government and archives, through Gen. Dmitri Volkogonov, the Russian co-chairman, the Department of the Army was delegated as the implementing agency.

A multi-service group of experts in analysis, intelligence collection, Soviet affairs research and Russian linguists, dubbed Task Force Russia, was formed under the initial command of Col. Stuart Herrington, and given multiple tasks: assist the commission in getting word of its existence out to the Russian public in hopes some would come forward with information about missing Americans; interpret the information obtained from citizens and the Soviet archives; act as the eyes and ears of the Senate Select Committee; and serve as the liaison with family members who already were anxiously awaiting new documents and leads that might help resolve their individual cases.

At the Pentagon, another concession was made to the growing awareness that the POW/MIA issue, whether the bureaucrats who hated dealing with MIA families liked it or not, was gaining momentum in the Senate and in the media.

In February 1992, Alan Ptak, who had been a counsel to the Senate Select Committee on POWs and MIAs, was named to the post of Deputy Assistant Secretary of Defense for POW/MIA Affairs. The title was impressive, but Ptak said he ultimately found he was powerless to change the narrow focus on Vietnam.

"What was clear to me in those first couple of months" on Capitol Hill and at the Pentagon, said Ptak, "was that the lobby on behalf of the Vietnam War was so overpowering and so overshadowing of the World War II-Korea-Cold War (people) that there was a disproportionate amount of time spent."

The task force and the commission both sub-divided into four groups, each concerned with a different time frame: World War II, Korea, Cold War and Vietnam. Cole and his team of researchers, who had already established contact with the appropriate archivists and bureaucrats in Moscow, was under contract to work on all but Vietnam-related material, yet found themselves shunted aside by the commission and by Task Force Russia's superiors in the Pentagon, excluded from negotiations and discussions about how the research would be gathered, evaluated and presented.

The joint commission's members negotiated operating rules for their work that required that all interviews and research be done in tandem. The American side was obligated to give advance notice to the Russians about every person they wanted to interview, each archive they wanted to visit, every file they wanted to see, every MIA name they wanted to track down.

It appeared to ensure cooperation by reassuring the Russians that the research was historical, or "humanitarian," as Volkogonov termed it, and not aimed at current Russian intelligence. But the operating rules also gave Volkogonov and his deputies on the commission exclusive access to material that was eagerly sought by numerous scholars, journalists, families and human rights groups.

The rules also meant that any of the Russians opposed to the new openness could easily learn which former official or prison inmate was ready to give up secrets, which labor camp was about to be searched, and how much the American side already knew about cases they were asking the Russians to help them resolve.

It was an arrangement that assumed a great deal of trust. And trust was missing in spades. Ptak, who was present at the joint commission's first meetings in 1992, said it was obvious that "the mistrust that was on the table was phenomenal."

And not just between the Americans and the Russians, but between Russians, too—those who were anxious to learn the truth and put it behind them, and those still holding positions of power in the security services who wanted no part of the new, open dialog of reformist Russia. "They were about as friendly as king cobras," said Ptak.

When the joint commission began its work, Cole said, Volkogonov's staff quickly gathered up the materials his research team had managed to gather in the first several months and locked them away again. From the RAND project director's perspective, the task of getting information out of Soviet files and into the public domain had not just stalled, it was going in reverse.

In practical terms, Task Force Russia members said, the joint-interview and research-request requirements didn't always prove an insurmountable barrier to open investigation. Several times the Russians—strapped for funds and unable to travel to interviews or archival sites unless the Americans paid their way—urged them to proceed alone.

While they were concentrating on many of the same archives and tracking down many of the same witnesses as Cole, Task Force Russia's staffers weren't told of the RAND project, and once they became aware of it were ordered by Defense Department superiors not to have any contact with Cole or his staff, Cole and others say.

No matter what the Soviet archives might hold, and no matter what Cole or Task Force Russia might find to help achieve a full accounting of American servicemen, the major emphasis at the Defense Department level remained this: keeping the POW/MIA issue focused on Vietnam, and keeping any POW/MIA developments from harming any bureaucrat's career.

Cole completed the remainder of his research in Russia and the United States and, in February 1993, on another trip to Moscow, the chance to meet with Bakatin came again.

While having dinner one evening with retired KGB general Oleg Kalugin—who had his own stories to tell about Soviet efforts to recruit new agents among American POWs in Vietnam—Cole mentioned his attempt a year earlier to talk to Bakatin. Kalugin said that he and Bakatin were close friends. Did Cole want to meet him? In the morning? By midnight, Cole and Zamascikov had a 10 a.m. appointment at Reform.

With his RAND colleague serving as interpreter, Cole sat in Bakatin's cramped office with his long legs jammed between the grungy wall and the ex-KGB director's bare desk.

Deferring to Zamascikov's suggestion that it would be impolite to tape-record their conversation at their first meeting, Cole got straight to the point he was interested in, the topic he had wanted to talk to him about in December 1991—"I'm trying to figure out how many Americans were taken from Korea to the Soviet Union during the Korean War."

Without hesitating, Bakatin replied: "There weren't many, were there? About 25 or 30?"

When Zamascikov told Cole what Bakatin had said, Cole was stunned, and asked him if he was sure. Had the former head of the KGB actually just told them that 25 Americans were taken to the USSR from Korea?

"He's expecting a reply," Zamascikov said. "Yes," Cole answered. "That's consistent with my own research."

His own 18 months of research and interviewing at that point—including the testimony of an active-duty Russian military officer—had convinced Cole that what Bakatin had just told him was the most likely scenario. The stories of hundreds or thousands of American POWs being shipped from Korea to Siberia aboard trains were probably unfounded, he had concluded, "because there is no room in Korean War casualty data to account for" that many unresolved cases of MIAs.[2]

But Cole believed a smaller number of POWs could have been transferred—no more than 100, say, or 50. Those were the figures he had used the previous November when he had testified before the Senate Select Committee on POW/MIA Affairs.

By then, he had interviewed Gen. Georgi Lobov, one of the commanders of the Manchuria-based 64th Fighter Aviation Corps, the main Soviet military unit during the Korean War, retired colonel Victor Alexandrovich Bushuyev, Lobov's deputy intelligence chief, and other Soviet veterans of the Korean War interrogation setup.

And by then, Cole had seen the same intelligence reports every other researcher into the Korean War era had, the ones offering graphic but incomplete details—names, camps, locations, physical descriptions, etc.—indicating that American POWs were present in Soviet prisons during and after the Korean War. Given this strong evidence, despite the Russians' denials, "the possibility that American POWs were moved from Korea or China to the territory of the USSR cannot be ruled out," Cole had testified.

And now he had Bakatin's word for it—a man whose position would have given him access to just such sensitive secrets.

Cole decided not to quote Bakatin by name, but in his three-volume report for the Defense Department on his research into missing Korean War POWs, the information was there, attributed to "sources." One was a serving Russian military officer. The other was Bakatin:

"Two Russian sources have provided an estimate of the number of Americans transported to the USSR during the Korean War that supports this study's estimate," he wrote. "The first reported through mutual acquaintances that he had first-hand knowledge to the effect that 30 Americans had been transported to USSR territory. But he was not willing to report this information to U.S. officials. The second source, a former high-ranking KGB official, said in an off-the-record discussion that the "number of Americans taken to the USSR was quite small, 25 or 30 or so."

When Cole's report reached the Task Force Russia staff, they called and asked him if he would identify the anonymous KGB source. He agreed to see if he could get Bakatin to repeat his assertion on the record, and on videotape.

Within a week, using Zamascikov's contacts, Cole had an answer. Bakatin was willing, under three conditions: First, he would discuss the details only with Cole and Zamascikov. Secondly, said Cole, "he wanted a letter from the highest possible U.S. government official requesting his cooperation."

And third, he wanted there to be no publicity. "Having been accused of treason once," said Cole, "he was going to be very cautious on this issue."

But while Cole was still waiting for a final decision on this arrangement, a member of Task Force Russia's Moscow staff, accompanied by a KGB representative, was sent to interview Bakatin. Confronted with the original "25 or 30 or so" quote, Bakatin denied saying anything of the sort.

By approaching Bakatin "cold," rather than through an intermediary, Cole said, "they blew this fantastic chance" to bring the entire issue of POW transfers to the Siberia to the surface. It would be a long time before another witness with Bakatin's credibility would be willing to discuss such matters at all, much less knowing that his information was ultimately meant for public consumption.

Norman Kass, now executive secretary of the Pentagon department that took over the commission-assisting work of Task Force Russia, said the commission staff has no choice in dealing with any Russian witness. Approaching a potential witness in Russia without informing the Russian side of the commission "would be a violation of the basic rules under which this commission was set up," he said.[3]

Kass said the American side has conducted interviews alone only in cases "where the Russian side has told us, after we've invited them, you can go and check this on your own, you can go pursue it."

But he said "we make every effort to involve the Russians in this work so it's bilateral." If the Defense Department's POW/MIA analysts "acquire information from anything we do on our own, without their involvement, we feel that we're fully free to bring that up with the Russians and ask for their assistance."

Peter Tsouras, an Army intelligence analyst for Task Force Russia who vigorously pursued the POW-transfer scenario during the year the task force was in operation, acknowledged that joint commission rules required the American side to inform the Russians of leads they were pursuing. But he believes Bakatin's status as "one of a handful of people in Russia who could have first-hand knowledge" of what remained locked away in KGB archives about American POWs warranted a more flexible approach.

The confrontational approach to Bakatin left Tsouras thinking "It was almost as though it was intended" by some on the commission staff to force Bakatin to deny his private remarks to Cole. The Defense Department bureaucrats who tried to edge the RAND project director out of the research picture "would rather follow the rules and fail" than find a way to enlist Bakatin in the ultimate effort to dig out the truth, Tsouras said.

Kass said that Cole's anonymous sources "were a problem, because without knowing who's involved we would have a difficult time corroborating the information." Of course, in this case, Cole readily identified his source to the commission and the task force. It was the method of getting him to confirm something he'd already said in private that was at issue.

The rule about conducting all interviews with both American and Russian officials present and of keeping the Russians informed of American investigative leads was drawn to ease Russian fears that the American investigators were interested not in finding POWs and remains but in getting their hands on current KGB secrets—to placate those Russians who thought the real purpose of the search for MIAs was to compromise Russia's intelligence services.

The practice was the complete reverse of what had gone on since World War II, when Americans and Soviets didn't share secrets, they stole them from each other, often at great cost. But while policies can change in a day, and governments may declare a former enemy a current ally, minds and attitudes take longer.

A standard diplomatic courtesy between the United States and many countries, such a policy when applied to the issue of prisoners of war missing on the territory of a formerly hostile power raises more complex questions.

And in the case of investigating the missing U.S. POWs from the Korean War—the suspected interrogation and imprisoning of U.S. soldiers and airmen by a government covertly aiding the United States' enemy in the conflict—a policy of strict reciprocity could easily prove counter-productive.

Since the war is long since over, a potential witness's first reaction might be to tell what happened. But on reflection? In practical terms, how could a Russian citizen—bureaucrat, labor camp survivor, former interrogator, railway worker, retired border guard, military intelligence veteran or taxi driver—fail to weigh the consequences of telling a foreigner the truth about Americans held in the Gulag, and of doing so in the presence of a Russian official?

Many of the same people in positions of power and influence before Yeltsin's rise to power—the guards, the judges, government department heads, KGB officials and agents—remain in place, despite the pronouncements that everything has changed. Do they really want to hear the whole truth? What if they perceive it as damaging to stability?

Who will be running Russia tomorrow, or next year? Might they not see that this person or that person spoke out, and demand explanations for confessing such acts, or for saying that someone witnessed something, or heard or saw something that was so morally wrong and ugly that it was never mentioned in public, and all written records of it were suppressed?

Did it matter whether the truth—even though Yeltsin had said he would try to uncover the truth—embarassed or proved troublesome for him or Russia's new friends in the United States?

All of these questions might be in the minds of the Russians who, at first, freely responded to the advertisements and broadcasts and wrote letters or called the hotline. But Task Force Russia and the American side of the joint commission were determined to play by the rules agreed to. In the commission's July 1992 summary, one of the "important lessons" learned so far was:

"On some occasions, we made the mistake of interviewing Russian citizens spontaneously, such as by meeting unilaterally in a public place. This practice tends to reinforce residual Russian conservative suspicions about our activities (i.e. that our team is involved in inappropriate intelligence collection activities.) We will not repeat this error."

Yet in the very next paragraph, the problem is laid out succinctly:

"On the other hand, as should be clear from the series of unproductive interviews conducted on 2 June 1992 in the Ilyinka 12 offices [of former Russian advisors in Southeast Asia], the environment…is not particularly conducive to productive interviews.

"For example…Team members and interpreter report that the former Russian officers who were mustered by the Russian side of the commission to be interviewed were almost to the man quite frightened and reluctant to talk.

"Our challenge is to adhere to the principle of bilateral, open interviews, while somehow overcoming the natural reluctance and fear of many citizens to discuss such matters in such a setting so soon after the demise of Soviet power.

"We therefore strongly recommend that emphasis be placed on the acquisition of office space in a U.S.-controlled area such as the former Embassy building, in which we can conduct interviews of Russian citizens. We would, of course, adhere to the principle of bilateralism and invite our Russian colleagues to be present for all interviews; however, we believe that interviews will not yield a free exchange of views as long as they are conducted in Ilyinka 12."

But the problem of making potential Russian witnesses comfortable enough to talk about the policies of Stalin's and Beria's time—in a building where the Communist Party had conducted its uncomfortable business—seemed to worsen. In November, 1992, testifying at the hearings of the Senate select committee, Al Graham, then the committee's Moscow-based liaison with the joint commission said one cause was instability in the new Russian government.

Russians, Graham said, "see things sort of falling apart. Things were a lot easier when I was over there in May and June. It was a lot more open. Now, people are becoming very reticent to speak because they don't know, maybe tomorrow he's gone and if they speak, if they say something, they could lose their job, lose their pension or whatever."

No matter which American might ask the questions—a Task Force Russia interviewer, one of Cole's project staff, or a journalist—the calculation of risk by the Russian being interviewed would be the same. All of the efforts to unearth the secrets of the Soviets' past dealings with American POWs were probes that rubbed against the same nerve endings.

In general, Kass said, while Cole's project for RAND was supposed to be a parallel effort, there had been friction in coordinating his research and the work of the commission.

"There were times when one duplicated the other and it had all the ingredients of any relationship that is difficult," said Kass, "when you have two parallel efforts and you try to keep them in a way that one reinforces the other—you invariably come up with difficulties, and there were those here."

Since taking on the Korean War POW/MIA project in the fall of 1991—before the joint commission was even created—Cole had pursued, interpreted and drawn conclusions from many of the same documents and witnesses as Task Force Russia. Moreover, in the instance involving Bakatin and others, he and his researchers and sources in Moscow were able to retrieve documents and testimony about American POWs in the former Soviet Union before the commission or the Army's special working group.

Kass conceded that Cole started his work on Korea before the commission was even formed, but added that while "we benefited from having two sources of information of what was available out there," it led to confusion. "There were points when the relationship criss-crossed and became messy." Sometimes, said Kass, "it complicated the picture, muddied the water to an extent with the sources that were there."

As time went on, he said, "the two separate tracks began to blend, began to merge and the sources that RAND hoped would provide it a very different set of information, that would give it an exclusive take on what was going on, became more and more the people who were working with the commission...."

In the end, Cole's and the commission's encounters with Bakatin illustrated how tenuous and difficult the search for answers to these sensitive questions can be.

Instead of opening up a whole new layer of proof, the Bakatin episode was relegated to an anecdote in a think tank's report. Meanwhile, the Russians would continue to argue that there was still no convincing evidence of American POWs being interrogated on Soviet territory.

They would continue acting as though there had been some kind of protective wall between the Soviet interrogators in the Korea-Manchuria-USSR theater of war and the American prisoners last seen answering their questions.

* * *

The U.S.-Russian Joint Commission on American POWs in the Former Soviet Union was the product of two powerful desires that arose almost simultaneously in early 1992 in the capitals of two world powers who had fought each other for so long, mostly at a distance.

The United States wanted information.

Russia wanted respect.

In Washington, two determined and sometimes disputatious senators—Democrat John Kerry of Massachusetts and Robert Smith, a New Hampshire Republican—were preparing for what were expected to be ground-breaking hearings later that year of a Senate Select Committee on POW/MIA Affairs. A crucial and potentially important investigative track for the senators and the committee's staff led to Moscow, where reports were circulating that long-secret archives surely contained documents that would resolve the fate of numerous cases of Americans missing in confrontations with Soviet-supported allies in Korea, Vietnam and throughout the 45-year Cold War.

To build the groundwork for their committee's work on the angle of possible Soviet involvement with missing American POWs—and hoping to get their hands on some of the secret material that was beginning to surface in the new Russia—the senators and their aides visited Moscow in February.

The reform-minded, non-Communist government of Boris Yeltsin was trying to find its feet in those first, optimistic moments of post-Glasnost Russia, and was in search of ways to prove to the U.S., suddenly the world's sole superpower, that the new leadership was not only no longer an enemy, but was worthy of America's trust, friendship and financial support.

The result was an exchange of expectations. Kerry and Smith received a list of 536 names—510 purported U.S. military personnel and 26 believed to be civilians of various nationalities—culled from a number of still-unspecified Soviet archival sources. They were told that the people on the list were "U.S. POWs from the Korean Conflict who were interrogated by the Soviets, some of whom had then been sent to China."[4]

The list wasn't made public immediately. Smith, who could rightfully take credit for helping bring the joint commission into existence by his persistent entreaties to the White House and State Department, was concentrating much of his time and effort on the Korean War in an effort to balance a distinct tendency by the other members to focus on Vietnam MIAs. He and Kerry brought the list back and had it analyzed by military personnel and Senate staffers in an effort to learn more about the people named on it.

The result was Smith's announcement the next June that of the first 510, 146 couldn't be linked to the U.S. military, 265 were U.S. POWs who had been repatriated, and 125 were names of men who had been declared dead after neither they nor their remains returned from Korea. The latter, he argued, should be considered American POWs "who were interrogated by the former Soviet Union and possibly transferred to China."

While that was not an unreasonable judgment—some may well have been—the list of 526 was actually more complex, and contained less useful information, than it appeared at first reading. (See analysis, Chapter 8 appendix.)

In return, the Russians won another nod of approval from potential western benefactors, and an invitation to send an emissary to testify before the Senate POW/MIA committee. The visiting senators also warmly endorsed the idea of forming a joint commission to look into the entire subject of missing American and Russian POWs. The commission would be a two-sided, humanitarian effort, aimed not only at resolving the cases of American MIAs but also finding the Soviet POWs who were still missing from Moscow's disastrous war in Afghanistan. The U.S. promised to use its contactss among the Mujnadeen to find missing Soviet POWs from the conflict that had become a Communist quagmire.

In their terminology, the Russians delivered a vice presidential decree establishing an "interdepartmental commission for clarifying information concerning U.S. citizens missing in action on the territory of the USSR during and after World War II," with Gen. Volkogonov as chairman. President Bush named Malcolm Toon, a retired foreign service officer and former ambassador to Moscow, as the American co-chairman.

To help carry out the commission's mandate, and to serve as a liaison with the growing number of family members who had been hanging on Yeltsin's words and hoped that the commission would become a new and effective means of finding answers to their specific MIA cases, the U.S. government delegated the Army to form a special unit of analysts, linguists, interpreters, researchers and specialists, with a branch office in Moscow.

Dubbing it Task Force Russia, and placing in command Col. Herrington, a highly regarded counter-intelligence commander with impressive Indochina experience, the Army organized a multi-service group of more than 30 very committed, energetic and highly skilled uniformed and civilian experts.

From the start, the task force was squeezed into borrowed offices and quarters in Washington and Moscow. But esprit was strong, fueled by the idea that a fleeting opportunity was at hand to delve into a long-closed history, and the Russians—not all, perhaps, but enough—were apparently willing to look squarely and honestly at the past, at evidence that American POWs had been consigned to the Gulag or the grave on the soil of the former Soviet Union.

The documents from the former Soviet archives began arriving slowly, then in thick packets. They ranged from lists of World War II air crews that were stranded on Soviet territory, and helped to returning home, to the names of American citizens who had immigrated to the Soviet Union with their parents, in the 1930s, and forced to take on Soviet citizenship.

But what seized the world's attention in the commission's first year were a comment by Yeltsin that started a controversy both Russian and American officials tried to squelch, and a search that promised a shocking find but trailed off in the remnants of the Gulag.

In June 1992, Volkogonov delivered a letter to Kerry and Smith in which Yeltsin acknowledged that a dozen Americans shot down over Soviet territory during the 1950s were kept in Soviet prisons and psychiatric clinics, and that hundreds of U.S. servicemen were held prisoner in the Soviet Union during and after World War II.

The imprisoned pilots were believed to have been casualties of secret reconnaissance flights, similar to that of Francis Gary Powers' U-2 shootdown in 1960. But the U.S. had never publicly announced the loss of any other aircraft on secret missions. The net effect was that of a top-secret toppling of dominoes, in which one country, by tipping over one of its secrets, knocked another country's secret into view.

A Pentagon spokeswoman observed that the U.S. had been "aware of the losses," but otherwise the U.S. government had little to say. Yeltsin's letter said the fate of the downed pilots was being investigated. None of the pilots was named.

As for the World War II prisoners, Yeltsin said some were held in isolation for a year or more. And he made the first mention of Soviet records dealing with Korean War POWs, saying the Soviets had interrogated at least 59 of them. That was a reference to the number of interrogation "protocols" the Russian side of the joint commission would make available from Korean War-era papers.

But Yeltsin's real eye-opener came in an answer he gave to a question he was asked on NBC television, about whether American POWs from Vietnam were transferred to the Soviet Union.

"Our archives have shown that it is true," replied Yeltsin, "some of them were transferred to the territory of the former USSR and were kept in labor camps. We don't have complete data and can only surmise that some of them may still be alive." He repeated the assertions in talks with Bush and at a press conference the next day. But no one seemed to want to take him at his word.

For the next several days, Yeltsin's people traveling with him to a summit with President Bush as well as his staff in Moscow expressed bafflement over his remarks. There was no evidence for such comments, they said. Gen. John Vessey Jr., Bush's special presidential envoy to Vietnam for POW/MIA affairs, said the claim "does not square with what we thought we knew. It's absolutely new information."

And Toon, eager to make the way smooth for the newly formed commission, suggested that Yeltsin may have simply misspoke.

While Yeltsin's comments about Vietnam POWs shipped to the USSR were being absorbed, a delegation of Russian and American officials were racing off to a remote Siberian labor camp in search of a man believed to be one of the U.S. POWs Yeltsin had been talking about.

But it was a strange and confusing story. The American prisoner, the reports said, was captured in Korea, not Vietnam. His name was either Martin or Markin. And he was either alive, or had recently been alive. One of the new task force's first investigations had just begun in a smog of media coverage and international confusion.

The case of "David Markin" began June 8, 1992, when a taxi driver from the Ukraine named Viktor Pugantsev arrived at the U.S. Embassy and asked to make a report in response to the joint commission's broadcast appeals for information. Pugantsev said he had been a prisoner in a Siberian labor camp from 1982 to 1986 with a man who said he was an American pilot who had been taken prisoner during the Korean War. His name was— depending on which disputed version one chose—either Robert Martin or David Martin or David Markin.[5]

Word of the "David Markin" sighting reached newsrooms in Moscow and the U.S. a few days later, and a joint team of investigators, accompanied by journalists, raced to the prison in question at Pechora, northeast of Moscow.

The prison's inmates and camp administrators remembered Pugantsev, but all denied knowing any prisoner named Markin, or Martin, or any American for that matter.

Pugantsev didn't give up trying to convince the Americans of his story, however. He volunteered the name of Vladimir Bageyev, a timber worker he said had also been an inmate at the Pechora camp at the time and who should remember the inmate who said he was an American POW.

Graham and another Task Force Russia staff member visited Bageyev at his home in Elista, Kalmykia, along with a representative of the Russian ministry of foreign affairs and Col. Viktor Borisenko, chief of the MVD in Elista.

Despite the presence of these rather imposing authority figures in his home, Bagayev confirmed that he did, indeed, remember a prisoner named "David Markin." He couldn't be sure he had been an American, however.

The Russian side of the commission responded to the growing confusion and controversy by declaring Pugantsev a huckster and liar. The Americans were left with doubts, a vague feeling that Pugantsev might have told them the literal truth. But it was far from a clean hit.

A prisoner calling himself David Markin might have claimed he was an American pilot captured in Korea—but neither the prisoner nor proof he existed was in hand. And no matching POW/MIAs showed up in U.S. military records.

All the leads at this point seemed to begin and end with Viktor Pugantsev—poor Pugantsev, whom the Russians treated like a crank.

But POW/MIA activists pointed out that journalists who went along with the investigators said the prison at Pechora had been freshly painted when they arrived. They said this was proof that the prison camp administrators had been alerted in advance that searchers were on their way to look for an American, and argued that a coverup was clearly in progress.

One moment, Yeltsin was announcing his government was going to track down any missing Americans in the Gulag, and the next, it appeared the Gulag had just swallowed another victim.

A few months later, when the Senate select committee was holding hearings, the case came up again. Asked about "Markin" when he testified, Volkogonov became visibly angry. "This criminal Pugantsev said he knew David Markin," he stated curtly. "We flew to the camp, but no one there including prisoners or guards had heard anything about him. Then Pugantsev said it was another camp...Pugantsev is a criminal with a long record...This Markin was supposedly from the Korean War period...Finally, we decided that Pugantsev wanted to disorient us for personal motives. He did all this on his own initiative. He wanted to go to America and promised to reveal a great deal."

No one pointed out to Volkogonov the obvious—no one except an ex-prisoner with a long record could have spied an American prisoner in the Gulag.

But by then, Sen. Smith's staff made contact with an American woman who claimed to have been engaged to a "David Markin" in the 1950s. She said he was a pilot who'd shipped out to fight in Korea and never returned. Volkogonov wasn't impressed.

"We can't exclude the possibility of a coincidence," he told the committee. "In Russia, Markin is a name almost as common as Ivanov, or Smith in America. We tracked 43 people with names like Markin in the camp system but there was no relation to Korea. They were all around 30 to 40 years old, so unless Markin was 10 years old when he was flying in Korea.... Still, we continue to follow up every lead. I'm becoming an expert on all these camps."

Pugantsev never got his trip to America, and the David Markin story faded.

Once the brief flurry over the Pechora prison sighting ended, the task force's Moscow staff began facing the day-to-day problems of dealing with the massive task of finding out where the Soviet records on American prisoners were physically located, of determining who could give them permission to review them, and of navigating the tortuous byways of one of the world's most imposing, and often impenetrable, bureaucracies.

Among the first problems the staff faced was a complaint from Victor Petrovich Kozlov, the Russian side's deputy chairman and head of Roskomarkhiv, the main archives of the Russian Federation, about the enormity of the task before them. Kozlov explained that while four of the federation's 18 archives probably held material of great interest to the commission, he had few funds with which to pay workers to review and declassify documents.

And while the American commission members and staff were permitted to visit the archives of the former Soviet Ministry of Internal Affairs, what they found there—card files, fingerprint records, indexes and dossiers on an estimated 25-million people, dating from the Communist takeover in 1917—was not heartening.

The Russians said if they were to conduct any research on POWs, they needed help in computerizing their archives. The budget for Task Force Russia was $9 million. Some of that would go to pay Russian researchers dig into the uncomputerized files that sat in musty stacks all over the former Communist empire.

Another problem noted in the joint commission's first months was that the media appeals "tend to attract swindlers and assorted kooks." That was obviously a cutting reference to Pugantsev, but on balance, the task force said the information they were receiving made the effort worthwhile.

Fresh reports of American POWs from Korea sighted in the Gulag came not only from Russia but from the newly independent Baltic states, where thousands of former inmates of Stalin's camps nursed long, unpleasant memories of the 1950s spent in meat-locker-cold camps that had housed millions of political victims of purges and repression.

Artur Roopalu, of Talinn, Estonia, said he spent two days in a transit camp near Vladivostok with two Americans in September 1951. He wasn't able to speak to them, because they were kept apart from the general camp population, but Roopalu said they were there when he arrived, and still there when he was moved to another camp.

Word around the Vladivostok prison, he said, was that many Americans were being shipped out of Korea to Khabarovsk, then to Magadan, then on to remote camps in the Kolyma oblast.[6]

From Lithuania, Apolinaris Kliveckas reported he had encountered an American POW from Korea while working as a doctor's assistant at a Gulag prison near Narilsk in 1952.

The POW was a U.S. pilot named "Robertson," he said, who told Kliveckas that he was shot down over North Korea, imprisoned in Manchuria, then shipped to Norilsk. Robertson told him his mother was Korean, his father European. When Kliveckas was released in January 1955, the American prisoner was still at the camp.

Kliveckas turned over two photographs of the man he knew as Robertson. He said that, after Stalin's death in March 1953, prisoners had been allowed to take photos in his camp, as long as the subject was smiling.

While waiting for access to archives, and trying to sort out the lines of authority that seemed to change almost daily under Yeltsin's authority, Task Force Russia's analysts worked at applying some of the newest leads to the list of MIAs. But conclusions were difficult to draw.

A former Gulag inmate living in Moscow said he had met an American pilot from the Korean War in a camp at Zimka. Shown a number of photos of American aviator MIAs, he selected four he said could be the prisoner he recalled. Matching the photos with his physical description of the man, the task force analysts leaned toward Air Force Lt. Donald E. Bell of Yuba City, Calif., as the most likely candidate. The Gulag veteran thought one of the other three photos was a better match, except of course for the fact that the man in the picture looked better fed than the man he remembered in prison.[7]

Some of the first attempts to approach Soviet military and intelligence veterans who were likely to have first-hand knowledge of the policies and practices regarding foreign POWs were rebuffed in short order.

A visit in mid-1993 to the regional MVD prison hospital in St. Petersburg to check out a report that some American POWs had been treated there began on a cooperative basis. The director welcomed the task force representatives and let them take a cursory look at the files. But moments later, after receiving a telephone call from his superiors, the director explained that he wouldn't be able to let the Americans look through the files themselves. He promised that his staff would review them and they would be informed if any information on American POW-patients turned up.

Unsurprisingly, no further information was ever received from the hospital.[8]

While task force members logged dozens of trips and interviews with Russian veterans, former inmates, human rights activists, aging dissidents, members of parliament, Yeltsin's cabinet and department heads within the vast Russian bureaucracy, the realization quickly set in that missing POWs were an issue Americans cared much more about than Russians.

The Russians—who could look back on the unrecorded deaths of millions of their own soldiers, relatives and friends during World War II—had difficulty relating to the American concern for the fate of long-missing soldiers and pilots. And they had other problems—their daily bread and shelter—to worry about.

In a summary of Task Force Russia's accomplishments, Gen. Bernard Loeffke, who had been summoned out of retirement to act as the top uniformed member, remarked that he often heard from Russians "that the U.S. POW/MIA issue 'is dead.' The most common reason given for the lack of Russian interest in this issue was the overwhelming problems the Russians themselves face ...."

But he argued that the biggest reason for a lack of commitment "to solving the problem of the fates of U.S. POW/MIAs who were held in the

Soviet camp system is at once more immediate and more superficial: this issue does not, at present, figure as a priority for President Yeltsin."[9]

The Russians appointed to the commission at least put on an appearance of concern, however, providing an office for the commission in downtown Moscow in a building that once served as headquarters for the defunct Central Committee of the Communist Party. A hotline was set up to receive telephone tips—subject to frequent periods of non-operation, due to Russia's abysmal phone system—and advertisements were published in various newspapers and broadcast on television soliciting information about Americans imprisoned in the former Soviet Union.

After seven months of work, in October 1992, Task Force Russia's analysts summed up their statistics to date: 849 pages of "original archives and related material" received from the Russians dealing with POWs from World War II on; 92 interviews with Russians and Americans, emigres, repatriated POWs, family members and journalists.

"Many difficult challenges" remained, the report admitted, after "modest progress." The Vietnam War working group had turned up little evidence of transfers from Indochina to the USSR. As for World War II, the evidence was that hundreds of American POWs liberated by the Red Army did not return, including some the Soviets "certainly withheld."

Regarding Korean War transfers, the evidence was "strong and growing" that "tens, if not hundreds" were taken alive and never repatriated. And the work was continuing.

"We visit ever more remote sites where our POWs may have been held," the 1992 summary stated, "and in the process we speak with local citizens and officials. We publicize our search through the national and regional media in Russia and the former Soviet Union, providing an address and telephone number for any residents who might wish to contact us with information. We spare no effort in this good cause."

But the Russian strategy was clear, the report said, pointing out that the vast majority of documents were handed over "with restrictive criteria"— meaning that "no Soviet culpability regarding U.S. POW/MIAs should be admitted or in any way indicated."

The impression left was that the Russian side "has a conscious strategy" to release "sufficient documentation to satisfy the U.S. side that serious research is ongoing," that "highlights documentation that shows that, whenever possible, the Soviets followed a positive, humanitarian line toward U.S. service members," and most importantly "shifts any blame that cannot be avoided onto third parties, such as China or North Korea."

Especially in the case of documents from the Korean War, the report said the documents that had been released had been "limited and carefully vetted to support the official Russian position that the Soviets had no direct contact with U.S. POWs in either North Korea or China and, further, that absolutely no U.S. POWs were taken to Soviet territory."

The Russians, it said, "have circled the wagons on this issue."

In November, 1992, as part of the Senate Select Committee's hearings on POWs and MIAs from Vietnam and Korea, Volkogonov was called as one of the key, high-profile witnesses.

The Russian side of the commission might have been "circling the wagons," as the Task Force Russia analysis concluded, but Volkogonov was also acutely aware that Cole's RAND report and testimony contained hard evidence that transfers of Korean War POWs to the former Soviet Union had occurred.

Volkogonov widened the wagon circle perceptibly.

Reacting to the growing body of evidence accumulating in the hands of Cole's researchers and the Task Force Russia analysts, he admitted there was "irrefutable evidence" that KGB and other Soviet officers had interrogated American POWs in Korea.

And because the KGB did it in Korea, "therefore, I do not exclude the possibility in Vietnam."

There were limits to Volkogonov's concessions, however. The "vast" number of documents he had personally reviewed from archives contained nothing, he emphasized, that indicated the Korean War interrogations took place "on Soviet soil" and nothing that supported the allegation that U.S. POWs from Korea had been shipped to the Soviet Union.

Moreover, he stressed, the GRU—Soviet military intelligence—was not involved.

The proof that interrogations took place, he said, rested on the word of two participants, retired Soviet colonels Alexander Orlov and Gavril Korotkov, and 49 interrogation reports that had been turned over to the Americans on the joint commission. Volkogonov said the head of the GRU in Korea "forbid any such participation in interrogation, but agreed to help with other intelligence work—he believed the KGB should handle any such interrogations."

Thus, he said, "I believe that the interrogations (in Korea) involved the KGB more than the GRU." The distinction between Soviet security and intelligence organizations had little meaning for the family members and other survivors in the hearing room that day. What ultimate difference would it make, after all, which Kremlin payroll the interrogators were on? The crucial point remained that answers to the fate of missing Americans were in Russian hands.

Task Force Russia's experts on the changing face of Russia's government, however, were fascinated by Volkogonov's assertions, and speculated later that his comments might reflect a power struggle between the security agencies.

To summarize the intensive investigations over the previous months, Volkogonov uttered a phrase that would be repeated over and over in future statements: "No American citizens are currently held against their will on the territory of Russia."[10]

The statement was intended to clear the air from Yeltsin's 1992 comments about American POWs still being alive, and the "David Markin" saga that followed. The finding—which not only Volkogonov but Toon saw as essential to future cooperation between the two sides—was intended to assure there would be no impediments—arising from this issue, at least—to the financial and material assistance the U.S. government had begun to furnish the new regime in Moscow.

To support his case that no American POWs were shipped north into the USSR, Volkogonov quoted from what he described as internal, classified correspondence between the Soviet Union's top security agencies just after the Korean War, saying no American citizens were in the agencies' "special prisons." The statement can be relied upon, he said, because "between themselves," the KGB, GRU and other Soviet security organizations "normally told the truth, although they lied to others...."

Volkogonov's testimony to the Senate committee delved into the entire range of inquiry by the new joint commission. He said no hard evidence had been found suggesting that American POWs from Indochina had ended up in the Soviet Union—only six deserters who stayed briefly, then moved on.

His figures for World War II-era U.S. prisoners who fell into Soviet hands when the Red Army liberated POW camps in Germany jibed with the numbers that the American side of the commission was coming up with through its own research and analysis of documents in the U.S. archives. Volkogonov said there had been 22,000 Americans among the many tens of thousands of allied POWs liberated by Soviet units at the end of the war. Of those, he said, 119 had "Russian, Ukrainian or Jewish names" which automatically earned them a ticket to a camp in the Gulag. Of those sent to such camps, he said, 18 died.

As for how the commission's work was perceived in Russia, Volkogonov acknowledged that, at first, there were "serious differences of opinion" the KGB, GRU and other security services, who refused to grant access to their files; but he said Yeltsin had ordered compliance, and the biggest problem at the moment was the huge volume of poorly organized, uncomputerized files that had to be searched and evaluated.

In December 1992, the task force presented the Russians with a detailed summary of known evidence that American POWs from the Korean War had been shipped to the Soviet Union—a harbinger of the lengthier and more detailed presentation of the case six months later.

In addition, the Americans asked the Russian side for help in arranging interviews with ten former Soviet officials who could be expected to buttress their case. The Russians issued a blanket reply: all ten, the Russians claimed, either didn't exist, were dead, didn't appear on any official government lists or organization rolls, or weren't willing or able to be interviewed.

That list of dead or impossible-to-locate officials included one retired Soviet general officer, Lt. Gen. A.M. Dzyza, whose long military career and later writings had been a matter of public—and published—record for 20 years. The Russians were willing to stand a little embarrassment in order to send a strong signal: we'll cooperate, but on our own terms. And you Americans aren't going to just march over here and start grilling our Korean War veterans about matters as sensitive as these.

Volkogonov said he'd heard rumors in Russia that a Soviet submarine lost in the Pacific in 1968 had sunk after colliding with a U.S. sub. Toon said the U.S. Navy had checked its records and found no U.S. sub was "within 300 nautical miles of your sub when it sank." Nonetheless, Toon learned that the Russian sub's bell had been salvaged and was in the CIA's custody.

He got the CIA to give it up, and presented the souvenir to Volkogonov.[11]

By early 1993, there were signs of strain in the cooperative relationship the commission members had endorsed at the beginning.

In February, a highly-critical article appeared in the newspaper Red Star, official publication of the Russian military. Entitled "Angels from the Pentagon and CIA," it accused the commission of distorting the POW/MIA issue to Russia's detriment, and complained that no sympathy was being shown for Soviet "defenders of the fatherland" during World War II.

The article claimed that if Americans lost airmen in Asian wars or in flights over the U.S. it was because of "suicidal" wars of "terror" waged by the United States, and the author invoked the U.S. use of atom bombs on Nagasaki and Hiroshima, Japan as an indication of how insensitive the Americans could be about victims of war.

For good measure, the article pointed out that while U.S. planes may have violated Soviet airspace during the Cold War, no Soviet planes crossed into U.S.-controlled airspace.[3]

While the Russian press is no longer a Marxist monolith, powerful groups in the government and military still speak through their favored publications, as in many societies. There was a message in the Red Star article. The question was, for how many members of the Russian side of the commission did it speak?

That same month, as a Russian representative turned over a fresh series of documents to the Moscow office of Task Force Russia, he advised the Americans there would be no more documents made available until after the next scheduled commission meeting in April.

Asked why, he said, "Every time I give you documents, it generates questions I cannot answer."[12]

He went on to say that the Russian researchers hadn't been able to turn up any new information on Cold War shootdowns, and that the Russians considered the Korean War period "a closed issue."

Volkogonov put the American side of the commission on notice in June, 1993, that Yeltsin wanted the commission to complete its work by year's end.

The American side's summary that June noted that the Russians had agreed to two more meetings, one in the fall and a "final one" in November or December.

The American side had its own problems coping with the voluminous records in U.S. archives—much of it still classified decades after the armistice at Panmunjom.

In June 1993, a Task Force Russia researcher ran across the records of Operation Wringer at the National Archives branch in Suitland, Md. The Wringer archive consists of about 40,000 files of the debriefings of German and Japanese World War II returnees from the Soviet Gulag. There were 289 cartons of German debriefings and 68 of Japanese.

Each returnee had been asked a long set of questions, including whether they had encountered any Americans while in a Siberian prison. The Wringer files held some potential for linking the information coming out of Moscow with actual MIAs. Some of the files that had already leaked or been declassified were the source of live-sightings disclosed in previous years, and the task force knew there could be even more material.

But there weren't enough researchers on the task force payroll to review them all. Exploiting all of the information that might be in Wringer debriefings would take numerous hours of slow, plodding work. The Wringer files would never remain unsearched long after Task Force Russia was history.

Meanwhile, time was running out for Task Force Russia. For a year, supported by Gen. Loeffke and Col. Herrington, the team of Korean War specialists had been carefully and methodically assembling the pieces of the USSR-POW-transfer scenario.

They had capitalized on the Orlov and Korotkov interviews that Volkogonov mentioned in his 1992 Senate testimony, checked out new leads, found other witnesses and laid out the evidence that had been in U.S. records all along.

But they had earned themselves some powerful bureaucratic enemies. And the job of pursuing that evidence and the individual cases it might resolve was about to be turned over to a newly created office under the Department of Defense—which had shown no real interest in either the MIAs from Korea or the answers the new documents and witnesses were providing.

Task Force Russia was to be dismantled.

First, it would fire its best shot.

Chapter Five

The Interrogators

"I also studied long reports based on interviews which Pak's interrogators had with American prisoners of war - including their recollections of where they had been fighting...tactics...battle plans...personal evaluations of their commanders."

—Pavel Monat. Polish military advisor
in Pyongyang during Korean War.

"We fully admit that some prisoners were interrogated by the Russians but they were turned over to the Chinese or the North Koreans. I would like to emphasize again that we focus on those (countries) for answers."

—Col. Alexander Orlov.
former POW interpreter for Russian interrogators
and now head of the Russian side's
Korean War working group of the joint commission.

One of the first Soviet veterans of the Korean War to speak openly about his experiences there was Gen. Georgi A. Lobov.

A tall, striking figure with gray hair and a general's haughty posture even in his declining years, Lobov saw the dissolution of the Soviet empire coming in 1991 and decided there was no good reason for keeping silent any longer. The days when the Kremlin could order entire divisions of troops and squadrons of planes to a distant battlefront like Manchuria and never inform the masses were over.

And the calm, inner satisfaction of having performed a dangerous and secret mission for your country—while most of your countrymen were never, and should never, be told what you did—was giving way to a notion that recognition, at long last, was due.

After all, a few of the fighter pilots who, like Lobov, had won medals there as Heroes of the Soviet Union, had already alluded to their exploits in books or newspaper articles, without saying where they had taken place.[1]

From his memento-filled flat in one of the towering Moscow skyscrapers that had been constructed expressly for high-ranking military veterans like himself, Lobov wrote a series of magazine articles about his tenure as commander of the Manchuria-based 64th Fighter Aviation Corps, the main Soviet military command during the Korean War.

The articles didn't delve into every secret program or covert operation the Soviets carried out in the Far East in the 1950s. For one thing, Lobov wouldn't have known about some of them. He was a combat commander, not one of these new political types who seemed to be more interested in psychology and trickery than prevailing in the thunder of battle.

But the articles were colorful, in a traditional sort of way, describing in detail the corps' mission, and the way the Soviet pilots in Chinese uniforms bravely flew their MIGs into numerically superior waves of American fighter planes.

In passing, Lobov also mentioned a number of the American pilots who had been taken prisoner. A mention of an American in a Soviet publication was always good for attracting a few more readers. Without saying so directly, Lobov made it clear that the Soviets had taken a particular interest in the American pilots and air crews, and had tried to learn a great deal about them, their training and their aircraft.

For an interview with an American reporter in Moscow in the fall of 1991, he arrived at the building that housed the Soviet Veterans' Committee dressed in his general's uniform. He brought along retired colonel Georgy Kuzmich Plotnikov, who had served with him in Korea as a high-ranking military adviser to the North Korean army.[2]

It was still somewhat new, this dealing independently with foreigners and their assertive reporters, who had none of the polite, deferential ways of the Soviet press. Lobov and Plotnikov answered all of the questions about American prisoners of war as though certain things were still secret.

Lobov would have had little reason to come into actual contact with American POWs, but every reason to want access to the intelligence that flowed from their interrogations.

Plotnikov had worked in the field as a military field adviser to the North Koreans, as well as an interpreter, and because he spoke English he hated to miss an opportunity to practice on a native speaker. He admitted interrogating an American POW or two, although he made it sound more like a social call than a grilling.

But in 1991, the United States and the new non-Soviet Russia were still feeling each other out, getting to know each other's fears and expectations under the new world order. So it would be left to others speaking out later to be more forthcoming about the secret Soviet interrogations in Korea.

As the doors to the old Soviet archives creaked open, and the living witnesses stepped forward, more veterans like Gavril Korotkov, Alexander Orlov, Viktor Bushuyev and Evgenii Pepelyaev would be heard from.

* * *

Orlov, a round-faced, barrel-chested veteran had commanded a tank regiment in World War II, then returned to Moscow to enter language school. When the senior Soviet advisers in Korea saw they had more American prisoners than English-speaking interrogators, they wired Moscow to send more. Orlov was among several dozen fresh interrogators and translators who were dispatched to Antung, Manchuria, where the 64th Fighter Aviation Corps was headquartered.

From there, after donning a Chinese army uniform so that he could blend in better among the Communist Chinese officers in North Korea, he drove down to Pyongyang, where many of the interrogations took place.

Orlov contacted Volkogonov in September 1992, and after his initial interviews on the subject was awarded a position on the joint commission, as the Russian side's top man on the Korean War era.

His accounts of the interrogations to the American researchers were usually couched in careful terms, stopping short of directly implicating himself or other Russians or the sensitive questions of how the questioning had taken place, and where, and what had happened to the prisoners who had spent time in the camps, even in the interrogation rooms, but had failed to come home when the war ended.

Orlov favored the "Chinese wall" argument, which he and others continue to cite as the prevailing method used by Russian interrogators when dealing with American POWs in Korea:

"As a rule," said Orlov, "the interrogations weren't eye to eye meetings. I can't remember names—what interested me was your radar technology. I recall a young American was brought in. He was seated behind a wall. I wore a Chinese uniform. There were a lot of Russian emigres in China.

"Of course, the U.S. pilots knew that Soviet pilots were flying" against them in combat.

Lobov had explained that, while his pilots were under orders to speak only in Chinese over their radios while on missions, most Russian pilots knew only a few Chinese words, not enough to communicate effectively while in flight.

"And when the bullets started flying," said Lobov, "you can imagine they used only the swear words—in Russian—they knew best."[3]

Bushuyev also came forward in November 1992. He had been Lobov's deputy intelligence chief during 1952-53, and told Task Force Russia's interviewers he organized the interrogation of American POWs and processed all the information, making sure his staff distributed the information and technical data to the proper authorities in Moscow as well as the officers and units in North Korea and Manchuria.

Bushuyev said he had never personally, directly talked to American POWs, but that "we had contacts with the American POWs, mainly the pilots. We weren't interested in anybody else."

Every American pilot who was captured, said Bushuyev, "with no exception," would be interrogated in Sinuiju, the North Korean city on the south of the Yalu River across from Antung, China.

The interrogation center was a "special building," he said, that the Soviet officers could actually see from across the river. "We would go there about twice a week to interroate the prisoners."

In the "special building," the arrangement was akin to a life-sized puppet show, as Bushuyev described it.

"We would enter the building from a different side before the POWs were brought there. We would go to our room and sit there very quietly. Only then would they bring in the POWs. We had no visual contact."

Soviet interrogators would write out the questions and give them to the Chinese to ask. "We would sit behind the wall, a thin, wooden wall, and the translators would sit with us. We were prohibited from actually seeing the Americans."

When that proved unwieldy, Bushuyev's superiors in the intelligence-gathering hierarchy found a Soviet officer who could be present in the same room with the Americans, but not be perceived as a Russian. The name Bushuyev said this interrogator went by sounded Russian: Kolya (a Russian nickname for Nikolai) Mankuev.

But, said Bushuyev, "he was a Buryat Mongol, looked Chinese. This Kolya Mankuev would go to that room and participate in the interrogations directly."

And the Chinese always acted as though they had territorial rights to the POWs. "Practically all of the American POWs belonged to the Chinese," said Busheyev. "The war was conducted not by the Koreans but by the Chinese and Soviets. The Koreans were under pressure and had no rights.

They would just load and unload stuff, build roads and that sort of thing."

But as for missing POWs, as Orlov and Plotnikov had, Bushuyev said he knew nothing of Americans being shipped to the former Soviet Union from Korean War POW camps.

"There was no need to bring Americans to Russia," he said. "Military personnel, location of bases and all that were already known. We had no questions of this sort. We had the planes as well as all their parts, so it didn't make any sense. If someone asked for political asylum we would have, but I haven't heard of any such cases."

Pepelyaev was one of the Soviet MIG pilots who flew against Americans in Korea. Much of the intelligence gathered from the American POWs was intended to assist combatants like him get an edge in the air battles over Korea. Pepelyaev was already a very good fighter pilot when Korea came along. He seemed to do even better in Korea, recording 19 shootdowns in aerial combat.

Pepelyaev said he never personally saw any American POWs, but remembered the special unit of 15 pilots, led by a Gen. Blagoveshchenski, that was summoned to the 64th Fighter Aviation Corps headquarters in Antung and given the task of forcing F-86s to land unscathed by surrounding them with MIGs in flight.

The ace fighter pilot said he couldn't think of a more "idiotic" idea. A more routine and practical method, he said, was for the corps' intelligence section to send out a search party when word of a downed U.S. aircraft was received. The corps also retrieved many of its own downed planes, said Pepelyaev.[4]

All of these Soviet veterans of Korea were ready to tell their stories to the joint commission and Task Force Russia, and over the course of the next year would find themselves regarded as the best sources for information about a highly classified operation no one had ever discussed openly and seldom even alluded to for several decades.

Now even the new president of the new Russia was interested in what they had done during the Korean War. Suddenly it was permitted to speak about such things.

The one with the most to say was Korotkov.

* * *

Col. Gavril Korotkov recalls that the questionnaires for the American POWs he interrogated in Khabarovsk during the Korean War were extensive, with about 150 questions on a wide range of topics, from training, assignments, strategy, order of battle and other military details to a prisoner's mood, morale and psychological attitude.

The POWs sometimes stayed for a few hours, at other times for several days at the Kamera Predvoritelnogo Zaklyucheniya, or Preliminary Confinement Facility. One of the questions Korotkov especially remembers asking, since it struck a chord deep in every Marxist-educated mind, was how much the American pilots got paid for shooting down a Russian plane.

The pilots usually said $100-$150. Korotkov always thought that was a measly sum, for a rich capitalist country like the United States.[5]

And when the prisoner was married and a caucasian, as were most of the ones Korotkov dealt with, it was routine to suggest that the Soviet government had somehow learned that the POW's wife was having an affair with a black man while he was risking his life in Korea.

The American prisoners never fell for that, Korotkov says.

As he or one of the other Soviet interrogators ran down the list of questions, aided by an English-speaking interpreter, they would look for an opportune moment to calmly and politely suggest that the American would be doing himself a favor if he agreed to come over to the Russian side. Things would go so much better all around if he would simply agree to cooperate in some future assignments, all very quietly of course.

"Our second task was to recruit," said Korotkov, "to turn some of them to our side." The Soviets had "special equipment," large radio transmitters they hoped to use to broadcast radio messages from Khabarovsk to the UN forces listening in the south, in Korea.

The Americans were uniformly polite in return, Korotkov says, but they always said no. "I can't recall a single instance" in which an American agreed to work for the Russians. "They were certain that they would get out of captivity anyway. They knew that they would return, and therefore they didn't want to collaborate with us."

Korotkov remembers the encounters with American POWs vividly. "It was a good opportunity to speak all the time with an American. That was good because I improved my own knowledge of the English language. I could talk with a real American."

When an interrogation session was over, the prisoner would be returned to his cell, often by the female Soviet Border Guard officers who had escorted him to the interrogation center. The POW's answers would be incorporated in the file that was kept on every individual prisoner, and copies would be prepared for distribution to various military and intelligence bases throughout the Russian Far East and to the Kremlin in Moscow.

Premier Joseph Stalin and his party leaders and ministers always took a keen interest in the information spilling over the edges of the hot war in Korea. It was a messy situation on the fringes of the vast Soviet empire that was consuming more attention and funds in the United States than in Moscow. Not to mention the lives of so many more American troops.

As for the prisoners, Korotkov said, when the interrogations were over they would have been sent to Soviet camps. "Without a doubt" they ended up in the Soviet Union, he said. He didn't witness it, but "I personally heard from many people at that time" that they did, he said. "They were shipped further on, to Siberia, beyond the border there, beyond Khabarovsk, somewhere in that vicinity."

They would have been hostages—to be exchanged for Soviet officers captured in Korea. "You know that our officers were taken prisoner in South Korea," he stated matter-of-factly. As a matter of fact, the United States had gone to great lengths to deny that any Soviets had been captured in the Korean War. But there had been hints, just a few, and a public announcement that had been quickly squelched.[6]

Meantime, Kortokov said, once headed for Siberia, the prisoners would have undergone a change. They would no longer be regarded as prisoners but spies, criminals. That would permit the application of an entirely different system of justice.

For example, he recalled the day just after the ceasefire in Korea, when a large U.S. plane, with perhaps 17 crewmen, was shot down not far from Posyet, south of Vladivostok. The Americans bailed out, and the Soviet specialists were very excited at getting a look at their survival gear.[7]

Most of the crew were rescued by the Russians, Korotkov said, but when he and his colleagues asked if they could speak to them, "we found out that they had immediately been whisked away across the border to the KGB."

As for the American survivors' status, "they were already not considered prisoners of war. They were already considered to be spies."

And since, he assumed, none of the Americans agreed to work for the Soviets, "they were formally convicted as spies and received their sentence, and were dispersed to camps...."

And today, more than 40 years later? "Since they weren't released, then they served their whole sentence. And many of course died there. I don't think any of them survived to today...didn't survive. Because the conditions of life were so hard...40 years."

Asked some months later why he believed none of the prisoners might still be alive, Korotkov said it was because no one had come forward.

"If they were alive anywhere," he said, "people would remember. You don't forget a thing like that."

* * *

Korotkov was a military political officer, a young captain in the Red Army when he was sent to Khabarovsk on Siberia's Asian border in the early 1950s to work as part of a special, secret team of analysts reporting to Marshal Rodion Yakovlovich Malinovskiy, commander-in-chief of the Far East Military District. The group was known as the 7th Directorate, and its mission was to extract useful information and intelligence from Americans taken prisoner in the Korean War. Recruiting any who could be recruited was a second important, if difficult, objective.

There were two main sub-groups involved in the interrogations: one, run by the GRU, or military intelligence, collected tactical and technical intelligence that would aid Soviet engineers and commanders in any future war with the U.S. The second, under the political directorate, focused on information that could be useful in propaganda programs and psychological warfare planning.

Korotkov said he worked closely with personnel from the GRU and KGB and the Border Guards. His assignment, like those of hundreds of other Russian military advisers and intelligence operatives who took part in the Soviet Union's covert war in Korea, was not to be discussed or revealed, even after the war had ended in a ceasefire and most of the American prisoners had returned home.

As years passed, and the Soviet veterans of Korea retired, tours in the Korean War theater were eventually counted as double or triple-time in service in the government's calculation of their pension benefits. But they noticed a curious thing: the name "Korea" never appeared on their military records. Like so many other missions beyond the frontiers of Mother Russia—in Africa, the Caribbean—the Soviet role amounted to conducting a secret war on the furtive edges of a very public war.

Service in Korea wasn't supposed to be discussed, even among the men who were there.[8]

As far as the majority of Russians and the rest of the world were concerned, Russia had mainly been a neutral observor in Korea. The fact that Russian pilots were flying MIG-15 fighters in air battles against U.S. pilots, however, was a poorly-kept secret. But the Soviet pilots, anti-aircraft troops and other military types dressed in Chinese or North Korean uniforms, and did everything they could to avoid capture. So the weak ruse of neutrality appeared to work.

Extracting information from American prisoners was another matter entirely. The Americans allowed to return would speak of it to their superiors, of course. But the U.S. government would not make it an issue, not wanting to cause the bloody conflict in Korea to ratchet upward into a full-scale land war in Asia.

Today Korotkov is a Far East expert at a government-supported academic and publishing operation, the Institute for Military History. For years, he was associated with the USSR's Institute of the USA and Canada, and the Scientific Research Institute of the Ministry of Defense. He is currently writing a book about one of the subjects he knows best, the Soviet role in the Korean War.

In June 1992, as the government of Boris Yeltsin opened a world of new travel and exchange opportunities to Russians, Korotkov was granted a visa to attend a seminar on the war in Seoul, where he confirmed that Stalin directed the North Koreans in "a kind of proxy war" against the U.S. and its UN allies. He described a trove of formerly secret documents containing the proof of Stalin's hidden hand in the plans for launching the 1950 invasion by Kim Il-Sung.

Many of the documents have since been released to Western scholars, who are using them to reconstruct the political history of the conflict.[9]

In August 1992, when he first began telling his story of secretly interrogating American prisoners during the Korean War to the Moscow staff of Task Force Russia, Korotkov had gone far toward convincing himself that the closed, repressive Communist world he had always known was gone, or disappearing fast. He assumed that some of his colleagues from the old days of the GRU, the Soviet military intelligence agency, and even some of the old-guard Soviet Army and Air Force veterans he had served alongside in Korea would do likewise.

He assumed that enough time had passed, and "it was permitted," as the Russians phrase such things, to tell the truth.

Some of the documents were already coming out. Lt. Col. Sergei Osipov, Gen. Volkogonov's principal assistant on the joint commission, would soon turn over the names of 109 American pilots taken directly from the records kept at Khabarovsk. Whether or not the documents would show it, many of these might have been men Korotkov had interviewed.[10]

Moreover, other veterans who had served alongside him as interrogators and interpreters in the Korean theater were likely to approach the commission and the other researchers from the U.S. who had descended on Russia after the collapse of the Communist Party to look in the archives.

They all had their experiences to tell, people like Plotnikov, Bushuyev and Orlov, who also had a retainer at the Institute of Military History. Of course some of the willingness to talk might stem from the fact that such a respected, "humanitarian" enterprise could be expected to furnish a kind of livelihood, as well as a chance to travel abroad, to the U.S. for commission meetings.

So Korotkov on Aug. 19, 1992, told the Americans what he knew.

• Hundreds of American POWs had been processed through the Khabarovsk interrogation facility throughout the three-year war. A few were flown in, but most started their journey to the Soviet Union at a POW "collection point" at Paektu-San, a famous mountain on the Manchuria-North Korea border, from there by train to the port of Posyet, then north through Ussurijsk to Khabarovsk.

• About 100 intelligence officers and interrogators had worked out of the Khabarovsk facility, all dedicated to the Korean War mission. One of them was a Soviet officer of Korean descent, which aided greatly in masking the number of Soviet officers actually involved.

• Acquiring the American POWs from the North Koreans was not a problem, because many of the North Korean officers had led Soviet army units during World War II battles against the Japanese in the Far East. But the Chinese were very reluctant to relinquish custody to the Russians. To get American POWs from Chinese-run camps it was often necessary to invoke higher authority.

• He could recall specific details about two American POWs he had personally interrogated, but the name of only one, a Lt. Col. Black.[11] He had also visited some of the prison camps in Siberia where Japanese POWs were still being held in the 1950s, but he saw no Americans there.

• While being interrogated, the POWs were always under the control of the MGB, the fearsome internal security police that a short time later would be called by its new acronym, the KGB.

While Orlov and other interrogators had traveled into North Korea, to Pyongyang, to conduct their interrogations, Korotkov said he was in Khabarovsk. "I was able to go to Korea once, but it was not linked with the interrogation of POWs. In Khabarovsk, we had a great collection of specialists who knew different languages."

Among the more than 50 people in his headquarters there were French-speakers, Turkish-speakers, "all the languages for the UN troops. We got information from POWs, from Americans, from the English and so forth. Our mission was to do a political assessment of the UN troops in Korea. Our commander was a member of the Military Council for the Far East, and he got permission from the Koreans and the Chinese for meetings. I don't know how it worked, but the many specialists each had two or three meetings, so about 100 POWs were interrogated.

"It happened in an area in the mountains where the border wasn't marked. Pilots were moved there by their guards. We went to Posyet, south of the lake country, where Korea, China and the USSR come together.

"We were definitely not in China. It was either Korea or the USSR. A female captain of the Border Guards took us there. She wore green tabs (on her uniform.) I wore a Soviet captain's uniform."

When Korotkov mentioned wearing his Soviet captain's uniform, he had fixed the location of the interrogations as well. Soviet army uniforms were to be worn only while on USSR territory. When traveling into Manchuria or North Korea, the Russians always changed into Chinese uniforms or wore civilian clothes. It was part of the meager disguise their superiors thought was sufficient to mask the presence of so many Soviet troops and advisors.[12]

And when Korotkov brought up female Border Guard escorts, the Task Force Russia analysts were handed a detail that also was more than colorful—it was crucial to their investigation. None of the repatriated POWs had mentioned female uniformed escorts at their interrogation sessions. Either Korotkov was throwing in details of his own creation, or no one who had been taken to Khabarovsk alive had ever come home.

Korotkov explained why the interrogations were important.

"We wanted to get first-hand information. And, although it wasn't a critical issue, we tried to turn them."

But, he quickly added, "I know of no case where an American had been turned—but Japanese, Turks, yes. They did radio broadcasts, or they wrote leaflets and so forth."

He said the most powerful Korean officer in the interrogation operation was a Soviet-Korean officer named "Pak" (a common Korean surname) who spoke English, Chinese and Russian. "He had power," said Korotkov.

And he confirmed reports that the POWs had been questioned by the KGB. "In Khabarovsk," he said, "I knew the KGB representative, since our work was related."[13]

Then came this revealing interchange. As Col. Herrington of Task Force Russia summed up the evidence for the case that the Soviets had transferred some of the American POWs from interrogations sessions to prisons or indoctrination camps—a conclusion that already served to explain the reports of Americans in the Gulag from Russian, Japanese and German former Gulag inmates—Korotkov stated flatly, "It's not a secret."

To which Orlov answered: "It's not a secret, but you still need documents."

Herrington continued: "You both said how important POW pilot interrogations were. You described how, from 1950 to '53, there was a secret war with Soviet participation. We know Moscow was worried that the USA would confirm Soviet involvement. So a POW interrogated by a captain in a Soviet uniform doesn't go back, it's a one-way trip."

Herrington's question was in the form of a statement. But the two former Soviet officers knew it required an answer.

"Yes," they said, nodding in unison.

But in keeping with Orlov's statement—"you still need documents"—the fact that no documents had surfaced that gave away the physical presence of American POWs on Soviet territory meant the Russian denials would continue.

How, then, the Americans wanted to know, had such an operation remained secret for so long? Surely many people who, like them, were still alive, would have to know of it.

Said Korotkov: "I think there are still people who know things...but who are afraid."

Might the POWs have finally renounced their U.S. citizenship, and thus be invisible to the average Russian? Korotkov was visibly moved: "As I knew U.S. officers, even privates," he said, "and I knew them well, they proved to be great Americans. Even in the Gulag these men would not have given up their citizenship. Their mood made me think they were assured, cocky, convinced that someone would come and get them."

Among the Russian interrogators, Korotkov said, "we discussed how difficult it was to work with the Americans. The tone of our conversation was that Americans were very self-assured, they never gave up hope."

* * *

The Americans on the joint commission, at least those who had supported Task Force Russia's efforts to confront the Russians with the import of their own disclosures, considered Korotkov a key link in their chain of evidence.

The Russians who believed it was still too early to disclose secrets from the 1950s involving intelligence matters recognized this too, and immediately launched into the task of discrediting him and his story. The effort began with questions about how the Americans had managed to cultivate this particular witness in the first place.

Even though a Russian official had been present at Korotkov's initial interview, as the commission's rules required, it was suggested that the Americans had somehow gone behind the Russians' backs. In some ways, it was a replay of all the other instances in which the Russians became convinced that the commission was simply an arm of U.S. intelligence, nothing more nor less.

It was similar to the "David Markin" episode, when Mazurov said he was positive that the Americans had set them up with that story, talking beforehand with Pugantsev (who had walked into the U.S. embassy unannounced) and using the allegations of Americans still held in the Gulag to force Yeltsin to do their bidding.

In the mind of Mazurov and others, it was all a grand, and not very well disguised, conspiracy to keep the Russians in their place, subjected to

America's ploys and strategems.

Perhaps the Americans had been convinced from the start that the transfers had taken place. Perhaps they were simply selecting the examples from their own massive files of classified intelligence reports that pointed toward Soviet complicity in some ugly crime against prisoners.

At the joint commission meeting in April 1993, Toon had given what he called a "personal observation." As a young foreign service officer, his first tour in the USSR was during the Korean War, "and there was no question in my mind that we were very close to being complete enemies. Our daily press expressed only abomination for each other.

"I had the gut feeling then that the authorities in Moscow would do everything possible to get their hands on U.S. POWs. If I had been running the Soviet Union back then, I would have done it....Rightly or wrongly, the feeling in my country is that you were involved."

To an American, it sounded as though Toon was only placing the discussions of the commission in their historical context. But repeated to the wrong ears, his observation could easily play into the paranoia and distrust expressed by certain members on the Russian side.

The Russian old guard representatives had their ways of dealing with these matters.

A young member of the new Russian parliament, Yuri Smirnov, had spoken out forcefully about the subject of missing American prisoners in the Gulag, saying it was a matter of human rights. Smirnov was also eager to begin restoring the neglected history of Russia's past war dead. Thousands had been buried without a trace, on Russian soil, but with nothing to mark their resting place.

He eventually came to the attention of Task Force Russia's staff as well as Paul Cole, the RAND analyst who was working on the Korean War era, and foreign journalists trying to track down information on the Siberian transfer story.

Smirnov said he had it on good authority—a military intelligence source on the Russian General Staff—that documentation for the POW-transfers from Korea to the USSR existed in military archives, but that it would not be disclosed.

Soon, Smirnov told Task Force Russia and the journalists who had begun calling him for interviews, he began receiving telephone calls from Russian security officials warning him to back off. The callers cautioned him that he was becoming far too interested in the POW/MIA issue for his own good.

All of this was the context for a followup interview a few days later for Korotkov. The Russians had suggested it. The Americans agreed. And some of what Korotkov had said the first time was now different.

Now he wasn't certain that the interrogations had been conducted in the Soviet Union, in the Siberian city of Khabarovsk, where Korotkov had been stationed and where Soviet intelligence ran its largest headquarters outside of Moscow.

It was possible they had been conducted somewhere else, perhaps in North Korea.

The best he could recall was that they had been carried out at some ill-defined place in the mountainous, unmarked border area where North Korea, China and the Soviet Union meet. It might have been the Soviet Union, or China or North Korea, he just wasn't sure. There had been no boundary markers or landmarks to help orient them.

The Americans knew of only one reason Korotkov might have changed his testimony: he had received a call the night before the second interview from Col. Vyacheslav Mazurov, the foreign intelligence representative on the joint commission. Mazurov had told him he might be present at the interview. That was a clear enough message for Korotkov.[14]

When the telephone call prior to Korotkov's second interview was mentioned in a report shared with the Russians, it got Mazurov's attention. He asked Volkogonov for permission to address the point, and in front of the Americans, gave his version:

"I exerted no pressure," he said. "If I wanted to exert pressure, I wouldn't do it by telephone, but by other means. I only wanted to insure that Korotkov gave true information. I called because the U.S. side claimed that Korotkov said POWs were transported to the USSR for interrogation." He and his deputies from the security service "even absented ourselves" from the previous day's interviews with Korotkov and Orlov "because we didn't want to influence their testimony."

Toon spoke up, using the diplomat's semantic footwork to avoid apologizing while seeming to: "If the implication that you applied pressure was unfounded, we apologize."

Korotkov spoke up to try to defuse his predicament: "The phone call was before the meeting," he said, "but there was no pressure. He (Mazurov) was only interested in insuring I would attend the meeting and he asked me to tell the truth. There was not any pressure involved. I'm a professor and a military officer, I speak only about what I know. No pressure was applied and will not be."

Then he went over his new version again:

"In one case, I spoke about meeting a U.S. POW on Soviet territory, then refuted it. There was confusion about this, I think, because I was talking about being stationed in Khabarovsk and then that it was possible to meet Americans, but it didn't mean this happened in Khabarovsk. It occurred on teritory that is ill-defined, there's no marking, you don't know to whom it belongs. It probably wasn't on Soviet territory."

Korotkov was rambling now, showing more signs of giving in to the reminders from the Mazurov faction that there were some matters that simply shouldn't be shared with their new allies from the United States.

At the April 9, 1993 plenary session of the commission, held in the Kremlin, Volkogonov stated that during the Senate hearings the previous fall, "I heard several times that Soviets took U.S. POWs—pilots. We have searched every source for U.S. pilots or POWs, regarding transfers to the territory of the USSR. Until today, we have found no evidentiary documents on the fate of the pilots. We have not found any individuals who saw U.S. pilots on Soviet territory with their own eyes, while the information from the U.S. side seems to be from second, even third-hand sources."

But despite the reminders, and Volkogonov's talk of "no evidentiary documents" found, Korotkov stood by most of his story. And some on the American side tried to show that they understood what he was trying to do and appreciated his good intentions.

"A brave man continues to speak out," Maj. Gen. Loeffke said of Korotkov in a "personal assessment" of the American side's progress the following month. "Retired colonel Korotkov continues to tell us of his personal role in interviewing U.S. POWs. It was obvious that he had been coerced to modify his story."

Korotkov had given in to protect the current Russian government from the sins of the past, Loeffke said, but not much. "The colonel was obviously willing to oblige the security services by not saying that (the interrogations) took place in Khabarovsk. But he was not willing to say that it did not take place on Russian soil."

And with indisputable detail and authority Korotkov had opened the door to linking the secret Russian interrogations of American POWs to the people who were the point of this whole exercise: the POWs who had last been seen and heard from answering the questions of Soviet interrogators.

* * *

The effect of Korotkov's testimony, even with his waffling on where the interrogations took place, was profound. By August 1993, Task Force Russia had completed a 77-page report concluding that American prisoners had been transferred to the USSR for interrogation, to exploit their knowledge and skills. The report featured interviews with Korotkov and a half dozen other witnesses to the process.

Orlov was a different story. Not only was his version of the interrogations more circumspect, it was articulated in a way that always made it seem that he and the other Soviet advisors and interrogators had to plead for cooperation and access from the Chinese and North Koreans.

But Orlov liked to throw in qualifiers that had little basis in fact. At the Antung, China, airfield when he arrived in March 1951, Orlov stated, "there was the 324th Fighter Aviation Division…it was the only airfield in China with Soviet aircraft."

A beginning student of the Korean War would know that wasn't true. U.S. aerial reconnaissance during the Korean War had revealed at least three Manchurian airfields that held Soviet planes. Had UN forces been permitted free rein to scout Manchuria, there's little doubt they would have found even more.[15]

The air battles were especially intense in April of 1951, Orlov said. The B-29s were bombing the bridges over which the Chinese moved into Korea—the Soviet aircraft were tasked to defend the bridges. "Our number one enemy was the B-29." Orlov was using reverse psychology, it would seem. By 1950, the B-29s were the oldest bombers in the U.S. Air Force. Many of the crews with World War II combat under their belts did acquit themselves well, but they were sitting ducks without some good fighter protection. So many were lost in the first year of the war that daylight raids were cancelled. Korea was the last war for them.

Orlov saw his story was going off track, and caught himself. "But the B-29 was slow, so it was easy for the MIGs to shoot them down. So F-84s started to cover them. The F-84s were also not a great threat, because the MIGs were better. But in December 1950, the F-86 appeared. It was based on the design of the Messerschmidt-262. The Sabre (F-86) and the MIG were equals, but the U.S. pilots were more experienced and they had high-pressure uniforms. They also had radar-assisted aiming, but the MIGs had the advantage of being closer to base."

Orlov and Korotkov had both been introduced to the full commission on the same day, Dec. 16, 1992.

Orlov began by relating how he was sent to Korea in March 1951 in a group of more than 60 people, and assigned to the 64th Fighter Air Corps stationed in Antung, Manchuria.

He said that during his first months in the war, "there were heavy dogfights" between the MIGs and F-86 fighters, and he worked on radio intercepts, to help the Russian pilots anticipate the American pilots' routes and maneuvers. And he said the American pilots' high-pressure suits were the object of greatest Soviet envy.

In May 1951, he said, he was sent to Pyongyang, to the headquarters of Kim Il-Sung, to interrogate American POWs. He said this was done by writing out the questions and giving them to Chinese officers or officials to ask.

But he recalled "two cases of direct contact" with Americans at the interrogation center. One was a Lt. Col. Black; his talk with him resulted in an article in Pravda, he recalled. He couldn't remember the other American aviator's name, but said his talk with him concerned "aircraft plans and tactics."

He said the Koreans were in charge of American POWs, and that his only involvement with them was to ask "tactical and operational questions."

Korotkov, when his turn came, explained that he had been stationed in Khabarovsk, a major Siberian city due north of the Korean peninsula, from 1950, soon after the war began. "As a professional," he said, "it was my work to analyze all sources of intelligence that came to us about U.S. forces in Korea."

He said the Chinese and North Koreans tried to "restrict" the Soviet personnel, but he, too, managed to make direct contact with two U.S. prisoners.

As for the interrogation process, Orlov emphasized that the Soviets had a strict rule forbidding him and other officers to question the Americans directly. (The Jan. 17, 1951 memorandum from Lt. Gen. Shalin to Lt. Gen. Razuvaev often cited by the Russians in this regard, as translated for Task Force Russia, specifies that the "translators are categorically forbidden to interrogate American and British POWs, or prisoners of any other nationalities." Razuvaev was the next Soviet ambassador to Pyongyang. He would succeed Gen. Shtykov in August of that year.)[16]

Orlov and other interrogators described a process in which the Soviets would write out the questions for the Chinese to ask.

Plotnikov described his encounters with American POWs as "interviews" rather than "interrogations" because his talks with them were more social than strategic or military. He recalled one "interview" with a U.S. Army infantry captain, a company commander from the 24th Infantry Regiment of the 24th Division. But he said he stayed away from military or intelligence questions, so as not to tip off the American that he was a Soviet advisor.

The method Orlov described coincides with the recollections of a number of repatriated U.S. pilots.

One of the interrogation reports in Soviet archives bears the name of Charles Maultsby, who was captured in November 1951 when his F-80 was shot down over North Korea. Maultsby said he never saw anyone he recognized as a Soviet interrogator during his captivity, but it was plainly evident that the questions he was being asked came from Soviets, not Chinese.

"The Chinese didn't know squat about our aircraft," said Maultsby.

They wouldn't have known how to ask the kind of technical questions that he had been asked about the airplane he flew. But he would sometimes give a wise answer to a question, hoping that by the time the information had been passed on, he would have been moved elsewhere.

"That caught up with me one time," he recalls. The Chinese had learned that Maultsby's squadron had begun swapping their F-80s for the more advanced F-86s. "They asked me, how do you change an F-80 to an F-86. It was such a stupid question. So I told them, you tie it between two trees and bend the wings back, and...."

The Chinese interrogators dutifully wrote down his answer to take back to the Soviet advisors. The wise answer came back to haunt him. When the Chinese discovered he'd been joking, they piled on the punishment.[17]

Asked if it was important for the MIG pilots to know as much as possible about U.S. aircraft, Orlov said, "Of course. We needed to interrogate these pilots. Before, when it was only the B-29 and F-84 and F-80, we had no need to interrogate them. I was a radio intercept (specialist), but I was used as an interpreter."

Orlov explained that a number of pilots would be asked identical questions, then the Russians would compare their answers, to see who was truthful and who was lying.

But Orlov insisted that the questions were always put to the Americans by the North Koreans, or the Chinese, not Russians. "We got answers back in a day or two," he said. "Then I translated the information from English into Russian. There were names, units, personal identification numbers, rank, date of birth, and so forth."[18]

Orlov, Bushuyev, Lobov and others who pushed the no-direct-contact scenario, however, stressed that it wasn't only a Soviet-imposed rule. The Chinese and North Koreans had made the attempted subterfuge necessary by being highly reluctant to turn over "their" POWs to the Soviets. Another Soviet document the Russians salvaged from the wartime archives dealt superficially with POW interrogations, but its true value is in illuminating the completely second-string role the North Koreans were playing by the end of the war, and how the intelligence-gathering process was in sad shape.

The document was written in January 1953 by a newly arrived senior intelligence advisor, a Col. Seregin, reporting to Soviet ambassador Razuvaev. As part of his orientation in the assignment, Seregin did a quick study of the situation in North Korea and made this report:

"1. The Korean People's Army (North Korea) is operating in the secondary sector of the front and is fully subordinate to the Combined Staff (the Soviet-Chinese command.) It does not have the right to independent planning and conducting of operations.[19]

"2. The intelligence directorate, and intelligence forces in general, do not receive due attention from the military command. The primary leadership staff changes often. The intelligence director is extremely poorly supported with materials, in particular with transportation vehicles and communications equipment."

Seregin's report to Razuvaev went on to outline just how slipshod and poorly orchestrated the Soviet-led intelligence operation was. The end result makes it plain that whatever the written policies and instructions from high Soviet officials, by the war's last year, in practical terms the operations in the Korean theater were seldom by the book.

"Reconnaissance missions are not assigned by the commanders of tactical formations, but by intelligence officers who, not having proper authority, do not always have at their disposal the means for organizing effective reconnaissance.

"Signals intelligence is extremely poorly organized. Air reconnaissance does not exist. The intelligence directorate does not have communications with partisan detachments operating in the enemy's rear. In view of the lack of communications and the difficulties of sending agents across enemy lines, covert intelligence does not have the necessary effect. The largest percentage of prisoners and captured enemy equipment goes to the Combined Staff; very little goes to our Korean comrades."

Orlov, while working in Pyongyang, had been part of that effort, which saw few benefits accruing to the North Koreans. It was their land, and their political goals that were at stake in the war. But the Chinese and Soviets had capitalized on an opportunity to weave the pursuit of their best interests into the Koreans' war of "liberation."

But he had presented the joint commission with a much different view of the intelligence setup in North Korea during his three-month tenure, when he said he handled only one to three reports a day.

"We didn't know how many people they actually questioned," Orlov said, "we just wanted the answers...we wanted concrete information. Whoever answered better received more and deeper questions...our specialists verified it in case it was disinformation. The North Koreans maintained strong effective controls."

As for whether the pilots were also interrogated by Soviet intelligence, Orlov said, "We didn't know what the KGB was doing."

How could the North Koreans have kept their Soviet advisers from speaking to the American POWs, Orlov was asked. "I was low-ranking," he said. "The bosses—there were lots of chiefs—made the decisions. Relations were official, there was no friendship. The guys with the big shoulder boards decided everything. And we had no base in Korea, just Kim's headquarters. It was in a forest in a valley."

He said they had to take cover in caves during U.S. air attacks. "We just called it Kim Il-Sung's headquarters," said Orlov.

Orlov said his group of interrogators reported directly to Col. Aleksei Ivanovich Zherabyatov, an officer of the GRU, Soviet military intelligence, and the head intelligence advisor to the North Korean general staff. He said his reports also were submitted to a Gen. Li, head of North Korean military intelligence who, Orlov believed, was also in charge of American POWs.[20]

Korotkov continued to attend the joint commission meetings, but his testimony had clearly put him on a hotseat. When Gen. Loeffke raised the subject of Korotkov's testimony about interrogating Americans in Khabarovsk, Osipov asked Korotkov: "You really think it happened through Khabarovsk?"

Shaken a bit, Korotkov answered: "I remember discussions. They said they'd brought some U.S. POWs. But I wasn't directly responsible. Still, these rumors seem to me not to be groundless...We can't say it couldn't have happened."

* * *

The documents the Russians produced did show that, at least for some period of time, Soviet military and intelligence officers assigned to the Korean theater of operations were under strict orders to avoid personal contact with American and other "foreign," or western, prisoners of war.

But as Orlov would admit, rules were not always followed to the letter.

For those who had delved into the memoirs of the survivors of the Korean War POW experience, their were numerous examples of this particular rule being broken. Consider the case of George Blake.[21]

Blake was a left-leaning British intelligence officer under cover as vice consul in the British embassy in Pyongyang when the Korean War broke out. He was taken prisoner along the British ambassador, Capt. Vyvyan Holt, and dozens of missionaries, White Russians and other civilians and repatriated with about 30 survivors of that group—through Moscow, incidentally—in April 1953.

While in prison camp, like many of the other diplomats and journalists who were there with him, Blake spoke frequently with the Russians who visited the camp. Blake says that, while the other prisoners were interviewed by a young Russian man "with pleasant, open features" that they nicknamed "Kuzma Kuzmich," his time was spent with a higher-ranking Soviet intelligence officer.

He learned some time later, he says, that this Russian was the chief of the agency's Khabarovsk station, for all the maritime provinces. He claims "the KGB chief" never told him his name.

While many of the other civilian POWs mentioned the Russian visitors in their accounts of their interrogation experiences, only Blake's was totally sympathetic, for in these meetings he was recruited into the KGB. Blake explained that from his perspective he wasn't so much recruited as accepted by the KGB, since he offered his services to the Communist cause before the KGB chief had time to wonder whether he might be a potential convert.

But Blake kept up appearances as a patriot among his fellow prisoners. "None of us guessed that Blake would weaken in these relentless brainwashing sessions by the Communists," said Commissioner Lord.[22]

"I remember his arrogance to the propagandists."

From his Korean War experience on, Blake was a spy for the Kremlin. He re-entered the British diplomatic corps, and was posted to West Germany, where he helped the Soviets and East Germans break up what had been one of the west's most useful intelligence channels—a tunnel running underneath the Berlin Wall that was used by western agents.

Discovered, arrested, convicted and sent to prison, Blake managed to escape in 1966 and flee to Moscow, where he lives today. Despite the widespread collapse of Communism, he professes to be undisturbed by the fall of Marxist ideology.[23]

It's not the Communist philosophy that has failed, he argues, but the earth's people who have failed—to live up to Communism's high ideals and standards.[24]

Philip Deane, then a young foreign correspondent for the London Observer newspaper, was also captured in Seoul when the North Koreans first invaded the south, and was held until March 1953. He wrote later of being "brainwashed" at the hands of a Russian official he nicknamed "Lavrenti," who smelled of rosewater pomade and over the course of many days insisted that Deane must be an intelligence agent.[25]

The Russian interrogators, just like the Russian artillery brigades and the communications units and logistics specialists, couldn't hide very easily in Korea, even in their Chinese uniforms. Air Force Lt. Col. Thomas Harrison told of being marched from one POW camp to another when a convoy of enemy trucks passed. All the men aboard were dressed in Chinese uniforms, "but they were all definitely caucasians, and the Koreans would point at them and say, 'Russki! Russki!.'"

Harrison's group of POWs saw another company of caucasians later on their journey, and "some of the men were dressed in black jackets and black boots. They didn't even make a pretense of being dressed as" Chinese troops, Harrison told his debriefers. And at Sinuiju, just south of the Yalu

River, they passed the Soviet anti-aircraft emplacements, and long lines of trucks loaded with Soviet troops. "I say they were Russians because the Koreans called them Russki. They didn't look like Chinese to me - they were all blond-headed, they looked just like you and I."

Sometimes the only way for an American POW to know who he was dealing with was by instinct. Cpl. Bennett V. Logan of the 24th Infantry Division said he was captured by North Korean forces, but one of the officers stood out.

"One of them spoke English and asked me a lot of questions about our weapons. He looked like an officer and about 36 years old. He was a tall fellow, about six feet, and heavyset. He spoke perfect English like an interpreter and at first I thought he was a GI. He didn't speak it like a North Korean would. He wore a mustache and sort of like a goatee on his chin. He had a scar on the left side of his face near his eye about one and one-half inches long, running up and down. He did not wear glasses. The reason I did not think he was a North Korean was because he had reddish-blond hair and was kind of red-faced. His eyes looked more American than oriental and he wore wide Russian bars from front to back on his shoulders. There were three bars of gold metal.

"His uniform was green-like with heavy woolen pants, heavy jacket, fur cap, and black boots with a thick heel. His pants were bloused in his boots. He kept trying to get a confession out of me and he kept smacking me with the back of his hand."

From Logan's ambiguous description of his interrogator, he might have been a Russian or another caucasian nationality. But lst Lt. Andrew Bigan of Waco, Tex., told debriefers there was no mistaking the nationality of the officers he encountered in Pyongyang.

Two Russian officers, he said, approached his mixed group of Turkish, South Korean and American POWs and "asked if anyone spoke Russian. I did not acknowledge my ability to speak Russian. Later these officers brought us two baskets of apples. Later on, I don't know how they found out I could speak Russian, they approached me, slapped me around, told me I was a traitor and put me into a hole in the ground where I stayed for three days."

But despite these numerous examples of Soviet involvement with American POWs—including the fact that the Russians did indeed win one very important recruit out of the process in Blake—when the U.S. government wrote its accounts of the POW experience in Korea, the part that Soviet interrogations played in the lives of the prisoners was relegated to a distinctly minor role. This was in keeping with the wartime policy of not referring to the Soviets as participants in the war itself.[26]

The U.S. military's evaluations of what American POWs endured minimized the part played by such men as Orlov and Korotkov.

A study done by the Army Security Center at Ft. Meade, Md., dated November 1954, included this section on "Interrogation by Soviet Personnel":

"Although many repatriates observed Caucasians in North Korea and believed that they were Russian, less than one-tenth of one per cent of the prisoners report having been directly interrogated by Soviet personnel.

"The few interrogations by alleged Soviet interrogators (in some instances the POWs could not be sure as to their nationality) were conducted primarily with USAF prisoners and were concerned, for the most part, with information pertaining to the Air Force. Nearly all of these interrogations were conducted in the early stages of the conflict (1950-51) and no individual POW experienced more than one. An exception to this statement involved the interrogation of a USAF lieutenant, who was questioned at SINUIJU shortly after capture and was later taken to ANTUNG, Manchuria, where he was interrogated eight or ten times by Russians.

"Later, at 'Pak's Palace' in Pyongyang, he observed that a Russian in civilian clothes seemed to be directing the questioning of the NK interrogators. This case appears to be one of the few instances in which the Russians had any kind of a planned program for the direct interrogation of an individual prisoner.

"Another POW relates that, at 'Pak's Palace' an individual whom he believed to be a Russian general officer attempted to question him at length about USAF techniques and equipment.

"From the above, it is perhaps safe to conclude that the primary role of the Russian interrogator in the Korean conflict was that of an observor and, occasionally, an advisor."

* * *

Those words might have been written in 1994 by Volkogonov, Orlov and the other Russian members of the commission, who by then were describing Korotkov's frank testimony as an unfortunate "incident" and of no real value in the joint commission's effort to find out what had happened to the missing American POWs in Korea.

Korotkov's reports, said Volkogonov, "once under examination are completely self-contradictory. He provided no detail that could be confirmed, in the end. I suppose his statement was more a hypothesis—it included nothing concrete."[27]

At the same meeting, Orlov characterized Korotkov's story as only fit for the press and "nothing of much use. This testimony was based on belief and conviction. Therefore, although a journalist might rest on the information, a serious researcher cannot. Similar information appears in our press which makes our work more difficult. Thus, we should observe to the press that Korotkov's statements are without rigorous basis or fact."

* * *

While much of the questioning and debate in the joint commission's sessions about the Korean War interrogations issue was expressed as though the versions given by Korotkov and Orlov were in conflict, it's clear from analyzing their answers that they are not mutually exclusive.

Orlov in Pyongyang, Bushuyev in Antung and Korotkov in Khabarovsk—all three could understandably have operated in parallel but slightly different modes, with different procedures and different—but mutually compatible—missions.

In the commission's August 1993 session, in fact, Orlov made this very point, although perhaps not intentionally. Asked if he had been part of Korotkov's group, Orlov replied:

"No, never. I never knew Korotkov back then. Korotkov was never in Korea or China." Were there two or more intelligence-gathering systems in operation then?

"At least," said Orlov, "more" than two, perhaps. "You know there were different levels of intelligence working. Now on interrogations. What do you call an interrogation? I just had questions. Some were translated from Chinese....I must also mention that, in my two cases, we didn't really see it as a formal interrogation. No 'fist-hammering.' I found a receipt for a brothel on one subject (POW), for instance."

Orlov's assignment had placed him at the main North Korean POW prison in Pyongyang, nicknamed "Pak's Palace" for the Korean interrogator by that name who earned a reputation among the American prisoners as one of their clumsiest yet most sadistic captors.

Hundreds of repatriated POWs gave their personal accounts of life in that place, and at least one mentions a Russian interrogator. But the Soviet interrogator wasn't Orlov.

Gerald Fink, a Marine captain, reported being interrogated by "a mountainous Russian woman so large across her posterior that she required the seating space of two chairs. She wore a filmy blue dress and cheap beads and earrings. To make matters more ludicrous, she wore Korean shoes which Fink later described as Korean 'boondockers,' a Marine term for field shoes.

"When the Russian behemoth asked through her interpreter why he had come to Korea, Fink replied, 'To kill communists.' He was promptly kicked and beaten with sticks."

Fink's debriefing continued, in the stilted style of a military chronicler, with his "inquisitor" accusing "all Americans of bestiality and of murdering women and children. Fink noticed three blond hairs that were growing from the tip of her bulbous nose. As the interrogation continued, he became fascinated by the hairs. The fascination grew into an obsession until, unable to restrain himself, he leaned forward and neatly plucked one of the hairs off her nose. The North Korean guards immediately set upon him with punches, kicks and severe blows with their clubs."

Fink, the report noted, spent the next three days in solitary.[28]

When it came to the names of individual American POWs they had encountered, the Soviet veterans gave Task Force Russia's analysts some information, but not much, to go on.

Lobov identified a half-dozen in his magazine series, all of whom were repatriated. And Gen. Sozinov, who preceded Lubov as commander of the 64th Fighter Aviation Corps, said he questioned F-86 pilot Capt. Walker "Bud" Mahurin, whose shootdown he had witnessed. Sozinov said he remembered the incident because the POW spoke Russian.

Mahurin told the Task Force Russia researchers that he doesn't recall being questioned by a Russian, but the interrogation might have been done the way Orlov said most of his were: second-hand, through the Chinese.

Orlov then suggested the encounter may have occured "by accident, when Col. Sozinov, as advisor to the Korean general staff, was in the area. As. Gen. Volkogonov stated, all advisors wore civilian clothes and gave themselves out as Pravda correspondents, so he could have asked questions without Mahurin realizing what was going on—and Mahurin spoke Russian, which was important."

Volkogonov ventured the guess that "it was not a traditional interrogation. He might have asked a few questions. Therefore, Mahurin does not believe he was interrogated."

Orlov and Korotkov said they remembered only one name of the hundreds they encountered, either written or spoken, during the war: a "Lt. Col. Black." Orlov said he remembered the name because the pilot was mentioned in a story he wrote at the time for Pravda.

Three pilots with that surname were lost in Korea: Air Force Lt. Wayne Forrest Black, a crewman on a B-29 shot down Oct. 23, 1951; 1/Lt. Shuman Harlan Black, an F-80 pilot reported MIA on June 14, 1951, and Lt. Col. Vance Eugene Black.

In a dialog at the joint commission's Sept. 1, 1993 meeting with Lt. Col. Robert Freeman of Task Force Russia, Orlov tried to convince the American analyst that the names of the pilots would have been of no interest to the Russians:

ORLOV: "I only knew the name of Black. Now I understand that my documents weren't formal, so those documents were lost. Anyway, no names were included.

FREEMAN: So you only reported information, not names?

ORLOV: Exactly. We wrote, 'POWs said that....'

FREEMAN: Then how did you evaluate the information, without knowing the sources?

ORLOV: What was important was the information, not names. Our reports would have given the specialties, pilot, navigator...

FREEMAN: But you need to know the education level, experience, their qualification on different aircraft...

ORLOV: The North Koreans gave us that. They already had it. Usually, it was just like that. But the Second World War was different, of course. We used a standard form. But in Korea, we used to send the same questions to several people. Then we gave a generalized report.

ORLOV's explanation failed to satisfy Freeman. The analyst pressed on:

FREEMAN: How could you tell which information came from which source?

ORLOV: We had records by specialty and there was a general list of all those interrogated at the beginning or end of the report.

FREEMAN: But some information would have been better than other information, based on the source.

ORLOV: Of course. If we would have been interested in further interrogations—but we weren't interested in that. We just did hasty interrogations.

FREEMAN: But how would higher levels (superiors) know whom to pursue further?

ORLOV: You see, we were working for the corps. Then there was the air advisor, Petrochev, whom I mentioned. He worked with the Koreans and he was subordinate to the General Staff. He was probably interested in broader matters.

FREEMAN: Do you know the name 'Kuznetsoz?' He prepared questions for the interrogation of U.S. pilots. It was in 1950.

ORLOV: It seems strange to me, since in 1950 there were no POW pilots.[29] The first aerial combat between U.S. and Soviet pilots took place on 17 December 1950. When our people arrived in 1951, those listed here, I was already gone. It was the second shift.

Finally, Orlov is led to concede that names were recorded at his level after all.

FREEMAN: But your description of how you conducted the

interrogations seems strange. They could have lied to you and you wouldn't have   known.

ORLOV: That's why we sent the same questions to different people in different camps. In April 1951, we were told to find out about the pressure suits and the range-finder as quickly as possible...well, probably we put down some names—I don't remember.

* * *

For months, the Russians on the commission insisted that a particular set of documents from Soviet military records, dating from January, 1951, proved that Russians never directly interrogated American POWs.

Reportedly a standard order that was issued routinely each year of the war, it stated that "our translators are categorically forbidden to interrogate American and British POWs, or prisoners of any other nationality."

Another, a telegram from Lt. Gen. V.N. Razuvaev, Soviet ambassador to Pyongyang from August 1951 to August 1953, to Lt. Gen. Shalin, included the notation: "General of the Army Comrade Shtemenko has written instructions on this telegram which forbids interrogation of American and British prisoners by our translators."

But later documents make it appear the policy was reversed while the war was still in progress and American pilots and troops were still being taken prisoner.

In April 1994, Defense Department POW/MIA Affairs Office investigators were shown a file at the Soviet military archives in Podolsk that included the following statement, dated Nov. 26, 1952, from the chief Soviet advisor in North Korea:

"Representatives of the MGB of the USSR and China came from Peking to conduct further prisoner interrogations, in order to gain more precise information on spy centers, landing strips and flights over the territory of the Soviet Union.

"The interrogations will continue in Pekton (Pyoktong.)"[30]

A later document, also acquired by the American side of the commission during 1995, also appeared to lift the prohibition. Dated Jan. 29, 1953, and addressed to three top Soviet leaders including Lavrenti Beria, then head of the MGB, the message reads:

"The minister of public security of China, having reported on 27 January 1953 to our advisor on this decision of the TSK KPK (the Central Committee of the Chinese Communist Party), requested that our advisor help the Chinese investigators organize the interrogation of the prisoners of war and oversee their work. The MGB advisor was ordered by us to render such help."

At the joint commission's meeting in April 1995, the representative of the Russian foreign intelligence service, Mazurov, took the American side to task for referring to these papers in the draft of an upcoming report on the commission's proceedings.

"I request that you show me the documents" related to the MGB interrogations of American POWs, he said. "If you are referring to document No. 333, Ignatyev's letter to Malenkov, then I cannot accept it as a legal document."

The meaning of Mazurov's allegation was clear. He was implying that the Americans had tried to pass a forgery to document their case of Korean War POWs being interrogated directly by Soviets. And as he made this patently false false allegation, he began to get exercised.

"The first time I saw this document was in August of 1994, when it was presented by the U.S. side. I have numerous times requested that you show me the source of this document. Let's determine where this document came from and what is the source."

The American side was dumbfounded. "I find this conversation to be truly unusual," said the State Department's John Herbst. "My understanding is that the document you are asking about was received by us from the Russian side....the Russian side now wants us to provide to them a precise archival citation!?"

Mazurov reconsidered. His point, he said, was that the Americans were citing these documents as support for the statement that Soviet intelligence Services were actively participating in the interrogation of American POWs.

There was only one representative of the KGB in Peking and Korea, Mazurov alleged. And he supposedly didn't participate in a single interrogation.

Chapter Six

Chain of Evidence

"It is a mystery that may be solved later."

—Gen. Dmitri Volkogonov,
Russian co-chairman of the joint commission on POWs/MIAs,
referring to evidence that U.S. POWs from the Korean War
were shipped to the former USSR.

"We have to stop paying attention to information from ex-inmates because they are unreliable. The relevant information can be had from official sources."

—Vyacheslav P. Mazurov,
Russian foreign intelligence service representative
for the Russian side of the joint commission,
at the September 1993 meeting.

The joint commission's Aug. 31, 1993 meeting—in the Kremlin, which provided the proceedings with more sense of ceremony than usual—marked a turning point in both the willingness of the Russians to withstand difficult questions about their dark past and the U.S. government's willingness to keep pushing for answers.

The afternoon session opened with Col. Sergei Mukhin, chief archivist of the Russian general staff, touting the hard work and long hours the Russian researchers had been putting in, and asking for more feedback from the Americans.

"Sometimes it would help to get the reaction of the U.S. side on how our information helps you," he said, "how it helps the families. Do these documents help or not? Did they help the families? In fact, we need a response to cheer up our archival workers, to convince them that their work is not in vain."

As though he knew what was about to come, Mukhin had also issued the Russian side's standard line: "I want to underline one more time that no evidence exists on the transfer of U.S. prisoners during the Korean War or the Cold War." Denial of any evidence of POW transfers to Siberia had become the Russian's mantra, a constant refrain.

But the Americans were geared to silence that argument. They had brought what the State Department's Richard Kauzlarich termed "our case that U.S. POWs were held as political hostages or as a source of technical labor in the Gulag."

Building on the material the Russians had turned over during the preceding year, and supplementing that with interviews and archival research in the U.S., Task Force Russia's analysts on the Korean War had wrapped up more than a year of painstaking work. Their 77-page report carried a straightforward title: "The Transfer of U.S. Korean War POWs to the Soviet Union."[1]

Prepared by the seven analysts and written by Peter G. Tsouras, the report was blunt and unequivocal. The first two sentences of the executive summary stated:

"U.S. Korean War POWs were transferred to the Soviet Union and never repatriated. This transfer was a highly-secret MGB program approved by the inner circle of the Stalinist dictatorship."

The report, quoting retired Soviet colonels Garvil Korotkov, Alexander Orlov, Georgii Plotnikov and general Georgi Lobov, and O. Delk Simpson, Philip Corso and other American veterans of the Korean War era, presented evidence from both Soviet and U.S. witnesses and archives pointing to the stark conclusion that the Russians had transferred some American POWs from Korea to the former Soviet Union—both through Manchouli and Khabarovsk.

One of the important missions of the 64th Fighter Aviation Corps, based in Manchuria, the report said, had been intelligence collection. The Soviets were operating a three-sided war command with the Chinese and North Koreans at the time. The intelligence they wanted was from the UN troops they were fighting against. Most of that, they believed, would come from captured Americans.

"A General Staff-based analytical group was assigned to the Far East Military District and conducted extensive interrogations of U.S. and other UN POWs in Khabarovsk." Khabarovsk was more than just a major city on the far eastern edge of Siberia. Beginning in 1945, it had also been a principal transit point for Japanese POWs held after World War II and recruited through intensive indoctrination for future assignments as Soviet agents. Khabarovsk was also the major regional headquarters for the KGB.

Of greatest interest to the Khabarovsk interrogators, the report said, were "a limited number of POWs with specialized skills, mostly F-86 pilots and other personnel for the purpose of technical exploitation." However, it noted ominously, "No prisoners were repatriated who related such an experience."

In other words, any UN POW interrogated in Khabarovsk never came home. If no more than that could be proved, it would be devastating. But there was more.

"Irkutsk and Novosibirsk were transshipment points, but the Komi ASSR and Perm Oblast (large regions in Siberia) were the final destinations of many POWs. Other camps where Americans were held were in the Bashkir ASSR, the Kemerovo and Archangelsk Oblasts, and the Komi-Permyatskiy and Taymyskiy National Okrugs."

The transfers of large groups of POWs to Siberia had also included thousands of South Koreans. But the emphasis in the report was on American POWs, and how this secret interrogation network explained why many of them came home.

The process the analysts had pieced together from their interviews and documents worked this way:

"The military intelligence officers uniformly describe a division of labor in which (North Korean or Chinese) Army personnel capture POWs, GRU officers conduct tactical and operational interrogations, and then POWs are turned over for custody and final disposition to the MGB. This system operated from before World War II to the present. These officers repeatedly assert that if any POWs were taken to the Soviet Union, it would have been a closely controlled operation of the MGB at the time."

Lobov and other air corps officers had explained that, as the war progressed toward a stalemate, and became more of a war testing-ground than a battle for territory, the Chinese and North Koreans had become less cooperative in making POWs available for Soviet questioning.

For that reason, a special group of Soviet pilots and specialists was deployed to Soviet headquarters and placed under Lobov's command to search for downed American pilots, so they could be exploited without going through their allies' channels.

The search team's efforts made another mission possible. Besides human intelligence, the Soviets had wanted to capture U.S. aircraft, specifically the F-86, then the most advanced fighter in the U.S.'s arsenal and the plane that had managed to take the measure of the new Soviet MIG-15, which the Russians introduced into air combat in Korea.

At the Zhukovski Central Aerohydrodynamics Institute and the

Sukhoi Design Bureau in Moscow, Task Force Russia interviewers had determined that at least two F-86s had been shipped there from Korea. No one they spoke to had met any American pilots, but one of the designers remembered an associate telling him he was taking part in the interrogation—in Moscow—of the pilot of one of the planes.

The institute staff they talked to said the planes had been stripped of markings and identification numbers, but the fuselage of one had been packed with sand. The engineers had surmised that the plane had made a forced landing on a beach or sandbar, saving it from being wrecked as most downed planes were. According to the faculty members interviewed, when the technical study of the F-86s was complete, the parts were destroyed.

The report also drew upon the long experience of some of its analysts with Soviet intelligence methods and personnel to peel back some of the protective covering that they were convinced the Russian side of the commission had been using to cloud the story.

Up to that time in the work of the commission, the analysis noted, "most of the information provided by the Russian side has been from former officers of the GRU (the Soviet military intelligence service). There has been a traditional rivalry and animosity between the GRU and KGB that may have influenced the uniform finger-pointing by the GRU officers interviewed by the U.S. side. Unfortunately, the Russian side has provided no former officers of the MGB/KGB as sources of information."

The only former MGB/KGB officers that had provided information, the U.S. researchers said, had been those discovered through their own research efforts. One of them, KGB Lt. Col. Valerii Lavrentsov, had told the task force that while investigating the history of Japanese and Korean POWs in the Russian Far East, he had come across information that some Americans may have been held in "special houses" in Khabarovsk while they recovered from wounds, then had been sent on to Moscow. He said he had found records of "unknown" people ordering food and drink for "special houses," but had not been able to determine who the recipients were.

And he agreed that the MGB/KGB "would have been the only organization with enough resources to accomplish that [transfer] mission, even if only a few Americans were involved."

He said the GRU could have been involved as well, and he speculated—along the lines of what Soviet defectors had told the National Security Council's Corso during and immediately after the war—"that the Americans could have been moved by either train, ship or air to the USSR, and that when they were in Soviet custody, their names would most certainly have been changed to Slavic ones. Lavrentsov suggested that an entire false background would have been concocted for each prisoner."

The report was extremely thorough, reaching back to a Central

Intelligence Agency document of November 1953 to indicate that there had been evidence in the U.S. government's possession even then of Soviet involvement in the POW structure and process in Korea. The document named the "secretary general" of the top secretariat for POWs, a man named "Takayaransky." In addition, "Director General of the POW control bureau was a Colonel Andreyev, USSR; its deputy director, Lt. Col. Baksov; for the North Koreans, General Kim Il, North Korean Army (alias Pak Dok San, USSR) and General Tu Fing, Chinese. The chief of the Investigation Section (one of the three components of the bureau) was Colonel Faryayev."[2]

And it offered page after page of detail. "The Soviet interrogation effort was largely disguised. Soviet interrogators, when present for interviews, wore Korean or Chinese uniforms without visible rank, or civilian clothes and in some cases were ethnic Koreans or other oriental Soviet nationalities. One Soviet officer Col. Georgi Plotnikov, called himself by the Korean translation of his name, Kim-Mok-Su, which means carpenter in both languages.

"Another Soviet officer was a Buryat Mongol. Most Soviet involvement was probably concentrated on the preparation and translation of collection requirements to be filled by their North Korean and Chinese allies."

And to offer a complete braid of evidence, the report included the testimony of a former Chinese "volunteer" in Korea, Xu Ping Hwua. While head of a division-level prisoner-capture team, he said he personally had turned over three American pilots to the Soviets, sometime between November 1951 and March 1952. Xu said that his superior officer had told him simply that "the Russians wanted the pilots."

The Task Force Russia analysts cited the examples of three MIA/ BNR(missing-in-action / body -not returned) pilots as possible targets of the POW-transfer program. And breaking down the casualty lists of F-86 pilots—whose MIA rate of 55 percent (31 of 56 pilots lost during the war) was higher, on average, than those of other aircraft—they listed the 31 who could have been captured and processed through the interrogation system the witnesses had described. All of them had been lost under circumstances that suggested they had been captured, not killed outright, when they went down.

Another important link in the chain was illustrated by Avraham Shifrin, a former attorney in the Soviet military defense industry. According to Shifrin, a Soviet air force commander had admitted to him he transported a group of American F-86 pilots out of Korea to Kansk, Siberia, on a clandestine flight during the war. He said the pilots were tightly guarded and wore civilian clothes.

And the report related the experiences of several 15 F-86 pilots who were repatriated from North Korea—including Roland W. Parks Michael DeArmond—to show that despite the Russian side's denials, and Soviet interrogators had been a common and visible presence in the POW camps.

They even addressed the question of how the Soviets could have gotten away with it. The answer: taking only those POWs who had been kept isolated, separated from the start from other American prisoners. Once American POWs made contact with others who were known by tyhe outside world to be prisoners then, the llikelihood rose that they would be repatriated.

The main reason those 14 F-86 pilots had been repatriated "may have been that they had been seen by too many people in the POW camp system. Having been formally enrolled in a prisoner of war camp, moving them to another country might have been considered too obvious. It is doubtful that there was any contact at all between the aviators who are still considered missing and thse who were repatriated. Whereas prisoner of war status may not have assured survival, it possibly assured accountability."

Adding credibility to this line of reasoning, the report argued, was the fact that, according to the summaries of known circumstances of loss for the 187 Air Force MIAs considered still unresolved (Air Force Manual 200-25, Jan. 16, 1961) none of the repatriated Air Force POWs reported any contact with any of them.

To add a visual dimension, the main interviews had been videotaped and edited into a short tape. Toon, who had supported the development of the report and frequently stated that he was convinced transfers had taken place, told Volkogonov and the other Russian members that the evidence the American side had been able to collect on the transfer issue "is too compelling to ignore."

The Russians certainly couldn't ignore it. But they could deny it. Faced with a mountain of evidence, they resorted to simply repeating that it wasn't enough, and came from tainted sources. There was no proof to the allegations, they argued. They insisted the evidence the American side had presented was "not credible."

The Americans had not only used the incriminating interview with Korotkov, they had obviously sought out sources of their own, people who could corroborate what Korotkov and other Soviet veterans had said. As for proving the interrogations took place on the territory of the former Soviet Union, Korotkov had stood his ground, or most of it, despite internal pressure.

At the August 1993 plenary, Volkogonov also tried to offset the impact of the Korean War-transfer report by bringing up the matter of Soviet MIAs. It was time to even the score, to make it clear to the rest of the world that humanitarianism on the POW issue is a two-way street, now that the Cold War is over. Volkogonov asked his American colleagues:

"What do you know about the fates of Soviet soldiers who became missing while serving abroad? Military aircraft and civilian aviation specialists who became missing without a trace while carrying out their military duty. We're not accusing anybody, but the times were as they were. The old Soviet leadership stuck to the Comintern doctrine of global confrontation and Soviet personnel were lost throughout the world, in Ethiopia, southern Africa, Yemen and in other places.

"Unlike the U.S. government, the Soviet government never cared about repatriating remains.

"But, in democratic Russia, we will try to right this wrong. Our request is this: if our U.S. colleagues know anything, please help us. We will present a list of missing persons today. Any information relating to these men will be appreciated."

There were, and are, some Soviet soldiers still accounted for from such Cold War battlefronts as Afghanistan. But, as Volkogonov admitted, not only had Soviet governments never displayed much interest in MIAs or war remains, but the number of Soviet military personnel "missing" in the classic sense is dwarfed by the number of Soviet citizens who over the past half-century absented themselves voluntarily from Soviet territory.

As for those taken away and held against their will, if Volkogonov wanted to find Russians who had disappeared since World War II, he might well look in some of the same records of the same Gulag labor camps where the U.S. government was looking for traces of Americans.

But on the issue of transfers of American POWs to the USSR, Volkogonov was unyielding. "There are no personnel who could serve as eyewitnesses," he said. "If the U.S. side has more evidence, we are ready to listen and to organize further expeditions, but most likely, this issue is exhausted. It is a mystery that may be solved later."

To a careful listener, that might have sounded like a tacit admission that what the American side had just presented was true. And an attentive listener would also have noticed that Volkogonov then made a detour onto safer ground.

"We've analyzed the materials and can state that, in Russia today, there are no U.S. citizens—no Korean War POWs—held against their will on former Soviet soil. The ministries for security matters conducted additional checks, and no U.S. citizens are being held against their will."

But the American side had discovered that, while the Russians usually dismissed their questions and discounted their evidence when they were all seated at an official meeting, the atmosphere was decidedly more friendly, and more forthcoming, at the coffee breaks.

At one of the breaks after the Russians had stiffened perceptibly at watching the video version of the Korean War transfer report, Gen. Loeffke approached Korotkov, and asked calmly where the Americans should look next for more information about the practice.

"There are two paths," said Korotkov helpfully. "Not all of the documents are open yet. I know there are documents they are not showing you. But I don't know exactly what has remained hidden." Then he launched into a rambling but passionate statement, urging the American side to not give up.

"You must find the right documents. A lot of documents are just stuck in boxes. I only want to say to you that the documentation from the 7th Directorate—the 7th Special Propaganda Department, which looked at the enemy—those documents aren't even available to us." Korotkov had been assigned to the 7th Directorate in Khabarovsk. He was telling the Americans the proof they were looking for was directly under their noses.

"That's one source. There are others, of course. Just plug away on the archives to which you have access. There're still lots of veterans to talk to—You must meet with them and fill in the picture." He was energized. He knew the Americans were close to putting a seal on the transfer story, and wanted to help close the door on the case.

"Point three: we're stuck in Moscow and St Petersburg. Look in the regional archives, like in Khabarovsk—I don't believe everything was destroyed. Try to get to Khabarovsk!"

The exchange between Korotkov and Loeffke even fired up the usually contrary and negative Orlov, who was listening in. "We will find you some people who know something."

"Not only people," Korotkov chimed in. "We'll find you documents."

* * *

That promising statement, however, presumed that Task Force Russia would be around to continue its pursuit of people and documents.

As the report was being presented, the Army's special task force was being dismantled (the official term was "reorganization") and the job of assisting the joint commission and exploiting the documents and information coming out of the former Soviet Union about American POWs was being absorbed by the Pentagon's new Defense POW/MIA office. The Task Force Russia analysts who had assembled the evidence and written the report were returning to their pre-project assignments, or moving onto new ones.

And the report itself had gained an extremely negative detractor: the POW/MIA office's acting director, Ed Ross.

News stories about the report had characterized it in much the same terms as used by Toon, Kauzlarich and the analysts who had produced it. But when Ed Ross was asked about it in Washington by an Associated Press reporter, he put it down as hard as the Russians had.

"There isn't one shred of evidence" that F-86 pilots from the Korean War were transferred to the Soviet Union, Ed Ross said. The 77-page report, he said, was comprised of "opinion" that wasn't supported by facts. And the reason for presenting it to the Russians on the joint commission was merely to "elicit or provoke some reaction."

Like Viktor Pugantsev and the alleged U.S. pilot "David Markin," the report on "The Transfer of U.S. Korean War POWs to the Soviet Union" was to be shunted aside as no more than unsubstantiated rumor. What made the criticism even more devastating was that it came from the very side of the commission —although assuredly not from the same people—that had produced the report in the first place.

But the policy of a U.S. government agency disowning its own investigation didn't stop there.

A newsletter issued by the POW/MIA office and reprinted in the June 1994 issue of The Graybeards, a magazine for Korean War veterans, charged that the report had been taken out of context and as a result "caused considerable confusion and misunderstanding" among some family members.

The report, the Defense Department said, "contains only a preliminary analytical assessment of the possible transfer" of U.S. POWs to the Soviet Union during the Korean War...The truth about this matter has yet to be determined."

By early 1995, the story of Korean War transfers was not only disowned by the Pentagon, it was out of the headlines. The Russians—with the support of those on the American side who had attacked the Task Force Russia report—remained adamant: there was no real evidence, no confirming documentation, to make a convincing case that Korean War POWs had been transferred to the former Soviet Union.

The joint commission, contrary to Volkogonov's earlier predictions, continues to function, meeting in Moscow or Washington several times a year. But the flow of information out of the former Soviet archives has slowed considerably. The Moscow hotline for citizens to volunteer information about Americans in the Gulag no longer operates, and few tips are received.

Within months of Task Force Russia's dismantlement, Ambassador Toon, who has consistently voiced support for the POW-transfer evidence accumulated by Task Force Russia, was charging the Russians with only going through the motions of cooperation.

Despite the "important progress" made during the actual meetings of the whole commission every few months, Toon told Volkogonov at the December 1993 session, "the interaction between our American and Russian researchers dies off as soon as I and my fellow commissioners leave Moscow." But the Russians could read Ross's heated attack on the Task Force Russia report. They knew the struggle to keep the secrets of the Korean War transfers intact had gone to them.

The cooperation on information about Vietnam continued to be particularly disappointing as well. Several times, Toon said, the American side had received replies to requests "that, frankly, are difficult to believe, such as 'no further information exists in Russian archives on Vietnam War POWs'...This, to me, is incredible."

There has been little change since then. James Wold, another Army general called out of retirement in the spring of 1995 to fill the Pentagon position once held by Ptak, is pessimistic about the outlook. He said the POW/MIA researchers—like many foreign researchers trying to gain access to the records in Russia—are finding "the KGB archives are still a closed book."[3]

As for the Russian side of the commission, "their position is that there is no evidence" that Korean War POW transfers took place, Wold said. "We are at an impasse with the Russians on that question, and that's why the KGB archive becomes very important. As pilots were captured, the KGB controlled that process. Unless we have that to confront them with, judging by the way they have resisted any further development of this question, it leads us nowhere."

* * *

Task Force Russia is history, but much of its work and many of its words are preserved in the printed record that the joint commission has kept since it was formed in the cooperative atmosphere that rose out of the chaos of Moscow in early 1992.

One especially telling document is an account of a conversation in September of that year, aboard an airplane en route from Moscow to Khabarovsk. The talk—which took place almost a year before the task force's staff of analysts produced the Korean War POW-transfer report—was between Myacheslav Petrovich Mazurov, the delegate on the commission from the Russian foreign intelligence service, and Col. Herrington, the Army intelligence officer who directed the day-to-day operations and research of Task Force Russia.

From the beginning, Mazurov had forged a reputation as a traditional, hard-line, Soviet-style thinker on the commission, very protective of his agency's reputation and secrets despite the rhetoric of cooperation from Yeltsin and Volkogonov. It was clear that he couldn't imagine the Americans not using the commission as a wedge for gaining an advantage on intelligence matters.

He asked Herrington why the CIA's representative on the commission hadn't been identified.

Herrington told him that while he and some others on the American side had intelligence backgrounds, the CIA had no role in the work being done on the POW issue, and that—as Toon and others had stated repeatedly—no one on the American side was using the commission as a stalking horse for conducting espionage.

Mazurov should put aside any fears that the Americans were looking for current secrets. They were only interested, Herrington assured him, in accounting for past casualties—through the shootdowns of the Cold War, the interrogation reports out of Korea, the prisoner counts out of that old war in Vietnam.

Mazurov wasn't convinced. The CIA wouldn't pass up a chance to benefit from the access being granted to the Americans on the commission, he said.

"I've known them for years."

Chapter Seven

Mathematics of the Missing

"A considerable degree of confusion has occurred because of the insistence for hard-and-fast figures regarding the obscure fates of those who were captured or other wise disappeared in enemy territory."

—Albert D. Biderman, in his book "March to Calumny" about Korean War POWs.

"Experience in the Korean situation indicates that although entry would not be refused, it would not be granted."

—Memo from the U.S. mission to the UN in November 1950 on efforts by the International Red Cross to inspect POW camps in North Korea.

When the Korean War ended in a cease-fire in July 1953, the U.S. military's task of trying to account for all of the American and other UN troops killed and taken prisoner in three years of fighting was far from over.

For the next two-and-a-half years, the Graves Registration Service's morticians and forensic experts applied their skills and the available scientific tools in matching as many sets of anonymous remains as they could—from those they had recovered and the Communists had chosen to hand back—with the names on the rolls of the still-missing.

When the Army's investigators had reached the limits of what could be determined from the evidence at hand, hundreds of sets of remains that had resisted their best efforts were placed in flag-draped coffins on board the cruiser U.S.S. Manchester and taken from Japan to Honolulu, where they were buried as unknowns at the American Battle Monuments Cemetery of the Pacific.

The first coffins bearing the "unknowns" reached Honolulu on Jan. 20, 1956. By March, the operation was complete.

The Army, whose Quartermaster Corps was in charge of the entire operation of collecting remains and accounting for the dead and missing, had ordered there be only "simple ship-side ceremonies" once the coffins reached Hawaii. The reason was that the government knew the more attention, the more controversy.

Maj. Gen. Kester L. Hastings, the quartermaster general, had written in 1954 that "an elaborate ceremony would result only in unfavorable publicity on this matter, which is extremely sensitive and certainly not one to be called to the attention of the civil population at this time."[1]

On the stone monument at the cemetery were inscribed the names of nearly 8,200 men who had not returned alive or dead from Korea. Thus began the sad mathematics of the missing from a war that left no neat sums behind.

Even 40 years ago, it was easy to understand how hundreds of bodies found on or beneath the cratered and bloody battlefields of a modern-day war would prove impossible to identify. War destroys, flesh is fragile.

But to understand how nearly 8,200 men could remain unaccounted for from the Korean War—thousands fewer than from World War II, but four times the number from Laos and Vietnam—it's necessary to add a qualification: It is certain many of them are dead.

Witnesses saw some of them die and, in some cases, helped bury them. The testimony to their deaths is in U.S. military records, while their bodies lie unrecovered, inaccessible. Others no doubt died unseen, in crashes, direct hits or explosions, blown away by the utter devastation of war.

But it's also necessary to remember where the dying and destruction—and the still-unresolved cases of "missing in action"—took place. They happened in a land sealed off for half a century.

Except for a few months in 1950 when United Nations forces carried the attack north of the 38th parallel and held territory that stretched all the way to the Yalu River boundary with China, the last time a U.S. military graves registration unit entered North Korea was in 1946.

The year before, the Soviet Red Army had stormed out of Siberia and through Manchuria to liberate the northern half of the Korean peninsula, while the U.S. Army was supposed to take control of the southern half.

The splitting up of territory was part of the allied accords, but the situation on the ground in Korea was not as neat as words and boundaries drawn on paper can make it appear. For a time, the U.S. military occupation force had liaison officers residing in Pyongyang, and the Soviet army had liaison officers living in Seoul.

It was a contentious relationship, with the Soviets bluntly refusing requests to trade weather data from the 11 meteorological stations in North Korea, and complaining that the American flag was too visible in the North Korean capital. The Americans were sore because the Russians tried to get every movie house in Seoul to show a movie extolling Soviet values and victories in World War II.

Then came the matter of the war dead. In April 1946, negotiations began over allowing U.S. authorities to remove the remains of British, Australian and American soldiers who had been killed in the north during the allied liberation.

A few months later, the Soviets granted permission and on July 3 a burial train proceeded to Hamhung with a party of 29 from the 107th Graves Registration Platoon under the command of Maj. Alfred C. Ranch. But instead of the four sites they had asked to visit, the Americans were allowed to go only to Hamhung and Pyongyang.

The Americans were not allowed to search the sites. No remains were recovered. The burial party returned a week later, empty-handed. It was not a good omen for the future of accounting for American troops in Korea.[2]

In 1953, as the Korean War drew to a close, both sides agreed on a plan—once the fighting had stopped—to let search parties from the opposing side enter their territory for the purpose of retrieving the dead.

But as with most other issues, the antagonists found the longer they negotiated, the more differences, acrimony and suspicion surfaced. When the armistice agreement was finally signed, it was clear that mutual distrust—that the burial parties wouldn't only search for bodies, they would spy, infiltrate, sabotage, and terrorize—would prevent the carrying out of the agreement to retrieve the dead.

Instead, each side agreed to disinter the other's dead from their territory and hand them back at the Demilitarized Zone. As with the supposed emptying of the Communist prison camps, this operation was to be unsupervised by any international organization.

This assured there would be no resolution of the missing, only a further confusion of numbers and names, based on hearsay, remembered in pain and fear, and lost in the fog of war.

Thus while the names of the 8,200 "unaccounted for" Americans include many—perhaps thousands—still buried at isolated sites, POW camp perimeters and cemeteries in North Korea, they also include an undetermined number of men who were taken prisoner, and were seen alive in prison camps, being interrogated or waiting to be repatriated, but never returned, dead or alive.

There are many phrases and acronyms that have been used to refer to them—missing in action/body not returned; prisoner of war/died in enemy hands; unaccounted for/presumed dead; declared dead/died while missing.

The phrases and acronyms emerged from the constant struggle during and after the war to compile up-to-date lists of casualties, those killed, wounded, missing and captured by hostile forces. Such lists always lag behind reality, but those in Korea were especially difficult to keep current.

Word that a soldier had been captured might come from his buddies, his commander, or other witnesses. But after capture he might have been taken to a different camp, executed in an atrocity, died of disease or malnutrition, killed trying to escape. The category of MIA—missing in action—was imprecise, but often the most accurate way to describe all that was actually known about thousands of men, month after month.

There were lists of those the Communists said had died in prison, or escaped. There were lists of American pilots and crewmen the U.S. Air Force said had bailed out over enemy territory but had been seen on the ground, alive and awaiting rescue.

There were lists of men whose families had received letters from prison, postmarked Peking, or whose name or voice had been heard over the radio by a special group of volunteers in New Zealand that monitored every Communist broadcast and passed the names on to the U.S. embassy in Wellington.

With the Communists using prisoners as propaganda—and in the case of South Korean soldiers, putting them back into combat against their former comrades in arms—their lists of POWs were by definition false and incomplete. None of the several hundred U.S. POWs they said had "escaped," for example, ever reached friendly lines.

When the first "official" lists of U.S. POWs were released by the Communists in September 1950, they included only 105 names. By that time, the Communists had boasted of holding thousands of prisoners.

As military analysts and personnel specialists in Korea and at U.S. Pacific Command headquarters in Tokyo struggled to keep up with the count of unverified captures, unseen bodies, "reported" crash and burial sites and the growing category of MIAs, a specter loomed over their shoulders. Always just beyond reach, north of the UN lines and extending to the Manchurian border and beyond, were the facts. They just couldn't get there to learn them.

In his seminal study for Rand Corp. of Korean War remains, commissioned by the Defense Department to recommend a strategy for recovering and identifying the MIA/BNRs in North Korea, Paul M. Cole referred to U.S. casualty data in the Korean War as "dynamic." That is a scholarly word for constant flux.

"During and after the Korean War," Cole wrote, "hundreds of

American BNR (body not returned) cases were progressively reclassified as many as four or five times, depending on how much information was acquired over time."[3]

The only POW count that the UN could be relatively sure of was the number of enemy troops they had placed behind barbed wire. But even that number eventually became troublesome. When the U.S. and its UN allies began to formulate the policy of voluntary repatriation, they had not counted on more than a small percentage of their Communist prisoners choosing to remain separated from the governments in Peking and Pyongyang that had sent them into the war.

In hindsight, it seems an ironic misjudgment, as though the dispensers and protectors of democracy in Korea didn't really believe in the attraction of it for those not raised to believe in it.

By January 1951, despite the intervention of hundreds of thousands of Communist Chinese fighters, the UN Command had regained control of most of South Korea, including Seoul, and had gathered up 137,000 enemy prisoners in UN stockades. MacArthur, facing more heavy fighting on a spit of land smaller than Wyoming, wanted them out of his way.

"Authority is desired to ship all POWs to the ZI (Zone of the Interior, military jargon for the U.S. mainland)," MacArthur's assistant chief of staff wrote to the joint chiefs.[4]

The memo proposed the enemy prisoners be put to good use. "POWs have been docile, cooperative and ready to work at all assigned tasks. Most are unskilled laborers with some semi-skilled workmen...There are 200 POWs who can understand and speak English sufficiently to transmit orders and instructions."

The facilities needed in the U.S. would only need to be "modest"—tents were recommended—and as for upkeep, "their food requirements are less than that of the occidental."

The joint chiefs were already beginning to shun MacArthur because of his open criticism of the administration's reins on his command. They were putting out lines of communication directly but quietly to Gen. Matthew Ridgway, who would be named to succeed him in April. They rejected the plan to send Communist POWs to the U.S.

Although German and Italian POWs had been shipped to the U.S. during World War II, some in the military leadership had evidently figured out that this was a dramatically different war.

For one thing, intelligence reports were saying that the Communists were secretly moving UN prisoners out of the war zone, behind the line of sanctuary that the U.S. and Britain had decided the UN forces should not cross. For the U.S. to ship Communist prisoners halfway around the world might undercut any criticism of that practice, and could justify its continuation.

Whatever their reasoning, the joint chiefs averted what could have been a major embarrassment by rejecting MacArthur's POW plan. As events—rioting, killing, the seizing of a U.S. general as a hostage at the UN prison on Koje-do—would later prove, the Communist prisoners were far from "docile."

But the joint chiefs' memo did give MacArthur an option that, had he chosen to use it, could have changed the course of the war, the negotiations to end it, and certainly the lives of all those taken prisoner in Korea.

The JCS authorized him to place his prisoners on an offshore island away from the battle area "to preclude their prompt return in number," which he did. But they added he could "release...any or all such PWs at such time and place and in such manner as will least interfere with current operations."

But MacArthur's command was fading, and the problem was left to his successors. Long after his departure, the POW problem—how and where to keep prisoners, when and how to return them, how to get our own back—grew and festered until it eventually became the war's central issue.

In any war, when combat troops are reported missing it is clear to the commanders in the field and the clerks who keep the rosters and morning reports which men are no longer present when a battle or mission is completed.

But in Korea, once a soldier was missing, even with reliable eyewitnesses to say what his location and condition were then, no reliable means existed to determine how much longer—given wounds, illness, torture, harsh climate—he remained alive.

The Secretary of Defense Advisory Committee on Prisoners of war estimated in a report dated July 29, 1955, that 2,730—or 38 percent—of an official 7,190 American POWs in Korea died in captivity. That rate is higher than for many wars, and some military historians say that is because the conditions in which prisoners were held in Korea were among the worst in any conflict.

Of course the death rate among those who were taken prisoner but never reached a POW camp—a category Cole refers to as "post-capture killed," is incalculable, although hundreds of victims of atrocities were discovered and figure into the final compilations for those killed.

A statement one ex-POW gave to debriefers soon after he was repatriated from a North Korean camp gives some idea of the conditions in one of the larger, better-known POW camps. The repatriate, Army Cpl. Walter R. Williams of the 718th Transportation Truck Co., was captured on Nov. 30, 1950, and marched first to a camp called "Death Valley," and later to Camp 5, the Communists' main camp on the Yalu River.

Williams said that two out of three of those in the camp when he arrived died before he was released. "During 1951 I was assigned to grave detail nearly every day. The greatest number of men to be buried in one day was 85 and there were never fewer than 12 a day in burial detail. Two to four men had to carry each body due to the distance from the camp to the places used for burial. Men died from the intense cold and lack of food and medical care."

There were, apparently, some outside observers to this parade of death. Unfortunately, they were not observers who took an interest in telling the world about it.

That winter, Williams noted, "some Russian military men were seen at the camp. They carried arms but I did not know exactly what their duties were. We thought they were administrative. One Russian instructor remained during the entire period in charge of the Turkish (POW) company."

The impossible task of arriving at exact, provable figures for the total number of UN POWs—let alone the breakdown by nationality, or by the camps or hideaways where they were held for varying periods of time—makes any percentage dealing with POWs' death rate an estimate, at best.

For instance, one report from the Korean War Crimes files said that of the 2,000 British and American POWs in Camp 1, half—about 1,000—had died. But a British report said there were no more than 1,600 POWs at the camp. Overall, casualty statistics showed the British with a generally lower POW-camp death rate than the Americans.

At Camp 3, according to another war crimes report, there were reported to be 400 to 800 British POWs. Yet when prisoners were exchanged, fewer than 50 British soldiers emerged from Camp 3. Either the death rate among British POWs at Camp 3 was astronomical, or there were far fewer of them in that camp to begin with.

One of the first serious treatments of the morass of unknown and unknowable casualty figures that blanketed the statistics from the Korean War was Albert Biderman's "March to Calumny." In it, he referred to the "limited precision" that was possible in discussing Americans missing behind enemy lines.

Clearly, he wrote, "precise figures cannot be determined" for POWs and those who died as POWs, and "the totals themselves are underestimates" that do not include "considerable numbers who were at one time or another in enemy hands—men who were killed in numbers of atrocities and others whose fate was never clearly determined."[5]

Even the atrocity figures, Biderman noted, are not easily analyzed as "front-line" atrocities or something else. "Mass killings of Americans included men who were shot at the moment of surrender—but also others who had been prisoners for weeks. In yet many other cases, the men simply disappeared after being cut off behind enemy lines, or from the groups of POWs they were with."

Of course, the fact that we know atrocities occurred is because some of the victims' bodies were found, and accounted for. Thus the estimated number of atrocities—another very dynamic figure—is not a number that can automatically be subtracted from the total of MIA/BNRs (missing in action/body not returned).

The more evidence a branch of the service demanded before declaring a missing serviceman to be "captured," the fewer the total number of POWs attributed to that service—and thus the higher the percentage of POWs in that branch some records would show had died while in captivity.

Until the war ended, the Air Force officially listed only four men as prisoners of war. Once POWs were repatriated, ample proof was forthcoming that many others had in fact been in captivity.

An Army study that tried to track death rates in Communist POW camps by month and year, to ascertain the survival rate, found a correlation between the length of time a soldier was held and his chances of survival.

The less time spent as a POW, as one might expect even without studying the data, the greater the chance of living long enough to be freed.

To help keep the numerous categories and sub-categories of dead, wounded and missing straight, U.S. military personnel chiefs dug into the Army's code books and came up with a separate shorthand vocabulary that left an indelible glossary on the lists and accountings of those who fought and died in Korea.

Anyone killed in action was "ETHER." An MIA was "GRAVY." Once confirmed as a POW, he became "URBAN." And anyone returned to military control, from a POW camp or elsewhere, was "BRICK." Japan-based dependents of those declared killed or missing in action were "BLUEWOOD."

The first official list of American POWs issued by North Korea reached the State Department, relayed by the International Red Cross in Geneva on Aug. 18, 1950. Fifty names were on the list, all U.S. Army and ranging from private to major. A second list containing 60 names, all U.S. soldiers who had been reported missing during July, was released on Sept. 14.

The lists were helpful, but suspiciously rounded-off—and far from complete.

In July, weeks before North Korea issued its first partial list, the New China News Agency in Peking published the names of at least 17 U.S. troops they said were prisoners of the North Koreans. None of the 17 was included on either of the two lists relayed weeks later to the U.S. by the ICRC.

For nearly a year and a half, until December 1951, the United States learned which of the missing men had become prisoners by reading the Communist press and monitoring the radio. Occasionally, the names of American soldiers and airmen would appear in the crude newspapers and propaganda leaflets the Communists distributed near the fighting front, urging UN troops to give up and go home to their families.

And once in a while a UN prisoner would be set free by the Communists, or liberated by UN forces advancing on a Communist position, bringing back word of others still being held, or already dead.

In New York, a small, leftist weekly, the National Guardian, published lists of hundreds of GIs who had signed "peace petitions" in prison camp. The names were published first in the English-language China Monthly Review in Shanghai.

As the list of missing soldiers lengthened, it became possible to shift more into the POW category because their families received letters from them, or allied intelligence agencies picked up reports of men held in secret camps. Fourteen countries in addition to the U.S. and South Korea deployed military personnel to the battle zone or the surrounding waters, and virtually all of them had some men taken prisoner.[6]

One break in the Communists' blackout on UN POWs came from a surprising source. In early October 1951, a Hungarian reporter, Tibor Meray, and a Polish correspondent were the first European journalists granted access to U.S. POWs. At a prison camp near Pyongyang, they interviewed and photographed more than a dozen.

Meray turned over the names and photographs of the U.S. prisoners to American reporters in Panmunjom, providing the West with the first pictures of Americans in captivity in Korea.

Now a recognized historian living in France, Meray said he was called on the carpet by his editors in Budapest for supplying the photographs to the American press, but was "saved" by the Chinese, who decided to exploit the issue for their own advantage.

Seeing the "powerful effect the fate of the POWs had on the American public opinion," said Meray, they summoned Wilfred Burchett, a prolific pro-Communist reporter from Australia, and began a steady stream of news coverage slanted to the Chinese perspective.[7]

Just before Christmas 1951, the Communists finally released their longest and long-awaited list of POWs. The Dec. 18 accounting of 10,500 POWs included the names of 3,198 Americans and brought great holiday rejoicing. There had been no news for many months about most of the men on the list. And for the military, it was gratifying to discover that many of the names matched those on its own POW list that had been cobbled together from a variety of sources, mostly the Communist media.

(On the same date, the UN Command reciprocated by turning over through the ICRC the names of nearly 170,000 North Korean and Chinese prisoners it was then holding.)

But the supposedly comprehensive list of POWs from Pynogyang amounted to just over a fourth of the 12,593 Americans then listed as missing in action. Not only were the names of 1,400 American MIAs that the Communists themselves had announced over radio were POWs missing from the list, so were more than half the 110 men named on the very first lists North Korea had issued in August and September 1950.

Another confusing puzzle stemmed from a cablegram that Jacob Malik, the Soviet Union's UN delegate, had distributed in New York the previous August that was purportedly signed by 37 American POWs. Of those men, only 12 were on the Communists' Christmas 1951 list. (Of the 25 omitted, only one was repatriated in 1953.)

Had the rest perished, or somehow been silenced in the intervening months? What about the other 8,000 still listed as MIA? Were most of them among the more than 6,000 U.S. troops that Gen. Ridgway had recently said were victims of Communist atrocities?

To some observers, there was no doubt that the discrepancy could be explained by the Communists' savagery.

"The smallness of the prisoner of war list," wrote Hanson W. Baldwin, The New York Times' military analyst, "should come as scant surprise to any who have served in Korea. Too many saw in months gone by when our troops were advancing in victory the bound bodies of our slain."

But the atrocity figures—except for the actual bodies recovered—were still estimates, like virtually every other statistic related to U.S. losses.

When the UN delegation at Panmunjom asked for more information about more than 1,000 non-Korean MIAs identified as prisoners on Communist radio broadcasts but missing from the POW list, North Korean delegate Gen. Lee Sang Kho replied that 726 "were either killed by air attacks and artillery fire during escort from the front to the camps, or escaped or were already released by our side, or died of disease." The remaining 332 names, he said, were still being investigated.[8]

President Truman cautioned the public to be skeptical about the POW list. There was good reason for skepticism.

Vice Admiral Turner Joy, then the main UN negotiator, lectured Lee that he ought to be able to account for more of the UN's MIAs on the basis of military realities alone.

Joy pointed out that much of the ground fighting up to then had seen United Nations forces retreating before an advancing Communist foe, giving up territory. This had been true in the first few months, when North Korea's troops had the aggressor's advantage, and again later when Chinese troops intervened and nearly succeeded in pushing the UN defenders into the sea.

Logically then, said Joy, the Communists should be able to account for the greatest percentage of soldiers who ended up behind enemy lines, dead or alive. Yet while the UN Command had been able to account for more than 60 percent of the Communists' 188,000 MIAs, the Communists had accounted for only nine percent (7,142) of the 88,000 South Korean MIAs and less than 30 percent (3,198) of more than 12,000 American and other allied MIAs.

(Of 1,500 British MIAs recorded by December 1951, more than half were on the Communist POW list, as were all ten of France's MIAs and Canada's lone MIA. Of eight Dutch MIAs, only one was listed, however.)

The fraction of South Korean MIAs on the Communist POW list was even more dismal. The 7,100 South Koreans the Communists claimed they were holding comprised only one-tenth of some 70,000 missing Republic of Korea troops.

Lee called Joy's argument "untenable," and said "in no war is there any determined correlation between the numbers of missing in action and prisoners of war." The Communists appeared to be doing their utmost to make that the case.[9]

The Communists did set some POWs free, issuing them "safe conduct" passes printed in both English and Chinese. An example was Pfc. Bill Beaumont of Pennsylvania, who safely returned to UN military control in March 1951 after two months as a POW. Lost, thrown away or turned in, Beaumont's safe-conduct pass was found later by UN forces and preserved among the many boxes of captured enemy records now on file in the National Archives.

But the Communists never released a list of those POWs, like Beaumont, they set free. From questioning all the returned U.S. soldiers, the UN could locate only 177 who had been "released" or allowed to escape. They were with few exceptions South Korean troops.

If so many U.S. troops were being let go at the front, said Joy sarcastically, "they must educate them in a hell of a hurry, if they turn them loose without getting their names."

The atrocities were part of the war's most gruesome calculations that figured into the accounting of the missing. Over the course of the fighting, U.S. estimates of Americans slain in acts of atrocity ranged from a few hundred to 8,000. Ridgway's 1951 estimate of 6,000 was repeated in October 1953, with a notation that this number was the result of separating "probable" victims from an initial "reported" list of 10,233, and that the accounts of POWs repatriated in the Little Switch (April 1953) and Big Switch (August-September 1953) exchanges had not yet been factored in.

A figure of 6,113 U.S. atrocity victims was also used that month by

Henry Cabot Lodge Jr., the U.S. delegate to the UN. A Far East Command memo makes it clear, however, that the investigation leading to this number had turned up only 216 eyewitnesses, and 511 bodies.[10]

Atrocities continued to be an issue in the war's aftermath, and a U.S. Senate inquiry in 1954, drawn from the testimony of 29 witnesses and a study of debriefing reports from repatriated prisoners, resulted in a figure of 5,639 victims, just among the military. Total atrocities of military personnel and civilians reached into the tens of thousands, the Senate investigators found.

The problem of missing prisoners was obviously tied very closely to how they were treated after capture. And the war was only a few months old when the UN Command concluded that, in their planning for a lightning attack on South Korea that would bring a complete victory and rout of Rhee's forces in 60 days, neither the North Koreans nor their Soviet advisers had given much thought to what would be done with prisoners.

A State Department intelligence brief concluded six months after the war broke out that "The North Korean army evidently did not develop policy and procedures for handling American prisoners of war until several weeks after the entry of U.S. forces into Korea. The initial phase of brutality toward American prisoners of war may be attributed at least in part to the fact that no over-all instructions outlining procedures to be followed in the capture and evacuation of prisoners had been given to combat units before June 25."

Minimizing what would later be exposed as a dominant theme—the slaughter and mistreatment of POWs—the report added there had been "isolated instances of summary executions and other acts of brutality perpetrated upon American prisoners of war," while the vast majority of POWs in the war's first weeks "were mistreated, deprived of much of their clothing (especially shoes), and paraded humiliatingly through the streets of Pyongyang. Even by North Korean standards wounded captives were not provided adequate medical care."

Toward the end of July, the North Korean command issued explicit instructions for handling enemy POWs. But not until Oct. 1, 1950, was a North Korean army order issued making the murder of military prisoners a court-martial offense—except in cases of "attempted escape."

Despite the new order, one of the war's most horrible atrocities— the Sunchon Tunnel massacre—took place after the order was issued, on Oct. 20, 1950. A trainload of American POWs was halted for some hours in a tunnel north of Sunchon. The next day, the bodies of 66 POWs were found beside the tracks. They had been taken into a field and told they were to be given supper when they were shot to death with automatic weapons by their North Korean guards.

The shooting went on for an hour. Twenty-one POWs survived to tell the story.[11]

The UN Command had its problems with prisoner treatment as well. On Nov. 2, 1950, in Seoul, the South Korean military executed 27 "convicted collaborators"—including a young woman with an eight-month-old baby strapped to her back whose crime had apparently been that she was the mistress of the Communist official who ran Seoul during the North Korean occupation.

While the high estimates of atrocities dimmed hopes that any U.S. soldier missing and not acknowledged a POW might still be alive in enemy hands, the Christmas 1951 list of POWs fostered optimism that the negotiations that had begun between the warring sides were producing some results, and spurred UN military officials into action.

The next month, in January 1952, the UN Command began mobilizing teams and drawing up plans to receive repatriated prisoners. Some officers were so eager to see an exchange come about that they suggested loaning U.S. military field ambulances to the Communists so they could transport the sickest and weakest prisoners from the prison camps to the exchange point.

Their optimism was premature. There would be plenty of time to prepare for a homecoming. The first official exchange of POWs was still 14 months away, and the transfer of the main POW population would not happen for nearly two more years.

Meanwhile, thousands of MIAs whose names didn't appear on the Christmas list would slip further toward oblivion. By the time it was possible to figure out what might have happened to some of them, they had been joined by thousands more.

* * *

This reciting of the fluid and imprecise statistics behind the Korean War POW/MIA problem might leave the impression that amassing such numbers and declaring someone a prisoner, or dead, was a matter of bureaucratic analysis, devoid of humanity.

Nothing could be further from the truth. Getting their hands on useful information about casualties involved work for the Army's badly understaffed Graves Registration personnel that was emotionally and physically taxing in the extreme.

In the first months of the war, U.S. troops followed the customary rule of creating temporary battlefield cemeteries for each division. As the UN Command took more and more ground in its drive north to the Yalu in the fall of 1950, the men who had fallen since the first U.S. combat troops had arrived the first week of July were buried in a series of cemeteries from Inchon on the peninsula's west coast to Wonsan and Hamhung on the eastern coast, and at several points across the breadth of North Korea.

But getting the dead to the division cemeteries wasn't a simple task. Describing conditions in the war's early months, Lt. Col. John C. Cook wrote that "Such remains as could not be moved because of the exigencies of battle were hastily interred in foxholes, shell holes, or any area of soft earth which permitted a quick burial. These isolated graves were not always marked, and even in cases where crude markers were erected, many were lost through the action of the elements or destroyed in battle. Still other markers were removed by natives or the enemy."[12]

There was worse to come. When the Chinese intervened in the conflict in October 1950, the UN withdrawal swept past many of those cemeteries in the rush to establish a defensive perimeter far to the south, around the port of Pusan. Graves Registration units began a frantic recovery effort to evacuate the cemeteries that were about to fall under Communist control.

The Eighth Army's cemetery at Inchon, with 870 graves, including 112 remains that had just been disinterred from Kaesong, farther north, was directly in the path of the advancing Communist forces. There was no time to spare. The lead Communist units were already at the outskirts of Seoul.

A platoon of graves registration soldiers, recruiting a few local laborers who agreed to delay their own retreat, began digging at the frozen ground with shovels on Christmas morning. "The exhumation by plot, row, and grave, with men of the platoon verifying the remains of each disinterred and noting any discrepancies on prepared reports" was the first phase of the evacuation. Then the sets of remains were wrapped, tagged and moved to a temporary mortuary at the port, for loading aboard a ship that would move them to safety in Japan.

The disinterment took three days. A month later, the job of the graves registration units got even tougher.

Korea was the first war in which the U.S. government attempted to embalm and ship home for final burial the body of every American casualty while the fighting was in progress. Previously, bodies of American dead had been placed in temporary graves until the war was over. In fact, thousands of World War II dead were placed in permanent graves in Europe, where they fell.

The policy change took place seven months into the Korean War, prompted by a public outcry over the perceived elitism of the U.S. military.[13]

Two days before Christmas 1950, Gen. Walton H. Walker, the Eighth

Army commander, was killed in a vehicle accident at Uijongbu, South Korea. Within a few days, his body was flown home for burial in Arlington National Cemetery. With that as a precedent, the families of regular soldiers killed in Korea demanded their loved ones also be returned to the United States. The new policy called for an even greater effort on the Army's part to deal with the war's casualties, just when the main military morgue in Kokura, Japan, was already working down a backlog of remains from the high casualty rates of the first six months of fighting.

At first, remains were taken to Japan by ship, often resulting in long storage in an unrefrigerated hold and the severe deterioration of remains. By the summer of 1952, air evacuation of remains had begun to speed the removal and identification of the dead.

But the efforts of inexperienced and undermanned graves registration personnel in the war's initial phase could not be reversed. Of the 7,924 burials done before the facility in Japan opened, 15 percent had been declared unknown.

"In addition, a number of discrepancies had been discovered in the records of those buried as 'known.' The primary reason for this large number of unknowns was the shortage of graves registration personnel supporting Army operations and the lack of training and experience of the medical technicians."[14]

Anatomical measurements and personal effects that would have aided later identification in many cases were buried rather than preserved, leaving future investigators little chance of correcting earlier mistakes.

The longer a name remained on the MIA list, the greater the likelihood that some clue would surface about the case, giving the personnel specialists a means of determining someone's fate.

But the first real flood of information didn't come until April 1953, with Operation Little Switch. On "humanitarian" grounds, both sides were to release those POWs in the direst need of medical attention. Meanwhile, talks would continue on how to deal with the rest. Operation Little Switch was a major disappointment, except for those prisoners who were freed, of course.

The Communists returned 149 Americans—mostly privates and corporals—and a handful of British and other allied personnel. They weren't what UN officials had been led to expect. More than a dozen were seriously wounded, but in general they were in good health, not in need of immediate attention.

Moreover, after debriefings, U.S. experts in psychological warfare concluded that every seventh or eighth man displayed a thorough indoctrination in, and tolerance for, Marxist-Leninist ideology. It's conceivable, of course, that the experts confused familiarity with indoctrination. There could be no doubt that the repatriates of Little Switch certainly had a lot of Marxist ideology pounded into them.

But if the experts were right, the Communists had apparently used Little Switch to reward some of their most apt and cooperative pupils (known as "Progressives" in prison camp jargon) with an early return home.

That observation led to one of the most controversial steps the U.S. military took regarding Korean War POWs: about 20 of the Little Switch returnees were sent to Valley Forge Hospital in Pennsylvania for mental and psychological tests, psychiatric evaluations and more debriefings to measure the extent of their "brainwashing."

If possible, they were to be "re-indoctrinated" in western democratic principles. (The British, who also had been warned that some of their repatriated prisoners would be coming home with their minds stuffed with Marxism, took a more relaxed view, announcing that their "brainwashed" ex-prisoners would simply be sent straight home, where they would no doubt find British life a good remedy for their warped ideology.)

But the U.S. military was vitally interested in what they and the rest of the Little Switch ex-POWs could tell them about MIAs. From the 127 Army repatriates, definitive information was gained about 8,093 other men who had been captured: either that they were dead, or had last been seen alive.

The signing of the armistice weeks later paved the way for the repatriation of the main body of POWs, in Operation Big Switch (Aug. 5-Sept. 6.) The number of UN POWs repatriated came very close to the figures announced prior to the exchange by the Communists. The final tally was: 3,596 U.S. (3,313 promised); 7,842 South Korea (8,186 promised); 946 U.K. (922 promised); 228 Turkey (228 promised); 40 Philippines; 30 Canada; 22 Colombia; 21 Australia; 12 France; 8 South Africa; 2 Greece; 2 Netherlands; 1 New Zealand; 1 Belgium.[15]

Another list from the Communists named 481 UN troops (438 U.S.; 33 U.K.; 1 Australia; 9 unknown nationality) they said had "escaped" or "died in prison." (Combined with earlier "died in prison" and "escaped" lists, the names totaled 1,022.)

Like the others, this latter list was highly suspect. But the U.S. military relied on it anyway as the sole basis for ruling some reported POWs dead.[16] It was most useful in those cases where it could be used to support the testimony of returned POWs.

And again, as was done with the Little Switch internees, the repatriates were asked to identify any fellow POWs they knew had died, or had been alive when last seen. From the 3,195 Army returnees in Big Switch, a study by the Graves Registration branch determined that information had been learned about nearly 20,000 other individuals.

But the sightings or other information could be months, or years—or one unrecorded atrocity—out of date. Even these new facts fell short of resolving all the cases still in the category of MIA.

The names and numbers didn't match. Some of those the repatriates said were dead had already been issued a "determination of death" based on other sources. Many of those mentioned by the early returnees as being "held back" by the Communists were freed later in the month-long exchange.

The inaccuracy of the Communists' various lists was evident from the start, but exactly how fraudulent their claims actually were was not clear until after the services had an opportunity to finish assembling a lot of the data they only received after the last list was passed.

An Army analysis in April 1956, for instance, pointed to the case of "Pfc. Billy W. Baker, USMC, whose body (was) positively identified (in) Operation Glory (the exchange of recovered remains) only after lengthy examination of physical health records. Baker (was) known to have been alive by Communists yet returned as unidentified body."

Operation Glory forensics had also yielded identification of 56 U.S. Army and four Air Force members.: "Some of the U.S. Army personnel were explained by the Communists as 'escaped.' Does this mean that remaining personnel (in the) 'escaped' category are also dead at hands of captors?"

Of five MIAs named in a 1951 Radio Peking report as in captivity, four were listed at the end of the war as "escaped" and the fifth "no data."

"We have evidence on 10 Air Force and 1 Navy personnel who were seen in captivity although Communists indicate as 'no data.' Four other personnel on whom similar evidence of Communist captivity exists (were) indicated 'escaped.' These 20 cases could be used (to) demonstrate inadequacy (of) Communist accounting."[17]

Whether the Communists' were guilty of bad accounting or bad faith, the facts were that during Operation Big Switch, both sides had found themselves engaging in a form of "chicken" with the POWs. UN officers kept daily tallies of the men returned, and several weeks into the process noted that many of the higher-ranking known POWs and Air Force personnel were still missing.

The UN side quickly inventoried its stockades and found, to its chagrin, that it had already repatriated a high percentage of Communist officers. It was too late to even the scales if the Communists did indeed hold back the officers.

Arguments were drafted on the "advisability of holding Communist POW as hostages, to be used as leverage when protesting against non-return of UNC pers(onnel)…." But it was decided it would be more advisable to carry forward with full repatriation, leaving the secretary of state to issue a strong demand for complete reciprocity.

In late August, however, while the Communists were engaged in their calculated release of POWs, Secretary of State John Foster Dulles issued a memo based on his best information at the time.

"The U.S. government believes," he wrote, "that some American and other United Nations military personnel, held prisoner by the Chinese and North Korean Communist forces in Korea, will not be returned to friendly control."[18]

He said the U.S. would demand the return of all POWs through the armistice commission that had been established to arbitrate all such disputes, but added the Far East commander "will use all possible means available to locate and recover those individuals interned within his area of responsibility."

A close reading of the memo raises the vital question of whether "within his area of responsibility" was meant to exclude Manchuria, the Soviet Union, and in fact any territory past the Demilitarized Zone.

The question is relevant because Dulles's memo went on to describe exactly where he thought the answers would lie:

"UN prisoners retained by the Communists will not necessarily be held in Korea, Manchuria or Eastern Siberia, but may be retained elsewhere in the Soviet orbit. (The message was sent to U.S. embassies in the major capitals of Europe and Asia.) The U.S. Government is anxious to obtain any information concerning these captives."

The UN Command went right to work on the new demands, handing the Communists a list of 3,400 UN troops still listed as MIA, including 944 Americans selected from the thousands of still-unresolved cases because they were all individuals who:

"(1) Spoke or were referred to in broadcasts from your radio stations.

"(2) Were listed by you as being your captives.

"(3) Wrote letters from your camps.

"(4) Were seen in your prisons."

Two weeks later, on Sept. 21, the Communists replied that most of the men on the UN list had never been their prisoner, and of the 900 who had been (including 112 Americans), all were now dead, had escaped or were "released at the front."

(They also pointed out that four men on the list of 944 "unaccounted for" had in fact been released during the just-completed Operation Big Switch, a sign that by this time, the perpetual listing and re-listing of names had reached certain human limits.)

No practical, peaceful means existed to allow the UN Command to press its demands for more information beyond the negotiating table. And the Communists had certainly proved they could give new meaning to the word recalcitrant.

The troublesome cases were actually more numerous than it appeared to those watching the combative theater of negotiators at Panmunjom.

A chronology of the process of declaring Korean War MIAs dead (under the Missing Persons Act of 1942, which set a one-year time limit for most situations) reveals that after the Big Switch exchange was completed, there were still 3,605 MIA cases in which there was "no information available" on which to make a determination.[19]

And a time limit was approaching. Findings of death were prepared "on those cases where we had no information," the summary states, because "the Missing Persons Act was about to expire (1 Feb. 54) and decision was made to get as many determinations made as possible before that date."

Another factor was cost. Hugh M. Milton II, assistant Army secretary, addressed this point in a January 1954 memo: "A further complicating factor in the situation (of unaccounted-for Americans) is that to continue to carry this personnel in a 'missing' status is costing over one million dollars annually. It may become necessary at some future date to drop them from our records as 'missing and presumed dead.'"

* * *

But the core of the search for missing American prisoners from the Korean War was, and is, not in the cost, but in the arithmetic.

For American POWs to have been shipped to Manchuria, or Siberia, or kept on communal farms in North Korea in sizable lots, there must be in the records an irreducible pool of POWs and MIAs for whom that is as good an explanation of their fate as anything else.

The place to look for this pool is among the thousands of men who were declared dead on the basis of little or no information.

The exact number of MIAs who were declared dead because no explanation of their fate could be learned before the allotted time ran out under the Missing Persons Act is, like most other numbers related to the Korean War, difficult to pin down.

But an approach is possible. In mid-October 1953, about 45 days after the last POW exchange, the Pentagon announced that 7,955 servicemen then carried as MIAs would soon have to be presumed dead. The total comprised 6,713 Army members, 671 Air Force, 493 Marines and 78 Navy personnel.

The Pentagon noted that some of the men had been missing since the first year of the war. But the process was already underway to end their missing status.

By the end of the year, the number had shrunk, but not by much. Citing the Missing Persons Act, the military said presumptive findings of death were being issued as of Jan. 1, 1954, for 3,600 MIA cases, and that another 3,800 cases would be carried as missing only until a year's time had passed.[20]

The chronology cited earlier indicates a slightly different total, but confirms that a rapid and massive countdown took place to eliminate all MIA cases by a certain date:

• 3,386 findings of death issued Dec. 31, 1953.
• 2,691 cases unresolved as of Jan. 4, 1954.
• 2,465 more findings of death issued by March 31, 1954.
• 226 cases "ready for dispatch" on April 1, 1954, "as the year required by the Missing Persons Act expires."

Biderman, who brought his own war experience to the subject and studied the war's statistics in the first decade after the armistice, asserts "there were at least 4,735 cases in which presumptive findings of death were made under the Missing Persons Act."[21]

Another means of estimating the number of no-evidence presumptive findings is to count the number of names among the 8,200 BNR (body not returned) cases for which the official date of death is Dec. 31, 1953 or later.

That figure is just over 4,100.

Does this mean that, since we don't know when or where they died, half the men listed as unaccounted for could have been alive—still in enemy hands, somewhere north of the 38th parallel—when the last prisoner exchange was completed in 1953?

Not exactly. The mathematics of the missing in Korea have more elements to take into account. A year after Operation Big Switch came Operation Glory.

In March 1954, the UN Command told the Communists it was ready to invoke the part of the armistice agreement that called for each side to allow the other's graves registration parties inside their territory to search for their dead. At the same time, it turned over to the Communists detailed information about the location of more than 800 isolated burial sites and 10 established cemeteries in North Korea where 1,715 UN personnel were believed to be buried.

The bodies in the cemeteries were well-identified when they were buried, but that had been years earlier.

As expected, the Communists had cooled on the idea of mutual search-and-disinterment parties. And the South Koreans were known to be reluctant to let North Koreans explore their zone. So the UN accepted the Communists' counter-proposal to have each side recover bodies in its territory and exchange them at the Demilitarized Zone.

The Communists submitted the alleged location of grave sites below the 38th parallel for more than 5,000 of their fallen troops and waited for an answer from the UN Command.

Acceptance of the Communist proposal, according to an analysis by U.S. Army officials in Japan, would mean an "early completion" of the task of recovery and no "opportunities for incidents" or clashes between the still-antagonistic north and south.[22]

But the analysis acknowledged that accepting it would also mean that a great many men would have to be declared dead without confirmation, with little or no evidence that they were dead. And it would allow the Communists to simply manufacture identities for sets of remains, using the names or personal items of prisoners still unaccounted for.

And there was another problem: the public not might think much of a plan that left the responsibility of accounting for Americans and other missing UN personnel to the very people suspected of lying about where they'd been for the previous four years.

But the final recommendation favored accepting the flawed, but realistic, counter-proposal. Continuing to press the Communists to honor the armistice clause for mutual recovery teams would mean an indefinite delay and assure that American dead "will not be recovered from N. Korea in [the] foreseeable future," the UN command's analysis concluded.

The stage was set for Operation Glory. From Sept. 1 to Nov. 9, 1954, the Communist side returned 4,089 sets of remains; 1,869 were "tagged" as Americans. As the coffins arrived on the UN side of the exchange point, they were loaded onto military trucks for a journey that ended at the morgue in Kokura, Japan.

Some came with dogtags or other items of personal identification attached, but each had to be checked forensically before an official finding could be issued. And there were some obvious problems. According to the information that accompanied the remains, the Communists' search had not been thorough.

The remains came from only six of the 10 established cemeteries the UN had identified for the North Koreans.

Thus the graves registration staff knew even then that they were working with the results of a limited—at worst botched, or at best half-hearted—recovery effort by the Communists.

But just how limited can be seen through the excellent efforts of Cole, the author of the Rand Corp. report on Korean War casualties. Cole visited the Central Identification Laboratory in Hawaii, the facility that succeeded the Kokura morgue and inherited its files on Korea, and did a detailed study of the records of UN cemeteries in North Korea and Operation Glory.[23]

When the rosters of identified remains brought back in Operation Glory are superimposed on the plot, row and grave locations in the UN cemeteries, the pattern of incomplete disinterment is clear: remains handed back in Operation Glory appear in random order on the list of men reportedly buried in a given location. The most thorough disinterments appear to have been done at Hungnam, Pukchong and Wonsan cemeteries, where row after row of named grave sites coincide with the names of U.S. casualties returned in the 1954 exchange of remains.

But even there, every dozen or so graves have been skipped. The names missing from the Operation Glory manifest, Cole notes, "were never exhumed and delivered, or were not buried in the first place." Given the opportunity, a mortuary team sent to the site might be able to determine which is true. But working solely from printed records it is not possible.

Ultimately, working with these same records of untended cemeteries in North Korea and the physical remains that were returned, the Army's forensics people over the next 14 months were able to match 1,010 of the remains the Communists had tagged as "American" with a name from the thousands that had already been assigned a "presumption" of death.

The remaining 859 unidentified sets were shipped to Hawaii for burial as "unknowns" from the Korean War.[24]

As of 1956, then, with the burial sites north of the 38th parallel closed to any outside inspection, and all possible forensic work completed on the anonymous remains that had been recovered or returned, the Army's mortuary operation moved from Japan to Hawaii.

The final 8,177 names of men who didn't return from Korea—both those for whom the military had records and witnesses testifying to their death and burial, and those who had disappeared without a trace—were recorded at the military monument in Hawaii.

One method of sorting out the possible transfer cases from this group of BNRs (body not returned) is to look not at the number of BNRs, but the number of rulings of presumptive death.

Since there were evidently about 4,100 cases (by name) in which a presumptive finding of death was issued before Operation Glory for lack of identified remains, 1,010 of those cases would have been resolved thanks to the identification made at Operation Glory. The return of remains would, in effect, have provided the evidence that was lacking when the finding of death was issued.

That would leave 3,090 cases (names) lacking a set of matching remains.

In addition, if all 859 "unknowns" from Operation Glory buried in Hawaii are actually U.S. military—far from certain, but possible—they should be subtracted, too.

That leaves, as a conservative estimate, at least 2,200 MIAs who could have been captured alive, but were not released and were not dead when the other American remains were returned.[25]

This method of applying some known quantities (names of MIAs; presumptions of death well after combat had ceased) to the larger statistics dealing with cases of the missing leaves a potential pool of 2,200 American POWs who were last seen alive during the Korean War.

It's not a precise figure. It's not an unshakable statistic. But as will be evident in the following pages, it's not an improbable one, either.

Xu Ping Hua turned over American pilots to Soviet officers and witnessed POW executions.

Photos by Laurence Jolidon

...ander Orlov, a ...red Soviet colonel, ...rrogated American ...Vs in North Korea; ...ds Russian investi- ...on of Korean War ...s.

...orij Pavlovich Derskiy, retired Soviet army ...nel, served as an advisor to the North Korean ...y and as an aid to the Soviet ambassador to ...h Korea. He prepared American prisoners for ...ment to the Soviet Union.

Valentin Pak, above, headed North Korean propaganda department during Korean War out of Soviet embassy in Pyongyang.

Gen. Yuri Yezerskiy, left, former prison camp administrator, saw American prisoners at Vorkuta he believes were from Korean War.

4

Photos by Defense POW/MIA Office

Because many U.,S. troops and aviators sent to fight in Korea were World War II veterans, a number of prisoners were survivors of POW camps Germany and the Pacific. One Korean War repatriate who h spent time in a Germa camp said the Germa experience was like a sabbatical — with chess games, books and beer, compared being a prisoner of t North Koreans and Chinese.

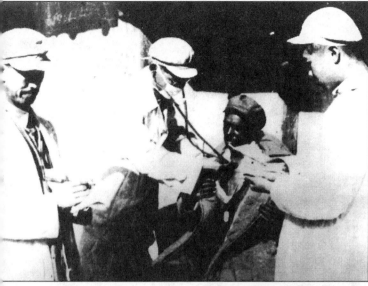

Most POW camps in North Korea were ill-equipped to provide medicine or medical help, but Chinese and Russians operated hospitals for their own military and diplomatic personnel. Some American prisoners were taken to Manchuria for treatment.

Photos by Defense POW/MIA Office

ading material in POW camps was limited to blications friendly to the Communist cause. The inese used Communist press and radio to issue ts of POWs' names, appeals to end the fighting.

5

Photos by Defense POW/MIA O[

Large groups of U.S. troops were captured in the first weeks and months of the war as the North Korean invaders stormed sou through thin defensive lines. Severe weather, poor medical care an harsh treatment woul take their toll on man POWs by war's conclu sion.

Photos courtesy of Valentin Pak

Soviet Gen. Terentii Shtykov (above left) was sent to North Korea as Moscow's first ambassador to the new Communist regime the Kremlin helped create. After building the North Korean military with the aid of Korean soldiers returned from helping Mao Tse-Tung's forces conquer China, Shtykov guided Kim IL-Sung (right) in his revolutionary ambitions. He was replaced in 1951, having wrongly predicted that the U.S. would not send troops to aid South Korea's government.

Photos courtesy of Valentin Pak

e Soviet Union's
bassy in Pyongyang
the 1950s served as
headquarters for the
ge Soviet military
d diplomatic contin-
nt sent to North
rea after World War
to consolidate a
endly government on
ssia's Far East
rimeter. During the
ar, bombing by United
tions planes reduced
ch of the capital to
bble, and the
ssians and other
viet bloc personnel
re forced to take
elter in basements
d caves in nearby vil-
ges.

In some larger camps, American prisoners were issued warm winter clothing, Chinese-made.

Army Pvt. Wildon C. East was reported missing in action in Korea in September 1950. His family in Arkansas received the post card below in 1992. They say it is East's handwriting.

TAKING TIGER MOUNTAIN BY STRATEGY
A Modern Revolutionary Peking Opera

People of Spadra, AR.
I was born in Spadra, AR
I enlisted in the U.S. Army
in September 1949. I am
still alive. I am sick, and still
a P.O.W. in North
Korea. M. W. C. East

RA 1828 1800

Pfc. Roger A. Dumas was a prisoner of war in Camp 5, on the Yalu River. When the war ended and prisoners were exchanged, he was led away by Chinese guards. His brother Robert believes he and other POW/MIAs from the war have been held on collective farms in North Korea.

otos by Defense POW/MIA Office

ither the United
tions nor the
ternational Red Cross
d any access to UN
soners during the
rean War. A substan-
l number of POWs
re shifted into
mps in Manchuria
d, according to intel-
ence reports, into
e Soviet Union, for
e as forced labor and
doctrination.

Charles Clifford-Brown, left, born in Los Angeles and Isaac Oggins, from Massachusetts, were executed while imprisoned in the Gulag on espionage charges, but prison authorities drafted false death certificates alleging they died of illnesses.

Giorgi Matveyivich Leivikov commanded anti-artillery brigade in North Korea; sent American aviator-POWs up chain of command to Barabash, USSR.

Photos by Laurence Jolidon

Sergei Kim, right, a Soviet-Korean born in Far East, translated for Soviet ambassadors to North Korea during the war.

Alexandrovich Viktor Bushuyev was deputy intelligence chief for Soviet air force in Manchuria during Korea War; organized interrogations of U.S. POWs.

Lee San Kho, former chief North Korean negotiat● at Panmunjom, later ambassador to Moscow; said all POWs released.

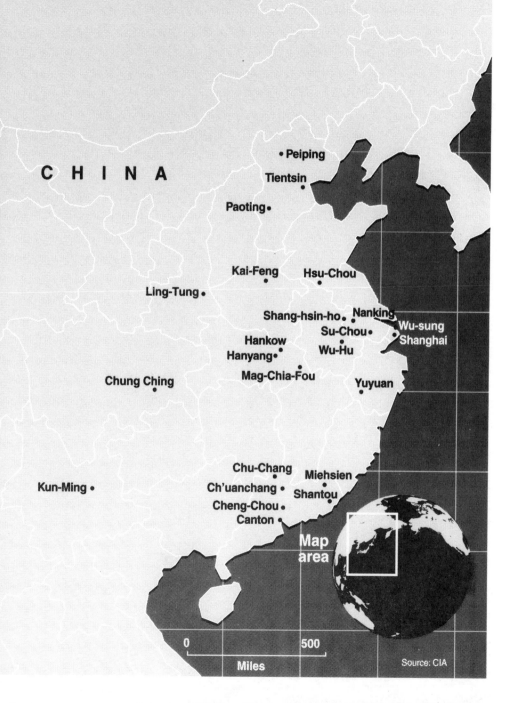

Locations Where United Nations POWs Were Reportedly Interned on Chinese Mainland During the Korean War

CHINA

• Peiping
Tientsin •
Paoting •

Kai-Feng •   Hsu-Chou •

Ling-Tung •

Shang-hsin-ho •   Nanking •
                                      • Wu-sung
Hankow •   Su-Chou •   Shanghai
Hanyang •   Wu-Hu •
        Mag-Chia-Fou •

Chung Ching •   Yuyuan •

                Chu-Chang •   Miehsien •
Kun-Ming •   Ch'uanchang •   Shantou •
             Cheng-Chou •
             Canton •

Map area

0   500
Miles

Source: CIA

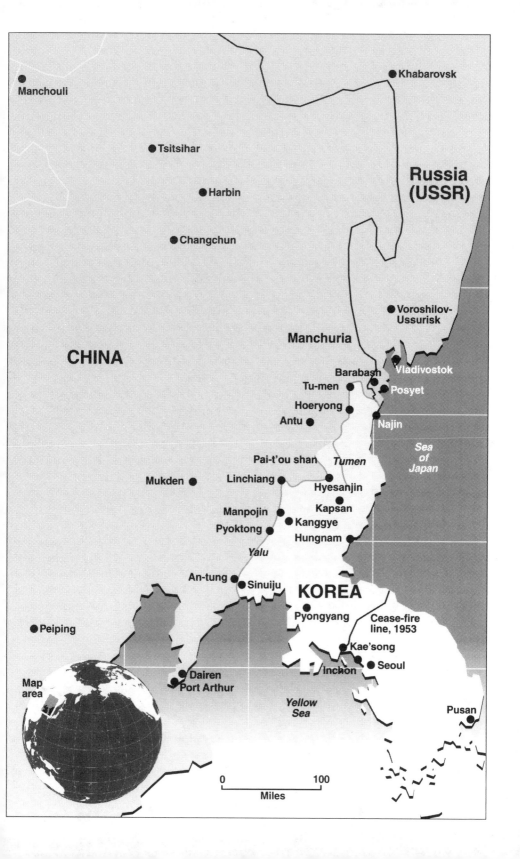

Chapter Eight

Documents, Documents

"It says, 'copies of crew members' registration sheets.' If you can make a list that says you have copies, where are the copies?"
—Acting U.S. Archivist Trudy Peterson,
to the Russian members of the
Joint Commission on American POWs in the former Soviet Union,
at August, 1994, meeting in Moscow.

"If we wait to receive the specifics and it turns out that these Americans are not alive, we can say that they died from American bombing."
—An April 6, 1953, message from Soviet official in North Korea to
Vyacheslav M. Molotov, Soviet foreign minister,
regarding American civilians who were POWs in North Korea.

One of the first discoveries American researchers made when the Russian government began handing over information from the former Soviet archives about missing American prisoners was that many of the "documents" weren't documents at all.

They were summaries of documents. Or lists of names culled from documents. Or partial Soviet files of documents that came from or referred to other, more substantive, source documents, which were not made available.

And in terms of numbers, even the lists weren't all they first appeared to be. The "List of 510" began with 537 entries, but after eliminating all the duplicated entries, shrank to a list of 494 military and 24 civilian names. The "List of 59" pilots is actually a list of 56 pilots. Those pesky duplications again. The "List of 262" interrogated pilots is actually a "summary" that lists fewer than ten names.

The Russians have provided the American side of the commission with two separate lists of more than 600 prisoners of war, several shorter lists of pilots whose names were reportedly found in the records of the Soviet air corps that was deployed to fight in the Korean War, and—largely for historical purposes—long lists of American military air crews who were temporarily detained in the Soviet Union at the end of World War II but eventually repatriated.

But the American side still doesn't know, and hasn't seen, which documents the names were derived from.

For example, after the Russians turned over a list of 99 U.S. Korean War POWs in December 1992, the American analysts noted that "The Russians did not provide any of the original documents pertaining to this list...but, as with every other list, only a digest of information prepared specifically for us."

Many of the U.S. POWs' names were attributed to "according to data of the Korean People's Army." But none of the "data" have ever been shown to the American analysts. North Korean records remain closed to U.S. scrutiny, as they have since the formation of the country after World War II.

The same imprecise derivation was true of the long list of names that was the first POW/MIA-related document released by the Russians to the U.S. government after the fall of the Communist regime. U.S. Sen. Robert Smith, R-N.H., was handed this list in February 1992 on a visit to Moscow, and made it public a few months later, after attempting to identify as many names as possible. The list consisted of 537 separate entries, divided into a list of 510 supposedly military names and 27 civilian names.

The list was titled, "American Prisoners of War—Data for 1950-51," and it quickly became known, erroneously, as the "510 List." (A revised version updated by the latest information appears in the appendix.) The number is misleadingly exact. Of 518 distinct names, at least 16 are non-American missionaries or diplomats. Names that are still unidentified could also be non-Americans.

But not only were the length of the list and the nationalities of the people on it subject to alteration. Smith said that when he was presented the list, he was told it represented the names of American POWs who had been "interrogated by the Soviets, some of whom had then been sent to China." The Russians maintain that Smith is mistaken, that the list is NOT an interrogation list. It's just a list of names, some of which are duplicated.

Every POW, repatriated or not, underwent some kind of interrogation by the Communist forces. And the Soviets did their share of interrogations in Korea. Whether or not each individual on the "List of 510" was interrogated by the Soviets—just because the list was provided to the U.S. in Moscow—is open to question. But the discussion shows what the American analysts were up against when the "documents" started to be passed.

Because of the public notice it received, the "List of 510" became a kind of standard by which much of the other information later turned over by the Russians had to be judged. If the first list of names received from them could not be subjected to rigorous analysis, how useful would the rest of the information be?

An independent analysis of the "List of 510" shows that:

1. A significant majority of names are Americans, both military and civilians. But many of the civilians are diplomats or missionaries of other nationalities (British, French, a Swiss, a Turk.)

2. Of the actual 518 total names, the first 340—except for a few—and some lower down on the list were all imprisoned at a single camp near Manpojin, North Korea. The camp became known as "Tiger Camp," named for the Korean military official who had led the American prisoners on a "death march" from Pyongyang to Manpojin. The POWs nicknamed him, in recognition of his cruelty, "The Tiger." The Tiger Camp was a significant but largely unpublicized camp farther northeast along the Yalu River than the cluster of large, well-known camps centered on the riverside city of Pyoktong. There were both military and civilian POWs at Tiger Camp, and Soviet officials and officers paid visits there.

3. Of the Tiger Camp POWs on the list, nine were reported by camp survivors to have died in captivity. The nine were also on a list of 147 U.S. POWs the Communists at the time of the armistice said had "escaped" from POW camps. None of these 147 men ever returned to military control. They are believed to be dead, but their bodies have not been recovered.

4. The name of Gen. William Dean, the highest-ranking U.S. POW of the war, is on the list. In his debriefings and memoirs, he said he was never interrogated by the Soviets. But Col. Grigori Derskiy, a Soviet advisor in North Korea during the war, said he questioned Gen. Dean not long after his capture in August 1950.

5. The name of George Blake, a British consul in Seoul who was captured and spent the war in Tiger Camp and other POW camps, does not appear. This is a telling omission. Blake became a Soviet agent, a mole in the British secret service, after he was repatriated, and subsequently was found out and sent to prison, only to escape and flee to Moscow where he lives today. He has published his account of being questioned by Soviet interrogators while a POW, in which he insists his conversion to Marxism pre-dated his meetings with the Soviets in North Korea. He recruited them

as his future bosses, in other words.

6. The list doesn't include a U.S. military officer named Black even though there were three U.S. officers named Black who were reported to be POWs and whose bodies were not recovered. Alexander Orlov, who worked as a translator and interrogator out of Soviet corps headquarters in Antung, Manchuria, said that he interviewed an American officer named Black for a newspaper story he wrote while in the war zone.

7. On the list are several U.S. soldiers—1st Lt. Stanley E. Tabor, Gilmer Newton (identified as an enlisted man) and Lt. James Lee Boydston—who are listed on U.S. rolls as KIA. Boydston's remains were returned; Gilbert is BNR, as a first lieutenant. The Communists' citing of ranks may be wrong; likewise, a prisoner might give an incorrect rank to the enemy. Clearly if they were KIA, the Soviets could not have interrogated them. But their identifications and other personal effects could have fallen into Soviet or Chinese hands.

8. The list mentions three Air Force POWs—Hart, Weese and Van Voorhis—who may have been POWs but who were MIA/BNR. They were reported by fellow crewmen to have survived a shoot-down of their plane, but were never repatriated. They were all from a B-29 crew whose other members were imprisoned in China for nearly two years after the armistice as "war criminals."

9. Fifteen on this list were among the first 50 POWs acknowledged by the Communists through the International Red Cross in August 1950. They were all then held at the Tiger Camp. The "510 List" should probably be renamed "Tiger Camp List."

The U.S. Army's special team of analysts, Task Force Russia, carefully worked the list with the help of the Pentagon's numerous data bases. Their first finding was that, while they did "not doubt that Russian officials may have described it in February 1992" as a list of POWs, "interrogated by the Soviets, some of whom were then sent to China," in the analysts' opinion, the description "does not withstand scrutiny."

Their other findings were that:

"b. Nothing in this list points to the Soviet Union as the custodian of U.S. POWs.

"c. The list is actually a composite of numerous separate files of different categories of personnel.

"d. The list purports to be of American POWs, yet contains in addition to POWs the names of missionaries, CIA personnel and personnel who were never POWs at all.

"e. The list purports to cover the years 1950-51, yet numerous personnel, such as the Arnold (B-29) crew, the two CIA employees, and others were captured by the Communists in 1952 and 1953.

"f. By compiling just a list of names rather than allowing access to the files themselves, the Russian side has shorn away most of the historical context which would have provided many more answers, especially for the numerous POWs who died in enemy hands or for those whose names cannot be identified.

"g. The list appears to have been hurriedly and carelessly put together by the Russians to satisfy the most superficial requirements of the U.S. side."

Other than that, it was a fine list.

The next significant lists handed over by the Russians were just-created rosters of American pilots and other airmen whose names had been culled from documents that were not released but which the Russians said had been found in the records of the 64th Fighter Aviation Corps, the major—but not the only—Soviet military organization involved in the Korean War.

The implication—always denied by the Soviets—was that the men on these lists had been interrogated by Soviet intelligence, either military or civilian. There was another batch of documents—40 at first, then 49, then 56, as more documents were passed—consisting of interrogation reports of individual pilots. These were the answers to the questionnaires that many American POWs were asked to respond to, covering the details of their unit, the training they'd had, technical information about the aircraft they flew, etc. The Russians maintain that, while the interrogation "protocols" as they call them were in their archives, for the most part they only wrote the questions for the Chinese to ask the POWs. That method was used, according to some repatriated POWs, but there was also direct interrogation of Americans by the Soviets.

With that list in hand, it was possible for the U.S. analysts to simply match interrogation subjects and returned aviators, and note the results. The main result was to find that 11 of the airmen on the list of those interrogated had never been repatriated. They were still MIA/BNR. And from the Russians' own admission, they had been last seen alive by their Soviet and Chinese interrogators. Here are the 11 men, never repatriated, for whom Soviet documents exist proving they were alive in their custody:

1. Hart, Alvin D. Jr. A/1C. (described as in captivity in debriefings of 1955 U.S. Air Force repatriates from China.) from Saginaw, Mich.

2. Weese, Henry Douglas, l/Lt. (same crew as Hart and Van Voorhis.) from Susanville, Calif.

3. Van Voorhis, Paul E. l/Lt. (survived a shoot-down, according to debriefing of 1955 repatriates from China.) from Glen Cove, N.Y.

4. Johnson, Johnny M. Sgt. MIA 23 Oct. 51; B-29 crewman.

5. McDonough, Capt. Charles E.; RB-45 pilot, shot down December 1950 captured, died after interrogation by Soviets.

6. Bergmann, Louis H. Sgt.—St. Paul, Minn. B-29 crew. MIA 12 April 1951.

7. Unruh, Capt. Halbert Caloway. B-26.

8. Tenney, Capt. Albert Gilbert. F-86.

9. Reid, Albert J. Jr. Sgt. B-29.

10. Harker, Charles Abbot, Jr. 2nd lt. F-84.

11. Niemann, Robert Frank. 1/Lt. F-86.

The Russians have turned over a substantial number of actual documents, too, making it possible to trace not only names but the shoot-downs that correspond in many cases to the reports of casualties or loss of aircraft that exist in U.S. records. But they don't always match, and that prompts long, involved discussions about which day a particular American pilot or soldier may have been in enemy hands, and whose map coordinates best describe the reality of the day, decades ago, when the men and their aircraft, say, were last seen.

The Russians say they possess records of 1,607 shoot-downs of American aircraft during the Korean War by Soviet aircraft or anti-aircraft batteries. That doesn't exactly correspond with the numbers the U.S. brought away from the war, but then the likelihood of that happening is next to zero. There were a lot of different people shooting at a lot of different aircraft for three years in the Korean War. And most of the time, they weren't as concerned about keeping score as they were about ending up on the wrong side of the scorecard.

The Russian side also has released a figure—not a list, a figure—of 262 U.S. Air Force fliers they say were downed in aerial combat or by anti-aircraft fire, who were then taken prisoner and, then, "passed through the interrogation point."

When the figure was announced, only four of the 262 were mentioned by name—all unit commanders: Col. John Knox Arnold Jr., of Tallahassee, Fla., Col. Harold Fischer, of Las Vegas, Nev., Lt. Col. Edwin L. Heller of Pennsylvania and Col. Walker "Bud" Mahurin. And the "interrogation point" was not described or identified.

Soviet veterans who participated in interrogations of American POWs, however, have mentioned at least two: at Sinuiju, North Korea, just across the Yalu from Antung, Manchuria, and in Khabarovsk, in the USSR. Intelligence gathered during the war said another Soviet interrogation center was located in Antu, in Manchuria not far from the Soviet frontier.

Despite announcing that 262 American aviators were interrogated, the Russians say they have been able to find interrogation reports for only 56 of the POWs. And they have yet to reveal the exact source of the 262 figure.

The 56 interrogation reports that have been released don't help explain much, either.

Some of the documents and lists record the personal effects—money, a unit scarf, photos, library card—that a downed pilot had in his possession.

The Russians say they're not sure why they have been able to locate only 56 reports, but that it may be because not every American aviator warranted an extensive interrogation.

Some of the 56 reports they released are from relatively low-ranking crew members and include routine information. One report consisted of only a few pages of questions put to a pilot who had only flown a few missions in Korea before being captured. And they don't include the interrogation report of some repatriated pilots such as Air Force Capt. Lawrence Bach, of Great Falls, N.D., who said they were questioned by Soviet officers. Bach, the first F-86 pilot shot down in the war and thus a high priority subject for Soviet interrogation, was interrogated by a number of Soviet personnel, who readily identified themselves as such, including a Soviet fighter pilot.

Nor do the 56 reports include one for Mahurin—one of the squadron commanders named in the summary of 262 interrogated pilots.

Orlov, in the September 1994 meeting, suggested one explanation: "There is no correlation between the 249 captured Americans and the 262. I believe that, just like in the "List of 59," there may be some repeat names or it may include some non-U.S. personnel. Again, I'm hypothesizing. I also believe that the number 262 referring to those who went through the interrogation point does not necessarily refer to people. It could have been just their documents..."

Thus there are lists of people, of POWs, and of interrogated POWs, but also lists of documents that refer to the personal papers of people who were not present when the original list was drawn up. If only the Russians could say exactly what each list they present does refer to.

The Russians have turned over two additional lists comprised of the actual names of pilots and crew members—one with 56 names and another with 71 names. They say these men were also interrogated while POWs.

The interrogations were conducted by Chinese and North Koreans, some of the former Soviet interrogators say, using questions Soviet intelligence officers posed in advance. Some names appear on both lists, others just on one. And the names on the lists of 56 and 71 don't coincide exactly with the names on the 56 interrogation reports that have been released.

The only explanation offered by the Russian side for that discrepancy is perhaps that the pilots' papers, or Soviet records pertaining to them, may have been the source for the name being listed, not the pilot himself. The answer would surely be somewhere in the original documents that formed the basis for the Russian list. The Russians say they don't know.

But the disparities remain unanswered, leaving the American side with questions and doubts about not only the documents, summaries, partial files and lists the Russians have turned over, but the ones they haven't yet revealed.

The Soviet interrogation reports citing individual POWs caused concern among the Russian representatives who were wary of how the POWs they questioned and who were repatriated would react to having the papers released. Viktor Mukhin, a Russian archivist, cited another reason: "First we gave you the list, then the interrogations, at your request. Why didn't we give you the interrogations immediately? Because, on our side, we feared repressive measures against your pilots. But Ambassador Toon repeatedly assured us it wouldn't ruin reputations, that nothing bad would happen. So Gen. Volkogonov said, 'alright, give them all of the documents.'"

Col. Sergei Osipov, one of the Russian representatives on the commission, has suggested that the names on the overall lists for whom there are no interrogation "protocols," or papers, "are from all sources in the ministry of defense, the ministry of security—we checked for the name of every POW, and as a result, the list contains every name, independent of whether or not detailed information was available.

"There was foreign information and even radio sources. For example, Herbert Lowe, lieutenant, we took his name from the address he gave on Pyongyang Radio. In the main political directorate, Mr. Korotkov prepared their documents and they used all kinds of information from the Chinese and Korean services and local press analysis. All of these names were included on our list. I assure you that if a name appeared without further explanation, we didn't know anything else."

The absence of some original documents in the material handed over by the Russians was explained by one Russian representative, who observed that from his experience in North Korea and Manchuria during the war, "documents don't exist for everything" having to do with POWs in Korea because "you could get sent back to Moscow for keeping records."

That reasoning flies in the face of the traditional view of Soviet officials and bureaucrats—even those involved in a large, semi-covert military operation in the 1950s—as dedicated record-keepers and paper-filers. Nothing the American representatives on the commission have seen so far leads to the view that records were not kept of the incidents that are under investigation. Whether or not they still exist is another question.

Occasionally, names of American POWs that have not been on any of the lists presented by the Russian suddenly surface in conversation among the commission delegates, in their working sessions. In the April 1993 meeting, Orlov added a couple of new names to the growing list of American

POWs who showed up in the Russian archives. He said "there is information of 2/Lt. Michael DeMoyne, on Lt. Smith, Lt. Harvey…that's what we just found and we're looking for more. However, there's a classification problem. I ask the authorities to accelerate the declassification process." The POWs were not further identified.

At the same meeting, Mazurov, the Russian security service representative, added a few more names to the list of American POW names found in the archives:

"…we can surface the names of Bergman, Louis, born in 1926, a master sergeant and a radio man; of Han, Joseph, born in 1919, a captain and engineer for radio location; and Kunega, Dedzin, born in 1925, a pilot. All were crew members of a B-29 shot down on May 10, 1951. We do not know anything more about them."

At the commission's meeting in August 1994, Mazurov made it clear that, from the perspective of the state security organization he represents, the American side has gotten everything it is going to get from archives dealing with intelligence and highly classified material.

"It is a fact," he said, "that I personally searched for documents regarding POWs. There were no such documents…In total, we have passed information to the American side on 530 people from the Korean War. This is fragmentary information; the final fates of these people cannot be determined based on these documents…Those persons who conducted this work and signed the documents bear the full responsibility for the information they provided.

"If we had not wanted to pass these lists, then there would neither be any representatives from our service here, nor would you have any list on these 510 persons, such as you do have."

He then launched into one of the Russian side's frequent denunciations of the testimony of Col. Gavril Korotkov, who has sworn that he was part of a Soviet POW-interrogation program directed out of Khabarovsk, in which more than 100 American POWs were questioned and attempts were made to indoctrinate and recruit them into the Soviet Union's service. He said that some of the POWs who were not repatriated were undoubtedly shipped elsewhere on Soviet territory.

"Understand that if we receive hard evidence, we can work with that. But, we cannot do anything with such evidence as given by Korotkov. We need documents, documents, documents."

* * *

One of the most provocative documents the Russians have released was an account of a conversation between Stalin and Chou En-Lai in which they discussed the POW situation in Korea. Stories about the exchange have described Stalin as proposing that the Communist forces in Korea hold back 20 percent of the allied POWs, presumably as bargaining chips.

But a close look at the memo suggests a different interpretation. Stalin says:

"Concerning the proposal that BOTH SIDES temporarily withhold 20 percent of the prisoners of war and that they return all of the remaining prisoners of war—the Soviet delegation will not touch this proposal and it remains in reserve for Mao Tse-tung."

The phrase "both sides" has been interpreted by the joint commission's analysts as referring to the Communist Chinese and the North Koreans. But that is hardly clear from the original memo, which leaves unstated the precise source of the proposal. Was it Stalin, or Mao, or some other party to the many-sided talks surrounding the issue of POWs at the UN, in Korea and many other venues? And did "both sides" refer to both Communist forces then fielding forces against the UN Command, or to the Communist and UN "sides?"

More documentation would appear to be necessary before coming to a final conclusion about what the Stalin-Chou memo actually says regarding the POW negotiations in Korea.

Later in the same memo, in a discussion about a proposal to hand over POWs to a "neutral" country that would determine their fates, Stalin's thinking is made clear. He worries about who will pay for the POWs' maintenance if they are sent temporarily to a third country, then says the proposal "could be accepted, but one must keep in mind that the Americans do not want to hand over all the prisoners of war.

"The Americans will keep some of them, intending to recruit them. It was like this with our prisoners of war; every day now we catch several prisoners of war whom the Americans send to our country. They detain prisoners of war not because, as the Americans often claim, the prisoners say that they do not want to return, but in order to use the prisoners for espionage."

In the immediate postwar years, the U.S. and Britain did dispatch numbers of trained agents selected from the ranks of Soviet dissidents and defectors back to their homeland, on missions designed to agitate for liberation from Soviet rule and to support the suppressed democratic forces still residing behind the Iron Curtain.

Those missions failed, but they apparently did not fail to come to Stalin's attention.

* * *

A few of the Russian documents are interesting not because they reveal what happened to any one individual, but because they shed light on the way the Communists were thinking about POWs during the Korean War—and they thought about POWs constantly.

In April 1953, the first POWs the Communists were to officially release were being prepared for freedom. In addition to a group of 147 military POWs, supposedly chosen because they needed urgent medical attention, the Communists had agreed to liberate a group of civilians they had been holding since the first days of the war, missionaries, diplomats and foreign correspondents from Seoul and Kaesong. There were three main groupings: French, British and American—and they were released in that order, returned to the west via Pyongyang and Moscow.

As this process got underway, U.S. authorities eager to learn who was about to be freed, and who had not survived the months of imprisonment, directed inquiries to the North Koreans via authorities in the Soviet Union, which acted as North Korea's official spokesman at the UN and in many other respects.

On April 6, 1953, a Soviet official, G. Arkadyev, sent the following telegram to the foreign minister, Molotov, in Moscow, asking for instructions:

"To our inquiry as to whether the People's Democratic Republic of Korea would affirm the request for repatriation of those still alive of the 13 American citizens located in North Korea and interned by Korean authorities at the beginning of the war; Kim Il-Sung stated that the government of the People's Democratic Republic of Korea would not oppose the repatriation of the aforementioned American citizens.

"As far as specific information regarding interned American citizens that are still alive, Kim Il-Sung added that it would seem advisable (rest of sentence underlined) not to give this information to the American charge d'affaires.

"If we inform the Americans now, that the government of the People's Democratic Republic of Korea is ready to repatriate the indicated Americans, but elaborate that they are no longer alive, this will create an unpleasant situation. If we wait to receive the specifics and it turns out that these Americans are not alive, we can say that they died from American bombing. As we have Com. Pushkin's resolution I suggest drafting a response to (U.S. Ambassador Jacob) Beam in the form of a verbal demarche."

Seven American civilian POWs survived and were repatriated that month. None of those who died in captivity were killed by American bombing, although American bombs did kill or wound some U.S. military

POWs in other POW camps in North Korea, where UN prisoners were often stockaded in unmarked buildings and pens.

* * *

One large batch of documents turned over by the Russians in April 1993 consisted of 351 pages of reports of Soviet anti-aircraft batteries stationed in North Korea during the war.

Because so many MIA reports deal with aircraft shoot-downs, and disappearances of aircraft, the material held the promise of providing the answers for at least some of the questions that remain about MIAs in Korea. But the papers lacked crucial information.

They did include the names of many Soviet military officers, since each report carried the signature of the reporting officer. But most of the documents are apparently immediate post-action reports, done by the ground crew commander and completed before the Russian search and salvage parties did their work, because they lack crucial information about the pilots or crews of the downed aircraft, except to note instances in which parachutes of survivors or U.S. search planes were sighted.

Before a shoot-down could be credited to a particular anti-aircraft battery, more investigation was necessary, Soviet veterans say.

* * *

Among the thousands of documents that have been released from the former Soviet archives over the past few years in the bilateral search for missing American POWs, a few illustrate both the powerful forces that were involved in keeping the truth hidden and the potential there is now for clearing the historical record of falsehoods and awful uncertainty.

One such document is a brief, two-sentence message sent on Nov. 3, 1951, from a "Boguslavskij" to "Comrade FOKIN." The message says:

"I am sending the responses to your questions via diplomatic mail on 5 Nov. 51. Prisoner FARLER's detailed testimony was sent by mail to Deputy Military Minister General-Lieutenant LOBANOV."

The message also bears several illegible signatures on the bottom of the page, but that is all. It seems to be a routine, ordinary document that would hardly be worth mentioning in the course of an international search for missing servicemen, much less singled out to be copied, translated and placed in the mounting public record of the first major effort to account for missing American POWs through the archives of a former communist superpower.

But the document is at least a sign that up to a certain date, presumably the first week in November, 1951, one U.S. prisoner was alive and being interrogated. "Prisoner Farler" was an American pilot, Air Force Capt. Hugh Phillip Farler, of Dayton, Ohio.

Farler was a navigator, bombardier and radar operator. The pilot of the plane he was on when it was shot down on June 1, 1951, Capt. Robert A. Fredericksen, gave a statement to Air Force investigators after he was repatriated.

He said Farler suffered a shrapnel wound in his right shoulder and severe burns on his ankles when he parachuted from their burning aircraft. Fredericksen was moved to Camp 5 and never saw Farler again, but other prisoners who saw him later at Pak's Palace, the POW compound in Pyongyang, said guards there placed Farler "in a hole for a long time" after which he died of beri beri and malnutrition.

In August 1953, when both sides in the war were obliged by the terms of the armistice to account for all of the prisoners in their custody, Farler's name was on a list of 1,022 names the Communists gave to the UN Command of U.S. prisoners they said had died in their camps.

His name was the third of nine Air Force POWs on the list, which noted that Farler died Dec. 22, 1951, of beri-beri.

Number five on the same 1953 list was Capt. Ronald Harry. The Communist prison camp authorities reported that he had died July 14, 1951, also of beri-beri.

It wasn't so. Ronald Harry was repatriated at the end of the war.

Chapter Nine

Taking the Trophies

"And when the search groups went out, they would make sure that they were able to verify, by taking the trophies, or by getting signed statements from the local authorities, from the Koreans."

—M/Sgt. Danz F. Blasser,
analyst for Task Force Russia,
describing how Soviet pilots or anti-aircraft batteries
were awarded credit for shooting down U.S. aircraft.

"Why were our search groups in such a hurry to seize the U.S. aircraft? Because there were incidents when the Koreans who arrived there earlier would take the aircraft into their possession.

—Retired Soviet colonel Alexander Orlov,
head of the Korean War Working Group for the Russian side of the
Joint Commission, at the September 1944 meeting.

Lawrence V. Bach Jr., of Grand Forks, North Dakota, was one of the first trophies.

Trophies could get rough treatment in Korea. And they always attracted a lot of attention from the Russians.

Bach's squadron of F-86 Sabrejet fighters—the first sent into combat in Korea—had only been flying missions against the Soviet MIGs for a few weeks when he was shot down over Sinuiju, North Korea, on Dec. 27, 1950. Captured by North Korean regulars, Bach was taken to their field headquarters where a Soviet officer questioned him with the help of an English-speaking Japanese interpreter.

Then more Soviet officers showed up, including one who pulled out his Soviet air force identification card, told Bach he was a fighter pilot, too, and said it had probably been him who had shot Bach down. Small, violent world, Korea. The Russians drove him across the river into Manchuria, where he was fed and held prisoner at a jet airfield near Antung.

At night, he shared a room with two of the Russians, part of the growing cadre of KGB and Soviet military intelligence personnel tracking the war and the UN prisoners who surfaced out of the daily fighting. The Russians were friendly enough and tried to fraternize when not working, Bach said, but during interrogation sessions they would threaten to hand him back over to the North Koreans if he didn't cooperate and answer their questions.

But they were too interested in what Bach might be able to tell them about this new, powerful fighter that the U.S. Far East Air Force was using. And they knew there was keen interest in the Kremlin as well. On Dec. 31, a copy of Bach's interrogation report recorded by the Soviet security officers was sent to Moscow, and soon it was being circulated to Stalin and the entire Soviet politburo.[1]

Bach spent the next two-and-a-half years in a rickety shelter on the fringes of what seemed like a large POW camp, in the company of a very few people, mostly Chinese and North Korean sentries.

From time to time, for nothing better to do, they would hustle him out of his hootch, order him to kneel on the ground, put a gun barrel in one ear and tell him it was all over.

Then he'd wait for the click, or the bullet.

It was always the click. Followed by laughing from the guards.

Ernest C. Dunning Jr. was another trophy, six months later.

Dunning, then a first lieutenant flying an F-80, was on a dawn recon mission on June 24, 1951, when he was shot down over North Korea. He managed to eject, but when he landed he was left with a broken leg, unable to run or hide. The North Koreans picked him up, but Chinese troops soon came along and—"thank God," he says, because the North Koreans were known to practice more cruelty on POWs—took him away.[2]

Dunning and his captors took shelter in a cave to avoid the bombs from American aircraft until later in the day, when a truck arrived "with two Russian interrogators," he recalls. They were dressed in civilian clothes, khakis, open shirts. "One of them was a pretty rough guy, short, heavy. He shoved me into the Chinese guards. Seemed kind of bitter. Slugged me around a little bit."

The other Russian "was tall, with glasses. That night they hauled me someplace in a truck. A doctor looked at my leg, but didn't do anything, except gave me a bottle of booze."

The next day, still somewhere in North Korea, a total of seven Soviet officers and NCOs appeared, and the interrogation started. "They wanted to know about people, who was in command and so forth." The interrogation lasted one to three days, he can't remember. "I'd lost track of time," said Dunning.

He was blindfolded and driven across a bridge into Manchuria. He knew he was in China because he could hear the bombs and see their flash as they struck Sinuiju, North Korea, to the south. By timing how long it took the sound to catch up with the flash, he calculated he was about 11 miles from ground zero on the southern river bank. He was kept there about ten days, by himself, no other POWs, in a three-by-six-foot room.

Sometime in July, he was driven back into North Korea, where he spent the rest of the war. "I never saw the Russians again," he said. "I don't know of anybody by name, but I'm sure there were some (fellow POWs) who were taken to Russia and killed there. They took me into China, and I'm sure they took some of our people up into Russia, too, and I think that's what they were thinking of doing with me."

That's what the Russians were thinking of doing with Roland W. Parks, too.

Parks, one of the last Korean War POWs to be released from prison—from China, in May 1955—believes he came as close as anyone to being shipped to the Soviet Union, and still live to tell about it.

"You don't know how scary that was," he said, "how close you can come to not being here." Here's how close he came.

On Sept. 4, 1952, Lt. Parks was part of an F-86 flight into MIG Alley over North Korea. When the MIGs came up to take on him and his squadron mates, a running air battle ensued during which he became separated from his flight. The last messages his buddies heard him broadcast were that his gyro and radio compasses weren't working and he didn't know his position. He couldn't see them, and they couldn't see him.

When his fuel was gone, Parks ejected. He was sure he was over a peninsula. What he didn't know until he hit the ground was that he had jumped into a Soviet military zone on the Liaotung peninsula of Manchuria, between the city of Dairen and Port Arthur.

The Soviet officers who began interrogating him suggested that if he didn't cooperate, they could just report he was killed in the crash of his plane and that would be the end of it. The Chinese didn't know he was there. His squadron sure didn't know.

"The Russians told me they were taking me to Moscow. I had told them I did not want to be turned over to the Chinese, and that's probably why they told me they were taking me to Russia. I thought they were taking me to the Siberian salt mines. I had made up my mind that if we kept going north toward Siberia I was going to go over the hill at all costs."[3]

After two weeks at a compound on the Soviet naval base at Port Arthur, Parks' concern grew. He was issued cold-weather clothing, boots, overcoat and heavy shirts, and ordered to put them on. "We're leaving," the senior Soviet officer told him. For where? "To Russia."

When he asked the Russians why they needed to send him to Siberia, Parks was told "because diplomats must resolve these cases, but you will go and be with other Americans like you."

In the end—Parks still doesn't know why—the Russians didn't take him to Siberia. Perhaps the Chinese outside the Soviet compound gates got wind of the fact the Russians were holding an American prisoner, and they said he's ours. For whatever reason, they turned him over to the Chinese. But not before trying to hide their tracks.

"The Russians took away from me everything Russian that they had given me, destroying any evidence that I had been in Russian hands."

Parks is convinced from his experience that while he was spared, other American pilots were not. Issuing him winter clothes for Siberia may have been a brainwashing gambit for him, or the Russians might have simply changed their minds. But he believes U.S. officials over the years have ignored the evidence that this was no game for a lot of U.S. POWs who found themselves in China—and a trophy for both the Chinese and the Soviets.

A significant share of the documents and testimony collected from Soviet sources by the American side of the joint commission deals with the small, elite group of men Bach, Dunning and Parks belonged to in Korea: fighter pilots.

Many of those fighter pilots who were repatriated tell similar stories about encountering the Russians, as interrogators and otherwise.

John W. Zwiacher and Michael DeArmond, two F-86 pilots who were held together as POWs for many months, had extensive dealings with Soviet officers. DeArmond's "whole interrogation in Sinuiju was run by the North Koreans and this Russian," he said.[4]

Zwiacher said for one week of his imprisonment, he was held at "an encampment of some kind." He was often blindfolded, but he could hear large power generators, men speaking Russian and the music of a balalaika, a traditional Russian mandolin-type instrument.

Zwiacher's correct conclusion: he was in custody at the site of a Soviet anti-aircraft battery.

Harry Ettinger, of Cardiff, Calif., was a Navy Skyraider pilot, shot down in December 1951 and held prisoner for the rest of the war. During the course of his imprisonment, he was marched to a number of different locations, "stopping at interrogation centers along the way." He remembers "a number of Soviet personnel" being in the Wonsan area, "and up in northwest Korea, they had some Polish troops."

He saw a lot of the countryside, the hard way. One North Korean captor tried to ransom him, he said, but to no avail. But despite his volunteering to give an account of his POW time in great detail, the Navy debriefers didn't seem very interested. "I was just missing, as far as the Navy was concerned. I was not debriefed on this. I gave them my story in about 800 quick words."

Joseph Hearn was an Air Force navigator captured in April 1951 who ended up in a camp near Manpojin that became known as "Tiger Camp" for the fierce madman who ran the place. He had many different interrogators, he said.

"The Russians threatened not to feed me" unless he talked, "but the Chinese treated me okay." The Russians wore civilian clothes, "two I definitely remember, because they worked in pairs. One would question you, the other one would get belligerent."

When they found out that a prisoner had a bourgeois family background, from the mercantile or professional class, "they didn't like that one bit," said Hearn. Anybody that was from the class of the workers, or the farmers," they had little tolerance for. That meant trouble for a number of pilots, who were frequently college-educated, from middle-class or upper-middle-class backgrounds.

They always seemed to get worse treatment than the rest, he recalls. Less food, more beatings, severe harassment, or often total neglect.

But his outstanding memory of North Korea, he said, is the sign he saw as he and some other POWs were being trucked across the Yalu River into Manchuria for a little more interrogation. The name of the company that produced the metal for the bridge was plainly visible on the struts as their truck passed by, said Hearn.

"It read, 'U S Steel.' I could never get over that. Here we were in one prison, going to another one, and the sign on the bridge says 'U S Steel.'"

And he knew they weren't anywhere close to home.

* * *

After Task Force Russia was disbanded in the summer of 1993, having argued the case for POW transfers that could have entailed close to 1,000 or more prisoners only to have the head of the Defense POW/MIA Office disavow the findings, some of the Pentagon analysts assisting the joint commission set a new direction in their research.

The 77-page report had been virtually disowned by the Pentagon officials supervising the research for the commission. But some of the analysis pointed in a slightly different direction.

By June of 1994, the Korean War working group had gone on record as saying that "large numbers of American POWs were not transported to the Soviet Union."

But a small number of American POWs—that was another matter.[6]

And based on the Korean War documents passed to the joint commission so far, if only a limited number of American POWs had been shipped to the USSR, they were probably fighter pilots—specifically, F-86 fighter pilots.

To test this "working hypothesis," as it was called, the analysts ran the MIA numbers: what percentage of various groups of MIAs, given the circumstances under which they were reported missing, could fall into the category of transferred POWs. The fighter pilots came out ahead.

They calculated the MIA rate among pilots of the various U.S. aircraft flown in Korea—the pilots who were not recovered, confirmed dead or repatriated and either were seen to bail out safely or were lost in circumstances that suggested they could have been taken prisoner—and then transferred.

The F-86 rate was based on 56 shootdowns. Of those incidents, only 15 pilots were repatriated from POW status, and one set of remains was returned, leaving 31—or 55 percent—as MIAs.

[Although a larger base figure might not change the MIA ratio, 56 shootdowns is a conservative number. The definitive study, "The United States Air Force in Korea, 1950-53" by Robert Futrell, cites 78 F-86s downed in air-to-air combat alone. Soviet anti-aircraft batteries also counted for hundreds of aircraft losses. And "operational failure"—engine trouble or fuel exhaustion and the like—could force a fighter pilot to eject over enemy territory just as often as a shell. The most incredible number comes from Soviet pilots who, according to Russian members of the joint commission, claimed to have downed 400 F-86s. At least one Soviet air force commander (Kozhedub) was relieved during the Korean War for padding his unit's shootdown totals.]

The American side's calculations placed the F-86 pilots at the top of the aviation MIA list—and made them prime candidates for a scenario in which highly trained, highly skilled professionals flying an aircraft the Soviets wanted to know everything about, were singled out to be exploited for intelligence purposes.

Another link in the fighter-pilot theory was the testimony of Avraham Shifrin, a former Soviet military attorney. Shifrin said a Gen. Djagadze, who was assigned during the Korean War to an aviation unit commanded by Joseph Stalin's son, Vasili, told him that during the Korean War he had ferried six U.S. pilot-prisoners from Korea to Kansk,in the former Soviet Union.[5]

There is universal agreement on the F-86 being the biggest intelligence target of the Korean War for the Communists. It was fast, deadly, the most advanced U.S. fighter at the time. And the Soviets were vitally interested in how it worked, what it could do and what it couldn't.

Korea provided a good test case for such a weapon, as well as the techniques for copying or countering it. And if the Cold War turned suddenly hot in Europe—where most bets said the real war between Communism and democracy would be fought—the F86 could be expected to show up there, too.

Orlov, who had been assigned as an interrogator and aircraft radio monitor at the headquarters of the 64th Fighter Aviation Corps, home base for Soviet pilots who had to take on the F-86 jockeys virtually every day of the war, made it clear that the sleek fighter was "of great interest to us" and that fresh intelligence from the pilots was crucial:

"As for the F-86, it was the only aircraft of U.S. production that was a rival to the MIG-15. So its tactics and characteristics were very important to the 64th Corps. We had a group of officers sent from the general staff to the 64th Corps specifically to find out about those planes.

"First, we had to organize radio intercepts to track takeoffs in order to allow our pilots to intercept them. But in April 1951, when there was heavy fighting over Antung, around the 7th and 12th of April, we first started capturing pilots and gear from F-86 Sabres. It was critical for us to get Sabre information.

"First of all, we needed to know about the pressure suits, the range-finders, the MK-18 (radar) sight, the catapult and rescue system…Our mission was to clarify these issues.

"The North Koreans kept all of the prisoners in their camps. We didn't know where they were. We organized our work. The air advisor to the Korean Army staff, Col. Petrochev and the intelligence adviser—I don't know what happened to him—well, Col. Petrochev told us what was needed. He gave us a list of questions, which we then wrote out in English, and the Koreans gave us a list of POWs.

"They were listed by speciality, not as individuals, but as navigators, pilots and so forth. We sent the questions to the POWs based on their specialties. We would hand over the questions to the Koreans and they brought back the answers. Then he would compile reports and forward them to corps."

"But sometimes…we had to break the rules to get information

quickly. That's why we met with POWs directly a few times. I took part in two such cases, and perhaps the others who replaced me did the same. In one case, that of Lt. Col. Black, the subject matter was not intelligence but political. It was for an article in Pravda, to 'reveal' the bad Americans.

"The reporter, Kravchenko, didn't know English, so he invited me to serve as his interpreter.

"We were in civilian clothes. We drove for two hours or so—there were no interviews at headquarters—but I don't recall exactly where the interview took place. The article was published on 14 August 1951.

"In the other case it was critical to get information to the design bureau on the range-finder and thusly, in the same manner, away from headquarters, we met a young pilot, maybe 20 years old, and had a long discussion. We tried to make corrections to the design we had. And that was all...We just wanted technical data. For example, at what distance could an F-86 engage? How did pilots fight G-stress? That's why those interrogations were not preserved. Of course, later, others did this work. But they probably worked under the same informal system."

While military officers like Orlov conducted some interrogations, and made preparations for others, some American POWs were also interrogated by Soviet security agents. They worked for the MGB, which later was renamed the KGB.

A telegram released by the Russian side of the joint commission dealing with the capture of 11 members of a B-29 crew shot down on July 24, 1952, said that they had already been interrogated by Soviet and Chinese forces. The telegram then adds:

"Representatives from the MGB USSR and China have arrived from Peking to conduct further prisoner interrogations, in order to gain more precise information. The interrogation will be continued in Pekton (Pyoktong)." Pyoktong was the site of a major Communist POW camp near the Yalu River border with Manchuria.

U.S. Far East Air Force commanders were keenly aware, since their pilots were flying sorties into North Korea and—although it was officially forbidden territory—Manchuria, that the "sensitive" items of equipment on the F-86, such as a new automatic gunsight and advanced radar, might fall into the hands of unfriendly military and intelligence officers. Air Force studies assessed whether the F-86 and other advanced aircraft should be sent to the theater fully equipped, or minus some of the latest electronic gear, to prevent it winding up on Soviet drawing boards. Few concessions were made to the potential loss of technology.

The three planes on the Soviets' most-wanted list were the F-86, the F-94, another interceptor-fighter, and the RB-45, a reconnaissance plane. With all of them vulnerable to shootdowns and accidents, "it can be assumed that Soviet technical intelligence personnel are available within the present theater of combat," one Air Force study said, "to exploit any such material possible."[6]

Some of those "Soviet technical intelligence personnel" thought they had bagged another F-86 pilot when Nick Flores, who had just escaped from a North Korean POW camp, was marched off to talk to them on Aug. 1, 1952.

Flores was a Marine corporal, a truck driver captured Nov. 28, 1950, near Koto-Ri, when Chinese divisions swarmed south, overwhelming the northernmost units of the UN forces. Taken to a North Korean POW camp, Flores made repeated attempts to escape, but was always caught.

On one attempt, he was well beyond the POW camp perimeter when he stumbled into a Soviet anti-aircraft battery that—unbeknownst to him— had just shot down an F-86. When Flores showed up in their midst—wearing an Air Force flight jacket and flying boots some of his fellow POWs had given him to wear for better protection against the elements—the anti-aircraft soldiers assumed he'd just walked away from the downed plane, and turned him over to Soviet military interrogators at the military airfield near Antung, Manchuria.

After four hours of stiff questioning, the Russians realized their mistake and sent him back to the North Koreans.

It's likely that Flores was mistaken for an F-86 pilot, Maj. Felix Asla, Jr. of La Grande, Ore., who was reported missing that day near where Flores was taken prisoner. The serial number of his plane paralleled the number on an aircraft mentioned in a Soviet operational report for Aug. 1, 1952. The aircraft was destroyed and the pilot died in the crash.

According to Air Force casualty data, Asla was in the midst of an air battle when he became separated from his wingman. He twice spoke over his radio, asking if the wingman could see him: "Red Two, do you have me?"

The wingman could not see him, but a U.S. pilot from another flight later reported seeing Asla's plane 15 miles northeast of Sakchu. It had lost its left wing, apparently from aerial combat, and was in a downward spiral from an altitude of 23,000 feet. An aerial search failed to turn up any sign of Asla or his aircraft.

He was never reported a prisoner and was not among the repatriated POWs.

Besides the intense and well-documented Soviet interest in trained F-86 pilots, who out-performed the Soviet pilots in the air by almost every measure, there is the fact that the aircraft itself was a prize trophy.

The Communist Chinese, who depended on the Soviets for all of their modern airplanes, operated a salvage yard in Manchuria during the war to which they dragged a number of downed U.S. planes. At least some were taken into China to use as evidence that the American pilots they were keeping in prison had conducted germ warfare, or had blatantly violated Chinese airspace (which numerous U.S. pilots did, despite UN rules of engagement that forbid flying or bombing north of the Yalu).

But better-preserved wrecks could be useful as training, design and engineering models once the new Communist regime completed its mission in Korea and set about building a military manufacturing base for a more modern Chinese People's Army air force.

And in fact, the Chinese didn't have to make do with scraps entirely. A U.S. Air Force intelligence "memorandum for record" dated Feb. 6, 1952, states "It is indicated that the Chinese Communists may have acquired a flyable F-86" and asks for an immediate detailed report "on missing F-86s and pilots for 26 Jan. 52."

Air Force casualty records of loss incidents list no F-86s downed on that exact date, but do record four during January 1952:

1/Lt. Frank L. Page, on Jan. 6; 1/Lt. Thiel M. Reeves on Jan. 11; 1/Lt. Charles W. Rhinehart on Jan. 29; and 1/Lt. Thomas C. Lafferty on Jan. 31. Only Rhinehart, of Brooklyn, Iowa, is on the Air Force's final MIA list. His aircraft flamed out at 41,000 feet, and he bailed out successfully at 4,000 feet, over water. A search of the area found no sign of him.

The Soviets also wanted the American planes as models, to study, test and observe in operation, as they had done with the U.S. transports and bombers they confiscated during World War II. The Soviet aeronautical engineering community was a proud one, but not too proud to take good ideas from the Americans, especially when they didn't have to pay for them.

Orlov, in keeping with his usual damage-control approach, maintained for some months after the fighter-pilot scenario came to the fore that only parts of U.S. airplanes were salvaged. "We shipped back all of the instruments we captured immediately," he said with an air of knowing authority. "But not whole aircraft. We were just interested in key instruments."

And Orlov's compatriot on the Russian side of the commission also put forward some counter-arguments. Col. Viktor Mukhin, chief of the archives of the Russian general staff, said whatever information the U.S. fighter pilots in Korea possessed would have been too "perishable" to be of much help over the long term.

Moreover, he argued, "it wouldn't have been wise to send groups into Korea and to organize the transport of aircraft under conditions of this difficulty," and finally, "no one would have wanted the bother of transporting them."

Unwise, perhaps, but not too difficult, and not too much bother at all.

A broad network of Russian witnesses have confirmed that fighter planes and at least one advanced U.S. helicopter were shipped back from forced landings or crash sites in Korea to the aircraft engineering and design laboratories in Moscow. The only question is how many, and whether the pilots went with them.

Gen. Lobov, the commander of the 64th Corps, said three operational F-86s were dismantled, crated and shipped back to Moscow during the Korean War. Lobov, in a Dec. 10, 1993 interview, said the first was delivered by the end of 1951.

"In 1952, two additional F-86s were captured, one of them on land (the pilot didn't run to the Yellow Sea), the second one a little bit later on the coastline while the tide was out."

Lobov said he didn't know the fate of the pilots of those planes.

Lobov tracked the intelligence collected on American pilots very closely, as would befit the commander in overall charge of all Soviet pilots in the war zone. Besides the interrogators, like Orlov, who dealt with the POWs once they were captured, his squadrons deployed "search-group expeditions" that were dispatched to the site of a crash or shootdown to certify the incident, evaluate the wreckage and channel any surviving pilots or crew to the proper echelon.

A Soviet aviation veteran of Korea, Valentin Sergeyevich Golobov, who served as an aviation mechanic with the 28th Guards, 151st Fighter Aviation Division in Antung, Manchuria, where Lobov's corps was headquartered, told the joint commission at the September 1994 meeting that the work of the search parties was highly compartmentalized and embedded in tight security, to prevent too many people knowing of their mission.

For anyone associated with the searches or the interrogations to retain "any kind of list or notes regarding any kind of protocols or any kind of notes," Golobov said, "was strictly forbidden. And if anybody showed any interest in any field other than the one he was working in, that usuallyh resulted in serious consequences, including reassignment to the USSR."

Paperwork was kept at a minimum, he said, to increase secrecy— which would explain the important omission on many of the Soviet shootdown reports turned over to the joint commission of the fate of the pilots and crews. "If anything occurred which should have been reported, the only way it was reported was orally, in person, and at the headquarters."

Golobov said the search groups "were made up of one officer and three or four soldiers" who traveled "throughout the Korean territory completing these missions." The search parties were responsible for two basic tasks:

"The first mission was to confirm from Korean agencies the shootdown of U.S. aircraft. The second mission was to destroy Soviet aircraft that crashed on Korean territory, and most importantly, to destroy their armament."

An example of the work of Lobov's "search-group expeditions" on an American shootdown can be found in the operational records of the 64th Fighter Aviation Corps obtained by Paul Cole as part of a six-month Soviet archive research project he undertook for the Defense POW/MIA Office.[7]

Just after 4 p.m. on July 20, 1952, 1/Lt. John Ellis, was among a flight of about 20 F-86s that encountered two MIG squadrons near the Suiho Dam, on the Yalu River. According to Soviet records, Ellis was shot down by a "Sr. Lt. Lepikov." The confirmation came from Lepikov's fellow pilots and gun camera film. Ellis was found alive on the ground and taken prisoner. He was repatriated at the end of the war.

In a telegram he sent to Moscow in 1952, Lobov wrote that on average, "70 Soviet servicemen participate daily in our search groups." He indicated that a special group of pilots under Gen. Blagoveshchenski sent to the war zone for the express purpose of capturing a fully operational F-86 by forcing it down in mid-flight weren't successful. But he said that enough U.S. planes made soft, forced landings on beaches, in shallow water or in rice paddies to provide the Soviets with several nice trophies.

He purported not to know the fate of any of the pilots involved in those incidents, either.

Col. Evegeni Pepelyaev was a Soviet ace of the Korean War, credited with 19 F-86 "kills" for one of Lobov's regiments. He recalled a specific F-86 incident on Oct. 6, 1951, in which a round from his cannon struck just behind the canopy of the U.S. plane.

He believes his shot disabled the plane's ejection mechanism, which would explain why the pilot didn't eject but instead rode the plane to the ground, where it landed on a beach along the Yellow Sea.

He said the pilot was rescued by a U.S. search-and-rescue team and the U.S. attempted to destroy the abandoned fighter by bombing it, but was unsuccessful.

That night, technicians from the 324th Division arrived, cut the wings off and hauled it to the airfield at Antung, Pepelyaev said, where he later sat in the cockpit and noted that all of the instruments and controls were still in perfect working order. He doesn't know what happened to the aircraft after that, but said it's possible it was taken to Moscow.

Pepelyaev said his regiment had the best combat record of any Soviet aviation regiment in the Korean War, responsible for shooting down 100 U.S. and other allied aircraft while suffering only 10 losses.

Yet because of political favoritism, Pepelyaev claimed, only one other pilot from his unit received a Hero's medal—Lt. Fyodor Akimovich Shibanov. Shibanov perished on Oct. 26, 1951.

Pepelyaev confirmed that when an enemy plane was shot down, the intelligence section would send out a search party. When one of the Soviet planes was downed, they would also form a search party and try to retrieve the pilot and wreckage.

He also recalled the project headed by Gen. Blagoveshchenski—but he recalled it with an air of ridicule, because as a fighter pilot, he regarded the assignment as "idiotic." Blagoveshchenski was dispatched to Antung in early 1951 with a detachment of 15 pilots, whose mission was to force an F-86 to land by surrounding it in mid-flight with MIG-15s. The motive was to capture one of the American high-altitude pressure suits the F-86 pilots wore.

Pepelyaev said such a method would be highly unlikely to succeed, and he doesn't know whether the force-down mission ever did entrap an F-86 but recalls that Blagoveshchenski's pilots, who rotated with his unit's pilots, left China to return to the USSR in October 1951.

The U.S. military was equally interested in learning as much as it could about the latest Soviet fighter, to assist American engineers and flight instructors in matching and exceeding the weapons and pilots they met in the skies over Korea.

Within months of the MIG-15 making an appearance in the Far East, the U.S. Air Force was circulating copies of Soviet instructional films for the aircraft through its top intelligence channels. Also helpful were debriefings from several MIG pilots who defected to the West in the early 1950s from Soviet air bases in Europe.

To minimize the chance that a MIG—or worse, a MIG pilot—would fall into enemy hands, the Soviet squadrons were under standing orders to not fly south of the 38th parallel. And there is no record that any Soviet pilots were captured by UN forces.

But with the help of a British naval salvage team, the U.S. was able to pluck one downed MIG out of the ocean just off the coast that was hauled back to friendly territory for study and appraisal.[8]

Orlov, who was not an aviator but had long experience as a ground monitor of U.S. aircraft, said in his opinion it wouldn't have been necessary to force down the F-86s, because they often arrived in "MIG Alley" year the Yalu low on fuel, having spent a considerable fraction of their total supply just reaching the MIGs' home base. If the MIGs simply kept the American pilots engaged long enough, he said, "bingo" an F-86 would be out of fuel and forced to land.

Korean War veterans who flew the F-86 made the same observation about fuel supply and distance from base to battle stations.

At the April 1993 joint commission meeting, Volkogonov detailed the kind of precise information Soviet intelligence possessed on U.S. air losses in Korea. His presentation left no question that the air war over North Korea, no matter being a secret war of not-so-covert support for an ideological ally, had produced volumes of paper and reports for Soviet intelligence:

"There are six files that bear on the fates of 100 or more U.S. pilots. These fall under 'operational actions.' There are six files on the shootdown of 140 U.S. planes by Soviet air defense forces in Korea. We have tried to do a map displaying the locations of the shootdowns, which occurred from 12 October 1951 to 20 May 1952. From these 140 shootdowns, we know 130 locations with an exactness down to 1 to 10 meters."

Besides the exact location, Volkogonov, the available information "describes the fate of every crew. In the archives, we often have the manufacturer's number of the aircraft and other characteristics…documents that contain not only time and place but characteristics and descriptions of what happened to the aircrews and pilots. There are special papers for every case. They are signed by the commander of the Air Defense unit—with maps."

The general said the Russian side was not yet ready to turn over the daily commanders' and individual battery logs of the 64th Fighter Aviation Corps, but he did not foreclose the possibility.

"We think the question cannot be closed," he said, "since the problem remains of the rumors of U.S. pilots on the territory of the USSR. The Russian side thinks that, if it is a myth, we will prove it. If it is a secret, we must find the evidence."

But Volkogonov either misspoke, or was misinformed. For while all the other details he described were provided, the majority of shootdown reports lacked the one piece of information that was so crucial to the U.S. task: whether or not the pilot or crew survived, and was taken prisoner.

Col. Mukhin followed Volkogonov, saying the Russian side's researchers had "worked through thousands of fat files and we've produced a list of 1,057 cases of U.S. shootdowns. This list gives information about air-to-air battles, with dates, times, types of aircraft engaged, the area, and even some data on crew fates."

In most cases, however, Mukhin conceded, "we found that the fate of the crew was unknown."

Several months later, at the 6th Plenum in August 1993, Volkogonov confirmed that Lobov and other witnesses were correct about planes being shipped back to Moscow, and gave a progress report on tracking down one F-86 that was seen by a number of people at the design laboratory:

"It was forced down by a Soviet pilot, but there were Koreans everywhere on the ground. It was forced down on the coast, where it's rocky, and it was a rough landing. Our pilot inquired and was told the U.S. pilot died, but he did not see it personally. The aircraft was dismantled, because the design bureau was interested in sub-assemblies. We contacted the design bureau to try to locate knowledgeable personnel. I think they may find some documents."

Orlov, conceding that his earlier denials were in error, added a few confusing, and contradictory, details: "Here's the pilot's picture in U.S. News and World Report. Our pilot was a famous pilot who downed 20 aircraft—during the attack he shot down the F-86, but the U.S. pilot managed to land near the coast on North Korean territory. The North Koreans rushed to the site. A boat approached and the pilot was taken away."

Then he catches himself. The pilot was taken away? So he survived? Suddenly the story he was so sure of begins to crumble and shake apart. He continues:

"But there are several different versions of the tale. Supposedly, the aircraft was taken to a tunnel by the North Koreans. The U.S. tried to bomb the transport unit, then the Koreans got it into the tunnel, disassembled it, and shipped it north.

"In another version, the pilot Avakumov says the transport of the aircraft he shot down was bombed. It's difficult to say exactly which aircraft was delivered to Moscow."

To be sure, Orlov and Mukhin argue that it would have involved too great a risk, but a number of former employes at the Moscow design laboratory have told the American side that the F-86 pilots did survive and were taken to Moscow along with their aircraft. Identifying numbers of one of the planes may yield a clue to its pilot, but thus far no individual pilot has been linked to any of the aircraft taken to Moscow.[9]

* * *

If the "working hypothesis" is true, that a limited number of U.S. aviators, primarily fighter pilots, were transferred from Korea to the Soviet Union, who were they?

The most likely cases would be aviators who are still unaccounted for and who were lost in circumstances that suggest they survived: forced landing on water, successful bailout, reported captured but not repatriated, disappeared without a trace.

They would be pilots like Lt. Robert F. Niemann, of New Ulm, Minn., or Capt. Albert Tenney, of Hyannis Port, Mass.

Niemann was reported missing on April 12, 1953. He was last sighted by his fellow F-86 pilots, according to Air Force Casualty records, flying at 40,000 feet, just south of the Suiho Reservoir, with a MIG closing in on him. He was declared presumed dead in 1954.

Tenney, another F-86 pilot, was reported MIA on May 3, 1952, on a combat mission along the Yalu River. He was diving low in an attempt to evade a Russian MIG when a fellow pilot radioed him to warn that he was too close to the ground and to pull up. His aircraft was last seen resting atop shallow water after striking the ocean's surface at a low angle about three miles offshore.

Both Tenney's and Niemann's name are on a list of Americans described by the Russians as "U.S. Air Force Personnel Shot Down in Aerial Combat and by Anti-Aircraft Artillery During Military Operations in Korea, Who Transited Through an Interrogation Point." The list was compiled in 1991 or 1992 from original documents in the former Soviet military archives and released to the American side of the joint commission.

But notes accompanying the list say Niemann "died in the Slodzio (Sinuiju) Region," but not when or how, and that Tenney died "in the vicinity of Myagou field," the name of a Soviet airfield just inside Manchuria.

The appearance on a list of airmen who "transited through an interrogation point," but are dead, leaves a number of large gaps and ambiguities that have still not been bridged several years after the first mention of these two pilots by the Russians.

In the case of Niemann, for example, it is now know that he underwent interrogation by the Soviets before he died. Viktor Bushuyev, a Soviet Korean War veteran who served as deputy chief of intelligence for the 64th Fighter Aviation Corps under Gen. Lobov, said he recalled questioning Niemann while he was recovering from wounds or injuries in a war zone hospital.[10]

He remembered him, Bushuyev said, because Niemann refused to answer any questions, saying "it was a violation of international law." But Bushuyev said he knows nothing of the actual circumstances of Niemann's death.

Despite Niemann's reported strict silence when faced by his interrogators, the Soviets were able to identify him from the personal documents they confiscated.

Likewise, in Tenney's case, the Russians acknowledge they confiscated a long list of personal documents and effects from his plane, including identification cards, a chit book, a photograph and a diary.

A search plane that viewed the area later that day reported North Korean vessels, indicating that Tenney could have been removed from the scene by enemy personnel, but no sign of Tenney or his aircraft. Another F-86 pilot on the same mission, William R. Nowadnick, has said that in a brief sighting just before he left the area, the downed aircraft appeared to be unscathed and he saw Tenney still in the cockpit with the canopy closed after the plane had come to rest in the shallow surf.

The circumstances of Capt. Tenney's downing and his aircraft's condition point to the possibility that his F-86 was one of those that officials of Moscow's aeronautial design institute said were shipped there from Korea in 1951 and 1952. In the case of one of the aircraft, Pavel A. Kovalskii, a design engineer, has testified that "we were puzzled by the fact that the aircraft was intact and only the presence of sand in the wheel wells and fuselage, were we able to deduce that the aircraft had landed on the beach...it must have been a wheels-up landing. There was no damage to the fuselage and there was no evident battle damage to the aircaft."

And if Tenney's F-86 was shipped to Moscow, there is at least a possibility that Tenney himself was shipped there.

A key piece of evidence that Tenney and his F-86 were Soviet trophies came from another F-86 pilot. Retired brigadier general Michael DeArmond, who was captured April 21, 1952, about 12 days before Tenney, said one of his interrogators showed him an officers' club "chit book"—a book of coupons used in place of cash—and asked what it was.

He told DeArmond the pilot who'd carried it had died when he crashed in the Yalu. The chit book belonged to Tenney.

But DeArmond noted that the chit book was dry, and showed no sign of having ever been in the water.

The fact that Bushuyev confirmed that Niemann was alive in Soviet custody for some time, presumably before the notation on the Russian list of pilots reports he died, provides some basis for believing that Tenney, also reported dead—was also held for some time in Soviet custody.

For any POWs—Niemann, Tenney or anyone else—who were being interrogated or watched over by the Soviets when they died, at the very least Soviet records ought to show how long they lived and where their remains can be located.

The Russians say they have looked, but have not yet been able to find any more information about either missing pilot.

They were trophies then. They're absent files in the archives now.

Chapter Ten

The Eyewitness

"I believe it was our division policy to turn over all (American) pilots to the Soviets."

— Xu Ping Hua, former Chinese People's Army soldier who
said he personally transferred American POWs to Soviet officers
who then shipped them to Soviet territory.

"I believe that someone had let Red China know that if they did come into the war, their mainland would not be attacked."

— Gen. Mark Clark, former United Nations commander in the Far East
during the Korean War, on April 27, 1956.
Like many in the U.S. military he believed spies or pro-Communists
had betrayed U.S. negotiating and policy decisions to the enemy
while the war was being waged.

When Xu Ping Hua turned the American pilots over to the Soviet officers at Changge-dong North Korea, in the winter of 1951-52, it was a little bit like handing them over to people from his own military, the Chinese People's Army "volunteers."

After all, the Soviets were wearing Chinese military uniforms much like his own. They were all over North Korea and Manchuria, easily identified by their speech and stature but supposedly the unseen hand in the war, the secret advisors and war experts and, as emissaries of Stalin, the suppliers of morale and materiel. But it was the Chinese "volunteers" like Xu and his men who contributed the blood and the fighting spirit.

They, the Chinese, were responsible for the deciding force, the massive armies of infantry troops who went directly, relentlessly into battle against the Americans, the other soldiers from the UN allies across the sea and the South Korean troops.

Xu gave the Russians the pilots. But he got a receipt. He always demanded a receipt.

Mao Tse-Tung dispatched many divisions of troops to Korea in the fall of 1950 to fight off the United Nations army, led by the military forces of the United States. The American and other UN troops had not only defeated the North Korean army in the south, despite the North Koreans' surprise invasion, they had recaptured the southern capital of Seoul, consolidated their gains through the center and along the eastern coast, and continued to move deep into North Korea. By November 1950, they were threatening to come across the Yalu into Manchuria.

The entry of China's soldiers had dramatically changed the tide of the war. They had turned the UN onslaught back on itself, forcing a bloody retreat out of the frozen November mountains of the north. And by 1951, with the war settling into a steady contest of wills, with the Chinese and North Koreans defending their very soil, and the Americans filling the skies with a virtual storm of bombs, rockets and napalm, the prisoners taken on both sides became the biggest pawns of all, as big as the question of where the opposing armies would draw the line that everyone finally agreed would have to be drawn.

A line had to be drawn so that the storm of bombs and the taking of prisoners could stop.

The exploitation of the Americans and other educated prisoners from the UN forces became an enterprise of its own, as the Soviets attempted to extract what intelligence they believed would assist them in their expected faceoff with the United States in Europe, and the Chinese sought to pull their peasant military force and proud new revolutionary regime into the modern age by draining the same prisoners of all the technical knowledge and propaganda value they could offer.[1]

The North Koreans were third in line in this process, unless—as sometimes happened—they got to the prisoners first. They had been fortunate in that regard. The war's most prominent American prisoner— Gen. William F. Dean, the commander of the 24th Division and a former military governor of South Korea, a true prize catch—had fallen into their hands only a month or so after the war had started.

But as might have been expected, they didn't know what to do with him, exactly. They kept his capture absolutely secret for awhile, then when the Soviets found out they had him, they asked the Russian ambassador's advice.[2]

In the early months of the war, when the majority of UN prisoners were from the infantry, artillery brigades and the advance observers the American units sent forward to aid in the bombardments, the North Koreans took the majority of prisoners. But just as they needed help planning and fighting the war, they also needed assistance in holding, indoctrinating, exploiting and organizing the many thousands of prisoners who had survived the battles and the forced marches to the rear.[3]

That's where China came in. As the UN forces pushed farther and farther north, to the very banks of the Yalu, the large, transient population of UN POWs had to be moved as well. The UN had already telegraphed its intention—against the heated objections of MacArthur—to give the Communist forces a sanctuary. They would have Manchuria, free of attack. The UN side was even debating whether it should allow its pilots to attack the bridges over the Yalu that the Communist divisions needed—except in winter, when the river froze to a sturdy depth—to reach the battle areas.

The prisoners could be put in safekeeping in Manchuria. The ones who might be of more than usual interest or assistance could be taken even farther, to cities on the huge mainland of China itself. Everything beyond the Yalu belonged to the triple-sided forces that flew the Communist banner. The prisoners could be moved, interrogated, even left in North Korea in unmarked prisons, if they didn't cooperate, to experience the same terrible storm of bombs that the North Koreans and their Chinese and Soviet friends suffered each and every day.[4]

And once they were moved, the transactions could begin.

Xu Ping Hua dealt in POWs in Korea. As head of a collection team for the 164th Chinese Division of volunteers, he was responsible for seeing that UN prisoners were moved from place to place, according to the instructions of his superiors.[5]

When he agreed to tell his story in February 1993 to Task Force Russia, the Pentagon's team of military analysts who were seeking information about what had become of American prisoners who never returned from Korea, he wanted them to be sure he was sincere. He had no reason to curry favor with the U.S. government. He had already moved legally to the United States, and so he assured them that he would "honestly and truthfully describe events that I've personally witnessed, heard or experienced. I do not say anything that I don't have personal knowledge, experience of, or eyewitness account of. If I don't know, I don't know."

Xu Ping Hua, the eyewitness, could tell the Americans what had happened in Korea, because he was there. He was the link between Manchuria and the Russians:

"I have personally witnessed and experienced the following two events," said Xu. "First, I have personally witnessed the POW management—management of sick or wounded POWs. I have personally witnessed the killings (of these sick or wounded POWs) around me."

Xu's testimony about the execution of POWs raised an old, never-settled issue. The atrocities leveled on UN troops in Korea were the subject of numerous studies, books, congressional hearings and great soul-searching. Nevertheless, the United Nations never took up the subject in a comprehensive way that would satisfy today's international courts and societies around the world dedicated to seeking justice in cases of violations of POW conventions.

Should it be necessary, Xu added, "I have no problem to take the stand as material witness." But he turned quickly to the matter of living prisoners of war, and the transactions that took place on the edge of the front lines in Korea.

"Secondly," he said, "I have personally witnessed the transferring of three pilots to the Soviets."[6]

He said he could not remember the names of the pilots he handed over to the Russians, if he ever knew them, but he is sure he obtained a receipt. He said he made at least two trips to Changge-dong to hand over American pilots. Each time there were about ten Soviet officers present, he said, all wearing the Chinese People's Liberation Army uniform. Some of the Soviet officers were of Asiatic origin, he said, but they were Russians nonetheless. "While some don't look like caucasians, they all speak Russian," he said.

The Soviet officers seemed interested only in taking the pilots and leaving, Xu said, with the translators who had accompanied them to the pickup point. "They were speaking Russian while pointing at the three pilots," said Xu. "We took the jeep parked outside of the prison and went back for a rest. Those pilots were taken away in a jeep in less than an hour—very quickly."

The next step, said Xu, was a trip north for the pilots. "Our division chief told me that the Soviets specifically requested that we turn over the pilots to them," he said. "He told me on that day that the pilots were going to be transferred to the Soviet Union. I believe it was our division policy to turn over all (American) pilots to the Soviets. The example I've provided exemplified the policy."

The testimony of Xu Ping Hua illustrates that, just as they took control of the fighting, the Chinese communists took control of the POW system, while using North Korean troops as guards, but that they cooperated with the Soviets when it suited their purposes.

But while the Chinese administration of the POW camps stabilized what had been a chaotic situation under the North Koreans, it also meant that learning where UN prisoners were being kept became a constant guessing game. The guessing game continued to the end of the war, even after the Communists returned about 3,600 live American prisoners.

Even when the Chinese passed information to the UN about the location of POW camps, it was quickly found to be incomplete or misleading. When the Communists passed the location of camps, the U.S. Air Force would immediately lay on a photo reconnaissance mission to ascertain the situation at each location. An Air Force report from Feb. 16, 1952 provides an example:

"Camp surveillance: Of the 11 PW camp locs (locations) listed by CCF delegates at Panmunjom, 25 Jan. 52, 3 have recvd photo recon coverage. Results as follows:

1. No evidence of PW markers as promised.

2. Low-altitude oblique photography of Taru-gol (Pukchin, Camp No. 11) offers rather positive proof that camp does not exist.

3. Chittong (Kangdong, Camp No. 8) is not capable of containing the 1,592 PWs said to be interned there. Nearby mining area at Taosong-ni presents similar aspect.

4. Toryong-dong (Pyongyang, Camp No. 6), claimed to contain 2 PWs, cannot be identified fr aerial photography."

These and similar reports throughout the war provide substantial evidence that the Communist POW camp system was multi-layered. But were there also, in fact, separate systems for each of the Communist countries that had dealings with UN POWs?

Did the North Koreans allow the Chinese to run most of their camps, but maintain others themselves?

Did the Russians, in addition to helping direct and staff the interrogation sections in the Chinese-run camps, have a separate line of contact with camps operated solely by North Koreans?

Did the Russians—after letting the Chinese and North Koreans winnow down the large body of prisoners to those men whose skills and knowledge were of special importance to them in the global battle with the United States—operate a completely separate system of camps, or safehouses, within the war zone, in addition to their interrogation centers on Soviet territory?

If so, where were they?

The most comprehensive study of U.S. POWs in Korea, completed at the Army Security Center at Fort Meade, Md., in November 1954, backed up the standard line used throughout the Korean War. The study asserted that all of the Communist POW camps were in North Korea, located "either on the Yalu River or within six miles of its banks."

An accompanying map showed a cluster of camps along a 50-mile stretch of the Yalu, 80 miles northeast of the mouth of the river and centered roughly on the city of Pyoktong, where Camp 5—the headquarters camp—

was located.

That cluster of camps—the Army Security Center study identified 20, but most public accounts mention fewer than a dozen—on the edge of the Yalu eventually became the stereotype for thinking about and discussing the POW situation in Korea.

The stereotype was a product of the Communists' propaganda. The existence of camps throughout North Korea and Manchuria—and the isolation of some individuals and small groups of prisoners in mainland cities such as Shanghai, Canton and Kunming—was known by U.S. authorities very early in the war. U.S. search and rescue teams were sent to many locations many miles distant from the Yalu in attempts to rescue American prisoners. Some succeeded.

Why the Army would keep POW camp intelligence secret during the war is easy to understand. But why the military would choose to ignore much of the information available in its own records about the POW camp system in assessing the war once it was over is difficult to fathom, except as part of a concerted and continuing effort to calm public fears over what might have happened to thousands of still-missing men.

A few Western reporters covering the war in Korea occasionally reported—on the basis of anonymous sources—that the Communists were holding Americans prisoner in mainland China. The stories naturally prompted families of MIAs to write their representatives in Washington, eager to know why the U.S. appeared to be ignoring them.

The Army's family liaison office helped quash the reports.

"I have made careful inquiries concerning that matter," read a letter sent by Lt. Col. Tench Tilghman, in March 1953, to several members of Congress who had been asked about the reports. "...and I find that the Department of the Army has no information to substantiate or to refute the allegation that American prisoners of war are being held on the mainland of China."

It was true that, over the course of the war, many of the prisoners the communists acknowledged holding were shuttled to a series of 8-12 camps near the Yalu River, most of which came into existence in the spring and summer of 1951.

Before then, thousands of POWs were sequestered in locations whose names—"The Valley," "Mining Camp," "Bean Camp," "Peaceful Valley," "Death Valley"—indicated the virtual absence of facilities.

Deprived of adequate shelter, clothing, food or medical care, the men held in these camps through the fierce Korean winter of 1950-51 died by the hundreds. Some camps were no more than mine pits, dank caves, or flimsy grass-roofed shacks and lean-tos, where the rags and food morsels of the newly dead passed quickly down to the ranks of the dying, and the mortality rate exceeded 50 percent.

At least six repatriated Marine POWs—Pvt. Alberto Pizarro-Baez, Cpl. Nick Flores, M/Sgt. Frederick J. Stumpges, 2/Lt. Carl R. Lundquist, 1/Lt. Felix L. Ferranto, and Col. Frank H. Schwable—were taken into Manchuria for medical care or interrogation, or both.

Pizarro-Baez spent four months in a Manchurian hospital. Flores—apparently mistaken for a downed pilot because he was wearing an airman's flight suit and flying boots—was taken before a group of Soviet interrogators.

Once he convinced them he was not an aviator, he was sent back to a camp in North Korea, and he was eventually repatriated..

With these experiences of individual POWs, and covert contacts in Communist-held territory, the U.S. military and intelligence community had a much more extensive POW system under scrutiny during the war than described in most post-war studies. There were in fact dozens of camps, temporary and permanent, through which large groups of prisoners were transferred and shuttled until the last few weeks of the war.

This extensive, fluid, POW camp network, according to intelligence received during the war, included large groups of captured U.S. personnel used as forced labor in sawmills, coal and mineral mines, construction gangs and in the restoring of railyards and other vital facilities damaged by allied bombing.

Necessarily, the network covered much of North Korea, coast to coast, from the mouth of the Yalu northeast to Manpojin, and in major population centers like Hamhung, on the east (Sea of Japan) coast, as well as Manchuria and elsewhere in mainland China. A CIA map showing the locations where UN prisoners from Korea were kept listed 24 separate locations. (see map.)

A handwritten Soviet document released to Task Force Russia in 1993 and labeled "Document given by the Chinese side in 1951" purports to list five "North Korean camps" that then held about 2,650 Americans and another few hundred Turkish, British and French POWs.

The total number of POWs listed—2,925—indicates that it is far from a comprehensive tally.

The vast majority—about 2,200—are listed at a single camp. One of the five camps is listed as having a total of two U.S. POWs—perhaps one of those the Air Force's photo reconnaissance people couldn't find.

But the strangest aspect of the "North Korean camps" list handed over by the Yeltsin government are the names—"Khekiseki; Ts'kotsin; Sukan; Kinka; Pyongyang."[7]

Only Pyongyang—the North Korean capital then and now—corresponds to an actual placename. The rest might be code names, or the result of multiple translations.

Hyon Suk Chong, a South Korean who worked as a special intelligence agent (Code Name "White Tiger") for the U.S. during the war, parachuted into North Korea in 1951 to locate a POW camp for American pilots.

While Hyon manned a radio in the mountains near Kapsan, his operatives tracked down the location: a prison in Musan, 100 miles to the northeast, on the Manchurian border.

The agents told Hyon that by the time they reached the prison, "the pilots had been moved into Manchuria."[8]

By 1952, U.S. intelligence was able to sketch a profile of the Communists' POW camp system. A July 17, 1952, report said the system was being directed from the War Prisoner Administrative Office in Pyongyang. The 30-person office, under a "Colonel No-men-ch'i-fu, an intelligence officer attached to the general headquarters of the Soviet Far Eastern Military District, controlled prisoner of war camps in Manchuria and North Korea."

There were three types of camps:

"Peace" camps, where prisoners who showed pro-communist leanings were held, were deep in Manchuria. The largest, at Chungchun, held 2,000 men.

"Reform" camps, where prisoners with useful skills were subjected to Communist indoctrination techniques, were also in Manchuria.

A public set of "normal" POW camps, for prisoners who would be exchaned, were all in North Korea.

"Prisoners in the peace and reform camps will not be exchanged," the intelligence memo stated forebodingly.

The fact that the American POWs who were repatriated spoke mainly of the camps listed in Army study and other military accounts of Korean War POWs is further evidence that the Communists, in the end, returned only SOME prisoners, from SOME camps.

The neat image of a "cluster" of POW camps along the Yalu is also shattered by another CCRAK report from March 1953, just prior to the "Little Switch" exchange of POWs.

The report said that, for the previous six months, one of the largest POW camps for Americans was a schoolhouse in Anju, well south of the Yalu on North Korea's west coast.

"POWs are being transported to the camp directly from the front," the report states. "In September 1952, an international investigation party, composed of a Soviet escort, an interpreter, a Hungarian and a Czech visited the camp and questioned prisoners for name, age and home town. Soviet advisers often visit the camp."

As late as August 1952, the Army's joint U.S.-South Korean CCRAK teams (Combined Command for Reconnaissance Activities Korea, which sent agents into North Korea to gather intelligence, reported a POW camp in a former brick factory in the Pyongyang region, at Huandong, well south of the Yalu.

The camp reportedly held about 300 U.S. POWs, a third of them Air Force personnel. A separate camp at a former brickyard near Pyongyang held "24 UN downed airmen."

That same fall, another CCRAK team reported 600 American POWs being held along with 1,500 South Korean troops at the former Unsan gold mine, only some 25 miles north of Pyongyang.One of the earliest reports of where American prisoners were being held in large numbers is contained in a U.S. military intelligence bulletin dated Oct. 1, 1950. Interrogation of captured North Korean troops had yielded a long list of POW sightings, including 800 being held at a girls high school in Pyongyang, 3,000 near the Hamhung railway station, 400 in a former Japanese army barracks in that same capital, and 200 at an elementary school in Manpojin, in north-central North Korea on the Manchurian border.

But the North Korean prisoners said the "largest PW camp in North Korea"—at that time—was a training camp for the North Korean Army's 15th Division, in the city of Hoeryong.

The North Korean prisoners reported seeing 4,000 POWs in a school near the Hoeryong railway station on Aug. 10, 1950, and another 500 in a Hoeryong municipal office a month later.

The prisoners' nationality is not specified in the reports, but two of the North Korean prisoners said "several thousand PsW, all thin and sickly looking," had been taken to Hoeryong from Pyongyang because of UN air raids, and that "high-ranking Russian officers (were) observed entering this PW camp in September."

Hoeryong is in the northwestern tip of North Korea that juts like an arrowhead into a notch between China and the former USSR. The city lies on the Manchurian border, only 40 miles west of the Russian border.

With the United Nations forces advancing closer and closer to the Yalu, it would make sense to move any prisoners believed to have any value, either as intelligence sources or bargaining chips, far from the fighting.

The "several thousand" prisoners of Hoeryong have never been seen again.

* * *

The Chinese archives dealing with the Peoples' Liberation Army "volunteers" who participated in the Korean War, and the large role Chinese officers and officials played in the administration of POW camps, are largely unseen by western scholars or governments. Some material has been published in memoir form, but the original source documents that could undoubtedly assist in resolving many cases of missing UN POWs remain out of sight and reach.

Nevertheless, using publicly available materials, Task Force Russia analysts were able to begin the process of uncovering material only the Chinese would have. The Pentagon's analysts have now uncovered a number of references to American MIAs in Chinese publications.

A Peking publication, Chinese Military Power Almanac, 1949-1989, dated 190, says Chinese Korean War Volunteers Battle Records say that "American Ace" Maj. George A. Davis was shot down by Zhang Jihui on Feb. 10, 1952. Another text, Korean War Logistic Work Experience, Summary, Pictorial," endorsed by former Chinese president Yang Shang kun, contains a picture of Maj. Davis and a closeup of his dog-tags. The caption states that Maj. Davis was dead.

Davis was also mentioned by Soviet air force general Lobov in his memoirs as one of the American pilots his crews were responsible for shooting down. The find in Peking suggests that the Chinese hold more information—at least burial site information, if not relics or personal effects—related to U.S. pilots that were shot down by Chinese-manned batteries, or otherwise fell into exclusive Chinese custody.

The Task Force Russia analysts also found indications that the Chinese "may have further information on the fate of the crew of a B-29 shot down on 10 June 1952 over Gwagsan." The pilot in that incident may have been 1/Lt.Wilbur Eugene Lewis, whose B-29 disappeared without a trace during a night bombing raid on Gwagsan on June 10, 1952. U.S. records show that two B-29s were lost that night. The other plane was totally destroyed and its crew members declared KIA while their remains were not recoverable.

A Chinese publication dated 1990, The War to Resist U.S. Aggression and Support Korea, refers—apparently mistakenly—to the destruction of three B-29s during a nighttime raid on June 10, 1952, on Gwagsan railroad bridges.

* * *

Some of the American prisoners in Chinese hands were captured not in North Korea but on Chinese territory. Those the Chinese held the longest were in this category.

Two CIA agents, John Downey and Richard Fecteau, were captured Nov. 24, 1952, when they flew deep into Manchuria on a secret mission to attempt to contact anti-Communist guerrillas. They were held until the 1970s, when they were released as part of the rapprochement between the Nixon Administration and Mao Tse-Tung that eventually led to the re-establishment of diplomatic relations.

The capture of Downey and Fecteau apparently didn't spook the CIA's operations chiefs into suspending operations, however, because, according to a document from Soviet archives turned over to the American side of the joint commission, a few days after the capture of Downey and Fecteau another U.S. aircraft was seized by Communist troops after it landed behind enemy lines in Girin province.

In the Dec. 3, 1952, incident, two unnamed U.S. Army lieutenant colonels were reported captured along with the aircraft's crew as they flew into Manchuria with new instructions for agents in that region.

A special message from a Soviet security official assigned to Port Arthur, China, relayed news of the capture first reported by a Chinese security official, Li Nan. The message said the two U.S. officers had been lured into a trap set by the Chinese counter-intelligence forces.

The lists of missing American POWs carry no reference to any Army officers captured in Manchuria. And it's possible that the Chinese failed to distinguish between Air Force and Army officers, or that the prisoners posed as Army officers as part of some evasion plan. But the Soviet message about the capture leaves no doubt that some Americans were captured.

"On 5 Dec of this year (1952), LI-NAN, Head of the Directorate for State Security, Chinese People's Republic, Port Arthur Region, informed the Department Head of the Counterintelligence Department, MGB, 39th Army that on 3 Dec of this year in the province of Girin, as a result of a ploy conducted by the Department of State Security, Northeast China, an American aircraft was allowed to land.

"Among the aircraft crew members were two intelligence offices, Lieutenant Colonels of the American Army, who arrived to brief agent-saboteurs that were earlier dropped into Northeast China.

"The above-mentioned American intelligence officers are in Mukden." That would be Mukden, as in, the Korean War POW camp at Mukden, China, considerably north of the Yalu River.

* * *

In comparison to the North Koreans, the Chinese enjoyed a relatively good reputation among UN prisoners when it came to how they were treated while in captivity. Frequent references appear in debriefing reports of repatriated POWs to their relief when they were turned over to Chinese guards. The testimony of Xu Ping Hua alters that perception dramatically. So does the recollection of James E. Gunnoe Jr.

Air Force lst Lt. Gunnoe was captured the day of his shootdown, June 8, 1952, and repatriated in September 1953, during Operation Big Switch. U.S. military interrogators were very interested in some of the things he told them he was ready to talk about at his debriefings. He had been a POW for 15 months, and he had seen and heard some things that other POWs had not. For instance, he said one of his Chinese questioners had mentioned that Air Force Lt. James Van Fleet, Jr., the son of the Army commander, "was a prisoner of war and living." Another had said he was dead.

Because of his father's position, the young Van Fleet—reported missing on his first B-26 flight of the war—was one of the better-known MIAs in Korea. Gunnoe said that after Lt. Van Fleet was reported down in enemy territory, it was common for other B-26 crews, when they were flying close to the area where Van Fleet's plane had last been seen, to be asked to check for any signs of life.

"If you couldn't get to your target," Gunnoe said, "or if you were passing by there on a mission, they would have you fly over and see if you could pick up anything."

Once Gunnoe was a prisoner himself, he had more to worry about, however. The Chinese were engaged in an intense propaganda campaign to link American pilots and air crews to an alleged campaign of biological— or "germ"—warfare. The B-29 and B-26 crews were especially subjected to this line of interrogation, he said.

While he was undergoing his daily interrogation, sometime in early August 1952, Gunnoe said his captors led him outside. His Chinese interrogator told him an "execution was to be held in my presence for my benefit," and moments later, a group of Americans were marched out of a nearby building and made to stand not far away. They were wearing U.S. Air Force flight suits and were obviously American airmen, he said.

The men were a B-29 crew, the Chinese told him. The dozen or so men were escorted to within 30 yards of where he was standing. When a squad of Chinese soldiers appeared, "the crew was lined up abreast and faced by the firing squad at a distance of approximately 30 feet."

Some of the men in the B-29 crew "broke down emotionally," said Gunnoe, and he heard some ranks mentioned, but no names. "At the motion command of the interrogator, the Chinese fired and continued firing until their weapons were empty. I believe there were ten Chinese using 30-caliber rifles."

They led Gunnoe back inside his "bunker," and from the entrance he could see the prisoners' bodies being carried away. "I could not see the actual placing of the bodies in the grave," he said, "but I did see the Chinese covering the grave."[9]

Gunnoe said he mentioned the incident to military debriefers when he was first released, but was told to save a fuller account for when he was back stateside. He was eventually summoned by military investigators to give a sworn statement at Wright-Patterson Air Force Base, Ohio, in February, 1954.

But he said he was never asked to look at photographs of missing airmen in an attempt to identify those who were executed that day.

It would have been a large stack of photos. By August 1952, quite a few B-29 crews were missing in action in North Korea.

Chapter Eleven

Footprints in the Snow

"It was the view of the Department of Defense that Major McDonough's name should not be included among the 450 (passed to the Communists for information about their fate)...this case is one with serious domestic public relations implications...."

> —Oct. 1, 1955, letter to the State Department
> from Gen. G. B. Erskine,
> assistant secretary of defense for
> special operations.

"We had our wings sticking over in China, because we were photographing the (Yalu) river every day. Particularly that time of year, after the Chinese invaded, we photographed the river every day so they could count the footprints in the snow to see how many came over."

> —Louis Carrington, of Tyler, Tex.,
> a retired Air Force pilot who flew bombers during World War II
> and was part of an RB-45 reconnaissance plane detachment
> during the Korean War.

A Willys Jeep wouldn't have been a normal target for a U.S. Air Force strafing attack in every country of the world in December, 1950.

But up along the Yalu in North Korea—where the Communist military and political elite and their Soviet mentors and suppliers drove around in American-made trucks and cars that had been given to the Russians under Lend-Lease, and passed on to their poorer relations the Chinese and North Koreans—it was.

So when the American fighters spotted the Jeep coming across the Yalu bridge and into Sinuiju, they came in low with guns blazing. The Jeep's two occupants leaped out of the boxy, thin-shelled vehicle and dove into a roadside ditch to escape the gunfire from above. When the American planes passed, they climbed back in and continued their journey south, to the headquarters of the North Korean air force.

In the U.S.-made Jeep on that clear, icy day were a North Korean Army general, the head of his country's tiny air force, and Pavel Vasilyevich Fironov, a young political officer for the Soviets' 29th Fighter Aviation Regiment then stationed in Antung, China.

The North Korean air force commander and the Soviet officer were going to investigate an incident of great importance to their joint war effort. Ten days earlier, Soviet MIGs based near Antung had shot down a new type of aircraft the U.S. Air Force had begun flying extremely close to the North Korea-Manchuria border. One of the Americans on board had been captured. They were on their way to ask him a few questions.

"Our radar determined that an aircraft was approaching," said Fironov, "that was unfamiliar to our radar operators. We knew it wasn't a fighter. We weren't sure whether or not it was a bomber or a transport, but we knew we'd never seen a signal like that on the radar."

The Soviet air defense commanders at Antung had scrambled several waves of MIGs to intercept the strange new plane, but it was cruising too high. "Our pilots tried but could not manage to reach the aircraft," said Fironov. "Suddenly he began descending. This gave our pilots the opportunity to shoot him down."

Four MIGs got the lone American plane within range, at about 7,000 feet, and rounds from their cannon tore into the big plane. But the solid hit was scored by only one of them, Aleksandr Fedorovich Andrianov. He can still see the moment he fired in his mind's eye. His shell hit the plane's right engine, setting it on fire.

If the American pilot "had not gone into a turn," recalled Andrianov, "we would have still been chasing him over Korea." At first, he and the other Russian pilots weren't sure what kind of plane they were chasing northeast along the Yalu. But as they got closer and could count the four engines, "we then recognized the aircraft as an RB-45A," one of the U.S. Air Force's long-range photo reconnaissance planes. "We did not know that it was in fact unarmed."

Andrianov, referring to the heavy competition among the MIG pilots for credit for shootdowns, said the four of them involved in the RB-45 attack couldn't decide who should get credit for the kill, since all of them had scored hits, so they drew cards—for the Jack of Clubs. Andrianov won, which entitled him to the 3,000-ruble bonus that went with an RB-45 shootdown.[1]

As the badly damaged and smoking RB-45 angled downward out of control, at about 2,000 feet a parachute appeared over the snow-covered, heavily forested area.

"All of my colleagues saw only one parachute as well," Andrianov remembers. "None of us saw any other parachutes. Although I have heard that others jumped, we did not note any other parachute."

Andrianov watched the plane descend, crash and explode into flames. He couldn't watch the parachute all the way down, because he lost sight of it against the white snow as he pulled up to avoid crashing to earth himself.

Perhaps he didn't see other parachutes emerging from the doomed plane for the same reason, because they were invisible against the snow.

It was apparently a week or more later that Frionov and the North Korean air force commander arrived at the North Korean aviation headquarters, where they interrogated a healthy-looking American prisoner who said he was a colonel and the pilot of an RB-45 that Soviet MIGs had shot down over the Yalu River.

Frionov had no reason then to doubt the American prisoner's story.

Now he does. Because the American he spoke to was undoubtedly an aviator, but not the pilot of the RB-45 that had crashed in flames over North Korea about ten days earlier. The pilot of that plane was a young captain, not a colonel. And the young pilot was not healthy and fit at all when he was finally picked up by North Korean or Chinese troops. He was badly burned from landing in the wreckage of his plane and severely frostbitten from walking barefoot for days on the icy ground.

When Fironov decided to tell his story about talking to the American prisoner he saw that day in North Korea, he didn't close the book on a long-unresolved case of missing POWs.

He opened a whole new chapter.

* * *

In the multiple mysteries left by the unresolved cases of missing American prisoners in the Korean War, the story of two Air Force officers, Capt. Charles McDonough and Col. John R. Lovell, who were in an RB-45 photo-reconnaissance plane shot down Dec. 4, 1950, by Russian fighters, stands out as one of the most perplexing and frustrating.

McDonough was the pilot. On board were two other crew members, a co-pilot and navigator, and Lovell, a passenger—but not an ordinary passenger, apparently. Lovell worked high in the Pentagon's hierarchy, in Air Force intelligence.

Because McDonough was put briefly in the same small prison cell in Sinuiju, North Korea, with another U.S. pilot who was able to relate the story when he was repatriated two-and-a-half years later, it's known that he bailed out, managed to elude enemy troops for a few days despite serious burns, frostbite and injuries, but eventually was taken prisoner and interrogated.

He reportedly told the other American prisoner that he was the only one who had managed to parachute to safety before the aircraft crashed in flames.

No one aboard the RB-45 came back from the war.

McDonough was last seen alive, but weak, wounded and very ill, being transported away from other U.S. POWs in a small, wooden cart. His interrogation wasn't finished, but the guards who took him away indicated he was to be given medical care.

In May 1951, a U.S. intelligence analyst monitoring a Communist Chinese broadcast in the Far East heard Col. Lovell's name mentioned during the reading of a list of UN prisoners of war. But neither man's name ever appeared on any of the lists the UN Command made public of missing officers and enlisted men they had reason to believe were prisoners in enemy hands.

Both of them certainly qualified for those lists. But for some reason, the U.S. government didn't want the enemy to know that they were missing.

That is virtually all that was known about the incident for years—until the Soviet Union collapsed in 1991 and Russian president Boris Yeltsin announced that there might be some American POWs still alive on the territory of the former Soviet Union and that he was ordering his government to determine if they were.

That sent the U.S.-Russian Joint Commission into action digging into the archival documents and remaining witnesses that are able to tell the story of the Soviet role in the Korean War. And with that, the families of McDonough and Lovell—primarily their daughters, Jeanne McDonough Dear of Fort Worth, Tex., and Nancy Lovell Dean of suburban Virginia—began their own odyssey in search of secrets that they hoped would be among those starting to seep out.

Sharing leads and moral support, the two women hoped that some new information on their case would surface thanks to the Russian and U.S. governments and the joint commission on American POWs in the former Soviet Union. The secrecy and security classification surrounding the information in U.S. archives and military records proved almost as difficult to deal with—in some cases, more difficult—than the famously forbidden records in the former Soviet Union.

But they eventually grew impatient with the commission and struck out on their own in a search for more answers, cultivating people more expert in research and the ways of the Russian bureaucracy than they would ever be. Along the way, they grew to distrust and not appreciate what they saw as the government's bumbling and insensitive ways of dealing with the Russian commission members and family survivors like themselves.

Because of the grit and determination of these two women, more is known about the McDonough-Lovell shootdown and interrogation than most longstanding, unresolved POW/MIA cases from the Korean War.

Unfortunately, however, their long search for the facts is also evidence that the U.S. government has expended too little effort and concern in recent years in helping Korean War POW/MIA relatives cope with the difficult, excruciating work of putting a small piece of a big war back together— their small piece.

As a result, the families and survivors learn that sometimes the best way to deal with governments and official channels is to work around them, not through them.

On Sunday, Dec. 18, 1994—44 years after Capt. McDonough is believed to have died—Jeanne McDonough Dear held a memorial service in his memory at a small Fort Worth chapel. Air Force F-16 jets flew overhead in a missing-man formation as Dear, with her mother, husband, daughter, other family members and friends around her, stood in silent tribute.

Over years of searching, Jeanne McDonough Dear had finally gathered enough information about the shooting down of her father's plane and his captivity to convince her that he had probably died while a prisoner on or about Dec. 18, 1950, from sickness and his captors' neglect of severe wounds and injuries he suffered in the shootdown.

The father she had never known, whose fate became so tangled in the crossed lines of family notification, military regulations and national security that his own government was reluctant to give his widow and daughter straight answers, was finally at peace in his family's heart.

Rev. Larry Zellers, a retired Air Force chaplain, conducted the service. Zellers was a Methodist missionary in Korea when the war broke out and spent nearly three agonizing years in Communist prison camps during the Korean War, only a few hundred miles from where McDonough's plane was shot down. After the flyover he was asked if he had anything more to say. "No," Zellers intoned. "There are no words left."

No words, perhaps, to express the relief and closure that came with knowing more than the families of Charles McDonough and James Lovell had ever known before. But the final chapter of the fatal mission of McDonough and Lovell, of their imprisonment, interrogation and death, wasn't written that somber December day in Fort Worth.

It's fair to ask now if it ever will be.

* * *

Capt. Charles E. McDonough, a tall, blue-eyed, 31-year-old pilot from New London, Conn., whose wife and baby daughter were then living in Glen Rose, Tex., was sent off to the Far East just before the Korean War to serve as the senior officer of a detachment of three RB-45 reconnaissance planes, jet-engined bombers that had been converted for use in photo reconnaissance.

Aerial reconnaissance work during the Korean War was conducted by a variety of aircraft, but much of the load was carried by converted bombers, a squadron of RB-29s and a small, three-plane detachment of RB-45s. Rigged with numerous large, powerful cameras, they made daily forays over the battlefields and invasion routes, photographing dams and power plants, highways and railyards, enemy locations and concentrations. With their photographs and visual data, Air Force intelligence was able to assess bomb damage and identify future targets, update maps, and multiply the military uses of reams of information about weather conditions, troop, train and convoy movements, the whole spectrum of data that a modern military force even 40 years ago consumed in great gulps.

McDonough's detachment of three RB-45s, dispatched to the Far East Air Force in Japan in October 1950, on temporary duty from Strategic Air Command. Their job was described as "vital penetration missions" and "pre-strike" photography. The aircraft were outfitted with 24 still cameras and a motion picture camera, with many different lenses. They were camera warehouses with wings.[2]

One of the RB45 detachment's main tasks was to constantly monitor the situation along the Yalu River, which divides North Korea from the Chinese province of Manchuria. "We were there every day, one of us," said Louis Carrington, of Tyler, Tex., an RB-45 pilot who served under McDonough. That put them right in the laps of the Russian MIGs.

"We would always photograph Antung, which is just across the river" in Manchuria, said Carrington. The MIG fighters would scramble from the base at Antung and chase the heavier, slower and unarmed reconnaissance planes as they flew north and east, the 200-mile-per-hour upper winds behind them.

Carrington recalls being shot at by the MIGs only a few times. "Mostly they were skittish," he said, "because the F86s were usually there."

But the speedy and deadly jet fighters weren't always there, and with no armament except a .45 pistol nestled in the pilot's shoulder holster, the RB-45 was designed for the sidelines, not the thick of the fight. "We just got up there in the middle of all those good air battles," Carrington said, "and watched them chase each other. Usually, we just continued photographing."

The planes were designed to fly with a crew of three—a pilot, co-pilot and navigator.

When McDonough's plane lifted off from the base at Yokuta, Japan, late in the morning on Dec. 4, 1950, his co-pilot was Capt. Jules E. Young, 29, of East Rochester, N.Y., and the navigator was 1st Lt. James J. Picucci, 32, of New York. As the detachment's maintenance officer, Carrington was out on the tarmac and watched them leave. The flight stands out in his memory because the aircraft McDonough normally flew was down for maintenance and the squadron leader "was flying my airplane. No one else had ever flown it before. I was seeing my baby off."

Just before the flight, "Mac" had introduced Carrington to another man who would be his passenger that day. He was Col. John Lovell, and he was part of the brass from headquarters.

"Jack" Lovell, then 46, was a man of achivement. A West Point graduate, Class of '27, who had coached the U.S. Olympic boxing team, a veteran of World War II intelligence operations, Lovell's presence on McDonough's plane speaks volumes about how sensitive any information about this particular flight and crew would be in case something went wrong. Between World War II and the war in Korea, Lovell had been a military attaché in Communist-controlled Romania.

Nancy Lovell Dean remembers that her father had an inkling that trouble was brewing, so he and her mother sent her out of the country. Soon the U.S. military attache and his wife were both placed under house arrest by authorities in Bucharest. Lovell was put on trial for espionage, convicted, sentenced to death, and finally expelled, returning to Washington in January 1949.

When war broke out in Korea, he was on the staff of Maj. Gen.Charles P. Cabell, chief of Air Force intelligence. His main duties, although not made public to this day, reportedly included acting as the chief intelligence briefing officer for Gen. Hoyt Vandenberg, Air Force chief of staff. Officers in positions such as his—possessing the national security secrets that go with such jobs—would normally not find themselves flying over enemy territory in wartime, risking capture.

Which means that the reason he was on board McDonough's aircraft that fateful day—never publicly stated by the Air Force—must have been of overriding importance to the Pentagon. Nancy Lovell Dean, based on her years of research into his career and the circumstances of his last flight, believes that he was on a top-secret, classified mission, perhaps to evaluate the RB-45 program, or collect personal impressions of the intelligence-gathering potential in the region for his superiors.

The Air Force was a relatively new service, desperately in need of the kind of skills and experience in fields like intelligence that regular Army officers like Lovell could provide. "He had a real strong sense for intelligence," said Nancy Lovell Dean, perfected in the years of battling to reclaim Europe from the grip of Nazi Germany. "The Air Force had all the pilots they needed, but they didn't have the other pieces." They needed the strong intelligence capabilities that a Jack Lovell could "bring across" from his years in the Army.

"All I know," she said, "is that my father was involved in estimates," the assessment of enemy war-fighting potential on the ground and in the air. The estimates most needed during the first months of the Korean War had to do with the military strength and intentions of three contiguous countries: North Korea, Communist China and the Soviet Union.

One of the best ways to acquire the information needed for an estimate, clearly, would be to see the situation up close, first-hand, judge the situation on the ground. Lovell was certainly able to get close to the enemy aboard McDonough's combat reconnaissance plane. No one had a finer look at the situation on the ground than the RB-45 crews.

Carrington's not sure why Lovell was on board that day. There was a kind of wartime tradition, he said, for staff officers to fly into a theater to qualify for a campaign ribbon. But that hardly seems likely in Lovell's case. Anyone wanting only a service medal could get it by going no farther than the landing strip at Pusan.

And Col. John Lovell certainly didn't need any more ribbons. "He was in harm's way repeatedly" during his distinguished career, said Nancy Lovell Dean. "He was not the kind of person who would deliberately set himself up to be killed." So it had to be fate, that some eagle-eyed MIG pilots just across the river in Manchuria were ready and waiting that December day as Col. John Lovell and Capt. Charles McDonough headed up to the Yalu, cameras rigged and loaded for estimate-shooting.

McDonough was turning left and downward, toward the crooked Yalu River glistening and snaking below him under an early afternoon sun, when Andrianov and the other Russian MIGs swarmed in and began firing at the silvery, unarmed plane.

The first rounds missed, but on a second pass, the MIGs did their damage, crippling two engines and setting the aircraft on fire. As the plane spun wildly out of control, McDonough managed to bail out, but came down amid the burning wreckage of his own aircraft.

The next day, his wife, Mary Jo, received an Air Force telegram saying the plane had not returned from the mission, adding: "All possible search completed."

The families of the other men on board the RB-45 received similar notices. But the following spring came one note of hope for Lovell's family. A communist broadcast had mentioned his name among the UN prisoners. But their hope was short-lived.

When the armistice was signed, and several thousand POWs were repatriated, Lovell wasn't among them. And one repatriated POW emerged with a detailed account of the shootdown that appeared to end all hope that McDonough or anyone on his aircraft had survived. But like every new chapter in the McDonough-Lovell saga, it also left many questions.

Having been shot down recently himself, Air Force Capt. Hamilton Shawe Jr., was enjoying some of the Communists' ricepaper-thin hospitality in a freezing jail in North Korea on Dec. 14, 1950, when North Korean soldiers threw another American pilot in the same cell. The other man's face and hands were severely burned, his legs were gangrenous from frostbite. He had received no medical treatment since parachuting into his burning plane some days earlier.

Shawe's cellmate was Capt. Charles McDonough.

Two days later, according to Shawe's account to Air Force debriefers, when guards removed them from their cell, they ordered Shawe to join "a group of prisoners starting a march to another prison camp...McDonough could not walk and was carried to an ox cart by fellow prisoners."

The North Koreans, according to Shawe's account, said McDonough "was being taken to a hospital for medical treatment, because he was suffering from frostbite and gangrene of both legs. He was not seen again by repatriates," the statement read, "and they reported his condition was so bad at that time that he was not expected to live."

A letter dated Sept. 21, 1955, from the chief of the Air Force casualty branch to the China desk of the State Department asserts that when McDonough finally jumped at 1,000 feet altitude, he believed he was the only man aboard the plane who had managed to bail out. Shawe's debriefing report says the same thing.

But the debriefing reports are undoubtedly sanitized. None mentions Lovell, for instance, presumably because his presence on the flight was highly sensitive.[3]

Findings of a presumption of death were issued for McDonough, Lovell and the crew, and no further information was released, officially. But Mary Jo McDonough wasn't content to let the matter drop.

With the help of her congressman, "pressure was brought to bear on the Air Force," said Jeanne McDonough Dear, and as a result her mother received a copy in early 1954 of the statement Capt. Shawe had signed at his post-release debriefing in 1953.

For the next few years, seeking out and organizing with hundreds of spouses and parents of Korean War MIAs who peppered Congress, the State Department and the White House with letters, telegrams and phone calls, she demanded that her government find out more—and tell them more—about what had happened to those who hadn't come home.

Then came a long, long silence.

In 1992, when Yeltsin gave his speech saying the former Soviet archives probably held more information about American MIAs, Jeanne Dear requested her father's file from the Air Force casualty office at Randolph AFB, Tex. When her mother had called in previous years, she had been told that her husband's records were among those destroyed in a fire at the St. Louis military records center in the 1970s. This time, the answer was different.

The casualty officer told Dear that her father's name was on a list of U.S. POWs from Korea culled from communist archives and turned over to American officials by the Russian government. The list, one of several that was provided to the U.S.-Russian Joint Commission, named dozens of U.S. airmen who had been interrogated by Soviet officers during the war.

That information sent Jeanne McDonough Dear into fulltime pursuit of all the information the joint commission was gathering on American MIAs in the former Soviet Union.

She also began to search for the families of the other crew members of the downed plane, the surviving members of the RB-45 detachment her father had commanded, and the repatriated POWs who had given statements about encountering or hearing of McDonough after his shootdown. She found next-of-kin for each member of the crew. And in the course of that search, she found Nancy Lovell Dean, who had also been stirred by Yeltsin's speech to resume looking for answers her family had never found 40 years before.

But when it came to learning more about their case from the bilateral program of searching for missing American and Soviet prisoners, the women hit a brick wall. The Russian representatives on the joint commission insisted that there was nothing more behind the list—only that McDonough's and the other names were passed on by the Chinese officials who ran the Korean War prison camps. Any further information, they insisted, would have to come out of Peking.

The U.S. side of the joint commission continued to raise the RB-45 case at meetings with the Russians, often in conjunction with other MIA pilots whose names were also on the list of more than 500 people who had "transited through" an unidentified Soviet interrogation point.

Jeanne McDonough Dear, however, was convinced that the details of her father's final hours and actions were contained in records the Soviets would not look for or would not release—and documents that lay stored in U.S. archives, some still classified more than 40 years later.

Nancy Lovell Dean, meanwhile, who had been a college freshman when the shootdown occurred, was conducting her own search for records of her father's service and status. After finding a report dated Oct. 5, 1950, over Gen. Cabell's signature, that discussed using the RB-45 for reconnaissance over the Soviet Union, she became convinced that her father had been somehow involved in evaluating that idea.

She thought he was probably an intelligence observor on the flight along the Yalu. But nothing was clearcut.

Nancy Lovell Dean's search was made more difficult by the fact that despite the 1951 radio broadcast out of China, Lovell had never been officially listed as a POW, only as missing in action. Nonetheless, she did track down a Dec. 14, 1954 report by the U.S. Far East Command that listed him among 71 men "positively identified as remaining in the hands of the Communists" after the final exchange of prisoners in 1953.

But the big breakthrough came from a different mountain of archives, thousands of miles away. In Moscow were some of the very documents they were looking for.

In late 1992, Paul Cole, a Rand Corp. analyst, was doing research for a Pentagon study of missing American POWs in the former Soviet Union, a study that was supposed to parallel the work of the Pentagon's own team of analysts dubbed Task Force Russia.

One day, he received two documents from his team of archive researchers in Moscow. What they said stopped him cold.

Originated by Soviet intelligence officials, and bearing the names or signatures of some of the highest-ranking Soviet military officials in the Far East and Moscow, the documents described how Capt. McDonough had not only been interrogated by Russians, he apparently had died in their custody.

One of the documents from Cole's Moscow research team, dated Dec. 18, 1950, was addressed to Marshal Pavel Batitskiy, chief of the Soviet general staff in Moscow. It read: "I am informing you that the pilot from the shot-down RB-45 aircraft died en route and the interrogation was not finished." It was signed by Marshal Stepan Krasovskiy, senior Soviet military adviser to the Communist Chinese army and commander of all the aviation units in the Far East of North Korea, China and the USSR.

But before he died, the Soviet report of his interrogation said, McDonough told them that when the RB-45 was going down in flames, "all three crew members bailed out. I saw one run off, I don't know where the other went to, and I landed where the plane crashed."

The new Soviet documents not only contradicted the old debriefing reports, they exploded everything the families had assumed they knew about the incident up to that time, and at the same time raised a multitude of questions. If McDonough had told his interrogators the truth, then all four men aboard the RB-45 had parachuted from the plane and at least one besides him had bailed out successfully.

But was it to cover Lovell that he had referred to them as three crew members, not two crew members and a passenger?

The one he "saw run off" could have been Lovell, or a crewman. But if anyone else had bailed out successfully, wouldn't they have tried to help McDonough first? Had a crewman or Lovell gone in search of help, but been captured, or killed, himself? And if Lovell had survived, had McDonough maintained the presence of mind—despite bad burns and frostbitten feet from walking days in the snow without boots—to not mention his name?

In a poignant note, report of McDonough's December interrogation said he was "in critical condition" and asked that Russian military advisers be used to help rescue downed American pilots in North Korea. We're left to wonder whether McDonough was speaking in general, abstract terms, which seems unlikely in the circumstances, or whether he was simply pleading with his interrogators to hand him back to his own country.

The longer of the two documents Cole's team found regarding McDonough's shootdown also confirms the reported transfer of downed U.S. aircraft to Moscow. "All of the equipment which has been found to be in good repair, details and apparatus from the enemy airplanes will be sent to your address," states the message from "Belov." Belov is believed to be Mikhail M. Belov, a Soviet advisor. The "address" of Gen. Batitski and the general staff of the Soviet armed forces was Moscow. (See *Appendix.*)

Pentagon officials passed copies of the documents to Jeanne McDonough Dear. But it was another matter to persuade the Russians to confirm them and add any more information they could. Now the ball was in the Russians' court. Cole's research had proved that, contrary to the Russian side's declarations, more documents on the McDonough-Lovell incident existed. All they had to do was look them up in the same archives. But that proved to be neither simple nor fast.

In the spring of 1993, Task Force Russia, the team of analysts and translators assisting the American side of the joint commission, logged in from the Russians an interrogation report on a "Chals Maktonat." That was McDonough, in fractured translation.

The document was dated Jan. 11, 1951, but the interrogation was conducted on Dec. 18, 1950—indicating that the gravely injured pilot had survived at least to that date. And the report noted that the interrogation had been conducted in English, then translated from English to Russian by a "Chinese comrade." The questions were "generated" by a man named Kuznetsov.

The documents Cole had found clearly pointed to direct Soviet involvement with an American POW, so as usual, the Russian side of the commission reacted defensively. When pressed for more answers, Orlov, head of the Korean War working group, insisted that Soviet archives held no more documents related to the case. He asserted that the interrogation might have been suggested by the Soviets, but had been carried out by the Chinese, and any further information would have to come from the government in Peking.

Cole countered with an analysis that accused Orlov of deliberate misinterpretation, pointing out that since both documents were addressed to and signed by Soviet officials, passed between Soviet commands, and through Soviet communications channels, "there is no evidence of Chinese involvement in any of this material."[4]

Nancy Lovell Dean wrote Orlov, attempting to prod him into turning up the information she was sure had to exist behind the Soviet documents Cole's researchers had discovered.

At the joint commission's meeting in September 1994, Orlov mentioned receiving her letter, and replied this way:

"Col. Lovell was a known intelligence agent, was a military attache in Romania, and according to our data, Capt. McDonough's testimony, he indicated that the crew consisted of three people. The radio operator was killed, one escaped, and McDonough was captured and died of his wounds.

"Now, all of a sudden, a fourth person appears among the crew of this aircraft. We have no information regarding this individual."

Orlov was choosing to define McDonough's three "crewmen" to include McDonough, although common military usage would distinguish between a pilot and his crew. And his characterization of Lovell was close to saying that this "known intelligence agent" deserved whatever he had received.

Willfully or not, Orlov was taking a murky, complicated incident and making it even murkier.

The surfacing of so much material—and even new witnesses who said they remembered the RB-45 shootdown—eventually forced the Russians' hand. In late 1994, at a joint commission meeting, Orlov presented a composite of the two documents Cole's team had first turned up two years earlier. The composite, apparently written by Orlov, omitted some of the names, dates and information on the original documents and stated that the RB-45 pilot "died during evacuation from the aircraft crash site."

Orlov's choice of words to describe McDonough's death again blurred the sequence of events. In fact, if the pilot had died "during evacuation" from the crash site, how would it have been possible to interrogate him?

Jeanne McDonough Dear attended a commission-sponsored "family forum" meeting in Virginia in December 1994 so that she could bring up the composite report of her father's death Orlov had composed. She was at a distinct advantage—she had seen the original documents used to draw up the composite report on her father's death.

Who decided to "sanitize" the documents the Russians were handing over in her father's case, she asked? "When I compare the original to those passed to the commission, they are different." Orlov said he produced the short version only to leave out information unrelated to the POW/MIA issue.[5]

While Orlov was trying to limit the information getting out about the McDonough-Lovell incident, Jeanne McDonough Dear had learned enough to convince her it was time to hold a long-postponed ceremony for her father.

She got in touch with the Air Force, and before long the fly-over arrangements were made.

The new Soviet documents had raised a lot of questions about Lovell and the others aboard the RB-45, but at least to her mind, Capt. McDonough's fate was as clear as it needed to be.

Jeanne McDonough Dear wrote the Pentagon's POW/MIA office asking that her father's name be removed from consideration by the joint commission. "My family considers the case closed," she said. "We now have the information we wished to gain."

But the POW/MIA office still considers the case open. The office's Korean War analysts heard of former political officer Frionov's connection to the incident, and he was summoned for an interview before Russian and American representatives.

They hoped he could at last bring some clarity to this long-clouded incident. They hoped he could help them follow the old footprints in the snow, and count again the number of parachutes and men who had slipped out of sight on the banks of the Yalu.

* * *

When Pavel Frionov and the North Korean air force general reached the aviation command post about 10 miles south of the Yalu, they found a congenial American prisoner who could answer all of their questions.

"He was a likeable person," Frionov recalled. "We got along well with one another. He was a very good artist. He drew our aircraft in great detail, and then he answered all our questions."

Not only that, the American colonel had an amazing amount of intelligence information in his possesion—a briefcase full of photographs of Soviet aircraft and biographies of all the key Soviet commanders.

The material in the American's briefcase was a real find, Fironov said. Included were Soviet aircraft that were still "strictly experimental and had not gone into serious production." And the biographies of the Soviet commanders included their birthdays, career histories, even notes on their morale.

Before the two-and-a-half hours of questioning ended, the American mentioned that he had a daughter at home, "and in accordance with the Geneva conventions, he asked that his life be spared."

Fironov passed this on to the North Korean general, who "nodded his head."

It was clear to the American analysts and interviewers when they began listening to Fironov tell about his encounter with the American aviator that, even though the prisoner had told the Soviet political officer he was the RB-45's pilot, and also the commander of his regiment, that Fironov had not been interviewing McDonough. And, perhaps, not Lovell either.

For one thing, McDonough had not been picked up the day of the shootdown. He wandered through the snow-covered countryside for several days, looking for food and help, before being captured.

Secondly, the prisoner Firinov questioned was in good health, not sick or injured. McDonough's feet were frostbitten from walking barefoot and he had suffered severe burns when he landed in the burning wreckage of his plane.

Then was it Lovell he had talked to?

None of the interrogation reports released by the Russians have mentioned Lovell or given any indication he might have survived the shootdown. But there was the one mention on a Chinese radio broadcast during the war.

And according to James Wold, Ptak's successor as deputy assistant secretary of defense for POW/MIA affairs, "a retired Soviet general living in Ukraine has claimed that Col. Lovell survived the crash and was captured by the Chinese."[6]

Marshal Krasovski's involvement indicates a high-level interest in the RB-45 aircraft and all who were captured.

The description of the briefcase sounded like something a top-ranking Air Force intelligence chief might have—although not necessarily on board an aircraft in a combat zone.

And Fironov had picked a photo of Lovell over a photo of McDonough, when asked to choose the best likeness of the prisoner he interrogated.

But the man Fironov remembered was too young to have been Lovell. And Fironov said he hadn't been able to verify the prisoner's claim to be a colonel. "I determined he was a colonel only because he said he was a colonel."

Was there another shootdown that Fironov might have confused with McDonough's aircraft?

Fironov had another story, a gruesome one, that only added to the lack of certainty about the prisoner he had interviewed.

At about the time of the McDonough-Lovell shootdown, he said, a caucasian POW was led into a North Korean village near the site of the shootdown, escorted by a Soviet political officer. His hands were bound and a sign hung around his neck. The sign read, "American War Criminal."

The prisoner was beaten to death by angry villagers, Frionov said.

He doesn't know the prisoner's name.

Chapter Twelve

Trains to Ussurijsk

"But General Dean still persisted on his loyalty to his fatherland. I have never seen in my life such a brave and sacred character. I thought that the American people were so happy to have this kind of a general in their army."

—From a statement made soon after he was captured by U.S. troops
by Lee Kyu Hyon, a North Korean soldier
who served as an interpreter for Gen. William Dean
when he was in a Communist POW camp in 1950.

"You take it and tap out and communications went from there to Voroshilov-Ussurijsk... headquarters of the Primorskij Military District. And the Primorskij Military District went to Moscow. We practically did everything through the Primorskij Military District."

—Retired Soviet colonel Grigorij Derskiy,
who as an aide to the Soviet ambassador to North Korea,
made arrangements for American POWs to be shipped to the Soviet Union.

Grigorij Pavlovich Derskiy is a retired colonel in the Soviet army who served in the Korean War as a military advisor to a North Korean Army division and as an aide to Gen. Shtykov, the first Soviet ambassador to Pyongyang.

He has grown grandchildren, a bad heart, a voice that trembles from his aging chest and a small military pension. When he speaks about the past, his dates are sometimes confused, his attention sometimes strays and he can be repetitive, but his grasp of details is excellent.

As for his service in Korea, when he was a young Red Army captain with a firm, square face and two young children, all that remains is part of the diary he smuggled out, a Russian map of Korea he carried through nearly a year of war, and his memories of the American prisoners he met there.

When he was ordered back to Moscow in the summer of 1951, accused of poor judgment and harming the war effort, the fighting was still in progress and the Soviet and Chinese officers at the border of Manchuria demanded that he give up all of the papers, documents and reports he had accumulated since arriving in North Korea in April 1950. He held back only what he thought might get him through the disciplinary action he faced. He didn't want another accusation lodged against him.

Just as they weren't supposed to tell relatives or friends back home where they were in the letters they wrote home with coded military return addresses, Soviet military personnel who served in Korea were not allowed to take anything out of the war zone that could reveal the fact that they and thousands of others were assigned there, both as advisors and combatants.

Derskiy, who had come to North Korea with his wife and two young children, a boy and a girl, but had sent them home earlier, took the train back to Moscow. He was ordered before a party disciplinary hearing and reprimanded, essentially told he would never make general.[1]

But he remained in the service and finished out his career as a military attache in Czechoslovakia. In 1993, long retired, Derskiy presented himself and his stories about the prisoners he dealt with during the Korean War to American researchers assigned to the U.S.-Russian Joint Commission, the bilateral committee that is declassifying documents from Soviet archives and interviewing witnesses in a search for American prisoners who ended up in the former Soviet Union.

Since then, the Russian members of the commission have tried to discredit him, to cast doubt on Derskiy's memories and take away his integrity.

They imply that Derskiy is no more reliable than any other old and shaky veteran who, for whatever reason, is lying about what he did and who he met in Korea. They say there's no truth to Derskiy's testimony.

Here's what Derskiy told the Americans who came to interview him:

• He questioned Gen. William F. Dean, the highest-ranking U.S. prisoner of the Korean War, while Dean was being held in North Korea in the first months of the war and, at Shtykov's request, made arrangements for him to be shipped to Moscow. There, Dean was to be questioned further and persuaded to say things that could be used for Communist propaganda.

• The Soviet advisor Derskiy appointed to escort Dean out of North Korea, a Col. Nikolaev, reported to him that he had left Dean with Soviet officials at the northern border on the Tumen River and that he would be taken from there to a military airfield at Voroshilov-Ussurijsk and flown from there to Moscow.

• In the fall of 1950, he captured an American pilot whose plane ran out of fuel and made a forced landing in a rice paddy near him. He waited with the pilot until other Soviet and North Korean soldiers came to salvage the plane, then arranged to ship the pilot first to Manchuria and then on to the Soviet Union. Derskiy later saw the American pilot among a group of U.S. POWs in Mukden, Manchuria.[2]

• He shipped from Pyongyang to Moscow a man he was told was an American intelligence agent who had been trapped in Seoul when the war broke. The agent, named "Andreyko," was caught with lists of U.S. undercover agents then active throughout the Far East and a cache of U.S. dollars. Derskiy arranged for him to be sent by train to a Soviet military base just across Korea's northern frontier and, from there, flown to Moscow to be interrogated and, Derskiy assumed, executed for spying against the Soviet Union.

For the initial phase of the war, Derskiy kept tabulations on U.S. troops who were captured by the North Koreans.

Derskiy said he spoke to Andreyko in Russian. "We didn't interrogate him because we were told to send him to Moscow. Protocol was not followed, we didn't interrogate him. We only asked him if these were his documents, various names, letters of recommendation and money. He said that they were. I said that he must sign the document listing all these items and he did."

So if Derskiy's recollection is correct, somewhere in the archives of the Soviet embassy in Pyongyang or the records of the MVD in the Far East should be a document, the receipt for all of the items confiscated from Andreyko.

Then Derskiy explained how the transfer would be done.

"I said the Koreans will accompany us as a guard and I have designated Col. Nikolaev, a political officer who was a fine attache and whom I trusted, to take you to the border."

Derskiy also said that the intelligence agent was a large man, and he was worried that he would be difficult to restrain.

"We had to have handcuffs sent up," he said, "because he was a powerful man and the Korean handcuffs would not fit his thick wrists. We handcuffed his hands behind his back and covered his hands so that others could not see that he was handcuffed and took him away."

Derskiy said the intelligence operative was taken by train to the Soviet border, and flown from there to Moscow.

And his fate? "I'm sure he was killed," Derskiy stated. "An intelligence operative, they wouldn't allow him to live."

Much of what Derskiy said in his accounts was further confirmation of what others have described as the Soviet role in the handling of American POWs in Korea.

There is no question, for example, that the Soviets searched for, selected and interrogated American prisoners face-to-face, and in some cases shipped American aircraft—perhaps with their pilots—out of the war zone back to Moscow for study and observation.

As for shipping U.S. prisoners to the territory of the USSR, Gavril Korotkov, who was stationed in Khabarovsk with a staff of dozens of interrogators and intelligence officers trained in English and many of the other languages spoken by troops in the multi-national UN forces, confirmed that certain selected prisoners had been taken there for interrogation.

Most of the POWs the Soviets had access to were already being held in camps, under North Korean or Chinese custody, and while their captors could be possessive, they were regularly made available to the Soviet interrogators, who composed most of the questions the prisoners were asked.

Xu Ping Hua, a Chinese People's Army officer who handled POWs on the Manchurian border during the war, has described personally turning over a number of American pilots to Soviet officers, after being ordered to do so by his commanders.

A few prisoners were acquired directly. Like prisoners from the sky, they literally fell into their hands. As Orlov, of the Russian side of the joint commission, observed, "There were times when pilots ejected from their aircraft and landed in the vicinity of Russian batteries. In those cases, of course, contact was unavoidable."

A former anti-artillery brigade commander in Korea, Giorgi Matveyevich Leivikov, of Chelyabinsk, said that very thing happened to his unit one day in late 1952 or 1953, when his brigade was stationed just north of the 38th parallel.

After shooting down an American plane one day, said Leivikov, parachutes appeared overhead and two Americans from the crew of the aircraft landed yards away from their gun emplacement.

He said his men captured the pair, but since none of his men spoke English, they couldn't speak to the Americans. When he reported the incident to his superiors, Leivikov was ordered to escort them to a nearby railroad terminus.

From there, he said, they were taken to the Soviet military region north of the Tumen River, to the city of Barabash, where he understood there was a collection point for American POWs. Leivikov said he assumed the Americans were to be held until the end of the war, then exchanged for Russian or Chinese prisoners.[3]

Derskiy's account of shipping prisoners out of North Korea to the

USSR coincided greatly with Leivikov's, in terms of the route and destination of American POWs. The area just north of the North Korean border both talked about, the Primorskij Military District, has long been a major military anchor of Russian fortifications and military bases because of its proximity to the borders of two other countries, China and Korea. At the time of the Korean War, a major Soviet naval installation at Posyet was also within the district.

Thus what Derskiy described was a second major transfer route—Trains to Ussurijsk—that comprised a parallel process to the one Philip Corso and others described as going through Manchouli, and from there into the prison camps of the Gulag.

Derskiy described an order that Shtykov issued requiring American pilots be sent to Mukden, "They were sent there," Derskiy said, "All fliers were sent to China."

But the main element that set Derskiy's story apart, and that gave it special importance, was the fact that he claimed to have dealt with the war's most famous prisoner, Gen. William Dean.

Dean, who had served as military governor of Korea after World War II, was made commander of the 24th Infantry Division in Tokyo when the war broke out. The division furnished the first U.S. combat troops sent to Korea to counter the North Korean invasion.

A tall, ramrod-type leader with a reputation of staying close to the fight and to his men once a battle was joined, Dean became separated from his troops when the North Koreans overran the town of Taejon, in late July, 1950. For the next month, he was a hunted man.

Trying to make it through the city, already bristling with North Korean armor, Dean was thrown from his jeep and knocked unconscious, but managed to elude the troops that occupied Taejon.

Armed only with a pistol, he wandered through the hilly countryside for several weeks, trying to make contact with friendly forces. But after 35 days, while still behind enemy lines, he was caught—betrayed to the North Korean authorities by some villagers he had asked for food, he said—and spent the remainder of the war in captivity.

Dean was initially held in a jail in the city of Chonju, while the North Koreans took great pains to identify him by comparing him with photographs in their files and running a kind of lineup in which he was shown to a number of South Korean prisoners, public officials who had met or known him earlier when he served in the U.S. occupation government. Several confirmed that the slim, erect prisoner with the gaunt face was Gen. William F. Dean.

For several months, while the U.S. military listed Dean as missing, then declared he was killed (he was awarded the Medal of Honor in absentia on Sept. 30), the North Koreans kept secret the fact that he had been captured. Various rumors circulated and unconfirmed reports came from captured North Korean soldiers and liberated American POWs—that the general was dead, that he was wounded, that he was in a North Korean hospital, that he was in a camp with other U.S. POWs, that he had signed a "peace appeal," one of the statements the Communists frequently issued with prisoners' names or signatures attached, attacking the UN cause.

Dean spoke about his experiences as a POW after the war at various press conferences, and recounted those years in a book, "Gen. Dean's Story," published after the war. In those accounts, he said that except for a few days in the fall of 1950 when he was taken into Manchuria, he was held in North Korea the entire time.[4]

He said he had been interrogated frequently, sometimes for days at a time. But he never mentioned being sent to Moscow, or talking to a Soviet military advisor named Derskiy. (Dean died Aug. 25, 1981, in Berkeley, Calif., at the age of 82.)

After Derskiy's interviews with the American analysts were discussed at a meeting of the joint commission, Alexander Orlov, head of the investigation into the Korean War for the Russian side, had a highly critical view of the retired colonel's testimony.

"It must be noted," Orlov said at the December 1993 session, "that much of his testimony is not trustworthy and is refuted by other evidence and documents. Therefore, doubt is raised concerning the remainder of his testimony." In other words, if one part of his story is wrong, the rest must be wrong.

But Orlov left the door open: "Nevertheless, we will continue to check his testimony."

Despite Orlov's attitude, however, the American analysts thought there could be something to it. They ordered a re-interview, and afterward included this evaluation in their next summary report in October 1993:

"Colonel Derskiy's testimony remains consistent and lends weight to other sources of information suggesting that the Soviets took U.S. pilots from Korea to the Soviet Union during the Korean War. Derskiy claimed that he had knowledge of the transfer to the Soviet Union of the late Major General William F. Dean, one unnamed American pilot, and one United Nations intelligence agent named Andreyko (American or British) to the Soviet Union.

"Derskiy was ordered by Colonel-General Shtykov (a senior advisor to North Korea) to assist in the transfer of General Dean to the Soviet Union. Furthermore, Colonel Derskiy had knowledge of a directive which required that captured American pilots were to be sent to the Soviet Union. Derskiy described the case of one American pilot he said was captured under these circumstances and taken to the border between North Korea, China and the Soviet Union for transportation to the Soviet Union."

Besides Derskiy's testimony to guide them, the U.S. analysts had a few documents related to Dean's capture that the Russian side had turned over to them.[2]

One was January, 1951, telegram from Razuvayev, then the top Soviet military advisor in North Korea, saying Kim Il-Sung had asked him for advice on what to do with Dean. But the more extensive document was a report from S. Ogoltsov, deputy minister of state security (MGB/KGB) to Stalin and his top ministers, dated Sept. 17, 1950, on Dean's capture. The letter said that as soon as Dean was reported missing, the North Korean "MVD Border Troops" instituted a search for him.

The copy of the report to Stalin that the Russian side turned over was not complete—the name of the MGB (KGB) advisor to the North Korean government was whited out. But it included some new information. Dean was not interrogated from the time he was captured, Aug. 20, until Sept. 8, Ogoltsov informed the Kremlin, "because he was seriously ill." During three days of interrogation that took place 8-10 Sept., however, the report said:

"Dean at first attempted to resist giving any testimony. But, after he was told that the American Government considers him dead and that he is completely in the hands of the Korean People's Army Command, he began to testify. So far, only insignificant testimony, in particular, the number of personnel and armaments of the 24th Division, which he commanded, was given.

"The interrogation of General Dean continues. Further results of Dean's interrogation will be reported to you."

According to Derskiy, as Stalin and the rest of the Kremlin leadership were being kept advised of Dean's medical condition and every answer he gave, he was being summoned by Shtykov to assist in getting the general to talk about substantive military and intelligence matters.

Officially, said Derskiy, his Soviet commander in Korea was Lt. Gen. Vasiliyev. But Vasiliyev was in the field most of the time, he said, and "when the war started I reported to and carried out orders from Col.-Gen. Shtykov," the Soviet ambassador to North Korea.

Derskiy had commanded a rifle regiment on the Volkhov front in World War II, where Shtykov had been a major wartime commander. "That is how we met," said Derskiy. "He trusted me completely."

A military attache at the Soviet Embassy was killed soon after the war started, said Derskiy, "and Gen. Shtykov entrusted me with that position."

Shtykov was disappointed with the North Koreans and their prize prisoner, Gen. Dean. Not only had the North Koreans not told the Soviets right away that they had Dean in their custody, now they weren't getting much information out of him. The Soviets had given the North Koreans a long list of questions to ask Dean, but the method wasn't working very well. "When we reviewed the questionnaire," said Derskiy, "and found out it was General Dean we saw that he had not answered any of the questions. It was as if he was trying to conceal state secrets. He didn't answer anything."

There were many things they knew Dean could tell them. After all, before taking command of the 24th Division, Dean had been a key figure in the military-supervised government that had helped create the new Republic of Korea under president Syngman Rhee.

"There was a lot that interested us," said Derskiy. "We didn't know how much, although we already knew how many artillery battalions, how many batteries per battalion, what type of batteries, the firepower of these batteries." But, he said Shtykov told him, "'We know that there are powerful weapons being deployed and that these weapons have long ranges, but we don't know the specifics on them…' There was nothing of value on the questionnaire."

Shtykov, said Derskiy, ordered him to go talk to Dean, to see if he could loosen him up.

"He told me to 'go and speak with him. He is, after all, a general…You went as far as the Elbe (River). Meet with him…Speak with him. Maybe he will tell you something else.'" Derskiy's regiment had been among the Red Army troops that linked up with American troops on the Elbe at the conclusion of the war in Europe.

Derskiy said he and an interpreter went to speak with Dean, who was then being held in Seoul, "under the cover of a correspondent from Red Star," the Soviet military newspaper. He and Dean talked about the American and Russian troops meeting to celebrate the allied victory at the time of the Germans' surrender, and how "we worked together and defeated fascism as allies." According to Derskiy, it wasn't long before Dean realized that he was a Soviet military advisor, not a Red Star correspondent, but that Dean was not surprised to find Russians advising the North Koreans.

He said that he and the general got on well. When Dean told him that he had no razor or towel, Derskiy asked the North Koreans to see that he was supplied some toiletries. Then he recommended that Dean be moved to Pyongyang.

After that meeting, "At first I lost contact with him," said Derskiy, "then Shtykov called me and said that he needed to be transferred to the Soviet Union." Derskiy said he set about arranging to do that, just as he had arranged for the intelligence agent, "Andreyko," to be shipped there a few months earlier.

Shtykov, said Derskiy, "told me that the general was going to be transferred to the Soviet Union but that no one was to know about it." Derskiy said he arranged for another political advisor, Col. Nikolaev, to accompany Dean on the train from Pyongyang to a Soviet military base just beyond the USSR border, at Vorosilov-Ussurisk. From there, he was to be flown to Moscow.

"I already knew him so we didn't handcuff" the general, as they had the foreign intelligence agent a few months earlier, said Derskiy. "He was transported in a separate car on the train. There was a guard on the car...He was transferred to the border location," southwest of Vladivostok.

Derskiy said Nikolaev later told him that "he went to the bridge" over the Tumen River, which is the boundary between North Korea and the former Soviet Union. "He stated that there were generals there. There were vehicles there to take him to the airfield." Derskiy said he was never informed of what happened to Dean after that.

Despite the positive evaluation of Derskiy's story by the joint commission's American analysts, based on what was known of Dean's captivity from the public record in the U.S., the Russians' criticism had a valid basis.

What was known of Dean's captivity suggested that Derskiy was lying, creating an exaggerated story to tell the Americans. The record showed that:

• The only interrogators Dean mentioned when he was released or in his later book were North Koreans.[4]

• The only time he mentioned leaving North Korea was when he was taken into Manchuria for four days in late October, where he was held in "a Chinese-type hotel." His guards had even steadfastly denied they were in China, saying it was a Chinese settlement within North Korea. Dean knew that they had crossed to the northern bank of the Yalu, however, which is the border between Manchuria and North Korea.

• The only Russians Dean reported seeing while a POW were a civilian he thought might be a technical advisor and several uniformed Soviet officers in the city of Manpojin, where he was held for part of his nearly three years in captivity.

• And the only non-Korean visitor Dean spoke of seeing while he was a prisoner was Wilfred Burchett, an Australian Communist newspaper correspondent. Burchett was granted access to a number of American prisoners in Korean War camps. His dispatches, published in Communist newspapers around the world, were among the torrent of Communist propaganda written, published and broadcast from the Communist POW camps during the war in a determined campaign to make it appear that even the U.S. soldiers fighting there were opposed to the United Nations effort.

But recently declassified documents in Gen. Dean's file, part of the record of his debriefings after he was repatriated, tell a much different story. They expand on what Dean said publicly after he was repatriated, and support Derskiy's account of POWs being sent to the USSR aboard trains to Ussurijsk.

The documents confirm that:

• The Soviets expressed a desire, as soon as they knew Dean was a prisoner, to have him transferred to Moscow,;

• That North Korean and Soviet officials made arrangements to do so, and word was received in North Korea that he had reached Moscow;

• And that, in fact, he may have secretly been transported there and back on a never-disclosed trip between Pyongyang and Moscow, either shortly after his capture or the following year.

Moreover, the debriefing papers say that when Dean was initially captured, he was among a group of American prisoners that included three other military officers and an American woman, who is not identified. Documents in the debriefing file disclose:

• A North Korean army major taken prisoner in October 1951, Mun Man Sun, told U.S. interrogators that he monitored a coded message on Sept. 3, 1951, to North Korean army general headquarters saying that "no announcement was to be made" but that the Soviet military headquarters for the Far East in Khabarovsk had informed the North Korean general staff "that Gen. Dean was to be sent to Moscow in Sep 50, exact day unknown."

Man Man Sun also said that in late August, 1950, while at the Soviet military advisory group's field headquarters in Pyongyang, a Soviet military telegraph operator, a non-commissioned officer named Chitov, showed him "a photograph of Gen. DEAN, a white woman, three white men and a Soviet Army colonel, a member of the advisory group attached to NKA Field HQ. Latter was dressed in civilian clothing, posing as a TASS correspondent. PW knows this man by appearance but cannot recall his name. Gen. DEAN and others in the photograph appeared well and did not appear to have been wounded or injured. Photograph had been taken on Capitol Building grounds."

Mun said the advance army headquarters received word on Aug. 23 of Dean's capture, in a message that reached the communication bureau while he was on duty there, and that the initial report stated Dean had been captured with "an American driver, two American officers and an American female."

He said a top secret message was then sent from the general staff headquarters to the 4th Division troops who then had the general and the other American prisoners in custody in a jail in the town of Chinan, ordering the North Korean troops to turn them all over to the chief Soviet military advisor in Seoul, Col. Kalinin.

• Lt. Kang Sok Kun, another North Korean POW who worked in the military communications bureau in Pyongyang, said he had seen Dean being driven away from North Korean army headquarters there in late August, 1950.

"Kang was told that the jeep was going to Antung City, Manchuria, and from there General Dean would be flown to Moscow.

"On 5 September 1950, Kang saw a copy of a secret message at the Communication Bureau in Pyongyang City the contents of which were as follows: 'General Dean arrived safely in Moscow.'"

• In March, 1951, U.S. forces interrogated a North Korean POW named Lee Qu Hyun, who said he had been assigned to act as personal interpreter for Dean while the general was being held in Pyongyang the previous September. Lee said another interpreter was assigned to accompany Dean when he was moved north at the end of September because U.S. troops were advancing on the capital. Lee later surrendered voluntarily to the UN forces. A report of his debriefing said:

"When Lee and the general parted, the general had recovered from the diarrhea and seemed to be in much better health. Lee believes that General Dean was taken to Manchuria or Russia although this is purely personal opinion."

And there is one more indication in Gen. Dean's papers that his captors took him out of the war zone—a two-month gap in the chronology of his imprisonment.

When he was repatriated, Dean told his debriefers each place he'd been kept and for how long—down to the day. Dean's prison chronology accounts for all three years—except the months of August and September 1951.

It's possible the omission was inadvertent. But no change of location is indicated—only a time gap.[5] (A complete chronology appears in *Notes and Sources*, p. 281)

* * *

The other document from Soviet archives the Russian side of the joint commission has released—a Jan. 21, 1951, telegram to Soviet generals Shtemenko and Vasilevskij from Gen. Razuvaev, then the chief military advisor to the North Koreans—is difficult to interpret. Apparently written a full six months after Dean's capture, and well after it was known that he was alive and a prisoner, the telegram summarizes what by then was an old story:

"The Koreans took American General Dean prisoner in the autumn of 1950.

"Surrounded, Dean had changed clothes and for quite a long time hid out in Korean villages. He was subsequently discovered and detained. The Americans announced at the time that Dean was missing in action. The Koreans did not announce Dean's capture and kept the matter a secret.

"Kim Il-Sung approached me for advice on the matter of what to do with Dean.

"I declined to answer.

"Request you tell me whether you have any kind of instructions on this matter from your side."

The wording suggests that Kim might have been considering some kind of offer—perhaps a swap—involving Dean.

The chronology of his movements while a POW that Dean provided to military debriefers after his release indicates that when Razuvaev sent his telegram, Dean had just been moved from Manpojin, near the Yalu River, to Pyongyang, the North Korean capital. The chronology shows that he remained in that area for the next two years, moving into caves and underground shelters as Pyongyang's above-ground structures were reduced to rubble by intense allied bombing.

When he was repatriated, Dean spoke of growing suicidal over his inability to cope with the stress of imprisonment while he was a captive of the communists. Perhaps the Soviets wanted to move the general to Moscow for closer supervision, but decided he was not psychologically capable of undergoing the strain of being hauled off to the seat of Soviet power.

His value as an intelligence source would diminish the longer he spent in a POW camp in North Korea, and the Soviets were clearly not pleased with what their North Korean agents had been able to pull out of him initially.

Once in Moscow, if his presence were discovered, it would have drawn more attention to the Soviets' role in the war than was obviously desired by either the U.S. or the Soviet Union.

So keeping a Moscow visit secret would have served both countries' interest by not raising international tensions any higher.

There would have been some witnesses. Perhaps they'll come forward.

And somewhere in the archives there should be a reply to Razuvaev's question:

What should be done with Gen. Dean?

* * *

The other key figure in Derskiy's startling account of serving as Shtykov's aide-de-camp and shipper of American POWs is the man he knew as "Andreyko," the intelligence agent captured in Seoul with rosters of underground, anti-communist operatives and a cache of U.S. money.

After all, if Derskiy's account of shipping "Andreyko" to the Primorskij Military District in July 1950 could be shown to be false, how much confidence should be placed in the stories about the American pilot, and about questioning Gen. Dean, and sending him off to the USSR on a train a few months later?

So whether Andreyko'was a real person, or a figment of Derskiy's imagination, is crucial in evaluating the growing evidence for transfers of American prisoners to the former Soviet Union.

Who was Andreyko?

* * *

In early July 1950, a few days after the invasion of South Korea, Capt. Grigorij Derskiy received an order from his superior, Col. Kuznetsov, at the Soviet military advisers' headquarters in Pyongyang.

Derskiy's principal duty since preparations for the invasion began in early 1950 had been to advise Gen. Lee Hung Mu, 4th Division commander, whose troops were involved in some of the heaviest combat against the United Nations force.

Derskiy was given a special mission: take charge of a captured American intelligence agent and prepare him to be shipped out of North Korea to the Soviet Union. He was to take the prisoner from a North Korean POW compound near Pyongyang to a railroad hub 40 kilometers away. There he would relinquish custody to another Soviet officer, Col. Nikolayev, who would personally escort the man on a train to the Soviet Union and turn him over to a Soviet general officer.

The assignment didn't cause the young Soviet officer anxiety or surprise him, as it might have some other Russians. For he had met Americans before, and liked them. He had fond memories of befriending U.S. soldiers in May 1945, when his rifle regiment was among the Red Army forces massed along the Elbe River, facing the Americans on the opposite bank.

They had merged their forces, cheered, linked arms and toasted their common victory over the defeated Nazis.

But things were very different only five years later in Korea. The U.S. troops were fighting again, and this time against a Russian ally, the North Koreans. The Soviets were "non-combatants," ready only to help the United Nations find a peaceful solution.

The posture of neutrality was an obvious sham. And as for handling American prisoners, it was obviously a dirty business for the Soviets to covertly interrogate and appropriate for their own purposes selected prisoners from a war in which they were providing the weapons, the expertise and the ideological backing, but none of the ground troops—none of the prisoners.

To Soviet dictator Joseph Stalin, prisoners—Russians in enemy hands as well as foreigners held by his forces—had always been one of war's most plentiful and expendable resources. Civilians or soldiers, Russians or foreigners, it made little difference; having been captured, they were all damaged goods.

Alive, they might offer intelligence or, at the least, badly needed, trained manpower. Dead, murdered in sufficient numbers as in the Katyn Forest, they could serve as object lessons of terror.

But the Soviet military command had ordered it, and so it would be done. Derskiy was told the American prisoner's name was "Lt. Col. Andreyko," or, because he was dressed in civilian clothes, simply "Andreyko. " He had been captured on June 28 trying to flee Seoul in a U.S. military jeep. He had been among the thousands who were prevented from escaping the besieged capital when South Korean troops blew up the main bridge over the Han River just after midnight to slow the advance of the North Korean invaders.

The North Koreans and their Soviet advisors had determined that "Andreyko" was working for U.S. or British intelligence because of the large amount of U.S. money in his possession and the documents he was carrying when captured: lists of undercover agents working for western intelligence agencies throughout North Korea, Manchuria and Siberia.

Since before World War II, intelligence agencies from several world powers—not only the U.S. and Britain but Japan, China, Germany and the Soviet Union—had worked diligently to install their own intelligence networks throughout the Far East.

After Japan fell, the battle among spies in the region narrowed, re-forming along Cold War lines: West vs East, the Communist powers vs the democracies.

The Soviets, with an estimated 2.7 million Japanese POWs from World War II salted away in Siberian labor and penal camps, had turned the Far East into a virtual spy factory by training select prisoners to be agents. Once repatriated to Japan, they would be available to carry out Communist sabotage, espionage or, at the very least, propaganda and harassment of western institutions and interests.

The Americans had just entered the espionage-intelligence game in Asia during World War II, modeling the OSS (Office of Strategic Services, forerunner of the CIA) after the British secret service. From 1945 on, U.S. intelligence efforts in Asia proliferated, but on a minor scale relative to Europe and the Middle East.

While the U.S. remained on the sidelines in China, the British—who retained a useful colony in Hong Kong—had made rapid accommodation with Mao Tse-Tung's successful Communist guerrilla movement. They were the real players in the region.

But with the list of names confiscated from the prisoner Andreyko, the Soviets and the Communist Chinese would be able to make short work of the network of anti-communist agents slowly built up since the end of Japanese rule in the Pacific.

The confiscated documents, Derskiy was told, allowed the Communists to shut down virtually all U.S. intelligence operations in the region north of the 38th parallel within a few months.[6] And to lock down the source of their lucky find and prevent word of his capture from leaking, they were separating him from the other prisoners and shipping him north.

As for the notion that an American intelligence agent could have been caught with a sheaf of classified documents, it is well to remember that the Korean War pre-dated the paper shredder.

The official and private reports of the June 1950 evacuation of the U.S. embassy in Seoul include notations that classified material was burned before the Communists overran the city. One account mentions that a huge mound of classified documents, set on fire in the embassy parking lot, lighted up the sky for hours the last night before the big evacuation. But that's no assurance that all the material that should have been was destroyed to keep it out of enemy hands.

On the contrary, when the UN forces re-took Seoul in early October 1950, a story in the New York Times describing the city after several months of communist occupation said classified U.S. documents could still be found lying in the street.

The story noted that all American officials had "left the city in haste. There was no time thoroughly to destroy all the confidential and secret memoranda and correspondence between Seoul and Washington, as well as other correspondence between the Korean government and United States representatives in Seoul.

"Upon their return to Seoul last week American officials found virtually the entire contents of desks, filing cabinets and safes strewn about as if by a cyclone. It was immediately apparent that looters, presumably

North Korean troops, had had no instructions about the documents.

"This is regarded by American authorities in Seoul as evidence that Russian political agents or military officers in all probability not only had not accompanied the invading troops but at no time following the capture of Seoul had evinced interest in the valuable papers available to any street urchin.

"The bulky United States papers lay rainsoaked in Seoul's muddy gutters. Whether all this resulted from the failure of some responsible North Korean or Russian official to collect them for their political or intelligence value or from the lack of any plan for the political as well as the military conquest of Korea. (sic)."

While Andreyko was his prisoner, Derskiy treated him as a fellow soldier, especially once the two men traded personal histories. They chatted about the irony of two men from Ukraine, both veterans of "The Great Patriotic War," meeting in this fashion, allies in one worldwide struggle ending up on opposing sides in a nasty little war on a divided peninsula.

Derskiy doesn't remember if he ever knew the prisoner's first name, but says Andreyko told him that his family emigrated from Ukraine to the United States in the 1920s, and that he had come to Korea while serving in the U.S. military's Pacific forces during World War II.

But once the prisoner was placed in a train car to be shipped north, the friendly chat was over. It was clear strict measures would be needed. "Andreyko was a big man, very strong" and "very athletic," said Derskiy. "The Koreans were much smaller, and were worried that he might overpower them. So it was decided that we should tie him up so that he couldn't escape."

As the North Koreans bound their imposing prisoner in lengths of rope so he couldn't wriggle free, Derskiy said he and Col. Nikolayev, the Soviet officer charged with taking him to the Soviet Union, traded helpless looks. Andreyko wouldn't be able to feed or relieve himself with his big hands tied behind him for days while the train made its way along the Korean coast to Barabash and Voroshilov-Ussurijsk. But they had no choice.

When the train began to pull away, Derskiy remembers, Korean children watching at the railroad siding jumped up and down and shouted excitedly, "They're taking the general away! The general is going away!"

To the children, a powerful-looking caucasian prisoner bound tightly so he couldn't run away could be no less a prize than a general.

Before long, Derskiy would spend time questioning a real American general—Gen. William Dean, captured in the fall of 1950 and held until the armistice almost three years later. But the first POW he was shipping to the Soviet Union from Korea wasn't a general.

In fact, except for the papers and money found on him, there was no actual proof of who he was, said Derskiy. He could have been one of the agents Stalin frequently complained of, the ones the U.S. kept sending into the Soviet bloc countries after World War II, to the Baltics, to Ukraine, Eastern Europe, Armenia, the Far East. Many were former Soviet soldiers who escaped from their native countries. They fled to the U.S., then volunteered to return secretly as a fifth column and foment trouble for the Communists.

They were in his jeep, but perhaps the cash and lists of agents belonged to someone else.

He could have been a lieutenant colonel, either then or during the war in the Pacific—or not. It would make little difference to the Soviet and North Korean interrogators who decided that a caucasian man in a jeep with a briefcase full of secret papers who had been unlucky enough to get trapped on the wrong side of the Han River bridge was a foreign spy.

And whether or not he truly was—as he told the Ukraine-born Derskiy—an American citizen and World War II veteran whose parents emigrated to the U.S. from Ukraine in the 1920s—that was irrelevant, too.

For if in fact he was the intelligence operative that the Soviets and North Koreans believed him to be, very little—if anything—of what he told Derskiy or his other escorts, interrogators and fellow prisoners can be taken literally.

By definition, and by dint of circumstances, he was someone in deep trouble, caught with the goods and prepared to say whatever he needed to say to escape his severe predicament.

Yet it is clear from the scenarios and descriptions given by two sources on opposite sides of the POW camp barbed wire—Soviet advisor Derskiy on one hand and the missionaries, diplomats and other civilian residents of Seoul who were taken prisoner in the war's first weeks on the other—that he is someone that all of them must have known.

• Derskiy knew him as Andreyko—a beefy, middle-aged but strong and athletic intelligence agent with a military background who was captured trying to escape Seoul in a jeep, then shipped out of North Korea to the USSR by the Soviets and never seen again.

• His fellow POWs from the White Russian community knew him as Andre Marzlitsky—a strong, middle-aged diver and engineer with a military background, a U.S. aid worker who spoke Russian and English, drove a jeep around Seoul and, once captured, was taken away for questioning by the Soviets and never seen again.

"I'm sure they wouldn't let him live" after reaching Moscow, Derskiy said. "Not an important intelligence agent like him."

His actual name, of course, could have been Andreyko or Marzlitsky, or something else—just as his actual job could have been to stay behind when the Americans left, at the risk of being caught, and he did his job almost flawlessly.

All we may assume, thanks to Derskiy and the civilian prisoners who survived the war as POWs, is that he left North Korea bound for the Soviet Union aboard one of the trains to Ussurijsk.

Chapter Thirteen

The Cancer Patient

"We have not been able to establish a single verifiable instance of the transfer of an American prisoner of war in Korea to the territory of the USSR."

—Gen. Dmitri Volkogonov,
chairman of the Russian side of the joint commission,
April 1995.

"Now the reason is clear to me. I know that the imprisonment of Mandra, a United States Marine, was a violation of international law and the Geneva Convention by the Soviet Union."

—Valerij Petrovich Pavlenko, former Gulag inmate,
on why Russian authorities would still be trying to conceal the fact that a Korean War
POW was in prison with him in 1979.

In 1978, Valerij Petrovich Pavlenko, a geologist with an interest in politics, was serving time in a Soviet prison camp near the village of Susuman, in the Magadan region of Siberia.

Earlier that year, at the age of 29, he had written a letter to Chairman Brezhnev, presenting his suggestions for rights to be included in a revised constitution that the party was then discussing. For that, he was "repressed," as the Russians term it, meaning he was first followed and threatened, then convicted on trumped-up charges and sent to the Gulag, and while he was in prison most of his relatives, including his father, who had fought in the Great Patriotic War against Nazi Germany, were placed under surveillance by the KGB.

The official charge against him was illegal possession of firearms. But he had a permit to own a small rifle that he kept at home for hunting, so he knew that wasn't the real crime. After his trial, the KGB director in his home town confided to him that it was not the gun that sent him to prison, it was his letter criticizing the draft of the constitution.

"Your father is highly regarded at work," the KGB agent told him. "How could you write such a letter?" Pavlenko officially apologized, writing a repentant letter, but that took nothing away from his sentence.

At Susuman, he was given the job of orderly in the prison hospital. One day he was transferred to a job in the cancer ward. That's where he said he met Phillip V. Mandra, a U.S. Marine taken prisoner in Korea.

The arrival of an American anywhere in the interior of the Soviet Union during those days would have been cause for a lot of attention and discussion. It was no different at the prison hospital in Magadan. When word got around that an American was in the prison's cancer ward, "everyone was talking about it at the time," said Pavlenko. The people who attended him every day referred to him by his last name, as "Mandra."

Pavlenko walked into the room where the American was being kept, sat down on his bunk and introduced himself.

"Just call me Phillip," the prisoner told him. Phillip Mandra had a terminal case of throat cancer, Pavlenko said, and looked it. Even though he said he was only 48, he looked much older, emaciated and balding, very tired-looking, with dark circles under his eyes and a yellow pallor to his skin.

"I will probably die soon," he told his new visitor. Pavlenko went to see Mandra from time to time, and they would talk. "I lie down and cannot fall asleep," Mandra told Pavlenko. "I think about everything, my past, of America, of my close ones."

When Pavlenko asked him what he had done to be sent to prison, Mandra told him a story that Pavlenko assumed was a lie, a made-up concoction, as many stories are in prison, not to impress or frighten but to keep other prisoners from knowing the truth, since the truth can make some people very angry.

"He said that on orders of the American Mafia he had carried narcotics into Austria in 1946, right after the war." When Pavlenko broke the rules of prison etiquette and asked Mandra how he had been arrested, he got more of the Mafia story, a tale of throwing the narcotics out a window but being caught with foreign currency. He also told Pavlenko that he had been born in Czechoslovakia, but that he lived in America and that he had a wife and child there.

Three or four weeks after he arrived at the prison hospital, in January 1979, despite the daily injections he was receiving, Mandra was dead.

By this time, Pavlenko had been transferred out of the cancer ward, but he was able to observe as the American prisoner's body was being prepared for burial. He saw that a tag with the name of the deceased had been attached to one foot, as was customary. The tag read "Phillip Vinyanimovich Mandra," he said.

Unlike the typical prisoner funeral in the Gulag, which is seldom more than a quiet putting away of the corpse, a burial document was prepared and Mandra was given a traditional burial, meaning a wooden marker at the site of the grave in the Susuman public cemetery.

Pavlenko and the other prisoners "could not leave the prison grounds," said Pavlenko, so the actual burial was carried out by the hospital's director, a Major Trusov. The entire event was carried out as though it was a matter of some importance to see that a U.S. citizen was buried in the proper manner, Pavlenko said.

Asked recently about his conversations with Phillip Mandra, and why he had disbelieved his story about his past (Mandra is an Italian name, not Czech), Pavlenko said that "I sensed that he devised his story as he went along," or that he was merely repeating "this version of his, (what) had been prepared ahead of time," but that the actual story of how he had come to be a prisoner in the Gulag "was necessary for him to hide."

He didn't believe Mandra's story about being a narcotics trafficker for the Mafia, he said, "because Philip was not that kind of person." He only knew the American briefly, but long enough, he said, to know he was not "a bandit. He is an intelligent, a very sort of 'wounded soul' person. He could not have engaged in the business of narcotics. I understood that he needed to tell me untruths."

Pavlenko learned after he was released from prison in Magadan, from an English-language book about American POWs he found in a store in Ukraine, that a Marine by the name of Phillip Vincent Mandra, of Queens, N.Y., was reported missing in action in the Korean War in 1952. Pavlenko is one of the dozens of Russians who have volunteered their stories to U.S. officials in the past several years about encountering Americans in the Gulag prisons of the former Soviet Union. The appeals to Russians to speak out have been published in newspapers and broadcast over television since 1992, when the U.S.-Russian Joint Commission was established.

In addition to those ads and appeals, a number of other private individuals, family members of missing American POWs and numerous human rights organizations from Russia and western countries have also circulated information about individual POWs and MIAs, asking for anyone with information— former prisoners, guards, officials, security agents— to step forward.

One of the most active and dedicated family members taking on this kind of campaign is Irene Mandra, the sister of Marine Sgt. Phillip Mandra.

For the past few years, she's pursued a number of leads about her brother's fate, especially those coming out of the former Soviet Union. She traveled to Moscow in 1994, while the joint commission was having one of its meetings there. She went hoping to meet a former colonel in the MVD, the internal security police, named Vladimir Markarovich Malinin.

As chief of the inspector general's division for the Leningrad (St. Petersburg) district, Malinin had been high in the internal affairs bureaucracy. He had made a career of police work ever since graduating from the KGB academy as a young man.

In the early 1960s, Malinin was visiting the KGB prison in Magadan. While talking to the prison commandant, in his second-floor office, Malinin looked out the window, into the prison exercise yard. There he saw a man, alone, walking slowly in a circle.[1]

The man was no more than 30 yards away. Perhaps sensing that he was being watched, he stopped and gazed upwards, giving Malinin a clear look at his face.

The prison commander told Malinin that the prisoner was an American spy who had just been transferred to the Magadan headquarters prison from a remote camp in the Gulag.

Three years later, Malinin was back in Magadan, visiting the same KGB offices. When he looked out into the courtyard from the commander's office, he saw the same man he had seen on the earlier visit.

When he heard about the U.S.-Russian Joint Commission's interest in American prisoners in the Gulag, Malinin volunteered his story. Analysts from Task Force Russia, the group of Army specialists then assisting the commission, showed him a number of photographs of missing American POWs.

Malinin picked out a photo of Sgt. Phillip Mandra.

Irene Mandra is still not certain whether the prisoner Malinin saw in the courtyard, or the prisoner Pavlenko befriended as he was dying of throat cancer in a Gulag hospital was her brother. They may not have even been the same prisoner. The prison rolls in the Magadan region of the Gulag go back to the 1930s, and number in the millions.[2]

* * *

After recalling the very unusual experience of encountering an American man in the prison hospital in Magadan, there was no doubt in Pavlenko's mind that "Phillip Mandra," the American who died of throat cancer in his prison hospital in 1979, is the missing U.S. soldier. And he believes there were probably very good reasons for the man to lie about why he was there.

"If he had told me the truth," said Pavlenko, "that he was an American prisoner of war, that he was an American Marine who had been captured in Korea, I would have of course sympathized with him. But people would have found out about it, people who would have simply had him killed, knowing that he had spoken the truth about himself.

"Because the Soviet Union held an American prisoner of war in jail and were breaking the convention of the status of prisoners of war which they themselves had signed.

"Therefore it's possible that Philip Vincent Mandra had been compelled to assume the conditions set but the authorities do not speak of the fact that he was a prisoner of war. Otherwise he would be held in solitary confinement in jail. He wouldn't receive any more such favorable terms such as being in the area among people.

"Therefore, he was simply held there, like a trophy in the jail."

Pavlenko was asked to fly to Moscow from his home in the Russian Far East to present the details of his testimony to both sides of the U.S.-Russian Joint Commission.

He presented essentially the same story he had since first contacting the U.S. consulate in Vladivostok, and added that his story is supported by the word of Gennadi Aleksandrovich Melnikov, who was the "senior orderly" or chief medic for the cancer ward where Mandra was hospitalized and who Pavlenko said befriended the American, too. At night, "they used to sit around and drink illegal tea together," he said. "He identified Phillip Mandra right away," he said.

Pavlenko told the commissioners he had attempted to find evidence to back up his story in 1993, when he returned to Susuman with the author of the book about American POWs where he had first learned of the Phillip Mandra case.[3]

He expected to find Mandra's marked grave. But when he reached the public cemetery, he was disappointed.

"Unfortunately, it had been a very severe winter," said Pavlenko. "There was much snow on the ground." But he was able to locate the prison doctor, Shpak, and Gennadi Melnikov, who still lives in Magadan. They remembered the American prisoner who had died in the prison hospital in 1979.

A representative of the American side of the joint commission, Jim Connell, interviewed Shpak and Melnikov, too, in March 1995. He reported that they said they remembered a patient who died of throat cancer who spoke English, but that they didn't know his name. Connell also checked the records of the prison hospital where Pavlenko said Mandra died.

The hospital records, Connell reported, show that only one patient died there of throat cancer in January 1979, but his name was listed as "Stepan Afanasyevich Mikhailetsky."

Pavlenko said he recalled that patient, too, but that it was not the same one as the American, Phillip Mandra.[4]

The Russian representatives on the joint commission have attempted to discredit Pavlenko's and Melinin's stories. And they have also begun to make it clear that by coming forward to tell his story about the American patient who died in a Magadan cancer ward, he has risked having his own life and activities re-investigated.

When called to Moscow to testify before the commission in April 1995. Gen. Maj. Kalinin, of the Russian Security Service, attacked Pavlenko's story, saying it couldn't be true because "since 1979, there has been a law that prohibits citizens of the USSR from being incarcerated in the same facilities as foreigners…so there is no way that a Soviet citizen could have been imprisoned with a foreigner."

Pavlenko answered that there was also "another law on the books that prohibited first-time offenders from being housed with repeat offenders," and since that law was frequently broken by the authorities, it would not be unusual for the law about separate facilities for foreign prisoners to be as well. The hospital drew its patients from four or five separate prisons within the Magadan area.

Then came this exchange between Kalinin and Pavlenko:

Kalinin: You are calling this individual "Phillip Mandra," and his identity has yet to be proven. I will do everything in my power to check out all of your testimony— in terms of where you were incarcerated and your duties. As to why you were the target of Major Trusa (Pavlenko had complained that the hospital director had made false accusations against him while he was working at the prison hospital) I will clarify that as well. You and I will discuss this matter later.

Pavlenko: How am I to take your last statement. As a threat?

Kalinin: No, I only meant that I will attempt to discern the relationship that existed between you and Major Trusa.

Pavlenko: I request that the commission protect me from the threats leveled by Gen. Kalinin. I have no intention of meeting with him.

Pavlenko said that after he was sent a telegram by the joint commission's American staff in Moscow, "the very next day my telephone was cut" and that the police attempted to break into his house.

Gen. Mazurov, the Russian side's representative from the intelligence and security agencies, interjected that Pavlenko had flown "freely" to Moscow from his home in Kamchatka. "If someone wanted to persecute you, you would have never left the city."

An American representative from the State Department, John Herbst, came to Pavlenko's defense: "We also feel that any person giving testimony here should not pay any penalty for such testimony. You should be able to do so freely without problems."

But Pavlenko left the commission meeting room with great pessimism about his story ever receiving a fair hearing.

Responding to Connell's remark that Melnikov, the close, tea-sharing friend of Mandra, had said he didn't recall the cancer patient's name, Pavlenko said when he had first talked to Melnikov two years ago, "he said that he definitely remembered the name Phillip. He could not remember the last name. He also told me over the phone that he recognized Mandra in a photograph."

But those were details. His visit to Moscow to tell his story about the American POW from Korea in a Siberian prison hospital had left him sure of only one thing:'

"I have no doubt," Pavlenko said, "that any search in the archives will prove futile.

"All data has been removed, and it will be very difficult at this time to find any documentation regarding this case, if any still exists. I fully understand my value as one witness is zero.

"The strength of my testimony is only as supported by witnesses such as Shpak, Melnikov and others who were there at the same time. The fact that other evidence will be repressed even today is obvious to me based on the words of Gen. Kalinin."

When Pavlenko had left, Orlov—who seldom misses an opportunity to mis-state, ridicule or minimize the value of any testimony that points toward Soviet responsibility for missing American POWs—gave this parting comment:

"In his testimony, the witness created for himself an image of an uncompromising fighter for justice. The person whom he called 'Mandra' he has presented as some kind of prison hero, who was encircled by an aura of respect and mystery. All this requires a very thorough check and double-check. Unfortunately, our past experience shows that some of the evidence acquired during the work of our commission has not been justified or proven.

"We are of the opinion now that the case as presented by Pavlenko better served his personal interest than the work of the commission."

Pavlenko's evidence was being disputed and his motives demeaned, but the Russian commissioners had lamentably made little effort to actually test or investigate his story. All Gulag witnesses are not equal in integrity, of course, and the search for missing prisoners of war has turned up a goodly share of money-seekers and mental cases. But judgments on the commission's Russian witnesses, by the Russian commissioners, are routinely rendered before any real checking has been done.

As to this specific case, it is difficult to see how Pavlenko's or Malinin's "personal interest" has been served, at least to date. Irene Mandra's personal interest in the truth about her brother, and the U.S. government's assumed interest in a full accounting of all prisoners of war, may eventually be served, once stories like Pavlenko's and Malinin's are treated as legitimate until proven false by all of the Russian-appointed representatives of the joint commission that has made this sad but important search its work.

Chapter Fourteen

Order of the Red Banner

"It is evident that the further we advance, the more questions arise. Things become less clear, not more clear."

—Gen.-Lt. Anatoli Krayushkin, Russian co-chairman of the Cold War working group of the U.S.-Russian Joint Commission on American POWs in the Former Soviet Union, speaking at the April 1995 sessions in Moscow.

"All such flights cannot remain a secret and probably a small percentage of aircraft would be destroyed...but not so great as to be prohibitive."

—From a February 1951 Joint Chiefs of Staff paper recommending a stepped-up program of aerial reconnaissance during the Korean War throughout the Far East.

In the joint commission's work of obtaining information from the long-closed Soviet military and ministry files on missing American servicemen in the former USSR, the fourth war—in addition to World War II, Korea and Vietnam—is the Cold War.

It involves the fewest cases of unresolved casualties—somewhere around 140—but some of the deepest secrets, and several of the most plausible sightings of Americans in Soviet custody, alive and not even close to being sent home.

The cases are so voluminous, so deeply immersed in decades of secrecy and revolve around so many ambiguous sightings, botched rescues, ghostly vessels, revised and refracted memories, differently tracked coordinates and outright lies that the joint commission members from both the U.S. and Russian governments settled on 10 cases out of the several dozen on (classified) record to attempt to crack. After more than three years, they had successfully resolved part of one.

The remains of Air Force Capt. John R. Dunham, whose RB-29 was shot down between Hokkaido, Japan, and the Soviet coast on Oct. 7, 1952, have been recovered from Yurii Island. The discovery was made after a Russian who had then been a young sergeant in the Soviet Border Guards admitted that he had participated in the recovery of the airman's body from the sea in 1952. He had also taken Dunham's Annapolis class ring from his hand as a keepsake. The ring has been returned to Dunham's grateful family, and Vassily Saiko, the former border guard, was invited to Capt. Dunham's funeral and commemoration ceremonies.

For decades, the Soviets were absolutely silent regarding the 1952 Hokkaido shootdown. Then came the fall of Communism. Saiko's confession and the disinterment of Capt. Dunham's remains.

And in 1995 came a report that another witness to the rescue-and-salvage operation saw two parachutes. Saiko said he had seen no chutes. In the business of resolving Cold War spy plane shootdowns, parachutes are a sign of life. There are still faint signs of life in the Hokkaido RB-29 case.

For the sake of comparison, while the other three wars involved large armies and squadrons of bombers and fighters pressed against each other in a mortal clash over cities, ideologies, countries, whole geopolitical regions, the Cold War was the largely invisible—but absolutely deadly—game of tag that began before, and lasted after, the hot wars in Korea and Indochina.

Because the thousands of missions involved in this atmospheric game were secret, those that were shot down by the Communists or simply went missing were almost always described as routine training or weather flights. Of course that was a thin excuse, and all parties recognized it. The weather is never so complicated or hard to fathom that you have to fly an airplane loaded with cameras (the 1950-vintage RB-45 had 24 cameras of varying sizes and lenses) and listening devices through it, and if you're flying a military aircraft unannounced over a hostile country, you're not training to do anything except bomb it, send long-range missiles crashing into it or land troops on it when the need arises.

The U.S. military could always cite the regulations that forbid its aircraft from approaching any closer than a certain distance—sometimes 20 miles, sometimes 40, the regulation was subject to change depending on the international situation. But somehow these aircraft or their wreckage and imperiled crews ended up closer than that to the beaches of the USSR, and it wasn't always the tide that brought them in.

For the families of those who were killed and those who may have survived, this high-flying contest of calculating and slit-eyed sizing up of each other's capabilities and intent has meant a dual-sided task: prying information out of the Russians, because they undoubtedly know what happened to at least some of the aviators who didn't come home, and prying information out of their own government, because it knows what their men were doing there in the first place.

It should also be said that it appears from the known history of the Cold War that the U.S. military sent a lot more flights over Soviet territory and near Soviet airspace than the reverse. Would the Soviets have matched the number of secret flights if they could? Probably not, since they could simply fly some agents over on commercial flights who would rent a flat in Brooklyn and get a lot of the job done without risking expensive aircraft.

That left the Soviet archives full of information about missing American men who were last seen alive losing altitude over, or floating amid debris near, Soviet territory, hoping to be rescued, with the nearest help coming from those they were spying on in the first place.

The U.S. government over the years had made frequent urgent appeals to the Soviet regime for information about the shootdowns, and for help in finding out the fate of the missing pilots and crews. The answers had always been no, or, we don't know anything about any American survivors from that or any other plane we've shot down.

Once the Cold War—the fourth war, the smallest but one of the most deadly wars—was over, you would think the entire truth could be told. You would think that Russian officials would be eager to clear the air on these cases, produce all the old files, seek out all the surviving witnesses, help recreate all of the drama and intrigue in an effort to prove that none of the missing men was mistreated and not a single report of airmen being dragged off to labor camps or psychiatric hospitals was true.

You would think so? Think again.

* * *

A. Denis Clift is the co-chairman of the Cold War working group for the American side of the joint commission. In April 1995, he asked the Russian representatives about a list they had recently handed over as part of their program to disclose information about unresolved cases of missing American servicemen from shootdowns near the Soviet Union in the 1950s and 1960s.

The document summarized cases of alleged violation of Soviet airspace between October 1951 and December 1952, during the heart of the Korean War.

"It strikes the U.S. side as unusual," said Clift, " that the document covers 25 incidents, but omits two of the incidents of importance to us which occurred in that time period: 6 November 1951 and 13 June 1952. We would like to consult experts who can help explain these omissions so that we are not left with more open questions."

(The two incidents he was referring to were two shootdowns over the Sea of Japan, just off the Soviet coast, one on Nov. 6, 1951, of a Navy P2V Neptune bomber, in which ten Americans were lost, and the other on June 13, 1952, of an RB-29 reconnaissance aircraft, from which 12 men did not return. They are two of the ten Cold War shootdowns the commission agreed to concentrate on most completely, in hopes of shedding light on the entire program of secret flights and unrepatriated survivors. In some cases, archival documents the Russians have handed over reveal that Stalin himself was kept informed of the incidents and their aftermath.)

Gen. Anatoli Krayushkin, Clift's Russian counterpart, replied: "I will make a note of it."

* * *

The Korean War and the Cold War were fought simultaneously by the U.S. Air Force and Navy, with their fleets of converted bombers and fledgling "spy" planes that in the coming decades would be quickly superseded by supersonic aircraft and space satellites.

And as the Korean War became more of an aviation battle between the U.S. and the Soviet Union, the Joint Chiefs of Staff decided that the war in Korea had shown just how much work remained to be done to protect the U.S. and its allies from the unseen threat of nuclear power in the hands of the Soviet Union. In January 1951, the joint chiefs approved a wide-ranging program of aerial reconnaissance for the Far East, which reconnaissance "should be conducted by high-speed aircraft relying for safety upon the advantages of surprise and speed."

"The United States now has in the Far East the following reconnaissance aircraft: 2 RB-45, 13 RB-29, 13 RB-26, 11 RF-51, 55 RF-80, 9 F4U, 6 F7F, 3 F9F, 9 P2V. It is believed these aircraft are adequate for the initial phase. The mission of this phase would be to determine the desired target complex, to indicate the frequency of coverage required, and to determine the necessary forces for sustained operations...On July 4, 1950, the Commanding General, Far East Air Force, stated that individual reconnaissance missions could be accomplished without detection over the following areas: Dairen-Port Arthur, Vladivostok, Sakhalin and the Kuriles."

But the military leaders knew the Communist Chinese and the Soviets, both strongly behind the North Korean aggressors, were not going to sit idly by and watch camera-laden U.S. aircraft whiz overhead in what were known as "Ferret" flights, or missions, snapping photographs of their dikes, industrial plants and troop concentrations at will. The advantages of an ambitious intelligence-gathering program would come at some price.

"Losses through 17 January 1951 in Korea have averaged one per cent of the effective reconnaissance sorties flown. It is assumed that future losses, although not prohibitive, would be somewhat higher, particularly in the Manchurian regions where Soviet air defenses would probably come into play either directly or indirectly." The joint chiefs were prepared to pay the freight for the Ferrets.

One of the first secret reconnaissance missions of the Korean War was flown on June 29, 1950, four days after the North Korean invasion. Ferret Mission No. 113 over Vladivostok, USSR, reported the following:

"An indication of possible build-up in shipping was reported. Spot reports covering this mission, and a follow-up report state that exceptionally bright return on an AN/APQ-13 (a type of camera) indicates considerable build-up at Nakhodka. This could be a possible indication of unusual naval and/or shipping activity in this area."

The Ferret flights were sometimes fishing expeditions, aimed at collecting any and all signs of potentially hostile activity, but more often were designed to bring back specific information for the use of the Air Force and other intelligence agencies. A request from the Strategic Air Command to its Ferret squadrons in the Far East dated Nov. 26, 1952 asked for "technical intelligence on certain Soviet radar," including the estimated power output and "exact physical appearance" of a Soviet radar unit located at Chongju, North Korea.

Chronologically, the first incident among the Cold War shootdowns-disappearances the joint commission agreed to investigate in depth was the unprovoked shooting down by Soviet fighters over the Baltic Sea on April 8, 1950—months before the Korean War started—of another Navy reconnaissance plane, a PB4Y2 Privateer. All ten men aboard were lost.

The Navy claimed for years that its plane had been on a "routine flight" from Germany, but it has been known since the 1970s that it was routine only for a special part of the Navy, because it was an eavesdropping flight, probing for signals from a Soviet missile base on the shore of the Baltic.

The Soviets claimed the unarmed aircraft fired at their pilots first. This was typical of the kind of blind faith in propaganda that the Soviets apparently enjoyed at the time. No reports of wreckage or rescue attempts surfaced, but a few years after the shootdown, credible reports were received by U.S. officials that some of the crew were seen in a psychiatric hospital in the USSR. An American released from the Gulag, John Noble, said another prisoner had seen and talked with members of the crew of this plane in Vorkuta, an infamous Gulag prison site.

One of the American prisoners had reportedly said he was serving a 25-year sentence for espionage—which sounded like the sort of charge the Soviets would bring against a foreign aviator caught trying to listen in on its missile-base communications gear.

In the first year of the joint commission's existence, most of the attention was directed at the POW/MIA cases from the Korean War and Vietnam War. But the Cold War cases were always on the agenda. And in fact, the Cold War cases draw on not only the massive archives of the regular military and diplomatic bureaucracies but another institution called the Border Guards, the guardians of the coastline of the former Soviet Union, where many of the Ferret missions that ended in tragedy seemed to end.

Yet one of the biggest revelations thus far came not from a Russian archival declassification but a Moscow military newspaper, Red Star, which published a diatribe against the joint commission's work in February 1993. Mixed with the diatribe was a mention that Red Star's editors had learned that "out of the 10-man crew (of the Privateer), one was rescued and the others perished." No survivors of the shootdown had ever been mentioned in the Soviet media or by Soviet officials in 43 years.

The Russian side didn't question or deny the report. Lt. Col. Sergei Osipov, the Russian side's key staff representative, said his staff "forgot" to tell the American side about the archival source for the Red Star report.[1]

The Russians eventually disclosed some minor operational details of the Baltic Sea incident, saying the Soviet interceptor waggled its wings to signal the American plane to leave Soviet airspace, and at 2,500 meters altitude, at 1740 hours, with the Americans still not obeying their commands, the Soviet pilots received orders to shoot. Once the plane was in the water, the Soviets mounted an extensive search effort that went on for three months, with more than 200 attempts to find recoverable parts as the salvagers tried to avoid the mines with which that part of the Baltic had been seeded. They reportedly found no bodies, no parts, only 10 oxygen bottles. And they weren't even sure the bottles were from the Privateer.

And in May 1993, the Russian side did present some archival documents on the April 1950 shootdown they described as still classified, but the reason for the classification was not apparent. They only described how the Soviet Navy had attempted to intercept the U.S. Navy Privateer, but heavy fog had kept their aircraft grounded until the American aircraft was almost out of sight.

The American side of the commission is still working to overcome the Soviet Cold War Syndrome in 1995. His team, Clift noted in March 1995, "has been trying for about a year to have a notice published in a psychiatric journal" seeking information about the live-sighting in Vorkuta of 45 years ago. The American analysts hoped to have the magazine publish a computer-enhanced photograph of Lt.(j.g.) Robert D. Reynolds, one of the Privateer's crew.

Unfortunately, he said, the psychiatric journal they were going to use has gone bankrupt.

Krayushkin suggested the Americans might want to utilize the mass media.

Then Clift brought up an example of reporting in the Russian mass media. This wasn't a document released from the archives by the Russian government's representatives either, but an article from the Aug. 29, 1992, issue of Izvestia, the Moscow general circulation newspaper. The article, Clift said, quoted a Viktor Shevchuk as saying "he participated in salvage operations for the plane and that part of a wing, part of the fuselage, and personal effects of one of the crew members were recovered."

As you might expect, he told Krayushkin, the American side would like to speak to Shevchuk, since never before—not in 45 years—had the Russian government suggested there had actually been some wreckage recovered from the Privateer in the Baltic.

"I will make a note of this," said Krayushkin.

And while Krayushkin was making notes, he launched into an explanation of how Izvestia might have found this Shevchuk fellow, and not the Russian Cold War working group:

"I know that we are still looking in the archives available to us (a clear hint that some hard-line outfits in the Yeltsin government aren't cooperating on the Cold War disclosure front yet); the archives of the Ministry of Defense and the Federal Security Service. But it is unclear which archives and which funds might contain relevant information. That is why I have given instructions for the work to continue. I can tell you that work in the Federal Security Service (successor agency to the KGB) archives has been going on since the beginning of the year, without results. Do not think by this that we are reluctant to search or that we do not know where to look.

"It is merely that up to this point we have no concrete results. And I will state as before that when we work together in a fact-finding capacity, whenever we find any document of interest, it is always declassified, and we hand over the complete document to you. I assure you that we have never tried to cover this information up. I am sure that my colleagues in the Ministry of Defense are doing as thorough a job as possible.

"But since you found new materials, such as the article about Shevchuk, and since the issue is not covered in full and you have doubts...." And so forth.

* * *

When it looks as though the Russians are still playing games with the information coming out of Soviet archives about missing American POWs, it usually involves a case of a Cold War shootdown.

But all of the blame doesn't fall on the Russians. Cold War shootdown family survivors have been among the American side's most loyal supporters, and angriest critics. Their requests for declassification of records that are now more than four decades old are often met with the standard line that "intelligence sources and methods" still require much of the information they seek to be kept from them.

Patricia Dickinson, of Newark, Del., sister of AD-3 Jack D. Lively, one of the ten crewmen aboard the Navy Neptune bomber shot down in November 1951, not only follows the work of the commission carefully, she attempts to accelerate their efforts by keeping a summary of known facts about the case updated, peppering the commission and its office of analysts and interpreters with letters suggesting questions and leads to pursue, and filing her own numerous requests for declassification of the records in the U.S. that her government has authority to unseal.

She tries to give the commission and the Russians credit for what they've managed to do so far. Like so many of the other POW/MIA families from the Cold War era, she can't quite understand why they haven't been able to do more. From a summary of the Neptune case she handed to the joint commission in March 1994:

"The U.S. position prior to the establishment of the Joint Commission was that this plane had been on a routine daily shipping reconnaissance flight, and was shot down by the Soviets over international waters. When this case was presented to the Russian side of the commission in 1992, our position was that this was an intelligence-gathering flight shot down over the Sea of Japan, overflying international waters.

"The Russian side included this case on their original list of ten Cold War incidents which they presented at the September 1992 plenary. They acknowledged shooting down this plane after it allegedly violated Soviet airspace.

"As a result of the commission's work, we know a great deal more about this incident than when we started. Soviet archival sources tell us that the plane was shot down by fighter aircraft and crashed into the water just 18 miles offshore. The Soviets mounted their own search effort with three cutters of the Maritime Border Guards, which found no trace of the plane. We know that the commander of the (Soviet) Pacific Fleet sent two messages on this shootdown directly to Stalin, thereby indicating the seriousness of the incident. There was no mention of survivors in these documents.

"Next steps on this case include the following: we have asked for Russian help in locating and interviewing the pilots that shot down this plane. We have asked for any gun camera photos, which we believe still exist due to the importance attached by the Soviets to the shootdown of an American plane."

But Pat Dickinson doesn't just keep her own family case updated. After the joint commission's December 1994 meeting, she compiled four pages of questions related to the Neptune incident, the agenda and priorities of the commission, the background of the Russian representatives and the precise points at which the Pentagon's current team of analysts ought to attack the remaining mysteries of her brother's case. The questions are also worth reading, for their remarkable insight into the complexities of the Cold War cases and for instruction on what it takes to cope with the bureaucracies and habits of secrecy that continue to keep much of the story of missing Americans in the former Soviet Union suppressed.

The first six of Pat Dickinson's list of 26 questions:

1. What is the established criterion for case priority? Would you please supply me with order of priority assigned to the ten shootdowns currently being investigated by DPMO (Defense Prisoner of War/Missing in Action Office) and the Joint Commission?

2. Is AD-3 Jack D. Lively (and nine fellow crewmen) listed in the names of American MIAs provided to the Kazakhstan government?

3. When checking card files in prison camps in the Soviet prison system, and selected American names are checked, whose names are checked? Who decides what names are checked and, specifically, was AD-3 Jack D. Lively checked?

4. Have you interviewed colleagues of Col. Korotov (one of the commission's witnesses in this case) yet? Was the information he gave corroborated by others?

5. Could we find out where Col. Osipov was assigned before coming to work for the Joint Commission? Where was he assigned in 1981-82?

6. Would you please inquire into the Nov. 6, 1951 shootdown in the Korean War working group, as the crew's names are carried on both lists (Cold War and Korean War)?

Pat Dickinson's letters to the Pentagon's Defense POW/MIA Office reflect the frustration felt by many families of the servicemen whose cases remain wrapped in questions:

"I remain doubtful that this case is being aggressively pursued by the staff of DPMO. I am very disappointed with the lack of interest, as evidenced in the minutes of the last plenary meeting. The information discussed was not presented correctly concerning a Japanese POW report of Americans in a camp named Sinda, and as a result it was brushed aside...What reports of intelligence sources and methods in 1951 would still be relevant today and require protection? Would they not be obsolete after 43 years? Does this protection directly involve the safety of my brother and his nine fellow crewmen or the crews of other aircraft shot down by the Soviets in the Cold War? I feel that to quote national security and keep documentation secret and classified on operations of 43 years ago is ludicrous...unless some of these POWs are still living under Russian control? If the cloak of national security surrounds this shootdown and many others like it, what recourse does that leave families searching for loved ones?"

As for the Russians' assertion that they have "exhausted" whatever documentary evidence they have on the Neptune shootdown, "The Russians have admitted shooting this plane down, but it seems they did not follow up with photographs, gun camera film and reports for final disposition and files. I find that very strange in a country noted for scrupulous record-keeping and the 'honor' bestowed upon those who protect their country from 'American aggressors.'"

And Pat Dickinson doesn't just keep the pressure on the commission and the Defense POW/MIA Office. She gives them leads to pursue. Here's one, from a November 1994 letter:

"We may be able to clarify the facts somewhat by obtaining the unadulterated report from the Chinese Security Forces on the capture of an American pilot on Nov. 6, 1951. Also perhaps they would give us a copy of the "top secret" presidium protocol No. 84 and address the report of five aviators brought to Sinda, near Khabarovsk, in 1952...one of which was named "Poll." There were two crewmen named Paul on the Neptune ...."

There are so many versions of the Neptune shootdown that have been offered at various times by the Russian government—at least four by Pat Dickinson's count—that establishing a reliable working version on which to base an investigation is difficult. One Soviet report claimed that the Navy reconnaissance plane Jack Lively and nine other Navy men were aboard entered Soviet airspace and flew over Vladivostok, drawing the Soviet fighters out to sea, where they shot it down. In all the versions, however, no wreckage or survivors were ever found.

And Dickinson, who has followed every word of the investigation into the Neptune shootdown that involved her brother, also keeps up with all of the other investigations the commission and the Pentagon's POW/MIA office is doing, or hopes to do, because she knows that information can come anytime, from anywhere.

An interview with a retired pilot involved in the shootdown of an Air Force RB-50 in July 1953, in the same area, east of Vladivostok, touched on her brother's case. The pilot who shot down the RB-50, Yuri Mikhailovich

Yablonovsky, knew the two pilots who shot down the Neptune. He had roomed with one of them and remembered the incident.

"I believe it was on the 6th of November," said Yablonovsky. "Two pilots from our 88th Guards Regiment, Lukashev—the flight commander, and another flier whose name I do not recall but I believe he was a senior pilot. They held the same rank structure as we had, a captain and a senior lieutenant. I believe that they shot down an aircraft in the area of Valentin Bay. As I remember it, it was Valentin Bay. It is east of America...east of Nakhodka. They shot down a Neptune. I know that they shot the aircraft down over the water at a low altitude and that the plane was destroyed. I further remember that they received awards just like we did. They awarded us...No, it was done in a secret, hushed fashion. I don't mean in a secret fashion, just without any fanfare. Yes, without any type of ceremony. They were presented their awards in the officers' house, in the fleet house. ..They both received the Order of the Red Banner. Admiral Kochubaev, a member of the fleet military council, presented the awards to them."

There it was. One name and two ranks and a quiet fleet house ceremony bestowing the Order of the Red Banner, awarded for their splendid marksmanship to many of the pilots who downed American reconnaissance planes, including the Neptune of November 1951, east of what the Russians used to call America Bay.

Now what about any survivors? Yuri Mikhailovich Yablonovsky had given Pat Dickinson more names to pursue, and more questions to ask.

* * *

The day the cease-fire took effect on the Korean peninsula, the Cold War resumed with a vengeance. As usual in the Far East in the 1950s, it involved an aircraft shootdown. And also as usual, it involved a dispute over where the aircraft was when it was shot down.

The unusual part was that it involved the shooting down of a Russian passenger plane by an American jet fighter. There were apparently no survivors, although as usual in such incidents, there was a discrepancy between the initial count and a later list of casualties.

The Soviet Union first charged that 15 passengers and a crew of six had perished on July 27, 1953, when U.S. fighters attacked an IL-12 passenger plane on a scheduled flight from Port Arthur, China, to Vladivostok. A list of the dead later presented by Soviet officials to substantiate a demand for $1.86-million in damages from the United States listed only 20 names, indicating either that the initial figure was incorrect, one person survived or the Soviet Union wished to keep the identity of one of the victims secret.[2]

The shootdown occurred at noon, just ten hours before the cease-fire took effect that was to end the fighting in the Korean War, and according to the Soviets, the attack took place about 75 miles north of the Yalu River boundary between North Korea and Manchuria, at a place called Khuadyan. They charged that four U.S. fighters were involved in the incident.

The coordinates that the Russians gave for the incident—and the map that appeared in Pravda with a story about the incident—placed it well within Manchurian territory. Throughout the Korean War, U.S. pilots had been forbidden to fly into Manchuria on combat missions, although it was well-known that many did on the basis of what was known as "hot pursuit" of the Soviet planes that were all based north of the Yalu. American reconnaissance planes, which were under separate orders to obtain intelligence, were understood to have entered Chinese airspace frequently as well.

The U.S. was adamant, however,—based on the account of the incident by the American pilot who shot down the transport—that the shootdown had taken place south of the river, over North Korean territory. The F-86 pilot who downed the Russian plane—Capt. Ralph S. Parr, Jr.—had flown more than 160 combat missions during the Korean War, and had nine MIG "kills" to his credit—one short of qualification as a double "ace.". His mission the day of the incident was to escort a Navy Banshee photo reconnaissance flight whose targets were several airfields on the North Korean-Manchurian border.

Parr admitted shooting down the transport—he said it bore a red star marking similar to those on other "hostile" planes he had shot down throughout the war. But only one other F-86—his wingman—had witnessed the shootdown. And the Soviets presented photos of a crashed plane, claiming it was the IL-12 that the U.S. had shot down. The photos showed a heap of metal on the ground in Manchuria.

One theory, advanced by Samuel Klaus, a State Department official who investigated a number of so-called Cold War shootdown incidents in preparation for having cases heard before the International Court of Justice at the Hague, held that the Soviets had actually lost another IL-12 transport in Manchuria at an earlier date and, when Parr shot down another, even though it was over North Korea, chose to charge him with shooting down the one in Manchuria.[3]

The Soviets didn't give the United States long to weigh the pros and cons of the IL-12 shootdown, however.

Two days later, Russian MIGs attacked a U.S. RB-50 photo reconnaissance plane over the Sea of Japan, just off the Soviet coast near Vladivostok. Of the 17 men aboard, there was only one survivor picked up by American search and rescue personnel. And just as the U.S. still doesn't know whether the transport plane that Capt. Parr shot down is the only one the Russians lost to American fighter planes, the U.S. still doesn't know what happened to the other crewmen who managed to bail out of the RB-50 two days later.

The buzz around the Soviet intelligence center in Khabarovsk on July 19, 1953, was the downing of a big American aircraft just off the Far East coast. Retired colonel Gavril Korotkov, a former Soviet military interrogator in Khabarovsk during the Korean War, said that when the aircraft was downed, "we were shocked that a big American aircraft, with 15 (sic) people on board, was shot down right after the armistice. The rumors in Vladivostok were that there were survivors—there were no facts, but in talking, we came to the same conclusion, that all might have survived because of the quality of the rescue equipment these pilots had."

The flotation, rescue and high-altitude flight gear of American pilots was very greatly envied by Soviet aviators whose equipment was not as advanced—yet.

When Korotkov and his colleagues in Khabarovsk learned that the U.S. aircraft had not exploded, but had sunk slowly, Korotkov added, "it was reasonable to assume they all bailed out near the Bay of Peter the Great, not far from Posyet. It's a comfortable place, with no big waves. We assumed the Americans had been rescued."

As it turned out, it wasn't comfortable at all. One American was rescued, although others were sighted; 16 were lost. The shootdown off Posyet was widely seen as Soviet retribution for the downing of the IL-12 transport two days earlier. One of the Soviet pilots responsible for the shootdown, Yuri Yablonovsky, told the joint commission that wasn't so. "No, not at all," he said. "I knew that crew (of the downed IL-12). How did I know? Because we flew to China and that plane accompanied us. So what kind of act of retaliation? We were on constant duty. It was daily. We sat months, years. During the summer we had to sit eight hours in the cabin...Please excuse me, but when we would get into the showers, everyone had a red spot here (indicating his buttocks.) Yes, all the time we sat. This was our ordinary combat duty. Not any worse than the other missions which they gave us."

So the shooting down of the RB-50 with its crew of 17 was not an act of deliberate revenge, just a welcome break in the boring and ass-numbing routine of the Soviet fighter pilots on constant alert around Vladivostok in 1953. Yablonovsky set the scene:

"We went on strip alert as a flight. We were on duty in pairs. The 88th Guards Regiment, our unit, was based there in the 89th Torpedo Division. I don't remember now what tie it was, but I remember that it was around 7 a.m...Rybakov and I received the command "Pair take off," and we took off...When they had directed us out to the coast, they gave us the order to search for the target. We didn't see the target. They gave us the order 'Go higher.' Well, higher we...Rybakov reported, 'I can't go higher. Cloud cover.' They told us 'fly under the clouds.' And I looked there and definitely saw on an intersecting path, that is, we were flying somewhat out to sea and he was flying somewhat parallel...So, we were flying like this, and that plane...it was a very beautiful plane, so big, and I saw clearly it was a B-50 or a B-29, that's what we thought...at that time I saw a tracer from the plane...Yes, from its machine gun...I was sufficiently far away that I didn't see whether it was the upper turret or from its tail gun...And then I turned and saw a tracer from Rybakov. I saw that its engine caught fire...I also opened fire, but I was far away. I tugged on the lever and at that time I saw the plane break apart...in the air. That is, it was like a small cigar. You could barely see the fuselage, and then that was all."

Yablonovsky said he understood that later that day an American aircraft carrier had moved close to the coastline to help search, "that major searches were being conducted, and that our people did not find anyone nor did they even get involved. This I remember also."

He also said he saw no parachutes, no sign of life from the sky or sea, and heard no mention of survivors in the days and weeks following the incident.

Before Yablonovsky testified, the Russians presented the American side of the commission with documents related to the July 29, 1953 shootdown of the RB-50, revealing that a total of 10 Soviet ships—nine Red Navy cutters and one cutter from the Border Guards unit—had reported to the search area while survivors would have been in the water.

During June 1993, Task Force Russia analysts interviewed Georgi Yakovlevich Kravchenko, a former sergeant in an anti-aircraft battery stationed near Vladivostok. He said that American pilots had caused "almost unbearable" tension, triggering calls to general quarters up to 18 times a day by buzzing the coast to within 25 kilometers of the shoreline. The Soviet guns had an 18-kilometer range.

But about 4 or 5 a.m., 29 July 1953, he saw an intruder airplane approaching and two Soviet planes race off to catch it. He saw the U.S. plane hit one of the Soviet planes, then the other Soviet plane fired and hit the U.S. plane, touching off a fire in its tail section.

He saw seven men bail out before the U.S. plane went down in the direction of Russky Island. Kravchenko remembers seeing three or four fishing boats in the area where the plane went down. He doesn't know for a fact, but he heard that an order had been given not to try to rescue the American survivors, and he said the story in the local newspaper didn't mention the parachutes he'd seen.

U.S. records show that the RB-50 took off at 3:30 a.m. from Japan, and at 5:41 the aircraft's radar "stopped working" for some minutes, but the plane regained its course and at 6:15, the plane was shot down by two Soviet MIGs. About six hours later a U.S. search plane from Japan made passes over the area of last radio contact and found nothing, then moved closer to the coastline. That afternoon, a search plane saw about six objects in the water that resembled U.S. survival vests and a total of 15 Soviet patrol boats between 4:09 and 4:30 p.m. At about 5:40 p.m., the co-pilot was sighted in the water and the search plane dropped a life raft to him and summoned a Navy ship. The Navy ship reached the rescue area at 4 a.m. the next morning and picked up Capt. John Roche, the co-pilot, from Soviet trawler No. 1423.

The Soviet Border Guard representatives say their records show there were no Soviet ships in the area of the shootdown that day, and they have no information about the fate of the U.S. crewmen. That contradicts directly the U.S. search party's report of Soviet rescue ships being on station that day. Someone's records are wrong.

As for patrol boats, Maj. Gen. Zaporoschenko of the Border Guards said, "The Soviet Border Guards were not equipped with patrol boats, only with light boats for (patrolling) 5-6 kilometers from the coast."[4]

Gen. Loeffke of Task Force Russia said Roche "was the last man out of the aircraft. That means more than 10 crew members parachuted before him. That's why we're so sure" there were survivors in the water for the Soviet vessels to rescue.

Moreover, said Loeffke, "the search-and-rescue aircraft saw those PT boats going in and out of the wreckage area. This was eight hours before our pilot was picked up by the U.S. Navy and 16 hours after the shootdown. To our logic, those boats must have picked up something."

Loeffke also said Roche felt waves from boats, heard the roar of boat engines around him, and heard another person cry out from the water, although he never saw anyone and only heard it once.

The Russians pointed out that in a report the Soviet navy commander submitted about the incident to the then-defense minister, Bulganin, there was no mention of survivors. "They would not lie to him about prisoners," said Prof. Pekhoia, main archivist of the Russian Federation, "it is absolutely unbelievable...if there were prisoners, the information surely would have been reported to the minister of defense." But how would the Soviet navy commander have a report to file unless his ships had been to the scene? Such are the routine mysteries of the Cold War shootdown investigators.

Toon, the commission's American co-chairman, then said he agreed that "it's highly unlikely that the Navy commander would lie to Bulganin," but he added that "knowing the old Soviet regime as I did—and do—I do not exclude the possibility that these records have been tampered with."

The message from Admiral Kuznetsov to Bulganin read: "This certifies that the aircraft was shot down...but no corpses or survivors were found by the border guards. The incident occurred 55 kilometers southeast of the island Askol."

A cynic might read the message critically and note that "this certifies" reads as though a subordinate has been asked to submit a document tailored for a specific purpose; and that "by the border guards" is a qualification that seems calculated to exclude only one of several agencies that could have reacted to the shootdown by sending water-going craft to fish for the fallout from the big American plane.

If an agency other than the border guards found corpses or survivors, perhaps it would be reflected in other archives, not the ones already checked.

Gen. Krayushkin will make a note of that.

Chapter Fifteen

Return Address: North Korea

"This return from North Korea was almost like coming back from the grave. In the midst of my happiness over my own return I am saddened by the thought that many of my fellow Americans are lying in unnamed graves in North Korea today."

—May 30, 1953, letter to the State Department from Nellie Dyer,
a Methodist missionary from Arkansas
who was held prisoner from June 1950 to April 1953
near Manpojin, North Korea.

"I saw Roger Dumas in 1956 in jail in Poktong (Pyoktong) North Korea."
—Walter EnBom,
a former enlisted man and repatriated prisoner of war,
in answer to questions posed for a federal court lawsuit by Robert Dumas,
brother of missing POW Pfc. Roger Dumas.

Most of the reports of live-sightings of missing American POWs from the Korean War date from the 1950s and 1960s.

But there are more recent reports, and reasons—call them signs, indications, or merely stubborn faith—to believe that despite overwhelming odds, some American POWs remain alive in North Korea, Manchuria or the former Soviet Union.

For these indications to be true, reality must conform to one of a number of possible scenarios. For example:

1. The North Korean government, which some policy experts describe as paranoid and which maintains tight, Orwellian control over one of the

most closed and heavily militarized nations on earth, was or has become deluded enough to believe that an act the West would call a crime against humanity is in North Korea's long-term interest. Pyongyang's ruling clique, acting like hermits without a conscience, but in keeping with their homebred philosophy of self-reliance, perpetuate the holding of American POWs decades after the war as secret hostages, bargaining chips in some future crisis with the United States and perhaps the rest of the world over, say, nuclear weapons.[1]

2. The nervous young revolutionaries in Pyongyang in 1953 initially held back American POWs out of distrust or for political leverage, either on their own initiative or at the suggestion of the Russians or Chinese, who also took their own share of POWs. By the time they were ready to release them, U.S. officials interpreted the offer as a demand for ransom and were not willing to bargain. Thus the POWs remain in captivity, an embarassment to the United States and useless to the North Koreans, who from their point of view see that the Americans haven't tried very hard to repatriate them anyway.

3. Many more American POWs from Korea converted to Communism and chose to remain behind than the 21 who were publicly identified, and the survivors among them remain sympathetic to those beliefs, sharing the arduous life of North Korean peasants and workers to this day. They are not hostages or foreign workers but foreign-born North Koreans, with Korean families and Korean names of their own.

4. The American POWs occasionally sighted were unacknowledged turncoats when the armistice was signed and watched silently from a distance when their fellow POWs went home to America. After a taste of North Korean life, however, they found the system unpalatable and began to stir up trouble and opposition. The North Korean regime, presided over from 1945 until 1994 by Kim Il-Sung, an autocratic dictator chosen by Stalin, excuted the ring-leaders and sentenced the rest to life on a communal farm.

5. American POWs held back in North Korea were freed from captivity some years after the war, when the U.S. was already involved in a new war in Vietnam and the plan to demand ransom was shelved. But they have not left, and do not try to escape, because the North Koreans have convinced them America would consider them traitors. They fear the consequences they or their families might face. Fewer remain each year, as the physical strain and mental anguish of 45 years in prison take their toll.

None of these scenarios is very pleasant. And some of them may be difficult to imagine, unless you know more than the average person about North Korea and the POW/MIA issue. But POW/MIA analysis is a lot like religion. You don't have to know something is true, or even believe it's true, for it to be true.

* * *

Robert Dumas, whose brother Roger is a Korean War POW missing since Nov. 4, 1950, lives in Canterbury, Conn., in a house where the basement is a virtual library-in-progress of documents and copies of documents and faxes of documents dealing with POWs and MIAs from the Korean War.

If fax paper, texts of congressional hearings, court transcripts and overdue telephone bills could bring someone back from a prison camp in North Korea, Pfc. Roger Dumas would have been home drinking coffee with his brother in Canterbury about seven hearings and a half-million faxes ago.

Bob Dumas has heard all of the arguments against his belief that there are still live American prisoners in North Korea held back from the Korean War. He's heard the arguments, the counter-arguments, the scenarios, the anti-scenarios, the can't-bes and the no-ways.

He's heard them and he always takes the same side. The yes side. He's not just sure they're there. Anybody taking the other side of the argument had better have proof they're not there, or he's going to have them believing they are there in about five minutes.

He's determined, obstinate and dedicated to his belief. He's a bulldog who never relaxes his jaw. He has never wavered. After all, he's been right before. In fact, and this is the incredible part, Bob Dumas has always been right.

When Roger was captured in 1950, Bob Dumas had just entered the Army and was training at a camp in Indiana. A letter from the Army adjutant general's office arrived at the family home in December, saying Roger had been missing in action for about a month. The letter added on a hopeful note: "Experience has shown that many persons reported missing in action are subsequently reported as returned to duty or being hospitalized for injuries."

Soon the Army shipped Bob Dumas to Korea, but he didn't want his mother to worry that she might lose another son there. So for months, he routed his mail through a friend serving in a military police unit in Austria. The letters he wrote home went first to a military post office box in Europe, then to Connecticut. His mother wrote to Austria, and his friend quietly forwarded them to Korea. Bob left out the stuff about being in the middle of a war.

As the fighting seesawed, and the Communists began broadcasting the names of some UN prisoners over the radio, Bob waited and listened in vain for a clue. He dreamed of finding Roger somewhere in Korea. He tried to get assigned to the 24th Division so he could track down soldiers who might know what had happened to his brother's outfit. When that didn't work, he wasn't fazed or deterred. Korea wasn't that big a place. Roger had to be there somewhere.

When his tour of duty was over 20 months later, Bob Dumas returned from Korea with no information beyond the terse declaration that Roger was still "missing in action."

In July 1953, an armistice was signed and the fighting ended. In August and September, about 4,000 U.S. prisoners were released and returned home, but Roger Dumas was not among them. The next year, the North Koreans handed over the bodies of about 1,000 other Americans who had died in combat and in POW camps north of the ceasefire line.

Roger Dumas wasn't among them, either. But then Bob Dumas didn't expect him to be.

For years, military officials told him whenever he asked to see Roger's military records that they didn't exist. This was in the old dark, dark days when only a few people among the millions in this country who are otherwise intelligent and caring people even were aware the United States Army, Marine Corps, Navy, Air Force, National Guard, Coast Guard and nurses' corps-plus armies and navies from 16 other countries—were all in Korea for about three years, fighting, killing, dying, taking prisoners and being taken prisoner.

The truth, of course, is that Pfc. Roger Dumas's military records from Korea are thick, smudged and extensive, down to his high school education and dental charts, and they've been on file somewhere in the U.S. government's custody from the very first day he was sent there in July 1950—by ship, just like Bob and two other Dumas brothers would be before it was over. Nevertheless, when faxed, government officials would regularly tell Bob Dumas that his brother Roger couldn't have been a POW in Korea and they wished they could prove it to him, but they couldn't, because unfortunately all of his brother's military records were destroyed along with the records of hundreds of thousands of other men who were never POWs in a fire at a U.S. military personnel records center in St. Louis, Mo.

That was an easy one. It only took about ten years to straighten out. Yes, there was a fire. No, all the records weren't destroyed. And most assuredly, Roger Dumas had been a soldier in Korea. Hell, Korea was practically a family tradition around the Dumas house.

Of six brothers from the working-class Dumas family in southern Connecticut, four served in World War II and three saw duty in the Korean War. Roger, the youngest, enlisted in the Army at age 17 and was just turning 19 when he was sent to Japan and then on to Korea a few weeks after the war started.

Assigned as a machine-gunner to the 24th Division, his regiment was overrun when Chinese troops launched their massive counter-thrust out of Manchuria that fall, forcing the UN into retreat and rescuing the North Korean army from certain defeat. That November, the Chinese took whole platoons of UN troops prisoner.

But proving that Roger had been among them was harder than cracking the St. Louis records-center fire case. All through the '70s and '80s, by fax, by letter and telephone, and by the basic, gut instincts that get an unbelievable number of soldiers from one end of a war to another, Bob Dumas tracked down a widely separated handful of men who had been in prison camps in North Korea with Roger. They all lived in the United States somewhere, within the sound of a fax beep, in Washington state, Texas, Oklahoma, California. He used the telephone. No problem. You couldn't expect the government to do this. The government probably didn't have enough telephones, or interest.

By this time, practically everyone ever associated with the POW/ MIA affairs offices in the federal government, Capitol Hill or New England had heard from Bob Dumas a number of times, some so often that they always seemed to be sick or on break when he called. But Bob was undaunted, would not be denied. He was close to pay dirt. Through the Freedom of Information and Privacy Act, the Red Cross, the Library of Congress, National Archives and anyone who would stand still and listen to him he was getting hold of POW lists and debriefing files and other formerly classified material that was once very sensitive, highly secret information.

Most of the papers mentioned the secret, actual names and military ranks of a lot of guys nobody had ever heard of except their friends and families. Their only distinction was that they had fought in Korea. And that their government seemed content to just put them on a list and file it away.

When the possibility that live American POWs from the Korean War are still being held is argued, someone usually makes the point that— with all due respect—what would the North Koreans, or the Chinese, or the Russians want with a bunch of no-name, low-skilled privates and corporals? Responses include the observations that: enlisted personnel may be more pliable; people with few skills and alumni contacts may be more willing to adopt a proletarian philosophy; sons of hod-carriers may be less prone to carp at Marxism's arduous existence for the masses than sons of yacht club members; and finally, Communists seeking converts were interested in numbers, not names.

This is a debate that can't be settled, of course, without access to the minds or memoranda of the Communist leaders who were making such decisions during the Korean War.

But it is worth noting that the U.S. Army's own counter-intelligence report on the POWs in Korea pointed out that enlisted men—not officers or

NCOs—were the prime target of Communist recruiting and brainwashing campaigns in Korea. The report said "it was not general pracice to attempt to indoctrinate officers as they were apparently considered to be hopeless cases due to their backgrounds and positions of authority."[2]

Some officers were convicted after repatriation of collaborating with the enemy guards and prison camp administrations. But of the 21 American "turncoats" who openly embraced communism after spending a few years in North Korean prisons, none was an officer.[3]

The debriefing reports Bob Dumas was interested in came from both officers and enlisted men repatriated during Operation Little Switch and Operation Big Switch, the POW exchanges between the UN and the Communists. Bob Dumas looked for reports from Camp 5. He'd heard that's where a lot of 24th Division POWs ended up. When the prisoners were released, the military debriefers had asked each one who they remembered seeing back in the prison camps.

The debriefing reports were a gold mine. George Rogers of Oklahoma had given the debriefers a list of some 60 men who had been in Camp 5 with him, including Roger Dumas. Walter O. EnBom and Cecil V. Preston also reported they'd seen Roger. Bob Dumas called them. One name would lead him to others. That's how he found Lloyd Pate and Bobby Caruth.

What they told Bob Dumas made him very angry, but not too angry to take it as a reason to hope. They all said Roger had been alive up to the time everyone else was released in the big POW exchange in August and September 1953.

What Caruth told him was the worst. Bobby Caruth and Roger Dumas had been in the same outfit, and were taken prisoner at the same time. When the Communists captured them, in fact, they tied Bobby's and Roger's hands "together behind our backs," Caruth remembers.

That forms the kind of bond that stays with a person for a long time after the ropes come off.

But on the day the men in their camp were to be exchanged, as he and Roger and the rest stood in line waiting to be put in a truck and driven to freedom, a guard went over to Roger and led him away.

"I said, 'Where you goin' Roger?'" said Caruth. "He shook his head he didn't know. And that's the last I saw of him."

That settled it. Roger wasn't just any prisoner of war anymore. He represented all the missing POWs who would have come home if they could have, if the Communists hadn't held onto them.

In 1982, Dumas filed suit in federal court to have Pfc. Roger Dumas—who had been officially presumed dead in 1953—officially re-declared a prisoner of war. This was only his first federal suit. There would be others. Filing a federal suit was a legal ploy meant primarily to take every cent of

Bob Dumas's disability money from the Connecticut highway department and, if possible, draw a little attention to the uncomfortable fact that for a long, long time, nobody with the authority and obligation to do so had been seriously looking for Roger or the other guys who never came home from Korea either dead or alive. There were only about 8,200 of them, round numbers.

It was a fair contest: Bob Dumas vs. the U.S. Army. They can both be as infuriating as a family of mosquitoes zipped inside a sleeping bag. The Army records-correction board had refused three times to hear the Dumas case before the federal court trial. And even after the federal judge, T. Emmet Clarie, orered the Army to hold a "full hearing" on the Dumas case, Army lawyers said the board that handles corrections of military records already had 30,000 cases pending. "I don't care if they get 30 million applications," said Judge Clarie.

Bob Dumas began using language like a club fighter uses his left jab. "This is the biggest military coverup in history," he would say. People still didn't listen, but it made him feel better. And besides, he was right. In the course of getting the federal court to order the U.S. government to do its duty and call a prisoner of war a prisoner of war, Bob Dumas unearthed a congressional hearing on POWs the U.S. military seemed to have forgotten and basically showed the U.S. government to be a liar and an incompetent one at that, with your permission, your honor, sir.

Bob Dumas presented all the ex-POWs who'd known Roger in camp. If they had been POWs, and Roger was with them, ergo, Roger was a POW. The logic of it all struck the federal judge as beautifully simple.

But the Army wasn't giving up that easy. The Army lawyers advised the court that at least one of the prison camp witnesses the plaintiff had managed to dredge out of his brother's non-existent military records had his brother confused with two other men with similar names who were POWs but were repatriated.[4]

Bob Dumas found the other guys the Army's lawyers were talking about. Different names. Different service numbers. Same war. Different POWs. Next witness.

Judge Clarie ultimately found for Bob Dumas, in a federal court sort of way. The presumptive finding of death should remain in force, but all Army records should be changed to reflect the fact that Pfc. Roger Dumas was, in fact, a prisoner of war in Korea. Not presumed dead, not anything else, just a prisoner of war.

Of course what Bob Dumas really meant by prisoner of war was, still alive in North Korea, under constant guard at some lousy labor camp. He didn't get that but he got a one-page statement from somebody in the Pentagon saying Roger was a POW.

"You know what?" he told me the first time I heard this story and he showed me the piece of paper. "Lookit. They just typed it. They didn't even have the decency to sign it."

It was 1989, and he'd been looking for his brother for nearly 40 years. But in a way, Bob Dumas was just getting started.

A few years later, the Soviet Union disappeared and North Korea, feeling lonely, decided to join the United Nations. Kim Il-Sung Inc. innocently sent a two-man delegation to New York—which anyone could have told them is only a short train ride from Canterbury, Conn. They opened an office with a telephone and fax machine.

Before you could say Panmunjom, Bob Dumas was faxing and calling, wanting to know when they were going to release Roger. It wasn't really fair. North Korea's only a small country. Bob Dumas is Brotherly Love. He tracked down Ambassador Ho Jong, head of the North Korean mission at the United Nations in New York. The North Koreans weren't terribly friendly at first. They didn't answer Bob Dumas's first 22 phone calls the first week. But the relationship grew.

Eventually, the North Koreans gave in and began meeting with him furtively for long, quiet talks in a hotel coffee shop near the UN headquarters. He would ask leading questions. They would say yes, we have live Americans. But help us get your government to recognize our government. They were crazy for recognition. Bob Dumas was crazy for releasing live American POWs. And would they like a photograph of Roger to send back to North Korea? It would help them pick him out of the soup line at the collective farm. No problem. More coffee? Wow, everything's expensive in New York, isn't it, Mr. Ambassador?

He got it all on tape. Took it back to Canterbury on the train. At every opportunity, Bob Dumas would try to get some politician involved. You can't fight the biggest coverup in military history alone. He'd call the Dukakis campaign, the Bush campaign, the Jesse Jackson campaign. Rev. Jackson was ready, all signed up—Jesse the Libya Liberator. But the trip never got off the ground—something about North Korea staying on the State Department list of countries supporting terrorism.[5]

Despite the sensitive issue they were discussing, between Bob Dumas and the North Koreans, it was all very cordial. When he got home from these trips to the hotel across from the UN, he'd call the Pentagon, a few reporters he's friends with, his congressman's office, the State Department's Asia desk and maybe Veterans Affairs and the White House and ask for the National Security Council people in charge of not negotiating with the North Koreans. He'd tell all of them what he'd told the North Koreans in New York. He'd tell them what the North Koreans said. Then he'd ask them what they thought, and what they were hearing out of North Korea. And he'd tape record those conversations, too.

There should be a wall at the National Archives reserved for the faxes and the tapes and the Amtrak ticket stubs from Bob Dumas when this is all over.

It's hard to say how much it had to do with the Bob Dumas-UN talks, but in 1991, undoubtedly noticing how much diplomatic progress Vietnam was making by giving up some American remains, the North Koreans started talking about doing the same thing. It was a big step. North Korea hadn't conceded a single thing on the POW/MIA issue since 1954, when the last U.S. remains were handed over in Operation Glory.[6]

Some remains were handed over with great ceremony, usually with a member of Congress in attendance. The U.S. military, assigned to guard the south side of the armistice headquarters at Panmunjom, received the coffins from the North Koreans in a solemn welcome and the North Koreans got their few moments of positive media publicity. The remains were a real disappointment, though. They were horribly commingled, and had obviously come from some warehouse, Out of more than 100 sets, the Pentagon got exactly one identified. And it didn't begin to satisfy Bob Dumas. The remains, the bones of dead Americans should be returned, he believed. But what about the live Americans, like his brother? They should come home first.

With a direct pipeline to the gentlemen with the keys to the collective farm, it wasn't long before Bob Dumas could visualize almost exactly where the farm probably was where they were holding live American POWs from Korea, including his brother Roger. He could do this because he had met and talked with a Romanian construction-design engineer named Serban Oprica.

Serban Oprica had seen the American POWs, in 1979, outside of Pyongyang.

Oprica emigrated to Connecticut from Bucharest in 1985. One day he saw a story in one of the state newspapers about Bob Dumas trying to get his brother Roger out of North Korea. He thought he could help. After talking to Dumas, he told his story to the newspapers, to his local congressman, to officials at the Pentagon, and testified before the Senate committee when it held hearings on POWs and MIAs from Korea. It's been seven or eight years since Oprica began telling his story. It hasn't changed.

Oprica was living temporarily in North Korea for several months in the fall of 1979, working on a Romanian foreign assistance project to build a factory in Pyongyang where television sets would be produced. The work week in North Korea is Monday through Saturday, but on Sundays, it was customary for his group of Romanian technicians to take a bus outing.

One Sunday, they were riding through the North Korean countryside, about three hours away from the capital, when they passed a group of about 50 men working in what looked like a cabbage field. All of the men were wearing gray, drab-looking work uniforms and appeared to be caucasians.

And the dozen or so nearest the highway as the bus passed, some 20 feet away, definitely had western features. One was a redhead. "I saw a person with a European face," said Oprica, "with blue eyes, very close to the bus. And I was very shocked. And everybody on the bus was shocked." The men didn't appear to be guarded, Oprica said.

When the Romanians on the bus asked their North Korean escorts about the men, they refused to say anything. But other Romanians who visited North Korea more frequently told him that the workers were American prisoners from the Korean War. The other Romanians behaved as though it was a routine thing to see American POWs working in the fields of North Korea.

At Bob Dumas's urging, Oprica wrote the Pentagon and arranged to talk with an official at the Defense Intelligence Agency, then the main agency in the Defense Department dealing with POW/MIA affairs. The DIA official asked him questions about what he'd seen in North Korea. Oprica heard nothing more from them.

Oprica wrote the FBI, members of Congress and other agencies of the federal government, repeating what he'd told the DIA, offering to supply the names of other people in Romania who could verify what he'd said and perhaps even provide more concrete information. He heard nothing from them.

Oprica also related some disturbing observations when he testified before the Senate in 1992. He said while he was in North Korea on another trip in 1980, he and his wife visited a museum some distance outside Pyongyang. The museum included displays of American military equipment and human parts. He said the "parts of American soldiers" are evidently displayed to instill rage against Americans in the Korean populace.

The "limbs, hands, heads" Oprica said he and his wife saw had been "put in alcohol, and they keep (them) to scare people...people all the time were pressured...the Korean people." He testified that the museum display has a Korean War theme. "They have a lot of American armament items. Uniforms, flags, everything."

It has been several years since Serban Oprica first told his story to the U.S. government.

Bob Dumas thinks the reason the government officials don't take more interest in what Oprica said about POWs working on vegetable farms in the North Korean countryside is because the responsible government officials already know it's true, and they just don't want to say anything about it. "They know they're there," Dumas says. "But if they admit it publicly, we'd have to do something about it, wouldn't we?"

Bob Dumas has a cynical attitude toward the government, cultivated through decades of trying to find out if they know anything about his brother, and when he finds out they do, getting them to tell him. It's a little bit like joining a club, and then finding out that you have to apply for membership again everytime you show up at the door. Bob Dumas has been dealing with the government, either on the telephone, by fax or in person, for a long time. He's managed to overcome a lot of the barriers the government erects, intentionally or not, to people like him—meaning people who think if the government can spend millions and millions of dollars getting troops to a place like North Korea to fight a war, and the soldiers spend three years fighting it, their government ought to spend a few dollars and however long it takes getting everybody back.

The Oprica revelation got Bob Dumas interested in the whole subject of live-sightings, which were big with the Vietnam MIA crowd but had not been widely discussed in the Korean War context. Bob Dumas started working on a better live-sighting context for Korea. Within the past few years, here's some of what has surfaced about live-sightings:

• In August, 1988, Pentagon intelligence sources were reporting that a U.S. POW from the Korean War had played a role in a 12-part North Korean film entitled "Unknown Heroes." The film is supposedly about counter-intelligence operations against UN forces during the Korean War. The POW "portrayed a British intelligence officer during the Korean War and spoke only English," the report said.[7]

The POW-film actor reportedly used the stage name "Louis," and his day job was as an English instructor at the foreign language department of Kim Il-Sung University.

• A later report, in July 1989, based on conversations with North Korean military advisors in Uganda, said "three U.S. personnel known among (North Korean) people as defectors form the Korean War remain in KN and are teaching English at the Reconnaissance Bureau Foreign Language College." The report added that one of the men is married to a Korean woman and the others are single. And two of them reportedly played parts in the "Unknown Heroes" movie: "Carl," a counterintelligence officer, and "Kelton," a civilian doctor.

• "Eleven American POWs from the Korean War are working as English teachers at the Foreign Language School, Reconnaissance Bureau, ministry of People's Armed Forces," according to another Defense Department intelligence source who offered the intelligence in February 1989. The Americans were reportedly not allowed to travel freely but are given escorted trips to historical sites and tourist areas.

• Another February 1989 report from a North Korean defector said the 11 American teachers are between 55 and 60 years old, "speak Korean fluently, and have completely adapted to Korean Life. All of the PWs have Korean wives and a few have children."[8]

• A heavily censored CIA report dated December 1990, subject: "Reports of Americans not able to leave" North Korea. According to agency informants, there are still "some Americans living there" but the government does "not allow them out" and they are "kept somewhere"...these Americans were 'left over' from the Korean War but (the source) never heard how many there might be or any other details about them."

There are many more reports such as these, and it's helpful to study them. They go back further in time, to the days at the very end of the war, some of them. But the live-sighting report that Bob Dumas obviously believes makes the best case for American POWs in North Korea after the war has been in his possession since his federal court suit in 1982-85. He's frequently tried to interest the Pentagon and various congressional offices and the White House in following up on it, but they never seem to get around to it.

This report doesn't say only that some Americans were seen in North Korea after the war was over.

It says Roger Dumas was.

One of the ex-POWs who testified they'd known Roger Dumas at Camp 5 was a man named Walter EnBom of Seattle, Wash. EnBom was a forward observer for an artillery brigade of the First Cavalry Division, a different outfit from Roger's. But they were taken prisoner about the same time and when the war was over, and Roger was not released, EnBom was repatriated along with Cecil Preston, Bobby Caruth and the others.

Then something happened to EnBom that didn't happen with any of the others. In 1955, EnBom re-enlisted, but in the U.S. Air Force, and was sent back to serve in South Korea. While on patrol along the DMZ, on Aug. 8, 1956, he and six other U.S. troops were captured by the North Koreans.[9]

The North Koreans held them for 15 months, and during that time EnBom was returned to Pyoktong, a city on the Yalu and the site where he and so many thousands of other GIs had been held prisoner during the war. That's where he saw Roger again.

Pfc. Roger Dumas, who had been waiting to be repatriated at Operation Big Switch in September 1953, was being held in the Pyoktong jail and "seemed to be physically well," EnBom said, but "his mind was gone. He didn't know his name, didn't recognize me, didn't know where he was."

That sad portrait emerged from answers EnBom gave to questions that were posed as interrogatories for the federal court suit filed by Bob

Dumas. EnBom also said Roger wasn't alone. He reported there were 15 to 20 other American and British men in the Pyoktong jail. They all told him they were unrepatriated POWs from the Korean War.

Apparently out of fear that the U.S. government and military will punish him for talking about his experiences, EnBom refuses to acknowledge what he said in the answers he gave to the questions for Bob Dumas's federal court suit. In fact, now he denies ever being a POW during the Korean War.

That's a more difficult thing to suppress than the later 15-month captivity, which the U.S. military said nothing about at the time. It's more difficult to suppress because there are all those friends who also saw Walter EnBom in the prison camps along the Yalu during the Korean War.

But he claims they're all mistaken—not just about the second time he was captured, but the first time, during the war. He acknowledges that one of the POWs in the photos that the other men at Camp 5 sent to Bob Dumas "looks exactly like me," but it's not. "I've never been a POW," he insists.[10]

Bob Dumas said he and EnBom last talked in 1985, after the federal judge ruled in his case. "Walter called and said, 'I can't talk to you any more, that's it,'" said Dumas. "He just doesn't want to lose his job." EnBom works for the U.S. Department of Commerce office in Seattle.

* * *

If you were an American POW who had been held back in North Korea when your fellow prisoners were repatriated in 1953, how would you let your family know you were still alive?

Pvt. Wildon East sent a post card. The card was inside an envelope The envelope was addressed with a flourish to "Honorable Mayor and the People of the Great City of Spadra...Spadra, Arkansas."

Wildon Chasten East, of Spadra, Ark., a rifleman with the 38th Infantry Regt., Second Division, hadn't been heard from since Sept. 1, 1950. That's when he was captured by the North Koreans. He had been in the first deployment of U.S. troops to the Korean peninsula after the North Korean invasion. The first units, known as Task Force Smith for the general who led them from Japan into battle, were ill-equipped and undermanned as a result of the rapid downsizing of the U.S. military infrastructure after World War II. Task Force Smith suffered an inordinate number of casualties—killed, wounded and missing. The men performed bravely, but against overwhelming odds. The U.S. military today uses Task Force Smith as a superb example of what should never be allowed to happen again.

A picture of Pvt. East, looking like the clean-shaven young soldier he was in 1949 when he joined up, was attached to the card inside, which read:

"People of Spadra, AR. I was born in Spadra, AR. I enlisted in the U.S. Army in September 1949. I am still alive. I am sick, and still a P.O.W. in North Korea." It was signed "Pvt. W.C. East" and had his Army service number along the bottom of the card.[11]

East's relatives, who still live in Spadra, in northeastern Arkansas on the southern edge of the Ozark National Forest, received the card July 1, 1992. A second letter from East arrived the next month addressed to Sen. John Kerry, D-Mass., co-chairman of the Senate Select Committee on POWs and MIAs, which was then preparing for hearings. The second letter contained a cryptic reference to "Remember Hudson Harbor" and "From: General Hyok Chan, North Korea...Co. Kang Tac Mu, N. Korea...From: Col. Han Se Con, North Korea."

Nearly three years have passed. No more letters or cards have been received by the family, according to Bobby Thomas, East's brother-in-law and the family spokesman. The FBI and the U.S. military have done some investigating, but beyond the FBI indicating that their agents are inclined to think it was a hoax, East's family has been told nothing.

"They've all been out here," said Thomas, "the FBI, the Army, everybody. But they don't tell us anything." Thomas and the other family members have done their own analysis, though, and they say the handwriting looks authentic, the service number and other data are correct, and the photograph is correctly identified. The caption below the photograph lists the date East was reported missing. Their conclusion is that Pvt. Wildon East wrote a post card from his prison cell or labor camp somewhere in North Korea, managed to quietly give it to someone who had access to one of the foreigners who have been allowed to visit North Korea under extremely tight supervision, and that person got it mailed to the United States. The letters were postmarked from Taejon, a city in South Korea.

"It's all real," said Thomas. He's confident the correspondence came from Wildon East. What he's not sure of is whether there have been any reprisals—since news reports in the U.S. about the correspondence enabled the North Koreans to be aware that the letters reached this country.[12]

Thomas doesn't think his brother-in-law, Pvt. Wildon East of Spadra, Ark., was the only American POW held back when the Communists returned many of them 42 years ago. And they may not all be kept in the same place. North Korea's not a big country, he notes, but it's big enough to have several places where American POWs could still be kept. It's a matter of whether they'll live long enough to be released.

"A lot of those boys have died by now," said Thomas. "But there's a lot left."

* * *

If Bob Dumas is wrong...and Serban Oprica is wrong...and Walter EnBom was wrong...and Wildon East's brother-in-law Bobby Thomas is wrong...

If all this business about the Pyoktong jail being full of Americans and Brits is bunk...

If a man being taken prisoner twice by the North Koreans and finding an old buddy from his first POW camp still there 13 years later, addled from isolation and mistreatment, is something out of a novel...

If American POWs from the Korean War working in a cabbage field outside of Pyongyang is an excuse to get called before a Senate committee to testify...

If the defectors who saw English-speaking POWs playing roles in a North Korean film about counter-intelligence agents created characters out of their own fevered imagination...

If the idea that a middle-aged American man in a North Korean labor camp could get hold of a postcard and some envelopes, write his family, and give the letters to someone who would see that they reached South Korea and have them end up at his family's little town in the Ozarks and a U.S. senator's mailbox makes absolutely no sense...

If they're all wrong, or overcome by delusions, and all of the thousands of men who were taken prisoner in North Korea more than 40 years ago were either already dead or returned by the Communists when the ceasefire was declared, then...

...there's still the matter of Ri In-Mo and Cho Chang-Ho.

Ri was a North Korean reporter during the war who gave up being a combat journalist and turned guerrilla fighter. On one stealthy mission behind United Nations lines with a group of subversives, however, he was captured by South Korean troops. But instead of being considered a prisoner of war, which would at least have made him eligible for repatriation when an armistice was declared in 1953, he was convicted of political offenses and sentenced along with a number of other guerrillas to a long prison term.

His prison sentence lasted 40 years. In 1991, Ri was allowed by South Korean authorities to file a petition to be returned to the north, and he became what in the international community is called a prisoner of conscience. Two years later, South Korea's conscience finally took effect and he was granted permission to return to Pyongyang, where he was reunited with his wife and daughter.

In heading back north, where the late Kim Il-Sung still ruled, Ri was going against the grain. The usual pattern is for North Koreans to come south, to escape the grinding poverty and strictly regimented political life of the Democratic People's Republic of Korea. The northerners who turn up in the south all give much the same picture of the place, a totalitarian society of 22-million people that is one of the most isolated and militarized in the world.

That's basically how Cho Chang-Ho described his life in North Korea, too. But when Cho made it successfully out of North Korea and appeared in Seoul in October 1994, he was not your typical North Korean defector. He was returning from the dead.

In 1951, Cho was a young artillery lieutenant in the South Korean army, fresh out of military school. During that year's massive Spring Offensive by the Chinese People's Army "volunteers," who had intervened to salvage the North Korean army from certain defeat at the hands of the United Nations' counter-attack, Cho found himself trapped in one of the most disastrous battles of the Korean War.

"In one week of fighting, our division lost 18,000 soldiers," he said, "killed, wounded, captured and missing." Cho's battalion was surrounded and he was captured at Inji-Kun, on the eastern coast of Korea, south of Seoul, and marched north. Over the next several months, as the war decelerated into a series of sharp battles through the center of the peninsula, Cho and the other troops captured in the spring offensive were moved between a succession of makeshift prison camps throughout North Korea. About 70 American troops captured in the same battles—those who didn't die of malnutrition or diarrhea from a diet of raw corn—were shipped to the large POW camps along the Yalu, while Cho and the rest of the South Koreans were taken as far as Aoji, in far northeastern North Korea, a few miles south of the Soviet border.

When the war ended in July 1953 in a ceasefire and armistice calling for the mutual exchange of all remaining prisoners, Cho wasn't brought to the exchange point at Panmunjom. By then, he was not in a prison camp, but—like Ri In-Mo in the south—in a civilian prison, charged with numerous offenses stemming from repeated attempts to deceive his military captors. "I kept trying to escape," he said. "Wherever they took us, I would try to get away." His imprisonment lasted 11 more years, until 1964.

At that point, things got easier, Cho said: "They put me to work in a coal mine." Life for even a typical, law-abiding North Korean with no criminal record, said Cho, "is the worst, the most terrible you can imagine," in terms of food (not enough), shelter (barely adequate), working conditions (inhumane) and liberties (non-existent). But for ex-prisoners with a record like himself, there is one more condition—no travel permitted, even within North Korea itself. He was married, with two sons and a daughter, and they shared his low social status, which meant the barest of necessities and the minimum of educational opportunities.

But in his small village on the Yalu River, a few people from the outside world—Chinese peddlers from villages in Manchuria, just across the river—could occasionally visit. Cho befriended one of them and asked, if he could somehow manage to reach the trader's village in Manchuria, if the peddler would help him get to the coast. The peddler said he would try. Cho gave the Manchurian a photograph of himself, and waited for an opportunity.

Finally, after dark on Oct. 3, 1994, just before the harsh Manchurian winter set in, he slipped across the river during a heavy downpour and headed for the peddler's village. From there, he made his way to the coast, talked his way aboard a small vessel belonging to smugglers, and sailed to a South Korean port.

Cho said he last saw American POWs before the war ended and large groups of prisoners were exchanged. But he understands that many more were not released. There were at least 400 South Korean soldiers he knew personally who were taken prisoner and, like himself, never repatriated. "If they weren't considered prisoners of war, but just prisoners, they weren't released," he said. "Most are dead now...there were 400 at one time...It took a long time for them to die...one by one."

Many American POWs died in the main prison camps on the Yalu not far from the remote village where he spent most of his decades of imprisonment and subsequent house arrest. And Cho heard of "mass burial sites" for American POWs in the villages along the northern stretch of the Yalu. But when the Americans who are buried there died, he doesn't know. During the war, South Korean POWs were separated from POWs from the U.S. and other western countries. After he was released from prison, he had no opportunity to travel and see for himself what might have happened to POWs who weren't exchanged. But many could have survived for a time after the war, he believes. They could have been held at many of the camps that the North Koreans supposedly emptied when the armistice was signed.

It was simply a matter of definition. When the fighting stopped, there could be no more prisoners of war still in North Korea. The remaining enemy soldiers had become criminals. The armistice agreement said nothing about releasing criminals.

Recently married to a Korean-American from Los Angeles, Sinja Yun, Cho has settled into his new life as a 65-year-old returned war hero. He posed for photograps in one of his old South Korean lieutenant's uniforms, complete with white parade gloves, pointing to his name on a wall plaque commemorating the thousands of South Korean soldiers who died in the war.

His newly published biography, "Return of a Dead Man," is on sale in Seoul and being translated into English. His five sisters who had given him up for dead dote on him. After recuperating in a military hospital from dehydration, he's taken on healthy coloring and appears much younger than 65.

"It was a miracle, a big miracle," he said, describing his escape from the north. Only when asked about the wife and children he left behind do his eyes reveal a slight tinge of regret at his daring departure. "There will be some reprisal," he said. "But not bad. I hope not bad."

Ri In-Mo and Chang-Ho Cho aren't really miracles, though. They're proof of a certain reality. The reality is that during the Korean War, the participants didn't merely take prisoners.

They took prisoners for a very, very long time.

NOTES and SOURCES

Where indicated, quotations and citations within the text refer to documents collected and translated for the U.S.-Russia Joint Commission on Prisoners of War by the Pentagon's Defense POW/MIA Affairs Office or (the short-lived agency) Task Force Russia, or to minutes of the commission's meetings. The following paragraph is standard issue and applies to all meeting transcripts since the commission's founding in March 1992:

"This transcript was prepared by a Task Force Russia officer with a high fluency in the Russian language who attended the working group session and took extensive, near-verbatim notes. It was then reviewed by other TFR personnel who were present and who are conversant in the Russian language. All paraphrased remarks are accurate in full detail as heard, while any portions of the text given in quotation marks are considered to have been recorded with a fully reliable level of accuracy."

Chapter One: *Caught in the Web*

1. Summary of security information, 441st CIC Detachment, 14 July 1950; CIC Report D3-9958 (5c), 6 July 50, "General Derevyenko in Communist China;" CCRAK (Combined Command Reconnaissance Activities Korea), 8240th Army Unit, 16 July 1952. Derevyenko's movements after suddenly departing Tokyo were a matter of intense interest to U.S. officials who had dealt with him in the allied council's deliberations. Army intelligence during the Korean War included reports that he had been promoted to marshal and placed in charge of a new Sinkiang Province command linking the new Chinese military and Soviet units in Asia. Meanwhile, the Australian embassy officials in Washington were told of U.S. intelligence reports that the Soviets had established a Japanese government in exile, complete with armed units staffed by Japanese ex-POWs, involving many of the Japanese Communist leaders Derevyenko had cultivated during his tour in Tokyo. (Aide-memoire, U.S. State Dept., Sept. 8, 1950.)

Pro-U.S. Japanese sources were reporting (State Dept., Bureau of Far Eastern Affairs, Nov. 20, 1950) that Derevyenko was heading up a special military training program for his new command made up of Chinese, Korean, Japanese, Mongol and Indochinese troops.

But a more ominous CIC report based on Japanese intelligence sources appeared in late September 1950, after MacArthur's troops made their successful Inchon landing. The Japanese report said after returning to Moscow, Lt. Gen. Derevyenko was executed for the sin of being wrong—assuring Stalin the U.S. would not intervene in the war.

2. Kathryn Weathersby, Kennan Institute for Advanced Russian Studies, paper presented at Seoul, Korea, June 13, 1995. Weathersby's analysis of the latest declassified files from the foreign ministry archives in Moscow makes crystal clear the degree to which Kim Il-Sung's government and policies were the creatures of Stalin—to the extent that a visit to the Lenin library by a ranking North Korean official required a resolution of the Central Committee of the Communist Party—and that Stalin's okay for the invasion was based on the presumption the U.S. would not intervene. Weathersby's papers also include the fact that Stalin set a price for his support: North Korea was obliged to make up for the USSR's "great insufficiency in lead" by shipping a "yearly minimum" of 25,000 tons. The North Koreans reportedly made their quota even during the war years.

3. Kyril Kalinov, "How Russia Built the North Korean Army," The Reporter, Sept. 26, 1950. Kalinov wrote that Stykov and North Korea's other Soviet military patrons understood that "without Korea, Vladivostok and Port Arthur have no military value," but that the Soviets were not plannng to turn the peninsula "into a bastion for an offensive in the Pacific."

4. Military Intelligence Section, Gen. Hqs., Far East Command, 30 Sept. 1950; source of report was a North Korean intelligence officer stationed in Seoul. Same source tracked the inpouring of Soviet supplies in the spring that were quickly hidden away in rural areas prior to the invasion.

5. Message, Amb. Muccio, Seoul, to State Dept., June 12, 1950. The ambassador, in the interest of correct terminology for a map of Korea, pointed out "Chagang province was created by Soviets as mineral, timber reserve with special USSR privileges. Its existence not recognized by ROK, US or any allied power outside Soviet bloc." He suggested using the standard name, North Pyongan province.

6. Stalin's military support of North Korea's effort can be viewed as sufficient or lacking, depending on the perspective. The North Koreans, seeing Soviet planes defending only as far south as the Yalu River, and providing no close air support, undoubtedly felt it was too little. But Soviet anti-aircraft and radar units were deployed throughout the war as far south as the fluid

front lines. Soviet fighter squadrons and other combat units did take casualties, although the number is uncertain. The closest thing to an official history of Soviet involvement in the Korean War, a book that covers all such wars "abroad" since World War II, states that 299 Soviet troops were killed in Korea—138 officers and non-commissioned officers and 161 enlisted. The officers were said to include 120 pilots. But Soviet veterans say casualties were actually much higher. Valentin Pak, head of North Korean military propaganda during the war, said (interview, December 1994) Soviet advisors told him that dozens of field officers were killed during three years of being on the receiving end of the Far East Air Force's daily bomb packages.

The Russian side of the joint commission asked the American side to help determine the fate of four Soviet MIG pilots who went down over North Korea. By consulting U.S. shootdown claims, Pentagon analysts were able to tell the Russians which U.S. pilots claimed MIG kills that matched in two of the cases.

7. Seized Enemy Documents, Gen. Hqs., Far East Command, Military Intelligence Section, Allied Translator and Interpreter Section, Item 15/201444.

8. "Uncertain Partners—Stalin, Mao and the Korean War," Sergei Goncharov, John W. Lewis, Xue Litai, p. 138-142. Kim apparently believed Korea would be a replay of the mass uprising that had just brought Mao to power in China. Syngman Rhee's government in Seoul was very unpopular. But the response to Kim's liberation troops was not as warm as he'd predicted.

9. Shabshin's role in North Korean affairs peaked when the UN intervention showed that Soviet presumptions in the region were misguided. He was last reported headed for Yugoslavia, where he saw another war as imminent (U.S. State Dept. messages from Berlin embassy, Aug. 5, 1950.

10. New York Times, Aug. 13, 1949.

11. Allied Translator & Interpreter Section, Far East Command, Interrogation Report No. 219, 29 July 1950; President Truman cited parts of this report in an April, 1951 speech.

12. New York Times, March 1, 1956.

13. Telegram from Seoul embassy to State Dept., 24 June 1950. The North

Koreans were moving into propaganda documentaries even then. What Muccio described as "2 strictly anti-US documentary films" produced in Pyongyang since 1946 had featured Russian actors portraying U.S. troops with "semi-pornographic" scenes alleging mistreatment of South Korean citizenry.

14. Seized Enemy Documents from joint cabinet ministers' building, Pyongyang; Nov. 6, 1950; Item 19/200753.

15. G-2, CINCFE, July 2, 1950; MacArthur Memorial Archives, Norfolk, Va. Source was a North Korean pilot shot down in first week of invasion, June 30, 1950. It was a bad war for North Korea's air force, which the Soviets had not built up like the armored units. And when the British, French and American missionaries and diplomats were released through a "flattened" Pyongyang in the spring of 1953, they reported the North Koreans had moved almost everything into caves, "complete with living quarters, offices, electricity, telephone."

16. Hqs., Far East Air Forces, bomb damage report from Jan. 31, 1951 to Jan 27, 1954.

17. Seized Enemy Records, Soviet mission, Pyongyang, Oct. 30, 1950; Item 17/201148. The list of attendees did not mention the location of the meeting, but the document was found in the abandoned Soviet embassy when U.S. troops occupied the North Korean capital.

18. Accounts of the civilians imprisoned by North Korea are a small library. Among the most thorough is "In Enemy Hands," by Rev. Larry Zellers. Philippe Gigantes, a London war correspondent writing under the name "Philip Deane" when captured also did a superb job in "I Should Have Died" of recreating the Communists' numbing attempts at "brainwashing" the intellectual crowd the North Koreans managed to imprison.

19. Drumwright letter to Amb. Muccio, July 5, 1950. The rumors of war in Korea were non-stop by the summer of 1950. Weathersby describes the situation that summer as "volatile."

20. A most astounding feat, fitting 690 adults and children aboard a Norwegian ship that had passenger berths for only 12. But Jean MacDonald, whose husband was a counselor at the U.S. embassy, was one of the evacuees and she swears the numbers are accurate. Not an inch of deck space was left by the time the ship lifted anchor. She said there was slightly more

room on the sea voyage from Japan to California.

21. The economic and educational ties between the U.S. and South Korea were extensive by 1950. Illinois Institute of Technology operated an institute in Seoul that trained technicians in fishing, farming and industrial occupations. Exchange programs abounded. A group of South Korean trainees from the Dunwoody Industrial Institute were scheduled to arrive in Washington, D.C., on Saturday, June 24, 1950, to inspect "industrial establishments" and "do a little sightseeing" before returning to Seoul July 1. Fortunate timing.
22. "In Enemy Hands," Zellers, pp. 29-37.

Chapter Two: *Trains to Manchouli*

1. Van Wees letter to President Clinton, Jan. 5, 1994.

2. Esquire, May 1953.

3. The CIA report is marked "Date Acquired 15 Jul 52" and "Date Distr. 2 Sept. 1952" but the report number is redacted.

4. Memo, State Dept. Bureau of Far Eastern Affairs, Dec. 22, 1952.

5. Memo, Department of the Army, Dec. 22, 1954. The two soldiers' story—that they were South Korean soldiers when captured by the Communists—was later verified. The refusal of the so-called Neutral Nations Supervisory Commission to investigate the soldiers' allegations was in line with the other actions of the commission, which tended to favor the Communists. One Polish guard assigned to the commission defected at Panmunjom. He told allied investigators that the "neutral" Polish delegation was seeded with Soviet plants.

6. Department of the Army memo to secretary of Defense, Jan. 29, 1954.

7. Guild was described by some as "a thorn in the sides" of the Pentagon and State Department for his campaign to draw attention to U.S. and UN inaction on the POW/MIA issue. But little came of the campaign. Korean War MIA families were largely silent on the issue until after the Vietnam War, when controversy over the MIAs from that conflict touched an old nerve.

8. New York Times, June 17, 1956.

9. Memo, Department of the Army, G-1, Asst. Chief of Staff, Personnel, April 29, 1954.

10. Message from U.S. consulate Hong Kong to State Dept., March 23, 1954.

11. Lt. Col. Corso's military intelligence career in the Far East and Washington, D.C., gave him an extraordinary view of the Korean War POW/MIA problem. He has given a step-by-step account of his positions in his November 1992 testimony before the Senate Select Committee on POWs and MIAs and in his interviews with Task Force Russia, Feb. 25, 1993.

12. Testimony, Senate Select Committee on POWs and MIAs, November 1992.

13. 6004th Air Intelligence Service Squadron, Report C-579, Sept. 17, 1951.

14. Aerial reconnaissance was developed to a science during World War II, and the Korean War gave it more impetus. A number of casualties from so-called "Cold War" shootdowns in the Far East during the Korean War were not considered combat-related only because, it can be assumed, all the emphasis was on keeping the war limited to the Korean peninsula. In any other war, a pilot or crew killed trying to photograph enemy buildups or movements on the periphery of the fighting would have been considered deaths attributable to that war.

15. New York Times, Aug. 14, 1954.

16. Rastvorov told the Senate judiciary subcommittee on internal security in 1956 that he and Sergei Tikhvinski, a Soviet intelligence officer active in postwar Japan and China, had been instrumental in the program to recruit Japanese agents: "After the second world war, the MVD Intelligence Service participated in the recruitment of Japanese prisoners of war in concentration camps, which existed all over the Soviet Union, particularly in the Far East area. In 1948 I participated myself in recruitment of PWs in the Far East area, especially Khabarovsk. The MVD Intelligence Service recruited approximately 400 Japanese prisoners of war to use as agents after their return to Japan...Some of them were put on ice temporarily, and we can assume that Mr. Tikhvinski will be engaged in re-establishing contact with some of these people, who up until now have not been active as Soviet

agents, but who are now important to Soviet intelligence because of their possible sensitive positions." Interviewed in December 1993 in Moscow, where he is on the faculty of an institute for the study of the Far East, Tikhvinski denied ever being a Soviet intelligence officer. He said all of his years in the Far East were spent pursuing a dual career as diplomat and Asia scholar.

17. After Corso testified about President Eisenhower's knowledge of the POWs' predicament, some Eisenhower scholars said they knew of no papers that would support such a contention. But the Task Force Russia people found papers in the Eisenhower Library they said persuaded them Corso's assertion was correct. The author's hunch, based on past experience with security classification rules, is that there are more Korean War-era Eisenhower papers somewhere that no scholar or reporter has been permitted to see and that therein lie the facts.

Chapter Three: *On Stalin's Instructions*

1. It was good of Mikhail Gorbachev, before he left office, to release the documents that laid out the responsibility of Stalin's regime for the massacre of 6,000-10,000 Polish officers in a Soviet POW camp in Germany in 1946. But the U.S. government has known since not long after World War II ended that it was Russians, not Germans, who did the killing. Some murders can't be well hidden.

2. The Soviets' stiff-arming of the UN debate over the non-return of POWs from World War II outlasted the Korean War. In September 1953, a report to the General Assembly said the effort had "reached an impasse" because the Soviets had refused to turn over names of prisoners they continued to hold. (New York Times, Sept. 2, 1953.)

3. New York Times, June 30, 1992..

4. Washington Post, Aug. 1, 1992. Volkogonov's effort to elicit appreciation for releasing the names of 39 Americans who had been imprisoned during World War II sagged a bit after some of the people on the list turned out to have been living in the U.S. for some years. But the stories of their escape from Soviet Russia were truly inspiring. When Joseph Marshall was freed from prison in 1956, he found his daughter living in Kazakhstan. He borrowed money to take the train to Moscow, but couldn't get past the Soviet guards at the U.S. embassy. Finally getting the attention of two

women as they left the embassy compound, he made contact with U.S. officials. He and four other members of his family reached the U.S. in December 1960.

5. Volkogonov, the author of books on philosophy, history and politics, brings a personal knowledge of Soviet repression to the study of Americans missing in the Gulag. His father was executed in the political purges of the 1930s and his mother died in exile. A lifelong military man, and respected scholar, he plays in the big leagues of historical analysis, having taken on hardliners in his efforts to write honestly of the sins of Stalinism.

6. To grasp the postwar Gulag in proper, horror-inciting context, the reader can't do better than consulting Nilolai Tolstoy ("Victims of Yalta;" "Stalin's Secret War;") or "The Last Secret" by Nicholas Bethell.

7. On the questionnaire in which Clifford-Brown's physical appearance is put in such minute detail, there were also multiple-choice categories (left blank) for identifying features including extra digits, warts, scars, tattoos, tics, gestures and stuttering.

8. Memo, State Department, Bureau of Eastern European Affairs, Aug. 6, 1956.

9. Abakumov was very powerful, but not for very long. A protege of Beria, by the time Stalin appointed him to direct all Soviet intelligence agencies, he had rivals in military intelligence with contacts in Stalin's circles. They presented Stalin with evidence that Abakumov was disloyal. That put a bullet in the chamber with Abakumov's name on it. In 1952, the gun fired.

10. Yeltsin's statement that some American POWs from Vietnam might be alive in Russia remains a problem for the Russian side of the joint commission. The standard line is that "no credible evidence" for either Soviet contacts or transfers of U.S. POWs from Vietnam to the USSR has been found. But the commission's May 1995 interim report says both sides consider the Vietnam War questions will "require substantially more work."

11. An insight into the difficulties of tracing anyone in Gulag records is gained from noting that the photos of Oggins were inscribed with "586. Ehgon-Ogens Khain-Sal Samoch." Because the cyrillic alphabet is different from the Latin alphabet, it's difficult to spell English names in Russian and vice versa. Perfectly simple names like Cox and Towers (two American servicemen freed in the 1950s) become "Koks and Tauehrs." John Helmut

Noble? "Dzhon Khellmut Noubl," etc.

12. Sudoplatov may be correct that Molotov feared the reputation of the American Communist Party would be sullied if a real Gulag ex-inmate could be brought before flash bulbs on Capitol Hill. But Oggins was safely tucked away in prison. He wasn't about to show up there even if he'd been spared execution. Testimony from Mrs. Oggins, perhaps? That's a different story.

13. Asahi Evening News, Tokyo, December 1956.

14. A report from the Russian Federation's Supreme Court in May 1992—in the flush of Russian democratic reform—informed Volkogonov that a special commission was created in Moscow in the spring of 1953, after Stalin's death, to study the subject of foreigners in the Gulag. The commission located 16,547 foreigners in prison, most of them German POWs. According to the information gathered by that commission, only eight of the foreigners were Americans; two were scheduled to be freed, the other six "were supposed to remain in prison to continue serving their sentences." (Task Force Russia document 2-72.)

15. Gen. Hqs., Far East Command, Military Intelligence Section, "Soviet Use and Treatment of Japanese PWs," Oct. 22, 1949; MacArthur Archives.

16. Kirichenko's report was based on documents the Soviet Union had previously insisted did not exist. And officially, there were only 26 cemeteries containing Japanese remains in all of Siberia.

17. Memo, Far East Air Force to CINCFE, 21 Oct. 1954.

18. Interview with author, November 1993.

19. Skardzius and Keburis both appear in Task Force Russia's report for June 19-July 9, 1993.

20. Interview with author, August 1994.

21. Task Force Russia interview, Oct. 27, 1992.

22. Message from USPOLAD, Heidelberg, to State Dept., Jan. 3, 1951.

Chapter Four: *Circling the Wagons*

1. Yevgenia Albats, "The State Within a State," p. 303.

2. Testimony before the Senate Select Committee on POWs and MIAs, Nov. 10, 1992.

3. Interview with author, May 11, 1995.

4. The release of the "510 List" came after 96 U.S. senators signed a letter to Yeltsin urging him to facilitate the release of intelligence reports and files that might hold answers to American POW/MIA cases.

5. The joint commission's American analysts appear to have shelved the Pugantsev story, for lack of corroboration. The Russian side never was interested in pursuing it too hard. But while no proof of a Korean War POW named "David Markin" has surfaced since the story broke in June 1992, the author's judgment is that it's too soon to rule that out. The story Pugantsev related included some details that would be difficult to create out of whole cloth. One element that didn't make the press coverage was that Markin supposedly underwent years in psychiatric hospitals where he was given numerous drug injections that brought on sleep and mental confusion. That would help explain why an American prisoner might not simply walk out of the Gulag once the Communist Party was history.

6. Task Force Russia report, 17-30 April 1993.

7. Lt. Bell, of Yuba City, Calif., was flying a B-26 on a night flight over North Korea on Jan. 26, 1952. He radioed word that he was "proceeding to attack three lights" that were five to ten miles in the distance. He was not heard from again.

8. The 1995 interim report of the joint commission notes that its American members in Russia "have been provided access to Russian archives, psychiatric hospitals, prisons, prison camps and military installations...." That much is true. But not always full access, as Task Force Russia's records show, and not often without weeks or months of preparatory negotiations.

9. By 1993, Yeltsin's concerns were primarily domestic. And in the POW/MIA search, the discovery by an American university researcher, Stephen Morris, of a document in Soviet archives that amounted to evidence that the Vietnamese had held back American POWs in the 1970s was causing

the Russians a great deal of discomfort.

10. This awkwardly-worded phrase was the Russians' defense against continued references to Yeltsin's earlier statement about American POWs still being held. To Ambassador Toon's credit, it cannot be stretched to rule out the idea that they were held in the past.

11. This presentation, done at a Pentagon news conference, provided a small piece of theater for an otherwise gray enterprise involving thick books of documents and translations.

12. This quote is as good an explanation as any for why more actual documents have not surfaced from the former Soviet archives on the topic of POWs and MIAs.

Chapter Five: *The Interrogators*

1. Besides Maj.-Gen. Lobov, 21 pilots were awarded the title of Hero of the Soviet Union for flying combat missions in Korea. The others were: Maj.Stepan A. Bakhaev; Capt. Arkadii S. Boytsov; Capt. Nikolai G. Dokashenko; Capt. Grigorii I. Ges; Maj. Anatolii M. Kavelin; Capt. Sergei M. Kramarenko; Capt. Mikhail I.Mikhin; Maj. Stepan I. Naumenko; lst Lt. Boris A. Obraztsov; Maj. Dmitrii P. Oskin; Capt. Grigorii U. Okhai; Col. Evgenii G. Pepelyaev; Mikhail S. Ponomarev; Lt. Col. Grigorii I. Pulov; lst Lt. Dmitri A. Samoilov; Lt. Col. Aleksei P. Smorchkov; lst Lt. Evgenii M. Stelmakh; Capt. Trofim P. Subbotin; Capt. Nikolai V. Sutyagin; lst Lt. Fyodor A. Shibanov; and Capt. Lev K. Kirillovich.

2. Interview with author, September 1991.

3. American pilots in Korea said that another tipoff that a Russian was in the cockpit was dogfight ability. Until late in the war, very few Chinese pilots could match the skills of the Russians, especially those who had seen combat in Europe.

4. Given the number of planes the UN and the Soviets lost over Korea, the search squadrons had their work cut out for them. The Chinese also retrieved downed U.S. aircraft and hauled it back to Manchuria. It's reasonable to assume that the Soviets supplied the salvage equipment and had the pick of crash sites, except in those cases where, Orlov said, the North Koreans took away parts before the Soviets could get organized.

5. Soviet pilots got bonuses, too, but in rubles.

6. The Soviets took precautions against being captured but with so many personnel in the theater, it stands to reason some were. An unnamed spokesman for the U.S. Army's Seventh Division told reporters a Soviet major had been killed and another Soviet officer taken prisoner in the Seoul-Suwon area in late September 1950 (New York Times, Sept. 24, 1950). And when American troops took Pyongyang, five men and three women described as Russian civilians were captured. The U.S. military said they were being detained "merely for their own protection." (New York Times, Oct. 30, 1950.) Soviet military personnel were required to wear either Chinese uniforms or civilian clothes while in North Korea.

7. This would be the RB-50 shootdown that was considered by U.S. officials a retaliatory act for the downing of a Soviet transport plane by a U.S. fighter on July 27, 1953, that took 21 lives.

8. A Soviet veteran in Bishkek, Kyrgyzstan, told me in 1994 that he had never mentioned serving with an anti-aircraft artillery battalion in North Korea to anyone, even his wife, in all these years.

9. Many of the Korean War-era documents have been translated and interpreted by Kathryn Weathersby for the Kennan Institute. They offer a full, new view of the Soviet patronage of North Korea, from teachers to automobiles, trains, planes, steam engines and oil, all to be financed with a $50 million line of credit from Moscow—in U.S. dollars.

10. There is no record that the list of 109 pilots referred to by Osipov has been released.

11. Both Korotkov and Orlov mention a U.S. POW pilot named Lt. Col. Black. Lt. Col. Vance Eugene Black was reported to have died in May 1951 while a POW. One document notes that he died of malnutrition at the "North Korean Interrogation Center" just outside Pyongyang.

12. Some Soviet veterans say they handed in their Red Army uniforms and were issued Chinese uniforms before they boarded trains in Siberia for the trip south to Manchuria and North Korea.

13. The KGB operation in Khabarovsk was sizable, and much of the agency's training of foreign agents reportedly was carried out there. The training

functions were in addition to a prison complex that could handle several thousand inmates at a time (The First Guidebook to Prisons and Concentration Camps of the Soviet Union, Avraham Shifrin, 1980.)

14. Only Mazurov and Korotkov know what Mazurov said to him in that call. Mazurov's attitude toward the evidence presented by the American representatives on the commission is a matter of record.

15. The photo reconnaissance missions laid on by Far East Air Force did find numerous airfields in Manchuria stocked with Soviet aircraft and operated jointly by Soviet and Chinese personnel. They were in the Manchurian sanctuary respected—in the main—by UN forces.

16. Razuvayev's appointment wasn't official until August. But according to a key associate and others who worked in the Soviet embassy at the time, his influence began to wane soon after the lighting invasion of the south turned into a protracted struggle.

17. Interview with author, June 1995.

18. Orlov at one point attempted to argue that the interrogators usually didn't bother with recording POWs' names. Here he makes the actual process quite clear.

19. Task Force Russia document 37-48.

20. There may not have been any North Korean official "in charge" of all UN or American POWs. The evidence from available records suggests that a number of individuals held some responsibility and that some of them shared responsibility with Chinese and Soviet officials..

21. Christopher Andrew and Oleg Gordievsky, "KGB—The Inside Story," p. 403-404.

22. Blake gives his reasons why in his autobiography with the telltale title, "No Other Choice."

23. Interview with author, June 1994.

24. Blake's blind devotion to communism puts him in sync with a sizable minority of Russian citizens today who would sooner have the politburo back than try to weather capitalism.

25. Philip Deane, "I Should Have Died," p. 5.

26. Once the fighting had stopped, the Eisenhower administration took some of the blinders off. A U.S. delegate to the United Nations charged the Soviets with supervising the torture and interrogations repatriated POWs had said took place at "Pak's Palace," the POW compound outside of Pyongyang. (New York Times, Oct. 27, 1953.)

27. There is nothing remotely "self-contradictory" about Korotkov's statements. He was evidently pressured into qualifying his assertion that the interrogations took place on Soviet territory. As for providing no detail that can be confirmed, that is true only if the KGB records for the interrogation center in Khabarovsk remain off-limits. The record of commission minutes show Korotkov trying to walk a fine line in front of Volkogonov, while privately telling Col. Herrington and the other Americans they were very close to the real story and to keep pressing for answers.

28. "The Problems of U.S.Marine Corps Prisoners of War in Korea," James Angus MacDonald Jr., USMC History and Museums Division, 1988.

29. Once again, Orlov futilely tried to rewrite the history of the war to prove his point. There were plenty of POW pilots in 1950, from B-29s, B-26s, F-51s, as well as from one of only three RB-45s flying missions over North Korea.

30. The MGB's China connection during the Korean War is testified to in Andrew and Gordievsky, p. 404: "China did...provide much intelligence on U.S. military technology obtained during the Korean War, and gave the MGB a base on Chinese territory, where it could train ethnic Chinese illegals for work against the Main Adversary (the U.S.) and other Western states. The MGB was also given unrestricted access to Western POWs held by the Chinese and North Koreans. Among them was George Blake."

Chapter Six: *Chain of Evidence*

1. The report was prepared by Peter G. Tsouras, Air Force Maj. Werner Hindrichs and Air Force M/Sgt. Danz Blasser, with the assistance of Air Force 2nd Lt. Timothy R. Lewis, Paul H. Vivian, Army Staff Sgt. Linda R.H. Pierce and Army Sgt. Gregory N. Vukin. Tsouras and Vivian are Department of the Army civilian employes.

2. Central Intelligence Agency memo, Nov. 12, 1953.

3. The interim report of May 1995 makes the same point in an oblique way, noting that "much archival work (is) yet to be done."

Chapter Seven: *Mathematics of the Missing*

1. Letter, Maj. Gen. K. L. Hastings to Maj. Gen. Ira K. Evans, May 24, 1954..

2. As of June 1995, the U.S. and North Korean governments were deadlocked over the subject of returning more U.S. remains from the Korean War. The U.S. offer stood at $1 million; the North Koreans demanded $22 million, plus trucks, according to Brig. Gen. James Wold, deputy assistant secretary of state for POW/MIA affairs. Pentagon officials involved in the negotiations insist that they do not consider the nearly $1 million already paid North Korea or any money it may pay in the future, as payment for the remains North Korea gave the U.S. in return, but rather compensation for the incidental expenses incurred in returning them.

3. Paul M. Cole, "POW/MIA Issues, Vol. 1, The Korean War," Chap. 2, Korean War Casualty Statistics.

4. Message CINCFE Japan to Department of Army, Jan. 3, 1951.

5. Albert Biderman, "March to Calumny," p. 97.

6. The POW/MIA figures for UN allies in Korea are smaller, but not much more solid than those for the U.S. Tim Carew's "The Commonwealth at War" calculates fewer than 100 MIAs at the war's conclusion from the UK, Canada and Australia. A UN breakdown counts more than 1,300 for the same three countries.

7. Tibor Meray letter to author, May 18, 1995.

8. In an interview in December 1993, Lee hadn't changed his position on POWs one inch since 1953. He swears North Korea returned every single one.

9. When all else failed, the Communists' usual response was that any bulge

in the number of UN MIAs could be attributed to UN bombing and air attacks—friendly fire, in other words.

10. Memo, Department of Army to CINCFE Japan, Oct. 30, 1953.

11. The Times, London, Oct. 23, 1950.

12. Graves Registration in the Korean Conflict, The Quartermaster Review, March-April 1953; Lt. Col. John C. Cook, QMC.

13. The change in burial policy is nowhere credited with having any effect on morale in the war zone. But the increased demands on the undermanned Graves Registration units was evident.

14. Graves Registration Service in the Korean Conflict.

15. Operation Big Switch records also report the return of three Japanese POWs. Japan was a silent UN ally in the war, contributing minesweeping vessels and crews.

16. Memo, War Claims Division, State Department, July 6, 1956.

17. Department of Army message to UNCMAC Korea.

18. Message, Dulles to major embassies in Europe and Asia, Aug. 26, 1953.

19. Report of Battle Casualties, Department of the Army, Jan. 22, 1954.

20. New York Times, Jan. 1, 1954.

21. Biderman, "March to Calumny," p. 99.

22. Message, CINCUNC to Department of the Army, July 10, 1054.

23. Cole, RAND Study, POW/MIA Issues, Vol. 1, Korean War, Chapter 2.

24. As with virtually every figure associated with Korean War casualties, there is not universal agreement on this figure. But even more difficult to reconcile is the fact that, in the summer of 1954, there were still several hundred—letters and memos cite between 500 and 600—unidentifiable remains still on hand when Operation Glory was just getting underway. If Operation Glory left another 850-plus sets of remains unidentified, then

the total number of unidentified remains left to ship out of Korea in 1956 would have been closer to 1,400.

As for the pool of MIA/BNR cases that can be considered in evaluating the evidence for POW transfers to the former Soviet Union, Cole has a much more scientific formula that leads him to basically the same figure the author's formula does. Here is Cole's formula, based on his extensive research in casualty data at the Central Identification Laboratory in Hawaii:

Missing in action at sea: 293.

Confirmed POW deaths (body not returned) 2,119.

Total U.S. graves on North Korean territory: 2,096.

U.S. burials related to aircrash sites: 412.

BNR cases outside Korea: 53.

BNR (died during marches): 959.

Postwar BNR cases grouped with war data: 13.

Total confirmed or documented BNR deaths: 5,945.

That leaves about 2,200 BNR names out of the 8,200 for the entire war as potential transfers.

Chapter Eight: *Documents, Documents*

The May 1995 interim report of the joint commission states that the Russian side has provided "more than 10,000 documents, many of which were once highly classified, bearing on U.S. POWs." Unfortunately, the search for POW/MIAs is not just a matter of how much paper gets turned over. A lot depends on what's printed on the paper.

Chapter Nine: *Taking the Trophies*

1. A true research project would be to determine how deeply Chairman Stalin dug into his prodigious in-box on those days when the F-86

interrogation protocols came in from Khabarovsk and Antung. Stalin is listed as the top recepient of a number of documents the Russians have released in the POW/ MIA category. Perhaps one day a Stalin scholar will be able to determine which ones he read.

2. Interview with author.

3. Interview with author

4. Interviews with author.

5. Shifrin, a former Gulag inmate, pursues leads from the office of his center for research into victims of forced labor in Jerusalem, a safe distance from Russia.

6. Memo, Far East Air Forces, Jan. 17, 1951.

7. POW/MIA Archive Research Project, Vol. 1, Moscow; Paul M. Cole, February 1995.

8. Several examples of allied salvage operations appear in "The Naval Air War in Korea," Richard Hallon, 1986.

9. The story thus far is that the tail numbers and other identifying marks on the aircraft were removed, thus making them untraceable. That depends on where the numbers were removed, and whether any good Soviet bureaucratic recorded the number to be rubbed off or painted over.

10. Interview with author, December 1994.

Chapter Ten: *The Eyewitness*

1. The Chinese Communists inherited a number of nearly new airfields the U.S. had laid down for the Nationalist regime, which couldn't hold power. But China's industrial base was meager, and made more so by the Soviets, who trucked off an impressive number of plants and factories in Manchuria when they seized that province from the Japanese.

2. The note from Razuvayev is discussed in Chapter 12.

3. The Chinese POW bosses picked up the receipt system the North Koreans

had begun to use in the war's first months. Captured enemy records include examples of receipts for American prisoners (example: "I certify that I have received 57 American prisoners, members of US 2d Infantry Regiment.")

A Chinese language manual entitled "How to Interrogate Prisoners of War" printed in March 1951, was a how-to lesson in selecting the most promising POWs for grilling.

4. The Chinese were still denying they had taken UN prisoners into Manchuria in March, 1952, when Rear Admiral Ruthven E. Libby, the UN representative at the Panmunjom talks, made it clear and public that U.S. officials knew they were. Libby said he had "convincing evidence: that the Communists had shipped UN POWs into Manchuria. A Communist prisoner, he said, had described in detail a POW processing center in Harbin, just north of Antung.

5. Xu, like other Chinese "volunteers," did not carry rank, only responsibility.

6. Xu's testimony, according to the minutes of the commission meeting where it was presented, drove the Russian representatives into a shocked silence.

7. Task Force Russia document 37-5.

8. Interview with author, 14 June 1994.

9. Sworn statement by James E. Gunnoe Jr., Feb. 18, 1954.

Chapter Eleven: *Footprints in the Snow*

1. The competition Andrianov metioned may help account for a number of attacks on unarmed reconnaissance aircraft such as the RB-45.

2.Memo, Department of Air Force, Jan. 10, 1950.

3. Air Force sensitivity over the case cited in letter from Gen. G. B. Erskine, assistant to the secretary of defense for special operations, to the head of Far Eastern Affairs at the State Department referring to the case as "one with serious domestic public relations implications," but not specifying what those implications were.'

4. There could be some Chinese involvement, if McDonough's plane actually

crashed in Manchuria, not North Korea. In that sector, a shot fired over one country could cause an aircraft to crash-land in another.

5. Orlov is suffering the consequences of the Russians' deliberate method of creating contemporary documents from consulting source documents, and then presenting the contemporary documents as released, or declassified. For some reason, the Russians prefer creating new, sanitized "documents" to blacking or whiting out the originals, a method that at least lets the recipient know where something was covered.

6. Joint commission minutes, September 1994.

Chapter Twelve: *Trains to Ussurijsk*

The story of Col. Derskiy's encounter with American POWs adds an historical dimension to the Soviet interrogation-and-transfer policy. As a Red Army officer at the end of World War II in Europe, he came to view U.S. soldiers as allies. For young veterans, it was disorienting to find themselves under fire by U.S. forces in Korea. Derskiy never reached the point of seeing the U.S. in the harsh light his Stalinist bosses wanted him to, and he paid a penalty for that. His account is based on an interview with Task Force Russia in October 1993 and my interview with him in December 1994.

1. Interview with author, November 1994.

2. Task Force Russia documents 33-26 and 37-2/3.

3. Interview with author, December 1994.

4. Maj. Gen. William F. Dean, as told to William L. Worden, "General Dean's Story.

5. There is no explanation on the list or elsewhere in the file for the missing two months. The missing time period comes after Dean is returned to Pyongyang in the summer of 1951, and American bombing has reduced the capital to rubble, forcing the North Koreans to live in caves. The list of places he said he was held and the dates, as they appear on Dean's chronology:

Chinan, South Korea: 25 Aug. 50.

Chonju, South Korea: 26 Aug. 50—27 Aug. 50.

Pyongyang, North Korea: 2 Sept. 50—7 Sept. 50.

Sunan, North Korea: 7 Sept. 50—2 Oct. 50.

Huichon, North Korea: 3 Oct. 50—12 Oct. 50.

Konhadong, North Korea: 13 Oct. 50—17 Oct. 50.

Manpojin, North Korea: 17 Oct. 50—27 Oct. 50.

Chian, Manchuria: 27 Oct. 50—31 Oct. 50.

Manpo, North Korea: 31 Oct. 50—12 Jan. 51.

North Pyongyang, N. Korea: 15 Jan. 51—17 July 51.

Pyongyang Area, N. Korea:17 July 51—30 July 51; 2 Oct. 51—29 Oct. 51
(cave)

Pyongyang Area, North Korea: 29 Oct. 51—10 May 52
(underground house)

Pyongyang Area, North Korea: 10 May 52—6 Feb. 53.

Kanggye, North Korea: 6 Feb. 53—16 June 53.

N. Pyongyang, North Korea: 17 June 53—28 June 53; 28 June 53—12 Jul
53.

Chun-ni, North Korea: 12 July 53—4 Aug. 53.
(SW of Sunan)

Kaesong, North Korea: 5 Aug. 53—4 Sep. 53.

The document bears the following typed note:
        "At no time was subject quartered with or authorized contact with
other PsW. All quarters were private residences other than periods housed
underground as indicated in chronology."

6. A roll-up of anti-communist agents during the Korean War is noted by David Wise in "Molehunt." He reports that a legendary White Russian who worked for U.S. intelligence in the Far East named Arseny Yankovsky (aka Andy Brown) was suspected of betraying them to the KGB. If Derskiy is right and the Soviets got their hands on a list of agents in Seoul, then Yankovsky, now dead, was probably not to blame for the agents being compromised.

Chapter Thirteen: *The Cancer Patient*

1.The joint commission's interviews with Malinin are part of the commission's papers. He had to be persistent to get U.S. officials in Russia to listen to his story. Despite the highly publicized program to encourage former Soviet security officials like him to be brave enough to speak up, he was rebuffed three times at the U.S. consulate in St. Petersburg (Newsday, Sept. 20, 1993).

2. Interviews with Irene Mandra.

3. U.S. side's interview of Pavlenko, March 31, 1995.

4. Joint commission session with Pavlenko, April 13, 1995. Records of death in the Gulag are far from trustworthy (Oggins, Clifford-Brown, Chap. 3). But if authorities were willing, and the grave Pavlenko describes so specifically can be found, an autopsy might assist this investigation. The reaction of local officials to Pavlenko's efforts to date, however, are not encouraging.

Chapter Fourteen: *Order of the Red Banner*

The ten Cold War shootdowns being investigated by the joint commission together account for the loss of some 90 American servicemen. Each of them involves specific pieces of evidence or documentation that point to Soviet involvement with possible survivors. The ten incidents are:

8 April 1950—PB4Y2 Navy Privateer, shot down over Baltic Sea, 10 unaccounted for.

6 November 1951, P2V Navy Neptune shot down over Sea of Japan, 10 unaccounted for.

13 June 1952, Air Force RB-29 shot down over Sea of Japan, 12 unaccounted for.

7 October 1952, RB-29 shot down over Pacific Ocean, 8 unaccounted for.

29 July 1953, RB-50 shot down over Sea of Japan, 13 unaccounted for.

17 April 1955, RB-47 shot down over Bering Sea, 3 unaccounted for.

10 Sept. 1956, RB-50 lost over Sea of Japan, 16 unaccounted for.

2 Sept. 1958, C-130 shot down over Armenia, 13 unaccounted for.

1 July 1960, RB-47 shot down over Barents Sea, 3 unaccounted for.

14 Dec. 1965, RB-57 lost over Black Sea, 2 unaccounted for.

Chapter Fifteen: *Return Address: North Korea*

My interviews with Robert Dumas, about his brother's case and the POW/MIA situation in general, stretch from 1988 to the present. To add one more descriptive phrase, if I—or you—were missing in action, I—or you—would want a brother like Bob Dumas.

1. The Democratic People's Republic of Korea, which is what North Korea calls itself, has earned its reputation as a small country carrying a big chip on its shoulder. And it sees no reason to tell the rest of the world much, even such mundane statistics as how many people live in North Korea. More of a worry is their militaristic attitude. U.S. intelligence normally ranks North Korea high. But using rare population figures, a new statistics-packed book, "Korea Approaches Unification" by Nicholas Eberstadt, pushes the size of the NK army even higher: to 1.25 million—six percent of a total 1987 population of 20.5 million. Fewer than a half-dozen countries in the world boast a military that big.

2. Interrogator's Guide, 441st Counter-Intelligence Corps Detachment; January 1954.

3. A number of officers among the repatriated POWs were court-martialed upon their return, however, for giving "aid and comfort" to the enemy. Of

more than 4,400 repatriates, officers and enlisted, 565 faced military boards or courts of inquiry for their actions while in captivity, according to adjutant general figures.

4. Bob Dumas cultivated friends in the government thanks to his unwavering stand, too. One sent him a copy of a 1982 Army memo discussing his federal suit and explaining that the department would be fighting his claim "because of the nature of this case and the undesirable precedent that might occur" by giving others grounds to claim POW status.

5. Letter from Rev. Jesse Jackson to Amb. Pak Gil Yon, Permanent Observer Mission of the Democratic People's Republic of Korea, Dec. 9, 1987.

6. While no remains were exchanged between the U.S. and North Korea from 1954 until 1991, the Chinese government quietly accepted 25-30 sets of remains of Chinese soldiers discovered in South Korea by U.S. troops during the 1980s.

7. The series of films were produced from about 1978 to 1983. The source of the report is a North Korean defector, of whom there is no recent shortage.

8. Age is an important element of live-sightings. A 20-year-old soldier captured in 1950 would be only 65 today. And some GIs in Korea were as young as 15 or 16 (the Army's a lot more strict these days.)

9. U.S. civil suit 93-0085, U.S. District Court, Washington, D.C., Robert R. Dumas vs the President of the United States of America, et al.

10. Interview with the author.

11. A postcard from a tightly controlled prison has historical precedent— John Noble, one of the best-known Americans released from Stalin's Gulag in the 1950s. Another inmate, the prison barber, had mail privileges through the International Red Cross, but he'd never received an answer. So he agreed to let Noble sign his name to a card—a dangerous move, since the guards knew every prisoner's history so well they could spot a new address. When a new censor was appointed, Noble wrote a distant relative in West Germany. She notified his family, and an appeal from U.S. authorities won his freedom.

12. North Korea doesn't let foreign visitors see much, and keeps its citizens isolated, but that doesn't keep its leaders, or the state officials who travel the world to drive a hard bargain with U.S. negotiators.

APPENDICES

SUBJECT: The List of 510

In February 1992, the Russians provided Sen. Bob Smith with a list of 510 names (TFR-3, 155-177), purported to be of U.S. Korean War POWs, and entitled:

LIST
American Prisoners of War
(Data for 1950-51)

{AUTHOR'S NOTE: THE FOLLOWING LIST REFLECTS MY ANALYSIS OF THE LIST SUBMITTED TO TASK FORCE RUSSIA. IT HAS BEEN REFINED ACCORDING TO INFORMATION AVAILABLE EITHER FROM REPATRIATED POWS, THE COMMISSION'S RECORDS OR IN OTHER RECORDS FROM THE DEFENSE DEPARTMENT, DEPARTMENT OF STATE OR THE UNITED NATIONS COMMAND. THE LIST RELEASED BY THE RUSSIAN GOVERNMENT WAS NOT EXCLUSIVELY OF MILITARY PERSONNEL. A COMPLETE ANALYSIS OF THE LIST AND ITS VARIATIONS APPEARS IN CHAPTER EIGHT.}

****

NAME	RANK/SERVICE	TYPE CASUALTY	UNIT
1. Barter. Charles Tracey,	MAJ, USA	DIEH/NR	24ID
2. Lantron, Newton W.,	MAJ, USA	RMC	24ID
3. Nugent, Ambrose H.,	CPT, USA	RMC	24ID
4. Anderson, Douglas R.,	CPT, USA	DIEH/NR	24ID
5. Green, Marin W.,	CPT, USA	RMC	24ID
6. Macomber, Wayne B.	1LT, USA	RMC	24ID
7. Minietta, Charles	1LT, USA	RMC	24ID
8. Bergman, William J.,	1LT, USA	DIEH/NR	24ID
9. Fox, Johnson, Ray A.,	PVT, USA	RMC	24ID

10. Marlatt, Herbert E.,	1LT, USA	RMC	24ID
11. Rountree, Wadie Jerome,	1LT, USA	RMC	24ID
12. Sirman, Donald S.,	CPT, USAF	DIEH/N	35FBS
13. Jester, William F.,	1LT, USA	DIEH/NR	24ID
14. Maynard, Edward Wiley,	CPT, USA	DIEH/NR	24ID
15. Thompson, Ray A.	CPT, USA	DIEH/NR	24ID
16. Kaiser, Henry G.,	SGT		
17. Gamboa, Milton S.,	PFC, USA	RMC	24ID
18. Spinoza, Floyed E.,	PFC		
19. Wilson, James E.,	PFC, USA	RMC	24ID
20. Cooper, George A.,	PFC, USA	RMC	24ID
21. Rager, Fred H.,	PVT, USA	RMC	24ID
22. Sizemore, Jesse L.,	PFC, USA	RMC	24ID
23. Deckard, Earnest L.,	CPL, USA	RMC	24ID
24. Domenech, Jaime O.,	CPL, USA	RMC	24ID
25. McComas, Charles M.,	PFC, USA	RMC	25ID
26. Krentz, Darrell J.,	PFC, USA	RMC	24ID
27. Grant, Eugene W.,	MSG, USA	RMC	24ID
28. Cagle, Leamon J.,	MSG, USA	RMC	24ID
29. Stanley, Robert Jr.,	PVT, USA	RMC	24ID
30. Jennings, Lacey Jr.,	PFC, USA	RMC	2053ASU
31. Martin, John A.,	SGT, USA	DIEH/NR	24ID
32. Roth, Jacob G.,	PFC, USA	RMC	24ID
33. Creel, Shelby G.,	PVT, USA	RMC	24ID
34. Davis, James C.,	PFC, USA	RMC	24ID
35. Rye, Jay,	SGT, USA	RMC	24ID
36. Johnson, George H.,	PFC, USA	RMC	24ID
37. Anderson, Lester E.,	CPL, USA	RMC	24ID
38. Heard, Lawrence A.,	CPL, USA	RMC	24ID
39. Tallon, Eugene P.,	PVT, USA	RMC	24ID
40. Harris, Billy J.,	PFC, USA	RMC	2ID
41. Preite, Augustine F.,	PFC, USA	RMC	24ID
42. Robertson, Clark H.,	PV2, USA	RMC	24ID
43. Soria, Edward,	PVT, USA	RMC	24ID
44. Hoffman, Clarence Jr.,	PVT, USA	RMC	24ID
45. Dunning, Raymond L.,	PFC, USA	RMC	24ID
46. Ferguson, Benjamin,	PVT, USA	RMC	24ID
47. Show, Andrew W.,	PFC, USA	RMC	?
48. Naville, Herman F.,	PFC, USA	RMC	24ID
49. Lawson, James L.,	PVT, USA	RMC	24ID
50. Cauti, Attilio P.,	PFC, USA	RMC	24ID
51. Longoria, George T.,	CPL, USA	RMC	24ID

52. Kimball, Reuben K., Jr.,	PFC,	USA	RMC	24ID
53. Durant, Frank C.,	PFC,	USA	RMC	24ID
54. Mata, Goya,	PFC,	USA	RMC	
55. Perry Glacel E.,	CPL,	USA	RMC	24I
56. Watkins, Fisher,	SFC,	USA	RMC	24ID
57. Sheffield, Edward C.,	PFC,	USA	RMC	24ID
58. Crespo, John T.,	PVT,	USA	RMC	24ID
59. Simpson, Raymond C.,	PVT,	USA	RMC	24ID
60. Paskovich, Michael M.,	SGT,	USA	RMC	24ID
61. Haggard, Billy M.,	CPL,	USA	DIEH/NR	24ID
62. Potts, Cecil S.,	PFC,	USA	RMC	24ID
63. Stice, Ivan E.,	PFC,	USA	RMC	24ID
64. Cossette, Joseph E.,	PFC,	USA	RMC	24ID
65. Hardy, Edgar Warren,	MSG,	USA	DIEH/NR	24ID
66. Deck, Kenneth F.,	SGT,	USA	RMC	24ID
67. Fontana, Anthony S.,	PVT,	USA	RMC	24ID
68. Goodwin, Jack P.,	PFC,	USA	RMC	24ID
69. Kennedy, French L.	PFC,	USA	RMC	24ID
70. Bailey, Harvey N.,	SFC,	USA	RMC	24ID
71. Villafana, David	PVT,	USA	RMC	
72. Fronaphel, Charles L.,	PVT,	USA	RMC	24ID
73. Hammett, Doyle W.,	PV2,	USA	RMC	?
74. Western, Robert D.,	PFC,	USA	RMC	24ID
75. Mickelberg, Albert,	PFC,	USA	RMC	1CD
76. Rhodes, Edward W.,	PVT,	USA	RMC	24ID
77. Tagget, Allen,	PFC,	USA	RMC	?
78. Struble, James T.,	PFC,	USA	RMC	24ID
79. Davidson, Charles W.,	PFC,	USA	RMC	24ID
80. Wilson, Donald E.,	CPL,	USA	RMC	24ID
81. Bolles, Lloyd Junior,	PFC,	USA	DIEH/NR	24ID
82. Johnson, Wayne A.,	PVT,	USA	RMC	24ID
83. Hancock, John W.,	PFC,	USA	RMC	24ID
84. Matern, Alfonzo D.,	PFC			
85. King, Edward M.,	PFC,	USA	RMC	24ID
86. Tadeki, Tomio	PFC,	USA	RMC	24ID
87. Corona, Jamie,	PVT,	USA	DIEH/NR	
88. Tamaye, Goichi,	PFC,	USA	RMC	24ID
89. Fortuna, Ernest A.,	CPL,	USA	RMC	24ID
90. Ghyers, Robert H.,	CPL,	USA	RMC	24ID
91. Boyd, William O.,	SGT,	USA	RMC	24ID
92. Gartin, John P.,	CPL,	USA	RMC	24ID
93. Hor, Charles C.,	CPL,	USA	RMC	24ID

94. Richard, Clayton E.,	CPL, USA	RMC	
95. Brantley, Charles P.,	CPL, USA	RMC	24ID
96. Varner, Russell Jr.,	CPL, USA	RMC	24ID
97. Sanders, Paul R.,	SGT, USA	RMC	24ID
98. White, Thaddieus,	CPL, USA	RMC	24ID
99. Reza, Timothy Jr.,	PVT, USA	RMC	24ID
100. Kostegan, Stanley	PFC, USA	RMC	24ID
101. McAndrews, Christopher G.	PFC, USA	RMC	24ID
102. Deming, William A.,	PFC, USA	RMC	25ID
103. Kemp, Robert A.	CPL, USA	RMC	24ID
104. Vigil, Juan J.	CPL, USA	RMC	24ID
105. Henson, Walter E., Senior	SGT	RMC	
106. Palacol, Sefronio,	SGT, USA	RMC	24ID
107. Mays, Jack T.,	PVT, USA	RMC	24ID
108. Nickells, Walter L.,	CPL, USA	RMC	24ID
109. Napier, Charles C.,	PFC, USA	RMC	24ID
110. Valdez, Glicerio,	CPL, USA	RMC	24ID
111. Apodaca, Tony,	PVT, USA	RMC	24ID
112. Panco, Charles H.,	CPL, USA	RMC	24ID
113. Colbert, James P.,	PFC, USA	RMC	24ID
114. Frost, Charles J.,	CPL, USA	RMC	24ID
115. Martin, Edwin C.,	CPL, USA	RMC	24ID
116. Randall, Elgin Vogala,	SGT, USA	DIEH/NR	24ID
117. Durham, Jesse W.,	PVT, USA	RMC	24ID
118. Heddinger, Charles L.,	PFC, USA	RMC	24ID
119. Williams, Henry D.,	PFC, USA	RMC	24ID
120. Robertson, Elmer L.,	PFC, USA	RMC	24ID
121. Oresto, James V.,	PVT, USA	RMC	24ID
122. Cummings, Richard E.,	PFC, USA	RMC	24ID
123. Trent, Eldridge S.,	CPL, USA	RMC	24ID
124. Jones, Dale Royce,	CPL, USA	DIEH/NR	24ID
125. Concepcion, Tommy J.,	SGT, USA	RMC	24ID
126. Leercamp, Henry G.,	SFC, USA	RMC	24ID
127. Baumgartner, Leroy B.,	CPL, USA	RMC	24ID
128. Vannoy, Hale,	CPL, USA	RMC	24ID
129. Laurent, Alfred V.,	CPL, USA	RMC	24ID
130. Pendarvis, Floyd M.,	PFC, USA	RMC	24ID
131. Cress, Patrick Jr.,	PFC, USA	RMC	24ID
132. Denton, Lee O. A.,	PFC, USA	RMC	24ID
133. Lewis, Robert E.,	CPL, USA	RMC	24ID
134. Bradford, Henry E.,	CPL, USA	RMC	24ID
135. Ampon, Jospeh Obonon,	SGT, USA	DIEH/RRG	24ID

136.	Brown, Joseph C.,	SGT, USA	DIEH/NR	24ID
137.	Smith, Robert L.,	PVT, USA	RMC	24ID
138.	Walintakonis, Joseph A.,	CPL, USA	RMC	24ID
139.	Martin, James S.,	CPL, USA	RMC	24ID
140.	Martin, Jack L.,	CPL, USA	RMC	24ID
141.	Hanhaback, John W.,	SGT, USA	RMC	24ID
142.	Fisher, Lowell D.,	PFC, USA	RMC	24ID
143.	Alford, Raymond K.,	PFC, USA	DIEH/RRG	24ID
144.	Graham, William M.,	SGT, USA	DIEH/RR	?
145.	Garcia, Francisco A.,	PFC, USA	RMC	24ID
146.	Franklin, John D., Jr.,	PFC, USA	DIEH/NR	24ID
147.	Atkinson, Rondal H.,	PFC, USA	RMC	24ID
148.	Strahan, Martin A.,	SFC, USA	RMC	24ID
149.	Rowe, Frank L.,	CPL, USA	RMC	24ID
150.	Myers, Max E.,	PFC, USA	RMC	24ID
151.	Majoria, Joseph Jr.,	PVT, USA	RMC	24ID
152.	Hubbard, William H.,	PV2, USA	RMC	24ID
153.	Justice, Richard D.,	PVT, USA	RMC	24ID
154.	Fancher, Harold S.,	CPL, USA	DIEH/NR	24ID
155.	Jester, William R.,	CPL, USA	DIEH/NR	24ID
156.	Tarbuck, Joseph,	PFC, USA	RMC	24ID
157.	Jenkins, G.W.,	PFC, USA	RMC	24ID
158.	Helmich, Robert P.,	PVT, USA	RMC	24ID
159.	Hays, Edward G.,	CPL, USA	RMC	24ID
160.	Smith, Donnal R.,	PFC, USA	RMC	24ID
161.	Nava, John,	CPL, USA	RMC	24ID
162.	Bingham, George M.,	CPL, USA	RMC	24ID
163.	O'Keefe, Arthur M.,	CPL, USA	RMC	24ID
164.	Trujillo, Daniel J.,	CPL, USA	RMC	24ID
165.	Sloan, Leroy,	CPL, USA	RMC	24ID
166.	Davis, George Parker,	CPL, USA	DIEH/NR	24ID
167.	Cogburn, James A.,	SGT, USA	RMC	24ID
168.	Connick, Karl F.,	CPL, USA	DIEH/NR	24ID
169.	Wood, William C.,	PFC, USA	RMC	24ID
170.	Roten, Ancil A.,	PV2, USA	RMC	1CD
171.	Ordonio, Phillip,	SGT, USA	RMC	24ID
172.	Goerlzer, James C.,	MSG, USA	RMC	24ID
173.	Watts, Roland,	SGT, USA	RMC	24ID
174.	Brunner, Clarence E.,	CPL, USA	RMC	24ID
175.	Warble, Dallas L.,	CPL, USA	RMC	24ID
176.	Sitler, Harold E.,	CPL, USA	RMC	7ID
177.	McClain, Edward M.,	SGT, USA	RMC	24ID

178. Lavange, Davis E.,	CPL, USA	RMC	
179. Thompson, Curtis A.,	PFC, USA	RMC	24ID
180. Jones, William J.,	PFC, USA	RMC	24ID
181. Shinagawa, Susumu,	PFC, USA	RMC	24ID
182. Malone, Haskel,	CPL, USA	RMC	24ID
183. Cantley, Bobby R.,	PV2, USA	RMC	24ID
184. Wilburn, William E.,	CPL, USA	RMC	24ID
185. Jiron, Amos A.,	PV2, USA	RMC	5044ASU
186. Baranksi, Alphonse A.,	PFC, USA	RMC	24ID
187. Tenario, Sam F.,	PFC, USA	RMC	24ID
188. Leblanc, Randsdall P.,	CPL, USA	RMC	24ID
189. Talbert, Marvin E.,	CPL, USA	RMC	24ID
190. Knowles, Billy C.,	MSG, USA	RMC	24ID
191. Hidalgo, Larry B.	SGT, USA	RMC	24ID
192. Archambault, Leroy,	PFC, USA	RMC	24ID
193. Escobar-Torres, Vic,	CPL, USA	RMC	24ID
194. Gaiser, Henry L.,	SGT, USA	RMC	24ID
195. Browning, Jack,	PFC, USA	RMC	24ID
196. Sanders, John D.,	CPL, USA	RMC	24ID
197. Arakaki, Henry T.,	CPL, USA	RMC	24ID
198. Oribio, Buenaventur,	CPL, USA	RMC	24ID
199. Hunt, James R.,	PV2, USA	RMC	24ID
200. Moreno, Raymond M.,	CPL, USA	DIEH/NR	24ID
or Moreno, Raymond,	PFC, USA	RMC	24ID
201. Eldridge, Johnny J.,	PFC, USA	RMC	24ID
202. Sawyer, Joe A.,	PV2, USA	RMC	24ID
203. Armour, Harlan D.,	PV2, USA	RMC	24ID
204. Harris, Thomas W.,	PFC, USA	DIEH/NR	24ID
205. Mason, Jack R.,	PFC, USA	RMC	24ID
206. Crews, William A.,	CPL, USA	RMC	24ID
207. Blue, Adelbert,	PFC, USA	DIEH/NR	24ID
208. Ferrell, Charlie E.,	PFC, USA	RMC	24ID
209. Scott, Amos L.,	CPL, USA	DIEH/RRG	24ID
210. Pipple, Howard,	PVT (Arty)		
211. Demeo, Joseph	PFC, USA	RMC	24ID
212. Martinez, Ramon F.,	PFC, USA	RMC	24ID
213. Bartlett, Wilmer A.,	CPL, USA	RMC	24ID
214. Scott, Eugene L.,	PV2, USA	RMC	24ID
215. Eaton, John Omer,	CPL, USA	DIEH/NR	24ID
216. Fleming, William C.,	PFC, USA	RMC	24ID
217. Colbey, Earl N.,	PV2, USA	RMC	24ID
218. Frazer, Charles F.,	CPL, USA	RMC	24ID

219. Cosby, Samuel E.,	CPL, USA	RMC	24ID
220. Hebert, Leonard,	SGT, USA	RMC	24ID
221. Freeman, Everett,	PFC, USA	RMC	24ID
222. McKinley, Ralph H.,	PFC, USA	DIEH/NR	24ID
223. Trujillo, Margarito,	PFC, USA	RMC	24ID
224. Shamwell, Robert L.,	CPL, USA	RMC	1CD
225. Dobson, Floyd J.,	PVT, USA	RMC	24ID
226. Brown, Gerard T.,	PFC, USA	RMC	24ID
227. Whitaker, Charles L.,	PFC, USA	RMC	24ID
228. Taylor, Calvin J.,	CPL, USA	RMC	24ID
229. Rodriquez, Lope G.,	PVT, USA	RMC	24ID
230. Kirk, James W.,	CPL, USA	RMC	24ID
231. Hallum, Leonard David	PFC, USA	DIEH/NR	24ID
232. Dean, Alvin Clinton,	CPL, USA	DIEH/NR	24ID
233. Sutton, Claxton G.,	MSG, USA	RMC	24ID
234. Dubose, Clyatt R.,	CPL, USA	DIEH/NR	24ID
235. Hardwick, Lloyd E.,	PV2, USA	RMC	24ID
236. Halbert, George R., Jr.,	CPL, USA	DIEH/NR	24ID
237. Thompson, Roy L,	PV2, USA	RMC	24ID
238. Roy, Floyd Alexander,	SFC, USA	DIEH/NR	24ID
239. Schlinghoff, Leonard M.,	PV2, USA	RMC	24ID
240. Koch, Kermit K.,	PFC, USA	DIEH/NR	24ID
241. Novobilski, Thaddeus F.,	PV2, USA	RMC	24ID
242. Rogers, George P.,	PV2, USA	RMC	24ID
243. Dickel, James P.,	PFC, USA	RMC	24ID
244. Stumpges, Frederick J.,	MSG, USMC	RMC	1MD
245. Charles, Ernest J.,	CPL, USA	RMC	24ID
246. Mascarenas, Candido,	PFC, USA	RMC	24ID
247. Martinez, Frank P.,	PFC, USA	RMC	24ID
248. Stone, Roy L.,	CPL, USA	RMC	24ID
249. Stick, Louis Jr.,	PFC, USA	RMC	24ID
250. Flack, Austin D.,	MSG, USA	RMC	24ID
251. Woodward, Thomas C.,	PVT, USA	RMC	24ID
252. Tyler, Charles R.,	CPL, USA	DIEH/NR	24ID
253. Vaughn, Lloyd Jr.,	PFC, USA	RMC	1CD
254. Holman, Albert C., Jr.,	CPL, USA	DMIA/NR	24ID
255. Robinson, Angus P.,	PFC, USA	RMC	24ID
256. Aldeis, Manuel A.,	MSG, USA	RMC	24ID
257. Smith, Charles C.,	PVT		
258. Duncan, James C.,	PV2, USA	RMC	7ID
259. Duty, Cermillus,	PFC, USA	RMC	24ID
260. McAlpine, Johnny Lee,	CPL, USA	DIEH/RRG	24ID

261. Ahern, Gerard,	PFC, UK	DIEH/NR	41BM
262. Newton, Gilmer G.,	PVT, USA	KIA/RR	24ID
263. Weidensoul, Floyd N.,	PFC, USA	RMC	7ID
264. Anguino, Benito J.,	PFC, USA	RMC	24ID
265. Gonsalez, Florentio,	PFC, USA	RMC	24ID
266. White, Richard L.,	PFC, USA	RMC	24ID
267. Wolfe, Charles J.,	PVT, USA	RMC	24ID
268. Bamford, Charles M.,	MSG, USA	DIEH/NR	15AAABN
269. Takeshi, Mukai,	PFC, USA	RMC	24ID
270. Bissell, James R.,	SGT, USA	DIEH/NR	24ID
271. Peterson, Donwin Ross,	CPL, USA	DIEH/NR	24ID
272. Simpson, Wayman E.,	CPL, USA	RMC	24ID
273. Skinner, William,	PFC, USA	RMC	7ID
274. Layton, Robert	1LT, USAF	DIEH/NR	28BS
275. Wilner, William H.,	COL, USA	DIEH/NR	24ID
276. Vancleave, Tommie M.,	PVT, USA	RMC	24ID
277. Underhill, Virgil E.,	CPL, USA	DIEH/NR	7ID
278. Addessa, Harry J.,	PFC, USA	RMC	24ID
279. Clark, Harry Bernard,	CPL, USA	DIEH/NR	24ID
280. Spencer, Charles L.,	PFC, USA	RMC	25ID
281. Larue, Charles B.,	PFC, USA	RMC	25ID
282. Barnes, Herbert R.,	CPL, USA	DIEH/NR	24ID
283. Furlow, Robert Daniel,	CPL, USA	DIEH/NR	24ID
284. Ragsdale, James N.,	SGT, USA	RMC	24ID
285. Chance, Adelbert W.,	PFC, USA	RMC	24ID
286. Skero, Charles M.,	PFC, USA	DIEH/NR	24ID
287. Kendall, Richard,	PFC, USA	DIEH/RRG	24ID
288, Anzaldua, Baldomero,	SGT, USA	DIEH/NR	24ID
289. Spencer, Richard S.,	PFC		
290. Boutwelly, Norman L.,	PFC, USA	RMC	24ID
291. Raymond, William H.,	PVT, USA	RMC	24ID
292. Torhan, George,	PFC, USA	DIEH/NR	24ID
293. Smith, Gerald J.,	PVT, USA	RMC	24ID
294. Cowart, William A.,	PFC, USA	RMC	24ID
295. Guidry, Joseph,	SGT, USA	DIEH/NR	24ID
296. Conley, James T.,	PFC, USA	RMC	24ID
297. Fitzgerald, Robert B.,	PVT, USA	RMC	24ID
298. Donner, Donald E.,	PFC, USA	RMC	24ID
299. King, Ralph E.,	CPL, USA	DIEH/RRG	24ID
300. Warren, Don L.,	PFC, USA	RMC	24ID
301. Langell, Irving Jr.,	PFC, USA	RMC	24ID
302. Merford, Beecher M.,	PFC, USA	RMC	

303. Cruz, Ruben D.,	PFC, USA	RMC	24ID
304. Cline, Oliver J.,	CPL, USA	RMC	24ID
305. Green, Paris L.,	PFC, USA	RMC	24ID
306. Creeson, Calvin C.,	MSG, USA	RMC	24ID
307. Starcher, Andrew J.,	SGT, USA	RMC	24ID
308. Patterson, Lewis J.,	PVT, USA	RMC	24ID
309. Kiyohiro, Tetsuo,	SGT, USA	KIA/RR	2ID
310. Moore, James R.,	PVT, USA	RMC	24ID
311. Izu, Isamu,	CPL, USA	DIEH/NR	24ID
312. Gavula, Stephan Jr.,	PFC, USA	RMC	
313. Hamilton, Merlin Jack,	SFC, USA	DIEH/RRG	24ID
314. Estabrook, Wilbert R.,	CPL, USA	RMC	24ID
315. Cortez, Ricardo,	CPL, USA	RMC	24ID
316. Cofer, James D.,	SFC, USA	RMC	24ID
317. Gomez, Joe or Joseph A.,	CPL, USA	RMC	24ID
318. Garcia, Andrew R.,	SFC, USA	RMC	24ID
319. Mellin, Raymond B.,	PFC, USA	RMC	24ID
320. Stearns, Minford L.,	PFC, USA	RMC	24ID
321. Mellin, Raymond B.,	PFC, USA	RMC	24ID
322. Tullio, Martin J.,	PVT, USA	RMC	24ID
323. Ollero, Luciano F.,	CPL, USA	DIEH/NR	24ID
324. Schmincke, Donald H.,	PFC, USA	RMC	24ID
325. Donahue, Jack F.,	PFC, USA	RMC	24ID
326. Mentzos, Paul,	SGT, USA	DIEH/NR	24ID
327. Shewalter, Earl W.,	CPL, USA	RMC	24ID
328. Rupp, Edward K.,	PFC, USA	RMC	24ID
329. Talbert, Joe or Joseph H.,	PVT, USA	RMC	7ID
330. Draper, Frank E.,	PVT, USA	RMC	24ID
331. Hackney, Raymon W.,	PFC, USA	RMC	3420ASU
332. Endris, Everett T.,	PFC, USA	RMC	24ID
333. Dirksen, Abraham Jr.,	CPL, USA	DIEH/NR	24ID
334. Berardi, Thomas Henry,	CPL, USA	DIEH/NR	24ID
335. Clint, Penn W.,	SGT, USA	RMC	2ID
336. Fanning, Clyde Anson,	SGT, USA	DIEH/RRG	24ID
337. Yoss, Raymond L.,	PVT, USA	RMC	24ID
338. Shimshock, John A.,	PFC, USA	RMC	24ID
339. Dunham, Leland R.,	LTC, USA	DIEH/NR	24ID
340. Bak, Joseph,	PFC, USA	DIEH/RR	24ID
341. Ales, Marion Louis,	1LT, USA	DIEH/NR	2ID
342. Bivens, William F.,	CPT, USA	DIEH/RRG	25ID
343. Boren, Claud W.,	CPT, USA	RMC	25ID
344. Brandt., Arnold,	LTC, USA	DIEH/NR	KMAG

345. Breton, Joseph E.,	1LT, USA	RMC	2ID
346. Bruner, Riley,	2LT, USA	RMC	25ID
347. Berry, Waldron,	1LT, USAF	RMC	6133TSW
348. Bach, Lawrence B.,	CPT, USAF	RMC	5AF
349. Harris, William R.,	CPT, USA	DIEH/NR	24ID
350. Gibb, Harry E.,	MAJ, USA	RMC	6ROKD
351. Gibson, Hal Thomas,	1LT, USA	DIEH/NR	25ID
352. Jackson, Walter I.,	1LT, USA	RMC	2ID
353. Jordan, Warren H.,	1LT, USA	DIEH/RRG	2ID
354. Dodd, Lyle E.,	1LT, USAF	RMC	307BG
355. Kahamiak, John,	CPT, USA	RMC	2ID
356. Caldwell, Howard O.,	1LT, USA	DIEH/RR	
357. Kaschko, Harold L.,	CPT, USA	RMC	2ID
358. Coleman, Norris L.,	CPT, USA	DIEH/RR	KMAG
359. Kopischkie, Carl E.,	MAJ, USA	RMC	2ID
360. Leamon, Nicholas J.,	1LT, USA	RMC	2ID
361. Magnant, Joseph A.,	2LT, USA	RMC	2ID
362. Manto, Joseph V.,	1LT, USA	RMC	2ID
363. Ivanushka, Michael,	1LT, USA	RMC	?2ID
364. Nehrling, Robert E.,	CPT, USA	RMC	2ID
365. Raskin, Alfred Jay,	1LT, USA	DIEH/NR	2ID
366. Roach, Paul Adams,	2LT, USA	RMC	2ID
367. Smith, Frederick A.,	CPT, USA	RMC	2ID
368. Sullivan, James E.,	CPL, USA	RMC	24ID
369. Fry, Charles A., Jr.,	MAJ, USA	RMC	24ID
370. Henslee, Allan M.,	1LT, USA	DIEH/RRG	1CD
371. Hornung, Frederick L.,	1LT, USA	DIEH/RR	?
372. Ellis, Alfred O.,	MAJ, USA	RMC	2ID
373. Erwin, Jeff D.,	2LT, USA	RMC	2ID
374. Pierce, Orville W.,	MAJ, USA	DIEH/RRG	2ID
375. Gaston, John R.,	2LT, USAF	RMC	51FW
376. Phillips, Eric Charles,	CPT, USA	RMC	2ID
377. Varner, Russell J.,	CPL, USA	RMC	24ID
378. Conley, James T.,	CPL, USA	RMC	24ID
379. Stearns, Minford L.,	PFC, USA	RMC	24ID
380. Brown, Gerard T.,	PFC, USA	RMC	24ID
381. Peppe, Isadore O.,	2LT, USA	RMC	24ID
382. Zimmerman, Stanley G.,	1LT, USA	RMC	24ID
383. Thomas, Mitchell C.,	1LT, USA	DMIA/NR/389	29REG
384. Smith, James Bryant,	CPT, USAF	RMC	5AF
385. Wirt, Frederick B.,	CPT, USA	KIA/RRG	24ID
386. McDaniel, William T.,	MAJ, USA	DOD/RR	24ID

387.	Holt, Crenshaw A.,	CPT, USA	DMIA/NR/389	24ID
388.	Clance, James Walter,	CPT, USA	DMIA	FEC
389.	Boydston, James L.,	2LT, USA	KIA/RR	24ID
390.	Blalock, Douglas W.,	2LT, USA	RMC	24ID
391.	Tabor, Stanley E.,	1LT, USA	DOW/NR	24ID
392.	Locke, William Davis,	MAJ, USAF	RMC	39FIS
393.	Mulock, Arthur F.,	1LT, USA	DMIA/NR	24ID
394.	Eltringham, Walter Stanley	Civilian	DIEH/NR	US GOV
395.	Dans, Louis Leo,	Civilian	Released	US GOV
396.	Booth, William E.,	Missionary	Released	Heaven
397.	Brown, Gerald,	LTC, USAF	RMC	6150TSW
398.	Lackner, Jospeh Carl,	WOJG, USA	DIEH/RR	2ID
399.	Kilby, Thomas E., III,	1LT, USA	DIEH/RRG	1CD
400.	Foss, Sheldon H.,	1LT, USA	RMC	25ID
401.	Nava, Adolphus,	CWO, USA	DIEH/NR	2ID
402.	Fedenets, Andrew,	CPT, USA	RMC	2ID
403.	Falls, Eino Erland,	CWO, USA	DIEH/RRG	2ID
404.	Stevens, James E.,	CWO, USA	DIEH/RRG	2ID
405.	Bagwell, Ralph Maxwell,	LT, USN	RMC	35AS
406.	Zacherle, Alarich L.E.,	LTC, USA	RMC	2ID
407.	Hume, Thomas A.,	LTC, USA	DIEH/NR	2ID
408.	Dean, William F.,	MG, USA	RMC	24ID
409.	*Clance, James Walter	Dup of #388		
410.	*Eltringham, Walter Stanley	Dup of #394		
411.	*Booth, William	Dup of #396		
412.	Jensen, Anders Kristian,	Missionary	Released	Heaven
413.	*Booth, William Robert,	Dup of #396		
414.	*Dans, Louis Leo	Dup of #395		
415.	Zellers, Lawrence Alfred,	Missionary	Released	Heaven
416.	Smith, Bertha	Missionary	Released	Heaven
417.	Rosser, Helen,	Missionary	Released	Heaven
418.	Dyer, Nellie,	Missionary	Released	Heaven
419.	Moreland, Joseph E.,	CPT, USAF	RMC	91SRS
420.	Rivers, Bernard Francis.,	TSgt, USAF	RMC	91SRS
421.	Koski, William Emile,	SSgt, USAF	RMC	91SRS
422.	Johanson, Charles Vernon,	SSgt, USAF	RMC	91SRS
423.	Combs, Edward D.,	SSgt, USAF	RMC	91SRS
424.	Hand, Donald L.,	A2C, USAF	RMC	91SRS
425.	Bass, Kenneth H.,	SSgt, USAF	RMC	91SRS
426.	Evers, Ernest Eugene	A1C, USAF	RMC	91SRS
427.	Arnold, John Knox, Jr.,	COL, USAF	RMC	91SRS
428.	Baumer, William H.,	MAJ, USAF	RMC	91SRS

429.	Vaddi, Eugene T.,	CPT, USAF	RMC	91SRS
430.	Elmer, Fred Allewelin,	CPT, USAF	RMC	91SRS
431.	Buck, John W.,	1LT, USAF	RMC	91SRS
432.	Brown, Wallace L.,	2LT, USAF	RMC	91SRS
433.	Brown, Howard W.,	TSgt, USAF	RMC	91SRS
434.	Kiba, Steve E.,	A1C, USAF	RMC	91SRS
435.	Benjamin, Harry M.,Jr.	A2C, USAF	RMC	91SRS
436.	Thompson, John Walker III,A2C,	USAF	RMC	91SRS
437.	Schmidt, Daniel C.,	A2C, USAF	RMC	91SRS
438.	Weese, Henry,	1LT, USAF	DMIA/NR	91SRS
439.	Van Voorhis, Paul E.,	1LT, USAF	DMIA/NR	91SRS
440.	Harris, Theodore Russell,	CPT, USAF	RMC	91SRS
441.	Streiby, Francis Allen,	2LT, USAF	RMC	91SRS
442.	Brazil, Kenneth S.,	1LT, USAF	RMC	91SRS
443.	*Clance, James Walter	Dup of #388		
444	*Booth, William	Dup of #396		
445.	Harding, Dick Erving,	Officer, USA		
446.	@Van Houten,	COL, USA	not POW	
447.	Brown	MAJ		4 R Co.
448.	@Anderson, Doresy B.,	CPT, USA	not POW	4 R Co.
449.	@Warren, John S.,	LT, US	not POW	4 R Co.
450.	@Johnson, James	LT, USA	not POW	4 R Co.
451.	Blakeley	LT, USA	not POW	4 R Co.
452.	@Buell D. Atwood,	LT, USA	not POW	4 R Co.
453.	@Baker, Raymond E.	PFC, USA	not POW	4 R Co.
454.	@Pucell, Edward	CPL, USA	not POW	4 R Co.
455.	@Miles, William T., Jr.,	SFC, USA	DMIA/NR	8086AU
456.	@Perry, Eugene	CPT, USA	not POW	8086AU
457.	@McGee, John Hugh,	COL, USA	not POW	8086AU
458.	@Witherspoon,	COL, USA	not POW	8086AU
459.	Blower	CPT		
460.	Poriaris, Estanisiao	MSG	RMC	2ID
461.	Mast, Clifford Henry,	SSgt USAF	DMIA/389	91SRS
462.	Downy, John Thomas,	Civilian	Returned	CIA
463.	Fecteau, Richard,	Civilian	Returned	CIA
464.	*Moreland, Joseph	Dup of #419		
465.	Halsverg	LT		
466.	Mokkey,	LT		
467.	Kervlend,	SGT		
468.	Hart, Alvin D.,	A1C, USAF	DMIA/NR	91SRS
469.	Halton, William T.	COL, USAF	DMIA/NR	18FBS
470.	Stiwell,	COL		

471.	Amerine,	LT		
472.	MacGhee, David	COL USAF	RMC	307BG
473.	Hedrick,	MAJ		
474.	Rase, Albert E., Jr.,	1LT, USAF	DNB/NR	91SRC
475.	Gilbert, John M.,	COL, USAF	KIA/NR	91SRC
476.	Brown,	LTC		
477.	Smith	CPT		
478.	*Magnant,	LT May dup #361		
479.	Breton, Joseph E.,	1LT, USA	RMC	2ID
480.	*Brunner,	LT May dup #346		
481.	Walker, John H.,	MAJ, USA	RMC	2ID
482.	Dawson, Perry Augustus,	CPT, USAF	DIEH/NR	
483.	Watson, Robert,	LT		
484.	*Lackner, Joseph Carl	Dup of #398		
485.	*Brunner, Riley	Dup of #480		
486.	*Fedenets, Andrew	Dup of #402		
487.	*Sheldon, Harvy	Dup of #400		
488.	Salting, Ben	LT		
489.	Fornes, William L.,	1LT, USAF	RMC	91SRS
490.	Albrecht, John A.,	CPL, USA	DIEH/NR	24ID
491.	*Arnold, John K.,	Dup of #427		
492.	Palver,	CPT		
493.	*Baumers, William H.,	Dup of #428		
494.	Kattering,	LT		
495.	Hensley, Bird Jr.,	SGT, USAF	DIEH/NR	620AWS
496.	Mekkoy,	LTC		
497.	Okkil,	MAJ		
498.	Dostoleks,	LT		
499.	Horton,	CPT		
500.	Roland,	SGT		
501.	Renshaw,	SGT		
502.	Mekgy,	MAJ		
503.	Kahl, Gordon King	MAJ, USAF	DMIA	13ABG
504.	Heris,	CPT		
505.	Strebe,	SGT		
506.	*Kahamiak, John	Dup of #355		
507.	Vinseni, Rassel D.,	Officer		
508.	Brown, Jeyms Thomas,	Officer		
509.	*Stearns, Minford	Dup of #379		
510.	*Brown, Herald Thomas,	Officer May dup #397		

****

"CIVILIAN" ENTRIES ON ORIGINAL "510 LIST" FROM RUSSIAN GOVERNMENT

The first list of names of prisoners of war from the former Soviet archives turned over to U.S. officials in February 1992 included 27 so-called "civilian" entries. Three names were duplicated, leaving 24 separate individuals. (The "military" section of the list also included civilians. They are identified as such on that list in the appendix).

The original list given to U.S. Sen. Robert Smith, R-N.H., included dates of birth but no nationalities. The first line of the entrIes below contains the information the Russian government provided. Further identification is from author's research.

1. Gimenez Varcis Dominadov. born 1927.
Dominadov is a White Russian surname, which is the most probable identification. At the Tiger POW camp, however, there was also a Pfc. Victor P. Jimenez, of San Antonio, Tex., reported to have died while a POW April 16, 1951.

2. Moratin Elas. born 1925.
Hamid, Moratiand. Turkish citizen.

3. Capt. Vilyam Holt. born 1896.
Captain Sir Vivyan Holt, British minister in Seoul. Repatriated from Tiger Camp, deceased.

4. Herbert Arthur Lord. born 1899.
Head of Salvation Army in Seoul. Repatriated from Tiger Camp, deceased.

5. Philip Deane. born 1923.
Correspondent in Far East for London Observer. Repatriated from Tiger Camp.

6. Cooper, Alfred. 69 years old.
British Anglican missionary bishop. Repatriated from Tiger Camp, deceased.

7. Norman Philip Owen. born 1916.
Owens. British embassy staff, Seoul. Repatriated from Tiger Camp, deceased.

8. Matti, Alfred Frederick.
Swiss, hotel manager, Seoul. POW in Tiger Camp; died there Nov. 30, 1950.

9. Perruche, Georges. born 1916.
French consul in Seoul. Repatriated from Tiger Camp, deceased.

10. Martel, Charles Emile. born 1909.
French embassy staff. Wife and daughter also POWs. Repatriated from Tiger Camp, deceased.

11. Chanateloure, Joan, born 1915.
Maurice Chanteloup, Agence France Press correspondent. (first name switched with Meadmore, see below.) Repatriated from Tiger Camp, deceased.

12. Meadmore, Maurice. born 1912.
Jean Meadmore, French foreign service. Repatriated from Tiger Camp.

13. Philip Deane (DUPLICATE)

14. William Booth (DUPLICATE)

15. Philip Crosbie. born 1915.
Australian Roman Catholic missionary. Repatriated from Tiger Camp.

16. Francis Canavan. born 1915.
Irish Catholic missionary. Tiger Camp POW, died there Dec. 6, 1950.

17. Bultlan, Joseph. born 1901.
Rev. Joseph Bulteau, French Catholic missionary. Tiger Camp POW, died there Jan. 6, 1951.

18. John Happy Bax. born 1895.

19. Philip Krosee. Father Philip Crosby (DUPLICATE.)

20. Tomas Green. born 1896.

21. Robert Wood. born 1919 .

22. John Cake. born 1901.

23. Kisch, Ernst. born 1899.
Austrian Methodist missionary. Tiger Camp POW, died there during war.

24. Smith, Helli. born 1904.
Possibly Pvt. Billy E. Smith, of Alabama, died in Tiger camp Nov. 4, 1950.

25. Phillip Simon. born 1912.

26. Robert Cooper. born 1917.

27. Charles William Anderson. born 1913.

KEY

RMC = Returned to Military Control (repatriated POW)
DIEH/NR = Died in enemy hands while a POW/body not recovered
DIEH/RR = Died in enemy hands while a POW/remains recovered
DMIA/NR = Missing, presumed dead/body not recovered
DMIA/NR/389 = Missing, presumed dead/body not recovered/on 389 List
KIA/NR = Killed in action/body not recovered
KIA/RR = Killed in action/remains recovered
DOW/NR = Died of wounds/remains not recovered
DNB/NR = Dead non-battle reasons/remains not recovered

Military Organizations

U.S. Army

1CD	1st Cavalry Division
2ID	2nd Infantry Division
7ID	7th Infantry Division
24ID	24th Infantry Division
25ID	25th Infantry Division
29REG	29th Infantry Regiment (attached to 24ID)
8086AU	8086th Army Unit KMAG
FEC	Far East Command
15 AAABN	15th Antiaircraft Artillery Battalion
307BG	307th Bomber Group
KMAG	Korean Military Assistance Group
6ROKD	6th Republic of Korea Division
ASU	Army Support Unit

U.S. Air Force

91SRS	91st Strategic Reconnaissance Squadron
5AF	5th Air Force
51FW	51st Fighter Wing
6133TSW	6133rd Tactical Surveillance Wing
6150TSW	6150th Tactical Surveillance Wing
39FIS	39th Fighter Interceptor Squadron
35FBS	35th Fighter Bomber Squadron
28BS	28th Bomber Squadron

U.S. Navy and U.S. Marine Corps

35AS   35th Air Squadron
1MD   1st Marine Division

United Kingdom

41BM   41st British Marines

TASK FORCE RUSSIA
INTERVIEW WITH GAVRIL KOROTKOV
November 1993

(Translator's note: the following is a translation of an interview conducted with a former Soviet interrogator, who apparently has detailed knowledge of the presence of American prisoners of war held in captivity in the former Soviet Union. This translation was made from a Russian transcription of the interview, which had been video-taped.)

INTERVIEWER: Tell me, please, based on your personal experience, what do you think of the suggestion that during the Korean War, American prisoners of war were sent to the Soviet Union for further interrogation?

KOROTKOV: Yes, I now think, and at that time I knew, and I now confirm that part of these prisoners of war, a certain group, were, of course in the Soviet Union.

Note: a brief conversation follows in which the details of the interview are worked out. The interviewer asks that the speaker begin with a brief personal history.

K: In July of 1950 I finished a special school, a special department of the Military Institute of Foreign Languages in Moscow. I studied there for five years. I went through special training, and in July I was sent to work in the (Soviet) Far East, since the war in Korea had begun. There was a large number of us specialists at that time stationed in Khabarovsk. I think that at different times there were 30-50, sometimes up to 70 people there. I already said, that our task consisted of gathering and analyzing material connected with the political situation, and the morale, primarily of American troops in Korea, and also other troops, the UN. I was personally involved with the analysis of the American problem - that was my specialty. So that's what our work was like, it required that we search for fresh sources, not just in the press, or from conversations. It required that we look for fresh sources among people, from among those who had been captured. So, we received information, that which they gave to us. They told us about different things. Our second task was to try to recruit, to turn some of them to our side. Well we had special equipment, over which we tried to use Americans, so that they would speak to the American forces with a certain message. We had these large, powerful transmitter stations there. So. I can't recall a single instance where someone or other of the American servicemen agreed to work with us (laughs). I don't know a single case. They were certain that they would get out of captivity anyway. They knew that they would return, and therefore they didn't want to collaborate with us. But, there among the other troops, especially the Koreans, they gladly crossed over and worked. But, as concerns the Americans.

INT: Did you personally interrogate American prisoners of war?

K: Yes, of course. I already said that by the nature of our service I was bound to meet them somehow. It was a good opportunity to speak all the time with an American. That was good because I improved my own knowledge of the English language. I could talk with a real American. But, the main thing was to get information from them which concerned us, and to try to clear up whether they were going to work with us or not. Therefore, I, over the course of probably two or three hours I talked with one American airman. A First Lieutenant I think he was. Yes, well, we talked about these issues that I described to you, I asked him questions and then drew up a report. We have these reports here, in Moscow. I know where they are kept.

INT: What we are concerned with is whether it's possible that they subsequently ended up in Soviet camps.

K: Yes, it's possible. Yes, of course they could have ended up there. Without a doubt they did end up there. Of course American Prisoners, a group of them from North Korea, could end up in the Soviet Union. And they did end up in the Soviet Union. It's hard to say how many there were, who they were exactly, but, that they did end up in our territory, and that they then ended up somewhere in the camps - that's for sure. I personally heard from many people at that time, from officers and from other talk, that some Americans were sent, well,...there. They were shipped further on, to Siberia, beyond the border there beyond Khabarovsk, somewhere in that vicinity. I heard about such things. Therefore I am convinced, and I confirm that this did happen.
INT: In your opinion, why would they be sent to the Soviet Union?

K: I think that the reasons are clear here. Well, in the first place to try to operate in new conditions, to, like we already said, to recruit. In the second place, they were hostages of sorts. Having these hostages on hand, we could then talk with the Americans - you know that our officers were taken prisoner in South Korea. For an exchange perhaps? Third, among them were specialists that we needed very badly. They knew the technology, they knew the situation. We would have needed these people on hand. And I know that some of the American pilots, who were in the Soviet Union, they helped, or told how, to install new equipment, which we were using, into our fighter aircraft. My colleagues in other departments, they told us that Americans helped us to do this. And who could have done this? Only prisoners of war. Well, and fourth, it's understandable. We were cautious. We assumed that among those who fell captive were not only flyers, but infantry, artillery troops, tankers, of course there were others who were captured. Among those, by this means, agents could have infiltrated us. If that was the outlook then, and we did have such cases, then naturally they would take him away, process him, check up on him, and if information was discovered, then of course he would receive the appropriate sentence and would sit in the gulag. He is a spy and that's that. Therefore they could (end up in the Soviet Union), that is either to work, or for political reasons, or to isolate possible spy agents. There. There were reasons. There was interest.

INT: You, when you were in Khabarovsk in 1953, tell me, please, what did you find out, what did you know about an American aircraft, a B-50, which was shot down not far from Vladivostok é in July, the 29th of July, 1953?

Note: the interviewer uses the more generic aircraft designator B-50 designating a bomber. Later in the interview, Korotkov uses the more precise term RB-50 designating a reconnaisance aircraft using a bomber platform.

K: I remember this incident very well. As a matter of fact, the war had just ended in Korea, the agreement concerning the cease fire had just been signed, and because of other missions I was at that time right there in Poset. That's near Vladivostok, Vladivostok is there across the gulf, Poset, in the region of Poset. And literally the very next day, this was the 30th of July probably, yes, it became very well known that near us an American aircraft had been shot down, a, as they said then, heavy aircraft, a heavy, in which there were very many people - later I found out that there were 17 men. So they said a heavy aircraft, and there were a lot of people. Yes, and that this aircraft was hit, and it slowly fell, and slowly descended into the sea. We also knew very well that these airmen, I think at that time they said all the crew, they parachuted out. The specialists then, I remember the conversation, that is, that the specialists were extremely interested, uh, with this equipment, the life support equipment, as a matter of fact I have pictures of it here. (points to his pocket). It was exactly this life support equipment that they had there. And our specialists were extremely interested. No, I remember this episode very well, because we thought then that they would take us to talk with these flyers, the Americans. Because we knew that many of them after they had landed were picked up. They were rescued, one of them died, but the majority of them survived. We then talked a lot, it would be good to talk with them. The war had sort of ended, but nevertheless, there were so many people, we could gather so much information. However, they told us that we would not be able to meet them. Some reasons or other. I don't know. When we tried, as specialists, to get information, "Is it forbidden to talk with them?", "Where are they?", then they said that we were forbidden to meet them. So, how many were there? Where were they? This they didn't tell us. But we found out that they had immediately been whisked away across the border to the KGB. Because there among us, let's say, were elements, units, bases, they had their own people. And they immediately snatched these people themselves. As a matter of fact, they already were not considered prisoners of war, that's where the problem was, that's why we weren't permitted. They were already not considered prisoners of war. They were already considered to be spies. And that's why we didn't have access to them. As to the fact that so many of them were picked up, and that many of them were alive, it turns out that there is no doubt about that. Then there was talk about it, that they had received so many Americans, so many Americans. And that's how it ended up. Later there was an official report about it, that there was this American plane, a reconnaissance aircraft, it had violated our territorial waters and had been shot down and that's that. But about how many people there were, or how many were rescued, and where they ended up, nothing was reported. Officially nothing. But we knew there that these people had been gathered up.

INT: You keep saying "we were told", or "it was reported to us", who told you? Who reported this to you?

K: Well, you know, in this big headquarters, in the general staff of the Soviet forces in the Far East, there was an extremely far-flung, and very rigid structure. Very diverse and far-flung. In the east we had contact with military intelligence and with representatives of the KGB, we had contact. They didn't give us all their secrets, and we also, but we had contact. Therefore, naturally we went to their representatives who were there in the element. These workers were of the so-called "SMERSH"- "Death to Spies". They were in the element. We immediately asked "are we forbidden to see them, after all you have them there". Well, he phoned, went someplace or other, to his own people, and they sent back that no, it is forbidden. I don't remember names of course. So there, well, for us there wasn't then something secretly, or, well I would say no big surprise that many American

airmen were there. I was completely surprised when the son, Anderson, came to Moscow last year. Yes. And when he found out about me, and invited me for talks, and twice with him we had these long conversations about this issue. I told him a lot of details, but, unfortunately, he didn't find any kind of hard facts. But I am completely convinced that his father was alive, I think he was among them. Because he was nowhere among those who perished, and so he would have received 25 years for espionage in accordance with Soviet law, and died in some camp. I think somewhere in the area to the east of Bajkal - There was one of those camps there.
INT: So what was the further fate of these airmen?

K: Since I assume that none of them agreed to work for us, didn't agree probably, then they were formally convicted as spies and received their sentence, and were dispersed to camps where they served this term and worked...there. And since the Cold War had begun, then naturally they were kept and not released. If the relationship with the Americans had worked out, then obviously they would have been freed earlier, and they would have returned alive. But, since they weren't released, then they served their whole sentence. And many, of course died there. I don't think any of them survived to today...did'nt survive. Because the conditions of life were so hard of course....40 years.

INT: But anyway there is now this joint American-Russian commission on Prisoner of War affairs. Why could they not, in your opinion, establish the fate of the flyers? Or that they died in the war?

K: This commission, uh, in the first place this is because a lot of time has passed and I think that many documents were simply destroyed probably. It's hard to say. In the second place, a lot of these safes in the agency of the former KGB to this day still have not been opened. They simply are not open, they just sit there. And to this day this mass of investigators simply doesn't have access to these documents. I am an expert member of this commission, and well, when we gathered there everything was going fine, until we got to this business. It turns out that no one is permitted there, nobody has been there with these documents. And their representative, who was with us on the commission, he said "we looked there, there are no documents", and that's all. So, therefore these documents weren't presented. They're not being studied. Second, I think they didn't succeed simply because the people are still alive who were somehow connected to all this. They are alive and they don't want this brought to light right now. There is no procedure for it, no methods, no system, they simply don't want to and that's all. Third, evidently, they didn't succeed because we are not organized,

the work is not laid out well. If some sort of group were specially created, if it were financed, and if it were given time and resources, then they would start to look. But there are no such people, no one is involved.
INT: But the Americans have a permanent (is cut off)

K: I see, yes, well, as it turns out the Americans themselves weren't given access to our secret archives, like a lot of them they weren't given access. I don't know the reason, it's obviously still, so to speak, a tradition, an old and continuing tradition. I am certain that there is still time and opportunity and that this will all be known. People will be found who will research this and piece this story together. I am certain of this. I would say it like this, that if they permitted me, and gave me everything - the means, the time, if they opened up, then I would dig it all up. I personally know where these things are, where to get them. I myself know. So there's why the commission was not successful...this isn't a completely hopeless matter.
INT Can you tell me where the documents are?

K: Well, they're in these KGB archives, which included at the time the border troops, internal troops, and...well this was part of a system. These are agency records, agency, so to speak governmental. And according to our laws access to them to this day is permitted only to government agencies. Former agencies. Now it's the security committee. And when you go around to them, and start to ask questions, you get "we just can't". Because of time limits for declassification, there are time limits. And the documents are absolutely classified. Declassification guidelines. So it's officially forbidden to disclose them. That's the kind of paradox you have. And so. But, as concerns, you know, further searches concerning this specific incident of the RB-50 aircraft, shot down on the 29th of July, I think the search must go on. If Anderson hears me or sees this, I think he should not lose all hope...he shouldn't. There will come a time and he will find out all the details of his father's fate. I wish this for him...I hope for this.

Footnotes:
Khabarovsk (4830 North by 13550 East) important industrial administrative center in the Soviet Far East. Near the Russian border with China, Khabarovsk stands at the crossroads of the Trans-Siberian Railroad and the Amur river, making it one of the most important trade centers in the Far East.
Vladivostok (4310 North by 13153 East) Most important port in the Soviet Far East and headquarters of the Soviet Pacific Fleet.
SMERSH - A Russian acronym formed from the words "Death to Spies". SMERSH was a special counter-intelligence unit formed to pursue and uncover people spying against the Soviet Union.

SOVIET MESSAGE RE:
DEC. 4, 1950 SHOOTDOWN OF RB-45

Copy No.2   Must be returned in 6 days to the
Adm. of the Gen. Staff of the Armed Forces
Ciphering No. 60118/sh
Correspondent 3   Given 12-12-50 9:00am
Received 17-12-50 12:33pm
(illegible) 8 Adm. of the General Staff of the Armed Forces
17-12-50   1:00pm

Cabled

Comrade Shtemenko
Comrade Batitskii

I attest:

An aircraft shot down on 12-4-50 of the B-45 type fell in a region 70 km to the east of Andun. The aircraft caught fire in the air and upon falling to earth burned up completely. The crew bailed out on parachutes. The pilot Captain Charles McDonough was taken prisoner.

Under interrogation he said:
The aircraft was shot down at an altitude of 30,000 feet.

The crew numbering 3 persons bailed out on parachutes. The navigator having landed ran off, where the radio operator disappeared to he did not see. The captive himself was burned and is in a critical condition.

The aircraft that has been shot down is of the RB-45 type and is of the 363rd detachment 5th squadron.

The detachment is based at Yokota Airdrome Japan.

In all at the Yokota Airdrome there are up to 100 aircraft of various types including only 3 of the RB-45 type.

Deciphered 17-12-50 4:00pm Sosin   111

Made 8 copies

(illegible)	__No.5 Malandin	__No.9 _____
Vasilevsky	__No.6 Agaltsov	__No.10 _____
Sokolovski	__No.7 Pavloski	__No.11 _____
Shtemenko	__No.8 Batitskii	__No.12 _____

__No. 15401__
2   17   12   1950

Chief of the Department
General Staff

(…)

(CONTINUATION OF ABOVE MESSAGE)

10
188
Page No. 2
continued Ciphering No. 60118/sh

570

At other airdromes there are no RB-45 aircraft.

The RB-45 aircraft is a modified B-45 assigned to aerial reconnaissance. It is different from the B-45 in that it does not have firing weapons and is fitted out with up to 10 air cameras. The RB-45 is now in a testing stage.

The RB-45 has 4 jet engines a maximum speed of 750 km/hr, a practical ceiling of up to 14,000 meters a radius of operations of up to 1000 km. In the tail portion of the fuselage is installed a radio locator with a detection range of up to 100 km.

Measures have been taken by me for a search of the downed airplanes.

All of the equipment which has been found to be in good repair, details and apparatus from the enemy airplanes will be immediately sent to your address.

I request your directives to the advisers located in Korea regarding the rendering of assistance in the search, the preservation and the sending of downed airplanes and details from them to my address.

Belov

No. 215/K

Sent Bantsekina 17-12-50 5:10pm /5/

SECOND SOVIET MESSAGE
REPORTING DEATH OF RB-45 PILOT

		(handwrittenComrade Vasilevsky
	Copy No.2	Must be returned in 6 days to the Adm.
Prohibited		of the Gen. Staff of the Armed Forces

Ciphering   No. 601120/sh

Correspondent 3   Given 18-12-50 8:25am   Received 18-12 12:00pm
(illegible) 8 Adm. of the Gen. Staff of the Armed Forces 18-12 12:30pm

---

Cabled

Comrade Batitskii

I am informing you, that the pilot from the shot down B-45 aircraft died on route and the interrogation was not finished.

I am sending you the material that I have on hand.

Krasovskii

No.221/K

Deciphered 18-12-50   1:00pm   Sheblikin

Made 8 copies	Lvova	1:30pm /1/___
(illegible)	__No.5 Malandin	__No.9_____
Vasilevsky	__No.6 Agaltsov	__No.10_____
Sokolovsky	__No.7 Pavloski	__No.11_____
Shtemenko	__No.8 Batitskii	__No.12_____

Chief of the Dept.
General Staff of the Armed Forces

No. 15435
(illegible)

SUMMARY OF SECOND MESSAGE
PROVIDED BY RUSSIAN SIDE OF JOINT COMMISSION

(TFR 242-2)

(illegible handwriting along left side of page)

To: Comrade SHTEMENKO
Comrade BATITSKIO

I am reporting:

The B-45 type aircraft was shot down on 4 Dec 50 in an area 70 km east of Antung. The aircraft caught fire while in the air and was totally engulfed in flames upon impacting the ground. The crew bailed out and parachuted to the ground. The flier, Captain CHAL'S MARTONAT (Charles McDonough), was taken prisoner.

The flier provided the following information during the interrogation:

The aircraft was hit at an altitude of 30,000 feet.

The crew, consisting of three personnel, bailed out and parachuted to the ground. The navigator landed and escaped. The status of the radio operator is unknown since he was not seen. The prisoner suffered burns and is currently in serious condition.

The downed RB-45 aircraft belongs to the 363rd Detachment, 5th Squadron.

The detachment is based at Yakoda airfield (Japan).

There are approximately 100 aircraft of various types located at Yakoda airfield, of which only three are RB-45's.

(Page is cut off at this point in the text. The following short clip has been attached with tape and does not appear to be part of the original.)

To: Comrade BATITSKIO

I am reporting that the flier from the downed B-45 died en route and the interrogation could not be completed.

All available information is being sent.

KRASOVSKIJ

U.S. SIDE'S EXPLANATION OF
'COMPOSITE' MESSAGE TFR—242—2

At the last plenary session the Russian side of the Commission passed two documents to the U.S. These two documents had been cut from complete documents and taped together on a single sheet of paper. They are translated exactly as provided and identified as Task Force Document (TFR -242-2).

About ten days prior to the Plenum, Professor Orlov passed to us a short handwritten note specifying information he had discovered in the Podol'sk archives. His note is translated exactly and is provided without a TAR number. Orlov also provided the archival citation for this document and has invited us to look at it. Our analysis suggests that Orlov's note paraphrases the TFR -242-2, however we will not know this until COL Parr travels to Podol'sk to review the document in place. It is likely that Orlov was trying, in his note, to present the information in a more positive light than did the original document.

****

HANDWRITTEN NOTE ON RB-45 DOCUMENTS
FROM COL. ORLOV

(TFR 217-1)

(The entire document is handwritten)

A/ Pr;pv1. Last names of American fliers mentioned in documents of the 64th IAK (Fighter Aviation Corps)

Captain Charlz Maktonat, crew member of an RB-45 shot down on 4 Dec 1950. Died during evacuation from the aircraft crash site. (TsAMO, f, 5, op. 918795, o. 120, 1. 559,574)

Selected Bibliography

Albats, Evgenia—The State Within a State; Farrar,Straus, Giroux, 1994.

Andrew, Christopher and Gordievsky, Oleg—KGB, The Inside Story; Harpers, 1990.

Appleman, Lt. Col. Roy E.—Ridgway Duels for Korea; Texas A & M, 1990.

Bethell, Nicholas—The Last Secret; Basic Books, 1974.

Black, Robert W.—Rangers in Korea; Ballantine, 1989.

Blair, Clay—The Forgotten War, American in Korea; Times Books, 1987.

Blake, George—No Other Choice; Simon & Schuster, 1990.

Bussey, Charles M.—Firefight at Yechon, Courage and Racism in the Korean War; Brassey's, 1991.

Carew, Tim—Korea, the Commonwealth at War; Cassell, 1967.

Cole, Paul M.—POW/MIA Issues; RAND National Defense Research Institute, 1994.

Conquest, Robert—The Great Terror; Oxford, 1990.

Conquest, Robert—Kolyma, the Arctic Death Camps; Viking.

Cookridge, E. H.—George Blake: Double Agent; Ballantine, 1970.

Crosbie, Philip—Pencilling Prisoner; The Hawthorn Press, 1954.

Dean, Gen. William F.—General Dean's Story; Viking, 1954.

Deane, Philip—I Should Have Died; Atheneum, 1977.

DeMille, Nelson—The Charm School; Warner Books, 1988.

Eberstadt, Nicholas—Korea Approaches Reunification, 1995.

Faligot, Roger and Kauffer, Remi—The Chinese Secret Service; Morrow, 1987.

Goncharov, Sergei, Lewis, John and Xue Litai—Uncertain Partners, Stalin, Mao and the Korean War; Stanford University, 1993.

Kennan, George—Russia and the West; Little, Brown, 1960.

LaFeber, Walter—America, Russia and the Cold War, 1945-1971; John Wiley & Sons, 1967.

Marshall, S.L.A.—The River and the Gauntlet; Warner Books, 1952.

Merrill, John—Korea, the Peninsular Origins of the War; University of Delaware, Murphy, Paul J.—The Soviet Air Forces; McFarland, 1984.

Nimmo, William F.—Behind a Curtain of Silence/Japanese in Soviet Custody; Greenwood, 1988.

Noble, Harold Joyce—Embassy at War; University of Washington Press, 1975.

Noble, John—I Was a Slave in Russia; Cicero Bible Press, 1958.

Ree, Eric Van—Socialism in One Zone; Berg; 1989.

Rigoulot, Pierre—Des Francais au Goulag, 1917-1984; Fayard, 1984.

Shifrin, Avraham—The First Guidebook to Prisons and Concentration Camps of the Soviet Union; Bantam, 1980.

Sauter, Mark and Sanders, Jim—The Men We Left Behind; National Press Books, 1993.

Scholmer, Joseph—Vorkuta; Weidenfeld & Nicolson, 1954.

Shultz, Richard H. and Godson, Roy—Dezinformatsia, the Strategy of Soviet Disinformation; Berkley, 1984.

Suvorov, Viktor—Inside Soviet Military Intelligence; Macmillan, 1984.

Toland, John—In Mortal Combat—Korea, 1950-1953; William Morrow and Co., 1991.

Tolstoy, Nkolai—Victims of Yalta; Corgi Books, 1977.

Volkogonov, Dmitri—Stalin, Triumph & Tragedy; Grove Weidenfeld, 1988.

Whelan, Richard—Drawing the Line; Little, Brown, 1990.

Young, Kenneth—Negotiating With the Communists; McGraw-Hill, 1968.

Zellers, Larry—In Enemy Hands, A Prisoner in North Korea; University Press of Kentucky, 1991.

Index

A

Abakumov, Viktor 50-51, 53
"Andreyko," 223, 226, 228, 232, 234-237
Andrianov, Aleksandr F. 206-207, 212
Antonov, Gen. Alexei 12
Arnold, Col. John Knox 162, 164
Asla, Maj. Felix 181

B

Bach, Lawrence V. 165, 173-174, 176
Bagayev, Vladimir 84
Bakatin, Vadim 69-72, 74-77, 79-80
Baker, James III 72
Baker, Pfc. Billy W. 151
Baldwin, Hanson W. 144
Batitskiy, Marshal Pavel 215
Beaumont, Pfc. Bill 145
Bell, Lt. Donald E. 86
Belov, Mikhail M. 12
Biderman, Albert 135, 141, 154
Black, Capt. Vance Eugene 104, 111, 119, 120
Blake, George 42, 114, 115, 116, 161
Blasser, M/sgt. Danz 173
Burchett, Wilfred 229
Busheyev, Victor Alexandrovich 75, 97-99, 103, 112, 118, 188-189
Byrne, Bishop Patrick 14

C

Cabell, Maj. Gen. Charles P. 211, 215
Carrington, Louis 205, 210-212
Caruth, Bobby 268, 274
Cho Chang Ho 277-280
Cho Sinja, Yun 279
Church, Brig. Gen. John H. 12